"This work contains chapters on a wide variety of interesting conceptual questions regarding toleration as well as sustained treatment of some vitally important practical concerns that have been somewhat missed by the literature until now."

— *Timothy Fowler,*
*University of Bristol, UK*

"At a time of heightened conflicts around the rise of extremist groups in societies world-wide, this volume provides timely and vigorous insights into the fraught relation between toleration and liberalism. The contributors engage with acuity and sensitivity historical and contemporary dilemmas over the role of tolerance within liberalism. This volume will provide crucial inspiration for scholars and researchers in the field."

— *Monica Mookherjee,*
*Keele University, UK*

# Toleration and the Challenges to Liberalism

This book explores the relationship between different versions of liberalism and toleration by focusing on their shared theoretical and political challenges.

Toleration is among the most pivotal and the most contested liberal values and virtues. Debates about the conceptual scope, justification and political role of toleration are closely aligned with historical and contemporary philosophical controversies on the foundations of liberalism. The chapters in this volume focus on the specific connection between toleration and liberalism. The chapters in Part I reconstruct some of the major historical controversies surrounding toleration and liberalism. Part II centers on general conceptual and justificatory questions concerning toleration as a central category for the definition of liberal political theory. Part III is devoted to the theoretical analysis of applied issues and cases of conflicts of toleration in liberal states and societies.

*Toleration and the Challenges to Liberalism* will be of interest to researchers and advanced students in social and political philosophy, ethics, and political theory.

**Johannes Drerup** is Professor of Educational Theory and Philosophy of Education at the TU Dortmund, Germany and Guest Professor at the Free University of Amsterdam, Netherlands.

**Gottfried Schweiger** is Senior Researcher in the Centre for Ethics and Poverty Research at the University of Salzburg, Austria.

# Routledge Studies in Contemporary Philosophy

**Social Functions in Philosophy**
Metaphysical, Normative, and Methodological Perspectives
*Edited by Rebekka Hufendiek, Daniel James, and Raphael van Riel*

**Microaggressions and Philosophy**
*Edited by Lauren Freeman and Jeanine Weekes Schroer*

**Cross-Tradition Engagement in Philosophy**
A Constructive-Engagement Account
*Bo Mou*

**Perception and the Inhuman Gaze**
Perspectives from Philosophy, Phenomenology, and the Sciences
*Edited by Anya Daly, Fred Cummins, James Jardine, and Dermot Moran*

**Logics of Genocide**
The Structures of Violence and the Contemporary World
*Edited by Anne O'Byrne and Martin Shuster*

**Revising Fiction, Fact, and Faith**
A Philosophical Account
*Nathaniel Goldberg and Chris Gavaler*

**The Indexical Point of View**
On Cognitive Significance and Cognitive Dynamics
*Vojislav Bozickovic*

**Toleration and the Challenges to Liberalism**
*Edited by Johannes Drerup and Gottfried Schweiger*

For more information about this series, please visit: www.routledge.com/Routledge-Studies-in-Contemporary-Philosophy/book-series/SE0720

# Toleration and the Challenges to Liberalism

Edited by Johannes Drerup and
Gottfried Schweiger

NEW YORK AND LONDON

First published 2021
by Routledge
52 Vanderbilt Avenue, New York, NY 10017

and by Routledge
2 Park Square, Milton Park, Abingdon, Oxon, OX14 4RN

*Routledge is an imprint of the Taylor & Francis Group, an informa business*

© 2021 Taylor & Francis

The right of Johannes Drerup and Gottfried Schweiger to be identified as the authors of the editorial material, and of the authors for their individual chapters, has been asserted in accordance with sections 77 and 78 of the Copyright, Designs and Patents Act 1988.

All rights reserved. No part of this book may be reprinted or reproduced or utilised in any form or by any electronic, mechanical, or other means, now known or hereafter invented, including photocopying and recording, or in any information storage or retrieval system, without permission in writing from the publishers.

*Trademark notice*: Product or corporate names may be trademarks or registered trademarks, and are used only for identification and explanation without intent to infringe.

*Library of Congress Cataloging-in-Publication Data*
A catalog record for this book has been requested

ISBN: 978-0-367-85746-2 (hbk)
ISBN: 978-1-003-01512-3 (ebk)

Typeset in Sabon
by Apex CoVantage, LLC

# Contents

Toleration and the Challenges to Liberalism: Introduction    1
JOHANNES DRERUP AND GOTTFRIED SCHWEIGER

PART I
Toleration and Liberalism: Historical Controversies    11

1 John Locke and the "Problem" of Toleration    13
   JOHN WILLIAM TATE

2 Toleration and the Origins of Liberalism: The Career of William Penn    36
   ANDREW R. MURPHY

3 On Liberalism, Liberty of Conscience and Toleration: Some Historical and Theoretical Reflections    53
   MARK A. HUTCHINSON AND TIMOTHY STANTON

PART II
Toleration and the Challenges to Liberalism: Conceptual and Justificatory Issues    77

4 The Mutual Independence of Liberalism and Toleration    79
   DAVID HEYD

5 Regimes of Toleration: Liberal and Republican    97
   CILLIAN McBRIDE

6 Liberalism and Toleration    114
   JON MAHONEY

7  Public Reason and the Burdens of Citizenship: A Case
   for Toleration                                                   129
   ANDREA BAUMEISTER

8  Modus Vivendi Beyond Toleration                                  146
   ROBERTA SALA

9  Toleration, Liberal Democracy and the Problem of
   Intolerant Doctrines: The Example of Right-Wing Populism         162
   ANNIINA LEIVISKÄ

PART III
Toleration and Liberalism in Context: Cases
and Controversies                                                   181

10 Religious Toleration, Education and the Headscarf Dispute        183
   JOHANNES DRERUP

11 The Harm Principle and Corporations                              202
   ANDREW JASON COHEN

12 Gypsy Traveller Nomadism and State Tolerance: A
   Liberal-Egalitarian View                                         218
   MARCUS CARLSEN HÄGGROT

13 Toleration as a Deep Practice, Legitimate Expectations
   and Refugees                                                     239
   GOTTFRIED SCHWEIGER AND CLEMENS SEDMAK

   Contributors                                                     256
   Index                                                            261

# Toleration and the Challenges to Liberalism

## Introduction

*Johannes Drerup and Gottfried Schweiger*

Toleration[1] is among the most pivotal and the most contested liberal values. Debates about the conceptual scope, theoretical justification and political function of toleration are closely aligned with historical and contemporary philosophical controversies on the foundations of liberalism. As Cohen (2014) has argued, it "is no exaggeration to say that the history of liberalism is the modern history of toleration" (p. 1). Since there is no canonical understanding of toleration, nor of liberalism in contemporary political philosophy,[2] the precise role of toleration in liberalism and the nature of a distinctively liberal conception of toleration remain disputed. These controversies are, among others, rooted in different interpretations of liberalism's core commitments and values – most importantly, competing notions of liberty and autonomy (Mendus, 1989; McKinnon, 2006; Gaus, 2018; Wall, 2015). Depending on the specific interpretation one uses to ground the normative basis of liberalism – for instance, in terms of negative liberty (Balint, 2017), personal autonomy (Raz, 1987), political autonomy and political respect (Nussbaum, 2011), the harm principle (Cohen, 2018) or moral autonomy and the right to justification (Forst, 2013) – different regimes of toleration and corresponding normative limits of toleration can be justified. Likewise, the specific conception of toleration that one regards as the most suitable and legitimate response to diversity in liberal societies and democracies (for instance, Galeotti's conception of toleration as recognition: 2002; or Forst's respect conception of toleration; 2013; see also Rossi, 2013) will depend on one's understanding of liberty in relation to other principles and values (such as equality, state neutrality and others; Fawcett, 2018) and hence on one's conception of liberalism (perfectionist, political liberal etc.).

Despite this diversity of approaches, it remains relatively uncontroversial that liberal conceptions of toleration assume that toleration is required by liberty (however defined) and that interference with liberty, rather than non-interference, is in need of justification (Balint, 2017). Therefore, competing conceptions of toleration and of liberalism in many respects share the same basic conceptual and normative structure and face similar theoretical and political challenges. The normative limits of toleration, for instance, usually also constitute the limits of liberalism (and vice versa). Justifications of these limits result in similar paradoxes (e.g., paradox of liberalism; paradox of drawing the limits of toleration; foundational paradox of toleration) and tend to evoke related criticisms (critiques of "illiberal" forms of liberalism or "in- or nontolerant" theories of toleration etc.).

Although toleration and liberalism are closely connected ideas, it would be incorrect to assume that tolerance is an exclusively Western or liberal notion. In debates about global history and philosophy, for instance, the idea that toleration is a characteristically liberal or Western value – which arguably itself is an "intolerant" assumption, given the history of "liberal colonialism" (Arneil, 2012) – is increasingly called into question (Nederman, 2011; Lacorne, 2019). Along these lines, it is disputed not only whether liberalism and toleration can be justified independently of comprehensive doctrines (Colburn, 2010; Quong, 2011; Cohen, 2015), but also whether the justification of toleration necessarily rests on distinctively liberal principles and values. This also holds for the practice of toleration in diverse societies, since one may assume that "even if tolerance is understood as distinctively liberal, its successful practice among citizens neither empirically nor normatively must rely on liberal reasoning" (Balint, 2014, p. 273). In the context of a pluralistic society we are facing a multiplicity of different, partly overlapping, partly conflicting theoretical conceptions and justifications as well as practices of toleration. Thus, one may argue that this "very pluralism seems to require pluralism of the ways to toleration" (Khomyakov, 2013, p. 237; see also: Walzer, 1997). At the same time others have argued that a justification of toleration based on, for instance, a conception of moral pluralism, which assumes that a plurality of incommensurable objective values exists, constitutes only one – controversial – view of the normative and social world among others (Forst, 2013), and therefore may be reasonably rejected as a ground for toleration by some individuals or groups. Similar criticisms, however, are also brought forward with respect to universalist justifications of toleration that claim to provide a universally shared (or shareable) normative basis, such as the right to justification, for dealing with toleration conflicts (Etinson, 2014; Galeotti, 2015a). While most authors nevertheless tend to assume that toleration and liberalism are inseparable with respect to their underlying principles and practices (see, for a critique of this position, Heyd, 2008), some authors are more sceptical, for instance, due to the misuse and "weaponization of toleration" in discourses about a clash of civilizations (Dobbernack and Modood, 2013, pp. 2–3). According to this critique, the dualistic worldview of a "muscular" form of "liberalism" (ibid.) – put bluntly: the tolerant West against the intolerant rest – provides justifications of questionable forms of intolerance towards minorities in the name of (certain interpretations) of liberalism´s core values (e.g., autonomy; see Galeotti, 2015b).

The ongoing debates about the dark – intolerant and illiberal – side of toleration and liberalism (Brown, 2006; see also: Di Blasi and Holzhey, 2014), as well as the possibility of a "tolerant" theory of toleration (Rawls, 2005; Königs, 2019), indicate that liberal conceptions of toleration do not rise "above the battle of values" (Williams, 1996, p. 25). They refer to tensions and conflicts that seem to be immanent to the politics and ethics of toleration in liberal states and societies (Drerup and Kühler, 2019). Both liberalism and toleration are ideas and ideals brought forward to enable and regulate civilized political disagreement and conflict, while they are at the same time also the objects and sources of disagreement and conflict (Newey, 2013). As allied and deeply ambivalent ideas, they constitute responses to the fact of pluralism and simultaneously reflect this pluralism in terms of a diversity of competing conceptions and justifications.

This volume sheds light on the complex and contested nexus between different versions of liberalism and toleration by developing critical reconstructions and discussions of their shared theoretical and political challenges. It provides an overview on defences and critiques of principles and practices of toleration in liberal states and societies by focusing both on historical as well as on more recent controversies and cases (such as debates about the rise of illiberal and intolerant forms of right-wing authoritarianism; see, for instance: Sunstein, 2018).

The volume is subdivided into three main parts. The contributions in the first part reconstruct historical debates about the in many cases troubled marriage between toleration and liberalism. The second part focusses on more foundational theoretical, conceptual and justificatory issues concerning toleration and contemporary challenges to liberalism. The third and last part provides discussions of conflicts of toleration in particular socio-political contexts.

Part I begins with a contribution by John Tate on John Locke, who is widely considered a foundational thinker within the liberal tradition, and one of the seminal sources of a distinctly liberal conception of toleration. But Locke began his intellectual career as a vigorous opponent of toleration in relation to matters of religion. Tate shows how toleration remained a problem for Locke throughout his intellectual career. By focusing on the discursive content of Locke's key writings on toleration, from the origins of his intellectual career to its culmination, he seeks to explain how Locke managed to overcome this problem of toleration and affirm it as both a means to ensure the outward expression of religious liberty and also a basis for ensuring civil peace and state security.

The next contribution, by Andrew R. Murphy, seeks to broaden the scholarly conversation on the history of toleration beyond the emphasis on Locke's *Letter Concerning Toleration*. It does so by exploring the career of Locke's contemporary, William Penn (1644–1718), who both theorized liberty of conscience in England and, when granted the opportunity, attempted to implement a tolerationist regime in Pennsylvania. Murphy's consideration of Penn's career and its context(s) focuses particularly on Penn's *Great Case of Liberty of Conscience* (1670) and *Perswasive to Moderation* (1685), and provides a window into the complex historical relationship between theory and practice as they pertain to liberalism and toleration.

Mark A. Hutchinson and Tim Stanton's chapter offers some historical and theoretical reflections on the relationship between liberalism and toleration. They show that the terms of that relationship as assumed in the minds of liberal commentators were established quite early, in the eighteenth century, and reproduced down to the present day in multiple versions of a grand narrative in which the liberal tradition originates in conscientious Protestant resistance to Catholic and Catholic-style persecution which, in 1688, would deliver limited government and religious liberty to all. Moreover, they argue that a habitual equation between toleration and liberty of conscience is operative in this context, legitimated by a reading of Locke which presents him as the intellectual mastermind of 1688, a founder of the liberal tradition, and an exponent of liberty of conscience. They suggest that hidden within the folds of this reading is an old idea, that progressive thinkers like Locke educate elites who in their turn restrain and re-educate the popular instinct to persecute. Finally, Stanton and Hutchinson use history to problematize the equation of toleration and liberty of conscience and give grounds for thinking that the old idea is alive and well in Rawlsian writing about liberalism, its history, and its relation to toleration.

Part II opens with a contribution by David Heyd, who criticizes the established assumption that the political virtue of toleration should be closely associated with the idea of the liberal state. Heyd argues that there is no conceptual connection between the two and that toleration may even be incompatible with political liberalism, both of the neutral state and of the perfectionist state. The main argument is that the role of the state is to apply an impersonal system of rights and duties while toleration is a personal attitude of individuals and social groups in their mutual relations. While respect for rights is a duty both of the state and its citizens, toleration according to Heyd is a supererogatory restraint which is exercised on a discretionary basis. This means that toleration may have an important complementary value for the life of citizens in the liberal state although the state itself cannot demonstrate it.

Cillian McBride's chapter focusses on the question whether toleration is inextricably linked to liberalism or whether is it possible to develop a republican conception of toleration. According to McBride, the permission conception of toleration is not distinctively liberal, so while republicans must reject it as a form of domination, that poses no challenge to the liberal respect conception. Liberals and republicans, according to McBride, can share equal respect as a common moral foundation. Where they differ is in their understanding of the contemporary *regime* of toleration. The liberal understanding of this assumes that states no longer tolerate and that toleration survives as a virtue or practice of individual citizens. To a republican, however, the contemporary toleration regime in fact displays significant continuities with the older permission regime (e.g., corporations enjoy considerable discretion to tolerate or not). According to McBride, republican toleration thus rests on a foundation of equal respect, but argues for a more domination-sensitive understanding of the regime of toleration.

Jon Mahoney's chapter discusses a variety of positions on liberal toleration as well as the challenge to liberal toleration posed by ethical pluralism. While political liberty is at the centre of liberal conceptions of toleration, liberal political philosophers disagree about the limits of toleration, whether equality is central to liberal toleration, and the toleration of illiberal religious and cultural practices, among other topics. Moreover, also some non-liberal states adopt a model of toleration, despite significant limitations on liberty. In addition to his systematic reconstruction of different conceptions of liberal toleration, Mahoney considers some recent work in comparative philosophy that emphasizes pluralism across traditions of political morality.

In the face of recent debates regarding the relevance of traditional conceptions of political toleration in a value-neutral liberal polity, Andrea Baumeister's contribution argues that the burdens of citizenship associated with the liberal commitment to justificatory neutrality provide distinctive grounds for acts of toleration, conceived as legal exemptions from generally applicable laws. She argues that although it is the state which secures toleration by granting legal exemptions, such acts of toleration are ultimately grounded in the relationship between free and equal citizens committed to the practice of justifying political power to one another. Toleration, thus, assumes a distinctive political role. By offering redress for the difficulties and limitation inherent in the search for a common evaluative standard, toleration, according to Baumeister, affirms the equal standing of citizens and helps to facilitate continued political engagement among citizens in the face of the plurality of conscientious commitments that characterize the modern liberal polity.

Roberta Sala's chapter focusses on the relationship between toleration and modus vivendi. Her overall aim is to defend an idea of modus vivendi as a strategy for the political inclusion of people who are not tolerant, without betraying the fundamentals of liberal democracies. To do that, she reconstructs and analyzes the essential meanings of the notions of modus vivendi and toleration. Sala shows how both notions can go in parallel when they are both adopted in the following political frame: a) modus vivendi can be the name for negative toleration as mere non-interference; b) modus vivendi can be the name for toleration as forbearance, hence it presupposes a negative even intolerant attitude towards the "tolerated"; c) modus vivendi can entail a positive idea of toleration as moderate recognition; that is, modus vivendi is here a strategy for intolerant people to be included into citizenry albeit under certain conditions.

Anniina Leiviskä's chapter addresses right-wing populism as an example of 'intolerant' doctrines from the perspective of the limits of toleration as they are delineated in three contemporary theories of democracy: John Rawls's political liberalism, Jürgen Habermas's deliberative theory of democracy and Chantal Mouffe's agonistic pluralism. She challenges Mouffe's argument that her agonistic pluralism, where the limits of toleration are drawn politically rather than rationally or morally, is able to provide a more satisfactory solution to the issue of right-wing populism than Rawls's and Habermas's theories. Leiviskä demonstrates that Mouffe's suggestion to include right-wing populists in democratic politics as legitimate adversaries is contradictory to the way she delineates the limits of toleration in her theory. It is further suggested that Mouffe's hegemonic approach to politics gives rise to both normative and political problems from the viewpoint of liberal democracy. She concludes by suggesting that while Rawls's and Habermas's theories provide a normative framework for delineating the limits of toleration in contemporary democracies and thus have philosophical and normative significance, also novel democratic interventions, which draw from an understanding of the causes underlying the rise of right-wing populism, are required on the level of political practices.

Part III begins with a chapter by Johannes Drerup, who provides a reconstruction and discussion of different, conflicting positions in the public controversy over a ban on headscarves in kindergartens and public schools. The wearing of headscarves in public institutions belongs to the classical topics and objects of debates about (religious) toleration and its limits. The topic (again) has become increasingly politically contentious in recent years, largely due the ban on the wearing of headscarves in kindergartens and primary schools in Austria and political proposals for corresponding bans in Germany. According to Drerup, opponents of headscarves in kindergartens and public schools appeal in part to a specific interpretation of the state requirement of neutrality. For example, they assume that the headscarf cannot be reconciled with the free and self-confident development of children and that it is an expression of religious coercion. Headscarf advocates, on the other hand, interpret the proposed ban as an expression of antireligious, intolerant and specifically antimuslim symbolic politics, and argue that it would amount to a restriction of the fundamental rights of parents and children (including their freedom of religion). Drerup begins with a clarification of the relevant principles of secularism as aspects of the more general ideal of state neutrality. Then he discusses the most important arguments put forward by the opponents of headscarves and argues that a corresponding state "unveiling decree" would be incompatible with basic principles of liberal politics and education, suitably interpreted.

Andrew Jason Cohen's chapter defends what may seem prima vista a surprising view: that John Stuart Mill's famous harm principle would, if taken to be what justifies government action, disallow the existence of corporations. His claim is not that harmful activities of currently existing corporations warrants *their* losing corporate status according to the harm principle. His claim, rather, is that taken strictly, the harm principle and the legal possibility of incorporation are mutually exclusive. Cohen argues that this view, which he does not attribute to Mill himself, should encourage us to think more about the nature of the markets within which business occurs. His basic argument is that, if the only justification for state action is rectification or prevention of harm, there is no justification for the corpus of corporate law as that law is state instituted for reasons not having to do with harm. He does not deny that the corporate model of the firm provides great benefit – by reducing costs that make goods and services less expensive for everyone (while also enriching a small group). He argues, however, that much of this benefit could be established without state intervention. Importantly, though, the failure to make that benefit possible, according to Cohen, is not a harm as that term is used in the harm principle.

Marcus Carlsen Häggrot's chapter discusses the question whether states as France or the UK should tolerate the nomadic lifestyle that still is maintained by a small but not insignificant number of Gypsy Travellers. Drawing on the twentieth-century policies of France and the UK, he suggests that a state might tolerate Gypsy Traveller nomadism in two distinct ways. It might permit nomadism but refuse to accommodate this practice in a wide range of policy domains (multi-domain-non-accommodation tolerance) or it can permit nomadism but oblige nomads to report regularly to police authorities (reporting tolerance). He further argues that from a broadly liberal-egalitarian viewpoint, neither form of tolerance is permissible. Multi-domain-non-accommodation tolerance runs counter to several liberal-egalitarian commitments, for example commitments to general health care provision and the right to vote. Reporting tolerance is objectionable, presumably on freedom-of movement grounds, but more importantly since it violates a foundational liberal ideal of non-humiliation. By developing a liberal-egalitarian critique of tolerance as a state response to Gypsy Traveller nomadism, Häggrot´s chapter advances normative thinking about the moral entitlements of minority groups and, as well, the conditions and cases in which tolerance is, or is not, called for.

Gottfried Schweiger's and Clemens Sedmak's chapter analyzes toleration as a deep practice and legitimate expectation expressed towards refugees. Toleration as a deep practice, according to Schweiger and Sedmak, includes a moment of adversity (experience of resistance), a moment of intensity (experience of effort and engagement) and a moment of commitment (an experience that requires endurance). They examine the question of the extent to which toleration as a deep practice is a legitimate expectation that both refugees and the population of the host society can place against each other. Thus, they are dealing with the criteria of legitimacy of toleration under non-ideal circumstances, in a particular asymmetric relationship. Finally, Schweiger and Sedmak consider empirical research data from stake holders of the second Humanitarian Corridor in Italy that brought 500 refugees on a legal pathway to Italy between November 2017 and February 2019, which indicate that the management of the expectations of social workers, refugees, volunteers and local politicians can been identified as a key factor in the integration efforts with distinct challenges to attitudes and practices of toleration.

## Notes

1. In what follows we use the terms *toleration* and *tolerance* interchangeably.
2. Both liberalism and toleration are thus sometimes interpreted as essentially contested concepts in the sense of W. B. Gallie (1955). See also Abbey 2005 and Bader 2013.

## References

Abbey, R. (2005). Is Liberalism Now an Essentially Contested Concept? *New Political Science*, 27(4), pp. 461–480.

Arneil, B. (2012). Liberal Colonialism, Domestic Colonies and Citizenship. *History of Political Thought*, 23, pp. 491–523.

Bader, V. (2013). Moral Minimalism and More Demanding Moralities: Some Reflections on 'Tolerance/Toleration'. In: J. Dobbernack and T. Modood, eds., *Tolerance, Intolerance and Respect*, 1st ed. Houndsmill and Basingstoke: Palgrave Macmillan, pp. 23–51.

Balint, P. (2014). Acts of Tolerance: A Political and Descriptive Account. *European Journal of Political Theory*, 13(3), pp. 264–281.

Balint, P. (2017). *Respecting Toleration*. Oxford: Oxford University Press.

Brown, W. (2006). *Regulating Aversion: Tolerance in the Age of Identity and Empire*. Princeton, NJ: Princeton University Press.

Cohen, A. J. (2014). *Toleration*. Cambridge: Polity Press.

Cohen, A. J. (2015). Contemporary Liberalism and Toleration. In: S. Wall, ed., *The Cambridge Companion to Liberalism*, 1st ed. Cambridge: Cambridge University Press, pp. 189–211.

Cohen, A. J. (2018). *Toleration and Freedom from Harm: Liberalism Reconceived*. New York and Oxon: Routledge.

Colburn, B. (2010). *Autonomy and Liberalism*. New York and Oxon: Routledge.

Di Blasi, L. and Holzhey, C. (2014). Epilogue: Tensions in Tolerance. In: L. Di Blasi and C. Holzhey, eds., *The Power of Tolerance*, 1st ed. New York: Columbia University Press, pp. 71–101.

Dobbernack, J. and Modood, T. (2013). Introduction. In: J. Dobbernack and T. Modood, eds., *Tolerance, Intolerance and Respect*, 1st ed. Houndsmill and Basingstoke: Palgrave Macmillan, pp. 1–20.

Drerup, J. and Kühler, M. (eds.) (2019). The Politics and Ethics of Toleration. *Critical Review of International Social and Political Philosophy*. [online] Available at: https://doi.org/10.1080/13698230.2019.1616876 [Accessed 27 Apr. 2020].

Etinson, A. (2014). On Shareable Reasons: A Comment on Forst. *Journal of Social Philosophy*, 45, pp. 76–88.

Fawcett, E. (2018). *Liberalism: The Life of an Idea*, 2nd ed. Princeton, NJ: Princeton University Press.

Forst, R. (2013). *Toleration in Conflict: Past and Present*. Cambridge: Cambridge University Press.

Galeotti, E. (2002). *Toleration as Recognition*. Cambridge: Cambridge University Press.

Galeotti, E. (2015a). Toleration Out of Conflicts. Review of Rainer Forst's 'Toleration in Conflict'. *European Journal of Political Theory*, 14, pp. 246–255.

Galeotti, E. (2015b). Autonomy and Cultural Practices: The Risk of Double Standards. *European Journal of Political Theory*, 14, pp. 277–296.

Gallie, W. B. (1955). Essentially Contested Concepts. *Proceedings of the Aristotelian Society*, 56, pp. 160–180.

Gaus, G. (2018). Liberalism. [online] Available at: https://plato.stanford.edu/entries/liberalism/ [Accessed 23 Mar. 2020].

Heyd, D. (2008). Is Toleration a Political Virtue? In M. Williams and J. Waldron, eds., *Toleration and Its Limits*. New York: NYU Press, Nomos series, vol. 48, pp. 171–194.

Khomyakov, M. (2013). Toleration and Respect: Historical Instances and Current Problems. *European Journal of Political Theory*, 12(3), pp. 223–239.

Königs, P. (2019). The Simplicity of Toleration. *Critical Review of International Social and Political Philosophy* [online]. Available at: https://doi.org/10.1080/13698230.2019.1616877 [Accessed 27 Apr. 2020].

Lacorne, D. (2019). *The Limits of Tolerance*. New York: Columbia University Press.

McKinnon, C. (2006). *Toleration*. Oxon and New York: Routledge.

Mendus, S. (1989). *Toleration and the Limits of Liberalism*. Houndmills and Basingstoke: Palgrave Macmillan.

Nederman, C. (2011). Toleration in a New Key: Historical and Global Perspectives. In: D. Edyvane and M. Matravers, eds., *Toleration Re-Examined*, 1st ed. London and New York: Routledge, pp. 69–82.

Newey, G. (2013). *Toleration in Political Conflict*. Cambridge: Cambridge University Press.

Nussbaum, M. (2011). Perfectionist Liberalism and Political Liberalism. *Philosophy and Public Affairs*, 39(1), pp. 3–45.

Quong, J. (2011). *Liberalism Without Perfection*. Oxford: Oxford University Press.

Rawls, J. (2005). *Political Liberalism*. New York: Columbia University Press.

Raz, J. (1987). Autonomy, Toleration and the Harm Principle. In: R. Gavison, ed., *Issues in Contemporary Legal Philosophy*, 1st ed. Oxford: Oxford University Press, pp. 313–333.

Rossi, E. (2013). Can Tolerance Be Grounded in Equal Respect? *European Journal of Political Theory*, 12, pp. 240–252.

Sunstein, C. (2018). *Can It Happen Here?* New York: Dey Street.

Wall, S. (2015). Introduction. In: S. Wall, ed., *The Cambridge Companion to Liberalism*, 1st ed. Cambridge: Cambridge University Press, pp. 1–18.

Walzer, M. (1997). *On Toleration*. London and New Haven, CT: Yale University Press.

Williams, B. (1996). Toleration: An Impossible Virtue? In: D. Heyd, ed., *Toleration: An Elusive Virtue*, 1st ed. Princeton, NJ: Princeton University Press, pp. 18–27.

# Part I
# Toleration and Liberalism
Historical Controversies

# 1 John Locke and the "Problem" of Toleration

*John William Tate*

## Introduction

Given the circumstances and the times in which he wrote, John Locke's primary focus on toleration concerned matters of religion. Religious toleration was a "problem" for John Locke in two significant respects. Firstly, it had potentially adverse implications for civil peace and state security. Secondly, it confronted him with what I call the "moral challenge" of toleration. The following seeks to show how Locke engaged with these "problems", overcoming them sufficiently to advance, within his political philosophy, arguments in favour of religious toleration justified in terms of (a) a normative commitment to individual liberty and (b) the pragmatic capacity of toleration to achieve objectives of civil peace and state security. The discussion traces the development of Locke's ideas on toleration from his earliest political writings to his most mature texts, and the shifts in position on toleration that occurred therein. It should be noted that whenever Locke refers, in these writings, to the "magistrate", he is using this as a shorthand description of those who exercise authorized political and legal authority within a polity.

## 1. The "Moral Challenge" of Toleration

It was the sixteenth-century Reformation, and its outcomes, which confronted political rulers in central and Western Europe with the practical political problem of how to ensure civil peace and state security within their borders between rival and, at times, belligerent adherents of competing religious faiths. Was the appropriate response to use the instruments of persuasion and force, at the disposal of the state, to enforce outward conformity to the state-endorsed religion upon all those subject to the state's jurisdiction? Or was the appropriate response to allow such adherents to outwardly express their different religious beliefs and engage in their rival ways of religious worship, so long as such liberties did not interfere with or undermine civil peace or state security? To this question – conformity or toleration – different ruling authorities gave different answers:

> It was absolutely impossible in the sixteenth century that the question of how governments should, or had best, deal with religious contumacy, or with "heresy", should not be widely debated and from many different points of view. It was a question which, however put, directly and acutely affected the lives of multitudes of men and women all over Western Europe. Every government had to make up its mind at least as to practical action; and that in face of all manner of difficulties and complications. To the question as a practical one put in general terms, every possible answer was given. It was maintained that under some circumstances it was expedient, under others inexpedient, to "persecute", and that the ruler had a right to judge and to act at his discretion. It was also maintained that he had no choice about the matter. It was asserted that he was bound to endeavour to stamp out false religion by force, if force were necessary; it was maintained, on the contrary, that he was bound, morally, to allow people to preach and worship as they pleased, so long as they did not break the peace or incite to breach of it. . . . "Toleration" as a practical solution of intolerable difficulties and "toleration" as a general principle of action in relation to religious differences, both appear quite early in the sixteenth century.
> 
> (Allen, 1960, pp. 73–74)

Indeed, the question of which policy (conformity or toleration) was the most appropriate for ruling authorities to adopt in response to the reality of religious difference was also affected by the motives and ambitions ruling authorities themselves possessed in relation to such difference. Most European ruling authorities in the sixteenth and seventeenth centuries were headed by individual monarchs. If their primary concern, in confronting religious difference within their borders, was a secular one – to ensure civil peace and state security within the areas subject to their jurisdiction – then they could choose between toleration and outward conformity on an entirely pragmatic basis, in terms of which policy was the most instrumentally effective in achieving such outcomes.

If, however, in confronting such religious difference, they were animated by religious motivations – perhaps a desire to advance what they perceived to be "true religion" – then toleration, as a policy, was likely to confront them with a "moral challenge". After all, a truly conscientious adherent of a salvational faith such as Christianity will be concerned not only about the eternal fate of their own soul, but also the fate of others. If they believe that there is only one "true religion", whose path alone leads to eternal salvation, then they will be extremely wary of tolerating the public presence of what they consider to be "false religions", not least because these, being permitted to openly practice, might ensnare the souls of others.

Consequently, the motives and ambitions that political rulers possessed in confronting religious difference had a definite impact on which policy – toleration or religious conformity – they considered most appropriate in such circumstances. If their motives and ambitions were religious, rather than secular, centred on the propagation of "true religion", toleration might appear to them as an irresponsible policy, since it allowed for the dissemination of what they perceived to be "false religions", and so endangered the souls of others. It was in this respect that toleration confronted such individuals with a "moral challenge", since any arguments in favour of toleration had to be balanced against these adverse consequences. As John Coffey points out, toleration was rejected as "irresponsible" by many sixteenth- and seventeenth-century divines in England precisely because of these consequences:

> To grant "the publique freedome of heresies", suggested [Thomas] Bilson, was to countenance the "murder of souls". [Saint] Augustine, Thomas Case noted, had declared that those who called for liberty of conscience only gained "'Libertatem perditionis', liberty to destroy themselves". Instead of shepherding their subjects along the path to heaven, towards true freedom, irresponsible magistrates allowed them the liberty to choose hell. In contrast, the godly ruler should compel the lost to come in to the banquet. "Mercy is cruel", said [Edwin] Sandys, "and why should not the church compel her abandoned children to return, if her abandoned children compel others to perish?"
>
> (Coffey, 2000, p. 35. My addition)

By contrast, a pragmatic choice between toleration and conformity, informed entirely by which was more effective in ensuring external (secular) objectives such as civil peace or state security, did not elicit a "moral challenge" at all. This is because such choice was not informed by the considerations of "true religion" or the eternal salvation of souls which underwrote this "moral challenge".

## 2. Individual Liberty and the "Boundaries of Imposition and Obedience"

John Locke came late to European debates concerning toleration. As explained earlier, these had emerged in the sixteenth century, in response to the religious division produced by the Reformation. Locke began writing on toleration in the second half of the seventeenth century, though even at this time within Europe, the divisions, first ushered in by the Reformation, were still deep and vociferous. Indeed, Locke believed that such divisions, within his own society of England, were endemic and ineradicable. As he put it, when it comes to religion, "every man in what he believes has so far this persuasion that he is in the right" (Locke, 1993a, p. 205), with the result that, in regard to such matters, "diversity of opinions . . . cannot be avoided" (Locke, 1993b, p. 431).

Locke identified the key contending policy positions, prevalent in his time, available to ruling authorities seeking to respond to the reality of religious difference. These were (as before) a policy of toleration (allowing for the outward expression of religious difference) and the forcible imposition, by these same ruling authorities, of outward conformity to the state-endorsed religion. Locke identified the absence of clarity which, he believed, characterized both these positions within his own time, as follows:

> In the question of liberty of conscience, which has for some years been so much bandied amongst us, one thing that hath chiefly perplexed the question, kept up the dispute, and increased the animosity hath been, I conceive, this: that both parties have with equal zeal and mistake too much enlarged their pretensions, whilst one side preach up absolute obedience, and the other claim universal liberty in matters of conscience, without assigning what those things are which have a title to liberty, or showing the *boundaries of imposition and obedience*.
>
> (Locke, 1993a, p. 186. Emphasis added)

Locke continued to wrestle with this question of individual liberty and the "boundaries of imposition and obedience" throughout his intellectual career. It was precisely this question to which the issue of toleration gave rise. After all, the scope of toleration defined what matters, within an individual's life, ought not to be interfered with, with the result that that which fell within this scope had, presumably, a "title to liberty". Everything that fell outside this scope, however, was, in Locke's view, potentially subject to the magistrate's command, and therefore fell within the "boundaries of imposition and obedience".

## 3. Locke's Persistent Interest in Toleration

The topic of Locke's first known political writings was toleration, and these appeared in the unpublished manuscript entitled *Two Tracts on Government*, believed to have been written by Locke between 1660 and 1662.[1] The subject matter of his final and unfinished written work was also on toleration, this being his *Fourth Letter for Toleration*, written in response to the Anglican clergyman, Jonas Proast, who was an enthusiastic advocate of the imposition, by the English state, of outward conformity to the Church of England.

The primary difference between these two texts, at either end of Locke's career, was that in the *Two Tracts*, Locke was an ardent opponent of toleration, insisting that this was not a responsible or prudential policy for the state to adopt in response to the reality of religious difference. By the time of the *Fourth Letter*, on the other hand, Locke had capped almost forty years as an indefatigable (but often publicly anonymous) champion of toleration.[2]

In other words, somewhere in between, Locke had reversed his position on toleration. Whereas toleration had at first appeared to Locke as a "problem" – something to be avoided if ruling authorities wanted to maintain civil peace and state security within the territories subject to their jurisdiction –in some respects it came to appear to him as a "solution", being considered a necessary means for the attainment of such ends, as well as an important means of individual liberty. On what basis, therefore, did Locke manage to shift his position on toleration, ceasing to perceive it wholly as a "problem" and instead conceiving it, in some respects, as a "solution" to the problems of society and state? It is to this question that the rest of this chapter is devoted.

## 4. Continuities in Locke's Political Philosophy

As we shall see, there are certain characteristics that persist throughout John Locke's writings on toleration, from his early anti-tolerationist writing, *The Two Tracts on Government* (1660–62), to later pro-tolerationist writing such as *An Essay Concerning Toleration* (1667) and *A Letter Concerning Toleration* (1689). One persistent characteristic, we shall see, is a commitment to a normative ideal of individual liberty – Locke, however, differing, in these texts, concerning the extent to which this liberty ought to be outwardly expressed. Within the *Two Tracts*, we shall see that he limits such liberty to a purely inward liberty of conscience, insisting, where necessary in matters of religion, on an outward conformity to the magistrate's command. In his later writings, his endorsement of a policy of toleration, involving limits on the magistrate's command, entitles such inner liberty to be outwardly manifest in freedom of religious expression and worship. In each case, Locke endorses individual liberty as a norm, but differs concerning the limits of its outward expression – that is, the "boundary of imposition and obedience" at which toleration of such liberty should cease.

The other source of continuity in Locke's political writings is that such limits on toleration, and therefore on the outward expression of liberty it makes possible, are determined solely in terms of secular, as distinct from religious, considerations – centred on the external consequences of such toleration for civil peace, state security, and other civil matters (such as the "good and welfare of the people") for which Locke (at least by the time of his mature political philosophy) believed political authority to be inaugurated.[3] We shall see that Locke therefore eschews matters of religious "truth", or other theological considerations, when determining the limits of toleration, instead seeking secular reasons for such limits that all can conceivably endorse, irrespective of their religious convictions.

Such continuities characterise Locke's writings on toleration. It is within the boundaries of these continuities, therefore, that Locke shifts from an anti- to a pro-tolerationist position.

## 5. Two Tracts on Government

Locke's discourse in the *Two Tracts on Government* begins from the assumption that, given religious differences and the character of the populace within England, civil peace is a fragile commodity. Locke identifies his own youthful experience of the English Civil War as evidence of this, declaring: "I no sooner perceived myself in the *world* but I found myself in a storm, which hath lasted almost hitherto (Locke, 1967a, p. 119). It is therefore in relation to the need to maintain such civil peace, and the state security that makes it possible, that Locke, in the *Two Tracts*, evaluates the demand (emanating from his textual antagonist, Edward Bagshaw) for religious toleration within England.

Locke's estimation of the fragility of civil peace arises, in part, from an evaluation of the English populace which is almost "Hobbesian" in quality. Locke declares that the "multitude" (the broad mass of the English population) is inherently unruly and possesses a propensity for upheaval and disorder. As he states: "Who knows but that since the multitude is always craving, never satisfied, that there can be nothing set over them which they will not always be reaching at and endeavouring to pull down" (Locke, 1967a, pp. 158–159; see also Locke, 1967a, pp. 149, 154, 158, 160–161, 161–162, 169–170).

It is precisely because of this ever-present threat of disorder from below that Locke, in the *Two Tracts*, countenances very few limits on government authority, perceiving such robust capacity for governance as necessary to avoid such disorder. In other words, Locke, in the *Two Tracts*, is (like Hobbes and for the same reasons) thoroughly "authoritarian" in his attitude to the scope of government:

> Nor will the largeness of the governor's power appear dangerous or more than necessary if we consider that as occasion requires it is employed upon the multitude that are as impatient of restraint as the sea, and whose tempests and overflows cannot be too well provided against.
>
> (Locke, 1967a, p. 158)

## 6. The Volatility of Religion

Locke perceives religion as foremost among those contentious and volatile issues likely to elicit disorder from the "multitude", since it is on matters of religion that passions are most aroused. This is due, not least, he says, to the fact that in matters of religion, individuals perceive "eternity" to be at stake, "men finding no cause that can so rationally draw them to hazard this life, or compound for the dangers of a war as that which promises them a better" (Locke, 1967a, p. 160). Further, because so much is perceived to be at stake in matters of religion, Locke insists that, on such matters, individuals will divide, vociferously, on the most trivial issues:

> And he must confess himself a stranger to England that thinks that *meats* and *habits*, that *places* and *times* of worship etc., would not be as sufficient occasion of hatred and quarrels among us, as *leeks* and *onions* and other *trifles* described in that satire by Juvenal was amongst them, and be distinctions able to keep us always at a distance, and eagerly ready for like violence and cruelty as often as the *teachers* should alarm the *consciences* of their zealous votaries and direct them against the adverse party.[4]

Given the propensity of religion to arouse such passion and disorder among the "multitude", and given the propensity of some, in such circumstances, to use religion as a "cloak" for their own profane ambitions (Locke, 1967a, p. 160), Locke insists that any policy of government, such as toleration, which allows for the open expression of religious differences, is inherently irresponsible, because it is precisely the expression of such differences, however small or trivial, which produces disagreement and therefore open conflict:

> I know not whether experience (if it may be credited) would not give us some reason to think that were this part of *freedom* contended for here . . . generally indulged in *England* it would prove only a *liberty* for *contention*, *censure*, and *persecution* and turn us loose to the *tyranny* of a *religious rage*.
> (Locke, 1967a, p. 120)

Referring to the English Civil War which overthrew the monarchy of Charles I, and perhaps to the Cromwellian Interregnum which came after, Locke identifies their origins, in part, in religious conflict, and a willingness to allow such conflict open expression: "[A] liberty for tender consciences was the first inlet to all those confusions and unheard of and destructive opinions that overspread this nation."[5] He insists that as "[t]he same hearts are still in men as liable to zealous mistakes and religious furies, there wants but leave for crafty men to inspirit and fire them with such doctrines" (Locke, 1967a, p. 160). As his "leaks" and "onions" comment at note 4 earlier makes clear, Locke insists, in the *Two Tracts*, that any open expression of religious differences, however trivial, can produce such conflict, particularly among those disposed to believe "God dishonoured upon every small deviation from that way of his worship which either education or interest hath made sacred to them" (Locke, 1967a, p. 161). He therefore insists that magistrates would be neglecting their duty if they didn't, in such circumstances, impose their interdiction to prevent such open expression of religious differences, thereby denying toleration in those instances when such expression is likely to lead to such conflict, or when religion is used by "deceivers" as a cloak for their own profane purposes:

> And here, should not the magistrate's authority interpose itself and put a stop to the secret contrivances of deceivers and the passionate zeal of the deceived, he would certainly neglect his duty of being the great *conservator pacis*, and let the very foundations of government and the end of it lie neglected, and leave the peace of that society is committed to his care open to be torn and rent in pieces by everyone that could but *pretend to conscience and draw a sword*.[6]

We see therefore, that Locke, in the *Two Tracts*, comprehensively denies that toleration is an appropriate policy for the state to adopt in response to the reality of religious difference. Such denial is premised on the fact that toleration leads to the outward expression of religious differences ("a liberty for tender consciences") which, Locke insists, is a likely source of conflict and upheaval. But what is also clear from this discussion is that Locke's refusal of toleration, or the limits upon it, is justified in purely secular rather than religious terms – because of the external impact which, he believes, the outward expression of religious difference will have on civil peace and state security.

## 7. Locke and Individual Liberty

While Locke conceded, in the *Two Tracts*, that the imposition, by the magistrate, of outward conformity in matters of religion did impose limits on individual liberty, he did not believe it expunged such liberty altogether, since individuals might still possess complete inward liberty of conscience in such circumstances. As Locke insists, so long as the magistrate does not insist that such outward conformity is "material" (a matter of religious conscience), it remains a purely "formal" matter, arising solely from the magistrate's command, and so binding the liberty of an individual's "will" (i.e. their outward actions) but not their "judgment" (conscience), with the result that individuals can engage in such outward conformity, in accordance with the magistrate's command, while keeping their inner consciences free on matters of religion (Locke, 1967b, pp. 238–239).

Locke's commitment to inward liberty of conscience as a norm within the *Two Tracts* is evident in his discussion of those commands of the magistrate which are "indeed opposed to the liberty of conscience" (Locke, 1967b, p. 238). Locke declares that if the magistrate (a) does insist that one of his or her particular commands is "material" (i.e. a matter of individual conscience), arising from divine injunctions, and so enjoins not only the "liberty of the will" (outward action) but also "liberty of judgment" (inner conscience), yet (b) this is not actually the case because the command arises solely on the basis of the authority of the magistrate alone, then (c) such commands are "indeed opposed to the liberty of conscience", with the result that (d) the magistrate "by such a law . . . ensnares the liberty of the conscience and sins in commanding it" (Locke, 1967b, p. 269. My addition).

Locke does not, in the *Two Tracts*, advance a right of resistance to such erroneous commands. But the fact that he is willing, within the *Two Tracts*, to declare a command by the magistrate "sinful" if it erroneously transgresses on the inward liberty of conscience, shows the extent to which Locke was willing, within that text, to accord an entitlement to such liberty even if he was willing to limit its outward expression entirely in terms of the magistrate's command.

Locke insists it is not possible for magistrates to gain access to or control over the individual's inner conscience. This is because such conscience ("judgment") remains outside not only the control of the magistrate, but also the control of the individual, who cannot help but believe that at which their judgment has arrived (Locke, 1967a, pp. 127, 129–130, 165, 167; 1967b, pp. 214, 238–239. See also Locke, 1993b, p. 420; 1993a, pp. 188–189). But individuals *do* have a choice over their outward actions (what Locke calls "liberty of the will" as distinct from "liberty of judgment") and it is at this level that the magistrate's demands for religious conformity are imposed (Locke, 1967b, pp. 238–239).

One reason "liberty of conscience" is a norm for Locke is precisely because of its necessity for sincere and genuine religious belief. As Locke states in *A Letter Concerning Toleration*, "saving religion" consists in the "inward persuasion of the mind, without which nothing can be acceptable to God".[7] In other words, at least at one level, "true religion", for Locke, is the religion that an individual believes to be "true", since only such belief is genuine and sincere, and so "acceptable to God", with the result that "men must in this necessarily follow what they themselves thought best, since no consideration could be sufficient to force a man from or to that which he was fully persuaded was the way to infinite happiness or infinite misery" (Locke, 1993a, p. 189). This assumption that only "sincere" belief is "acceptable" to God, and that it is only the religion in which an individual genuinely believes, on the basis of their own judgment, that can be "sincere", constitutes one of the bases by which Locke is able to uphold an ideal of "liberty of conscience" and arrive at the conclusion, evident in his later pro-tolerationist writings, that "[t]he care . . . of every man's soul belongs unto himself, and is to be left unto himself" (Locke, 1993b, pp. 405–406; see also Locke, 1993b, pp. 393–394, 396, 403, 405, 411, 412, 421–423).

## 8. The Difficult Issue of Religious "Conscience"

Yet while Locke perceives inward "liberty of conscience" as a norm (it being a part of the wider norm of individual liberty itself), nevertheless individual conscience is a difficult issue for Locke. On the one hand, as a Protestant, he believes that individual conscience, along with Scripture, is the source of the "rule of faith", the ultimate touchstone for individual religious beliefs and conviction.[8] He makes this clear in the *Letter*, at note 7 earlier, when he insists that only sincere religious belief (i.e. belief in accord with the conscience of the individual) is "acceptable to God", with the result that "[a]ll the life and power of true religion consists in the inward and full persuasion of the mind, and faith is not faith without believing" (Locke, 1993b, p. 394). Indeed, in the earlier *An Essay Concerning Toleration*, Locke identifies individual liberty, of which "conscience" is at the centre, with individual dignity, insisting that one is not possible without the other:

> [S]o chary is human nature to preserve the liberty of that part wherein lies the dignity of a man, which could it be imposed on would make him but little different from a beast
>
> (Locke, 1993a, p. 204).

And yet Locke also makes clear, not only in the *Two Tracts* but also in his later pro-toleration texts, that individual "conscience" can be a source of immense civil and political upheaval. He refers at note 6 earlier to the danger that "society" may be "torn and rent in pieces by everyone that could but pretend to conscience and draw a sword". The reason "conscience" possesses such unruly capacities is (as Locke points out at note 9) because there is "nothing so indifferent which the conscience of some or other do not check at", with the result that it is potentially unlimited in its claims. So for instance, Locke refers, in the *Two Tracts*, to recent "conscientious disorders" in England (Locke, 1967a, p. 120) and declares that a key problem for the state and civil society is that religious demands, arising on the basis of "conscience", are potentially unlimited, overriding civil and political restraints – and further, it is toleration that gives these demands open expression:

> Grant the people once free and unlimited in the exercise of their religion and where will they stop, where will they themselves bound it, and will it not be religion to destroy all that are not of their profession? And will they not think they do God good service to take vengeance on those that they have voted his enemies?
>
> (Locke, 1967a, p. 159)

The result is that even within his pro-tolerationist writings, such as *An Essay Concerning Toleration*, written in 1667, Locke nevertheless still seeks to place limits on the entitlements of "conscience", and therefore limits on the toleration that allows for its outward expression, precisely because of its potentially adverse implications for civil peace and state security:

> But yet no such opinion hath any right to toleration on this ground, that it is a matter of conscience, and some men are persuaded that it is either a sin or a duty, because the conscience or persuasion of the subject cannot possibly be a measure by which the magistrate can or ought to frame his laws, which ought to be suited to the good of all his subjects, not the persuasions of a part, which often happening to be contrary one to another must produce contrary laws, and there being nothing so indifferent which the conscience of some or other do not check at, a toleration of men in all that which they pretend, out of conscience, they cannot submit to will wholly take away all the civil laws, and all the magistrate's power; and so there will be no law, no government.[9]

## 9. "The Business of Laws Is Not to Provide for the Truth of Opinions"

So how does Locke resolve this paradox that, on the one hand, as a sincere Protestant, he respects "conscience" as a source of religious "truth" for individuals, and perceives the capacity to live according to "conscience" to be a fundamental condition of individual "dignity", and yet, on the other hand, recognizes that some expressions of "conscience" are a fundamental danger to civil peace and state security and ought to be overridden by the magistrate's command? In other words, in the case of "conscience", where does Locke draw the demarcation between toleration, with its guarantees of a "title to liberty", and the "boundaries of imposition and obedience"?

Once again, as in the case of the *Two Tracts*, the answer resides in the fact that Locke sought to draw this demarcation solely in secular terms, centred on the purely material interests of civil peace, state security, and the "good and welfare of the people" – these being the "civil" interests which all individuals shared, irrespective of their religious divisions, and which, he believed, to be the sole responsibility of governments.[10] Locke seeks to place limits on the toleration of "conscience" when it produces actions likely to endanger these "civil" interests. But at no point does he seek to circumscribe "conscience" in terms of its intrinsic content, centred on the "truth" or "falsity" of the religious beliefs or doctrines it seeks to espouse. This was one more means by which Locke dealt with the "problem" of toleration – by justifying its limits in terms of "civil" interests all shared rather than in terms of religious "truth" on which many were divided. Indeed we shall see that Locke insisted, on sceptical grounds, that any indubitable criterion of religious "truth" was unavailable.

So for example, while both Catholicism and atheism are a matter of conscientious conviction, Locke, nevertheless, in *An Essay Concerning Toleration*, denies toleration to Catholics, not on the grounds of the "truth" or "falsity" of their theological convictions, but because, yielding an allegiance to the Pope in Rome, these convictions are a threat to the security of the state (Locke, 1993a, pp. 202–203. See also Locke, 1993a, p. 197). Equally, Locke denies toleration to atheists on similar secular grounds. Just as Catholics cannot be trusted to abide by their 'oaths, promises, and the obligations they have to their prince' (Locke, 1993a, p. 203), because of their allegiance to a foreign power, so atheists cannot be trusted to do the same, given the absence of their belief in God:

> Lastly, those are not at all to be tolerated who deny the being of a God. Promises, covenants and oaths, which are the bonds of human society, can have no hold upon an atheist. The taking away of God, though but even in thought, dissolves all.
> (Locke, 1993b, p. 426. See also Locke, 1993a, p. 188)

In other words, it is not the theological error of not believing in God, or other factors internal to the doctrine of atheism, that is the basis for Locke denying toleration, and imposing the "boundaries of imposition and obedience", on atheists. Rather, as with Catholics, it is the secular consequences of this absence of belief, and its implications for state and civil society.

Locke, in *A Letter Concerning Toleration*, denies toleration to a range of other conscientious convictions, arising from religious doctrines, such as the doctrine that "dominion is founded in grace" or "faith is not to be kept with heretics" (Locke, 1993b, p. 425; see also Locke, 1993a, p. 201). Again the reasons for this denial of toleration are entirely secular – these "opinions" being "contrary to human society, or to those moral rules which are necessary to the preservation of civil society" (Locke, 1993b, p. 424).

In all the examples given, therefore, it is not any concern with "truth", religious or otherwise, that determines for Locke the scope of toleration, and therefore the "boundaries of imposition and obedience", when it comes to the conscientious convictions of individuals. Rather, it is the instrumental consequences of such convictions for civil peace or state security. Indeed, at one point in *A Letter Concerning Toleration*, Locke makes this position very clear, explicitly eschewing any consideration of "truth" in determining such matters and instead insisting the relevant appeal is solely to such secular considerations:

> If a Jew do not believe the New Testament to be the Word of God, he does not thereby alter anything in men's civil rights. If a heathen doubt of both Testaments, he is not therefore to be punished as a pernicious citizen. The power of the magistrate, and the estates of the

people, may be equally secure, whether any man believe these things or no. I readily grant that these opinions are false and absurd. *But the business of laws is not to provide for the truth of opinions, but for the safety and security of the commonwealth, and of every particular man's goods and person.*
(Locke, 1993b, p. 420. Emphasis added)

Locke's disregard of religious "truth", when it comes to determining the scope of toleration and the "boundaries of imposition and obedience", is also evident in *A Letter Concerning Toleration* when he extends toleration to entirely heterodox religious doctrines and practices, such as idolatry and animal sacrifice, which he himself, as a sincere Protestant, would have perceived to be entirely at odds with the will of God (Locke, 1993b, pp. 415, 417). The reason he does so is, once again, for the entirely secular reasons identified earlier, wherein, he says, such practices "are not prejudicial to other men's rights, nor do they break the public peace of societies" (Locke, 1993b, p. 417). But if there was a food shortage, whereby animal sacrifice as religious practice became a wasteful extravagance likely to harm the interests of civil society, then, Locke writes, 'who sees not that the magistrate, in such a case, may forbid all his subjects to kill any calves for any use whatsoever?' (Locke, 1993b, p. 415). Such an account forms part of my wider thesis that Locke sought, in significant but not always comprehensive ways, to separate his political philosophy from wider issues of Christian theology and religious belief in general. For my attempt to refute those who have sought to immerse the former in the latter, see Tate 2012; Tate 2013; Tate 2016a, pp. 4, 5, 17n, 98-99, 262n; Tate 2017.

## 10. The *Two Treatises* and a Right of Resistance

We have seen that Locke circumscribed the entitlements of "conscience", and the liberties and prerogatives individuals claimed on the basis of it, in terms of secular considerations centred on civil peace and state security. However by the time of his most mature political work, the *Two Treatises of Government* (1689), Locke has shifted from this position. This is because, in this work, Locke affirms a right of resistance to government for individuals when, on the basis of their conscientious convictions, they believe the magistrate is transgressing their most fundamental liberties, these being those liberties which such individuals, or their predecessors, inaugurated government to protect in the first place:

> For no Man, or Society of Men, having a Power to deliver up their *Preservation*, or consequently the means of it, to the Absolute Will and arbitrary Dominion of another; whenever any one shall go about to bring them into such a Slavish Condition, they will always have a right to preserve what they have not a Power to part with; and to rid themselves of those who invade this Fundamental,

Sacred, and unalterable Law of *Self-Preservation*, for which they entr'd into Society.
(Locke, 1965, II, § 149; see also Locke, 1965, II, §§ 131, 135, 168, 171, 222; 1993b, pp. 423–424, 432)

In the context of this right of resistance, Locke envisages the possibility of open conflict between those seeking to exercise such resistance and the government against whom it is exercised, whereupon, he tells us, the "appeal" (being subject to the resort to force) is to "heaven" (Locke, 1965, II, §§ 20–21, 168, 176, 241–242). We see the extent to which this position is qualitatively distinct from his earlier one in which individual liberty was limited by secular considerations of civil peace and state security. This is because, in the context of the right of resistance, it is civil peace and state security which are potentially *expendable*, it being these which are forfeited when individuals seek to overthrow the authority of government by force. Locke concedes that such resistance to government authority may or may not succeed, given the contingencies and exigencies involved in any resort to force (Locke, 1965, II, §§ 168, 208–209, 223, 225, 230). It is for this reason that he declares that in such circumstances the "appeal is to heaven". The only limit Locke seeks to impose upon such resistance is a *realpolitik* one, declaring that unless these dissidents have the support of the "greater part" of the "People", they are "sure to perish" at the hands of those they seek to oppose (Locke 1965, II, §§ 208, 230. See also Tate 2017, p. 118).

In endorsing such an open right of resistance to government, Locke moves well beyond the right of conscientious objection to state authorities he endorsed in *An Essay Concerning Toleration*, wherein he declared that individuals were entitled to disobey the laws or commands of the magistrate "so far as without violence they can", when these were contrary to "the sincere persuasions of their own consciences", but insisted they must also "quietly . . . submit to the penalty the law inflicts on such disobedience", and "by this means . . . secure to themselves their grand concernment in another world, and disturb not the peace of this . . . the interest of the magistrate and their own being both safe" (Locke, 1993a, p. 194). By removing entirely, within the *Two Treatises*, this "boundary of imposition and obedience", and allowing individuals to engage in full-scale resistance to government, refusing to submit to any of its "penalties" in the process, Locke endorsed nothing less than an entitlement to "revolution" within this text. Richard Ashcraft has sought to explain these more radical elements of Locke's political philosophy in the *Two Treatises of Government* in terms of Locke's involvement, at this time, in the first Earl of Shaftesbury's political opposition to Charles II during the period when Shaftesbury and his supporters were seeking to exclude Charles' brother, the Catholic Duke of York, from succession to the English throne (Ashcraft, 1980, pp. 431, 436–438, 449, 451, 466, 468, 474–475; Ashcraft, 1986, pp. 9–13).

## 11. Re-Evaluations

So we have identified continuities between Locke's early anti-tolerationist writing and his later pro-tolerationist writing, as well as qualitative shifts away from both in his *Two Treatises of Government*. We have seen that, even in his later writings, toleration is still potentially a "problem" for Locke and therefore requires limits – and this because individual conscience is still a potential source of civil instability and political upheaval. But toleration is also seen, in these later writings, as a means by which such instability and upheaval can be avoided. The result is that Locke breaks from the anti-tolerationist position of the *Two Tracts* and espouses, in his later writings, toleration as the preferred response of governments to religious difference within their borders.

How does Locke engage in this transition? How does he shift from seeing toleration as a source of instability (in the *Two Tracts*) to seeing it as a means by which such instability can be avoided, and a basis upon which the "magistrate" can establish "the peace and quiet of his people" (Locke, 1993a, p. 202)?

The answer is that Locke achieved this transition on the basis of a series of empirical re-evaluations. These evaluations are "empirical" because they involve an assessment, by Locke, of the actual material circumstances of his time and place, and the extent to which toleration, applied to those circumstances, and allowing for the outward expression of religious differences, will produce specific types of outcomes rather than others.

We saw that Locke maintained a normative commitment to individual liberty throughout his political writings, only differing between the anti- and pro-tolerationist writings in terms of the extent to which (given considerations of civil peace and state security) such liberty ought to be outwardly expressed. What allowed Locke to move from an anti-tolerationist position (in which such liberty, on matters of religion, was largely confined to an inward liberty of conscience) to a pro-tolerationist position (where it extended, via a policy of toleration, to outward religious expression) was an empirical re-evaluation of the extent to which this outward religious expression would produce the dystopian outcomes for civil peace and state security that he identified in the *Two Tracts*. Only if Locke was able to perceive a future for England in which the outward expression of religious differences did not result in such tumult and disorder would he be able to endorse toleration – a policy which enabled such outward expression – as an appropriate response to religious difference.

## 12. Empirical Re-evaluation

By the time of *An Essay Concerning Toleration* (1667) Locke had engaged in this empirical re-evaluation. He still identifies religious differences as a potential source of disorder but (as with the *Two Tracts*) identifies the primary source of this as residing in the motives of those who profess these differences, insisting that if such disorder results, it is "not the fault of the worship, but the men, and is not the consequences of this or that form of devotion, but the product of depraved, ambitious human nature, which successively makes use of all sorts of religion" (Locke, 1993a, p. 190). Unlike the *Two Tracts*, however, Locke is much more willing to conclude that in the absence of such nefarious motives, outward expression of religious difference will not produce any "disturbance of the government or injury of my neighbour" (Locke, 1993a, p. 189). As he states:

> Religious worship being that homage which I pay to that God I adore in a way I judge acceptable to him, and so being an action or commerce passing only between God and myself, hath in its own nature no reference at all to my governor, or to my neighbour, and so necessarily produces no action which disturbs the community. . . . If I observe the Friday with the Mahometan, or the Saturday with the Jew, or the Sunday with the Christian, whether I pray with or without a form, whether I worship God in the various and pompous ceremonies of the papist or in the plainer way of the Calvinists, I see nothing in any of these, if they be done sincerely and out of conscience, that can of itself make me either the worse subject to my prince, or worse neighbour to my fellow-subject. Unless it be that I will out of pride or over-weeningness of my own opinion and a secret conceit of my own infallibility, taking to myself something of a God-like power, force and compel others to be of my mind, or censure or malign them if they be not.
> (Locke, 1993a, pp. 189–190)

Further, far from perceiving toleration as an "inlet to all those confusions and unheard of and destructive opinions that overspread this nation" (such as Locke claims earlier at note 5), toleration, in *An Essay Concerning Toleration*, is presented as the most likely means of avoiding such upheaval and disorder. In other words, far from being presented as a "problem" for civil peace and state security, toleration is now presented as the "solution" most likely, in a context of religious difference, to achieve such objectives. The reason, Locke insists, is that toleration's alternative (an outward conformity, imposed by state authorities, on matters of religion) will produce more resistance to government, and therefore more disorder, than it is likely to avoid:

> [N]o man ought to be forced to renounce his opinion or assent to the contrary, because such compulsion cannot produce any real effect to that purpose for which it is designed. It cannot alter men's minds; it can only force them to be hypocrites, and by this way the magistrate is so

> far from bringing men to embrace the truth of his opinion of that, as that he only constrains them to lie for their errors; *nor doth this injunction at all conduce to the peace or security of the government, but quite the contrary, because hereby the magistrate does not make anyone to be one jot more of his mind, but to be very much more his enemy.*
> (Locke, 1993a, pp. 192–193, emphasis added; see also Locke, 1993a, pp. 204–205)

We see in the italicized section of this passage evidence of Locke's shift in empirical evaluation, wherein he concludes that state-imposed religious conformity, far from being a means to ensure civil peace and state security (as he assumed in the *Two Tracts*) will in fact produce more disorder than it will avoid. He makes the same point on a much more *realpolitik* basis in the same text. Addressing himself directly to the magistrate, and referring to the number of those within the polity with whom the magistrate may be at odds in matters of religion, Locke states:

> [I]f you think the different parties are already grown to a consistency and formed into one body and interest against you, whether it were the hardships they suffered under you made them unite or no, when they are so many as to equal or exceed you in number, as perhaps they do in England, force will be but an ill and hazardous way to bring them into submission.
> (Locke, 1993a, p. 207)

It is on the basis of this empirical reassessment that Locke then advances the propriety of toleration as a means for state authorities to respond to religious difference. Not only will such toleration expand the scope of individual liberty in matters of religion (thereby according with the norm of liberty that Locke has always advanced), but it will, at a pragmatic level, be much more likely to ensure civil peace and state security than the alternative policy (outward conformity) wherein such (outward) religious liberty is denied. Referring specifically to Dissenters in England, divided, as they were, into a multitude of minor sects, Locke, again directly addressing the magistrate, advances such pragmatic arguments for toleration as follows:

> People . . . that are so shattered into different factions are best secured by toleration, since being in as good a condition under you as they can hope for under any, 'tis not like[ly] they should join to set up any other, whom they cannot be certain will use them so well. But if you persecute them you make them all of one party and interest against you, tempt them to shake off your yoke and venture for a new government, wherein everyone has hopes to get the dominion themselves or better usage under others.
> (Locke, 1993a, p. 207; see also Locke, 1993a, pp. 197–198)

30  *John William Tate*

There has been some attempts within the literature to explain Locke's shift from an anti- to pro-tolerationist position in terms of his commitment to natural law. I have sought to refute such a thesis (see Tate 2017: 110–114). There has also been widespread debate within the literature concerning the extent to which Locke's volte-face on toleration can be explained by Locke's new-found association with Anthony Ashley Cooper, later the first Earl of Shaftesbury, whose household Locke joined in 1667, the year he wrote *An Essay Concerning Toleration* (Laslett, 1965, pp. 38–43; Cranston, 1952, pp. 620–621; Cranston, 1957, p. 113; Wootton, 1993, p. 18; Ashcraft, 1987, p. 21; Milton and Milton, 2010, pp. 27, 49–52; Marshall, 1996, pp. 49, 69; Dunn, 1969, pp. 28–30). For a discussion of this debate, as well as a more detailed account of Locke's shift on toleration, see Tate 2016a, chaps 2 and 3; Tate 2017.

## 13. The "Moral Challenge" of Toleration Revisited

Even if Locke was able to engage in the empirical evaluation that allowed him to arrive at such pro-tolerationist conclusions, this did not, in and of itself, override the "moral challenge" of toleration. After all, this "moral challenge" was premised not on concerns with civil peace or state security, but rather on concerns regarding "true religion" and the salvation of souls. Even if Locke did not believe that toleration led to adverse civil or political consequences, it was still possible that it led to adverse theological consequences, arising from the propagation of "false" religions that (from the perspective of a sincere Christian believing in only one doctrinal path to heaven)[11] potentially placed individuals on a path of eternal perdition. How did Locke, as a sincere Christian, overcome this "moral challenge"?

Whereas Locke's re-evaluation of toleration's propensity to produce civil or political disorder is empirical, the means by which he overcomes the "moral challenge" of toleration is epistemological. I have focused elsewhere on what Locke, in *A Letter Concerning Toleration*, offers as three distinct arguments (or what he calls "considerations") for toleration (Locke 1993b, pp. 394–396. See Tate, 2016a, chap. 5; Tate 2010). In addition, Locke offers a fourth argument for toleration that is premised on distinctly sceptical epistemological considerations (Tate 2022; Tate 2016a, pp. 129, 157–159, 226-236; Tate 2016b, pp. 670–671). This sceptical argument for toleration centres on the proposition that no one should use force to impose "true religion" because no one can ever ultimately *know* what the "true religion" is, it being entirely a matter of "faith", while any revelation of its "truth" (such as the faithful believe is testified to in scriptural sources) occurred too long ago for factual confirmation to be possible (see Locke, 1963a, p. 89; Locke, 1963b, pp. 144, 402, 419, 420, 422, 424; Locke 1963c, p. 561; Tate 2016a, pp. 129, 235–36; Tate 2016b, pp. 670–671).

Such scepticism, it is important to note, does not apply to the existence of God Himself. Locke believed it was possible, on the basis of human reason alone, to arrive at a knowledge of God's existence (Locke, 1975, Bk. I, chap. iv, § 17; Locke, 2004, pp. 278–279). But "true religion", in a Christian context, refers to the religion necessary for salvation, and it is precisely such "truth", "revealed" in biblical sources, that Locke believes is inaccessible to human knowledge, being dependent solely on human "faith" (Locke, 1963c, pp. 558–559, 563, 567). As Locke puts it to his antagonist Jonas Proast, who claimed precisely such knowledge of "true religion":

> You say . . . that "that one true religion may be known by those who profess it". . . . At first, it will be necessary to inquire what you mean by "known"; whether you mean by it knowledge properly so called, as contradistinguished to belief – or only the assurance of a firm belief? . . . If you mean, that the true religion may be known with the certainty of knowledge properly so called; I ask you farther, whether that true religion be to be known by the light of nature, or needed a divine revelation to discover it? If you say, as I suppose you will, the latter; then I ask whether the making out of that to be a divine revelation depends not upon particular matters of fact, whereof you were no eye-witness, but were done many ages before you were born? and if so, by what principles of science they can be known to any man now living?
>
> The articles of my religion, and of a great many such other short-sighted people as I am, are articles of faith, which we think there are so good grounds to believe, that we are persuaded to venture our eternal happiness on that belief. . . . But we neither think that God requires, nor has given us faculties capable of knowing in this world several of those truths which are to be believed to salvation.
> (Locke, 1963b, p. 424. See also Locke, 1963a, p. 111; 1963b, pp. 144, 402, 419–420, 422; 1963c, pp. 558–559, 563, 567; see also Tate, 2016a, pp. 157–159, 234–236)

The "moral challenge" of toleration derives its normative force from an assumption that one is in possession of religious "truth", and so can know and identify religious "error". Consequently, on the basis of sceptical assumptions that deny these possibilities, Locke avoids the "moral challenge" of toleration, because he denies the possibility that anyone can have indubitable knowledge of which religion is "true", and therefore knowledge of which religions preclude the path to individual salvation.[12]

## 14. The Two Arguments

This chapter has distinguished Locke's arguments for toleration premised on pragmatic and normative considerations. Arguments for toleration premised on pragmatic considerations, such as its capacity to secure civil peace or state security, may also avoid the "moral challenge" of toleration, since they are not dependent on the considerations of religious "truth" that underwrite that "challenge". But such pragmatic arguments are contingent, in terms of their cogency, on changes in empirical circumstance, or our assessment of these. For instance, if another process independent of toleration (such as enforced outward conformity in matters of religion) is perceived to be a more effective means of ensuring civil peace or state security, there is nothing intrinsic to the pragmatic argument for toleration that can counter this, since it lacks any commitment to the normative ideals (such as individual liberty) for which toleration is a necessary means. In this respect, such pragmatic arguments for toleration have circumstantial force, given the ends toleration is expected to achieve, but they lack normative force.

The alternative argument for toleration, premised on its capacity to ensure the outward expression of individual liberty, possesses such normative force. This is because the connection between such toleration and liberty is not contingent (dependent on empirical circumstances) but necessary, it being only toleration (not alternative policies like outward conformity) that can secure the conditions wherein such liberty (in terms of its outward expression) can be achieved.

## Conclusion

Locke never wholly rid himself of the "problem" of toleration. Even in his later pro-tolerationist writings, toleration still threatened disorder, because of the liberty it provided for (a potentially unruly) individual conscience, and for this reason required limits. But he did undertake a definite transition within his texts from an anti- to a pro-tolerationist position. To do so, Locke needed to engage with the "problem" of toleration, understood as both a threat to civil society and the state, and a threat to "true religion". Only by engaging effectively with this "problem" could he become the ardent advocate of toleration for which he is famous and inaugurate much of the toleration debate in what we now know as the liberal tradition.

## Notes

1. The *Two Tracts* were actually untitled and only discovered in 1947 when the Earl of Lovelace sold, to the Bodleian Library, a collection of Locke manuscripts (Abrams, 1967a, p. 3, 1967b, p. ix). It was the editor of the untitled manuscript, Philip Abrams, who gave it the title of *Two Tracts on Government*. He states: "Their polemical character, their similarity of form with the *Two Treatises*, and their underlying concern with questions of law and obligation will, I hope, justify this choice" (Abrams, 1967b, p. ix).
2. Concerning such anonymity, John Locke's *A Letter Concerning Toleration* (1689) was published anonymously, as was his *Two Treatises of Government* (1689). Locke's *An Essay Concerning Toleration* (1667) was unpublished in his lifetime.

3. On Locke's belief that government was inaugurated to achieve specific "civil" purposes, including civil peace and the effective governance that ensures this, see Locke, 1993b, pp. 422–423; 1965, II § 13, 21, 90, 94–95, 123, 127, 136–137, 171. By the time of his mature political philosophy, Locke insisted individuals left the state of nature and agreed to create governments precisely for these purposes – Locke, 1965, II § 87, 124, 131, 134, 192, 222. Locke believes that this process constituted the actual origins of governments (Locke, 1965, II § 14, 99, 101, 104, 106, 112). However he admits any evidence for this would be lost in the mists of time (Locke, 1965, II § 101).
4. Locke, 1967a, p. 121. See also 1967a, pp. 161–62.
5. Locke, 1967a, p. 160.
6. Locke, 1967a, p. 162. Emphasis added.
7. Locke, 1993b, p. 395.
8. Concerning the Protestant belief that individual conscience is the "rule of faith", as famously advanced by Martin Luther at the Diet of Worms in 1521, see Popkin, 1979, pp. 3, 7–10; Hughes, 1960, pp. 108–109; Chadwick, 1976, p. 56.
9. Locke, 1993a, p. 191.
10. On Locke's insistence, in the *Two Tracts*, that the authority of state authorities should be limited to these "civil" matters, with the result that any state regulation of religion should be justified solely in their (secular) terms, see Locke, 1967a, pp. 137, 145; 1967b, pp. 219–220, 237. Locke makes the same point in his later pro-tolerationist writings: Locke, 1993a, pp. 192, 193, 195, 1993b, pp. 393–394, 423. On Locke's belief that individuals established government authority precisely to achieve these "civil" purposes, see note 3. On the "good and welfare of the people", see Locke 1993a: 192.
11. Locke, at some points, conceded a belief that there was "one true religion" and that this was the sole path to salvation – Locke, 1993b, pp. 407–408; Locke, 1963a, p. 133; 1963b, pp. 320, 326, 327–328, 332–333, 356, 422. Yet elsewhere he declares that such an exclusive conception of salvation is merely an excuse for persecution, since "if there were several ways that lead thither, there would not be so much as a pretence left for compulsion" (Locke, 1993b, p. 406).
12. Locke was accused of scepticism, in matters of religion, by Jonas Proast, during their debates on toleration, and Locke denied the charge (see Locke, 1963c, pp. 562–563). On why Locke was in error regarding his repudiation of scepticism, and how he advances precisely the scepticism, in matters of religion, of which Proast accuses him, see Tate, 2016a, pp. 226–231.

# References

Abrams, P. (1967a). John Locke as a Conservative. In: J. Locke and P. Abrams, eds., *Two Tracts on Government*. Cambridge: Cambridge University Press, pp. 3–29.

Abrams, P. (1967b). Foreword. In: J. Locke and P. Abrams, eds., *Two Tracts on Government*. Cambridge: Cambridge University Press, pp. ix–x.

Allen, J. (1960). *A History of Political Thought in the Sixteenth Century*. London: Methuen.

Ashcraft, R. (1980). Revolutionary Politics and Locke's *Two Treatises of Government*: Radicalism and Lockean Political Theory. *Political Theory*, 8(4), pp. 429–486.

Ashcraft, R. (1986). *Revolutionary Politics and Locke's Two Treatises of Government*. Princeton, NJ: University of Princeton Press.

Ashcraft, R. (1987). *Locke's Two Treatises of Government*. London: Allen and Unwin.

Chadwick, O. (1976). *The Reformation*. Harmondsworth: Penguin.

Coffey, J. (2000). *Persecution and Toleration in Protestant England, 1558–1689*. Edinburg: Pearson Education Ltd.

Cranston, M. (1952). The Politics of John Locke. *History Today*, 2(9), pp. 619–622.

Cranston, M. (1957). *John Locke: A Biography*. London: Longmans, Green and Co.

Dunn, J. (1969). *The Political Thought of John Locke: An Historical Account of the Argument of the 'Two Treatises of Government'*. Cambridge: Cambridge University Press.

Hughes, P. (1960). *The Reformation*. London: Burns and Oates.

Laslett, P. (1965). Introduction. In: J. Locke and P. Laslett, eds., *Two Treatises of Government*. New York: New American Library, pp. 15–135.

Locke, J. (1963a). A Second Letter Concerning Toleration. In: J. Locke, ed., *The Works of John Locke*, vol. VI. Aalen: Scientia Verlag, pp. 61–137.

Locke, J. (1963b). A Third Letter for Toleration. In: J. Locke, ed., *The Works of John Locke*, vol. VI. Aalen: Scientia Verlag, pp. 141–546.

Locke, J. (1963c). A Fourth Letter for Toleration. In: J. Locke, ed., *The Works of John Locke*, vol. VI. Aalen: Scientia Verlag, pp. 549–574.

Locke, J. (1965). *Two Treatises of Government*. New York: New American Library.

Locke, J. (1967a). The First Tract on Government. In: J. Locke and P. Abrams, eds., *Two Tracts on Government*. Cambridge: Cambridge University Press, pp. 117–181.

Locke, J. (1967b). The Second Tract on Government. In: J. Locke and P. Abrams, eds., *Two Tracts on Government*. Cambridge: Cambridge University Press, pp. 185–241.

Locke, J. (1975). *An Essay Concerning Human Understanding*. Ed. P. H. Nidditch. Oxford: Oxford University Press.

Locke, J. (1993a). An Essay Concerning Toleration. In: J. Locke and D. Wootton, eds., *Political Writings*. London: Penguin, pp. 186–210.

Locke, J. (1993b). A Letter Concerning Toleration. In: J. Locke and D. Wootton, eds., *Political Writings*. London: Penguin, pp. 390–436.

Locke, J. (2004). Religion. In: J. Locke and M. Goldie, eds., *Political Essays*. Cambridge: Cambridge University Press, pp. 278–280.

Marshall, J. (1996). *Resistance, Religion and Responsibility*. Cambridge: Cambridge University Press.

Milton, J. R. and Milton, P. (2010). General Introduction. In: J. Locke, ed., *An Essay Concerning Toleration and Other Writings on Law and Politics, 1667–1683*. Oxford: Clarendon Press, pp. 1–161.

Popkin, R. H. (1979). *The History of Scepticism from Erasmus to Spinoza*. Berkeley: University of California Press.

Tate, J. W. (2010). Locke, Rationality and Persecution. *Political Studies*, 5(58), pp. 988–1008.

Tate, J. W. (2012). Locke, God and Civil Society: Response to Stanton. *Political Theory*, 40(2), pp. 222–228.

Tate, J. W. (2013). Dividing Locke from God: The Limits of Theology in Locke's Political Philosophy. *Philosophy and Social Criticism*, 39(2), pp. 133–64.

Tate, J. W. (2016a). *Liberty, Toleration and Equality: John Locke, Jonas Proast, and the Letters Concerning Toleration*. New York: Routledge.

Tate, J. W. (2016b). Toleration, Skepticism and Blasphemy: John Locke, Jonas Proast and Charlie Hebdo. *American Journal of Political Science*, 60(3), pp. 664–675.

Tate, J. W. (2017). Locke, Toleration and Natural Law: A Reassessment. *European Journal of Political Theory*, 16(1), pp. 109–121.

Tate, J. W. (2022). John Locke and Religious Toleration. In: M. Sardoč, ed., *The Palgrave Handbook of Toleration*. London: Palgrave Macmillan.

Wootton, D. (1993). Introduction. In: J. Locke, ed., *Political Writings*. London: Penguin, pp. 7–122.

## 2 Toleration and the Origins of Liberalism
### The Career of William Penn

*Andrew R. Murphy*

### Early Modern Toleration: Beyond Locke's *Letter*

Any account of the relationship between toleration and liberalism must necessarily include a close consideration of John Locke's *Letter Concerning Toleration*; this volume is no exception.[1] To be sure, Locke's account of toleration represents an important milestone in the history of the concept and its associated practices, and its publication in the wake of the 1688 Revolution (and alongside the 1689 Toleration Act), as well as Locke's prominent place in the philosophical canon, has lent it additional significance in the history of political thought.[2] At the same time, Locke hardly exhausts the early modern story of toleration, and he was in fact (as Tate's chapter lays out in detail) a rather late arrival to the tolerationist movement. In this chapter, I explore the work of one of Locke's contemporaries, William Penn (1644–1718), who not only theorized liberty of conscience in England well before Locke, but also, in his colonial undertaking in Pennsylvania, attempted to establish a society based on those principles.

As a matter of the historical record, Penn and Locke shared important personal and professional connections. Each one advanced Whig arguments during the 1670s, and their contact with each other was facilitated by mutual friendships with well-connected figures like Algernon Sidney, James Tyrrell, William Popple, and Benjamin Furly (see Marshall, 2006, pp. 489–490; Robbins, 1967; Scott, 1991, pp. 129–131; Ashcraft, 1986, pp. 515–516). Locke owned copies of some of Penn's most important political works, including *The Great Case of Liberty of Conscience* and each of the three 1687 *Letters from a Gentleman in the Country* (Marshall, 2006, p. 153; Ashcraft, 1986, p. 489). Yet Locke came to distrust Penn deeply during James's reign, viewing him as propagandist for a would-be tyrant. Despite the lack of any credible evidence, scholars (most recently, Miller, 2012, p. 51) continue to circulate the story of Penn securing a pardon for Locke during the latter's exile in the late 1680s.[3] During the second half of the 1690s, Penn had frequent conflicts with the Board of Trade, on which Locke sat, over his management of

Pennsylvania and the Crown's efforts to exert control over its American provinces (see Murphy, 2019, chap. 11–12).

Although Penn never attained Locke's canonical status, his career as a theorist and activist for liberty of conscience placed him at the forefront of the tolerationist movement for nearly a half century. A closer examination of that career can yield fruitful insights into the relationships between theory and practice, church and state, and religion and politics. If Locke's *Letter* has become the most renowned theoretical product of these early modern disputes over toleration, Penn's colony represents an attempt to institutionalize some foundational precepts of the tolerationist platform: not simply in England, where a precise constellation of political and religious forces would be required even to achieve the halfway measures of the Toleration Act, but in the setting-up of a new society in America.

Before proceeding further, a brief note on terms is in order, since Penn variously used both "liberty of conscience" and "toleration" to denote the goal of his political theorizing. Mary Maples Dunn has noted that Penn often used the phrase "liberty of conscience" to describe his theoretical or political ideal, and the term "toleration" in discussions of practical political realities (Dunn, 1967, pp. 47–48). It is a useful distinction, though the complete title of Penn's major 1670 publication – *The great case of liberty of conscience once more briefly debated and defended . . . which may serve the place of a general reply to such late discourses who have lately opposed a toleration* – shows that he used the terms more or less interchangeably at times.

## Toleration in Theory and Practice: The Career of William Penn

From the late 1660s through the early 1710s – a crucial period for both the theory of religious liberty and the maturation of the British colonial system – William Penn played a central role at the centre of English and American political life and in the campaign for liberty of conscience on both sides of the Atlantic. He published dozens of important works and became a national celebrity, a leading figure in the Society of Friends and activist in support of liberty of conscience. In 1670 alone, Penn published *The Peoples ancient and just liberties asserted* (1670c), a "transcript" of his trial for unauthorized preaching, which presented Penn as a heroic figure taking on the state-church establishment; and *The great case of liberty of conscience* (1670a), a systematic treatise presenting the main arguments for toleration in a succinct format. Five years later, in *England's Present Interest Discovered* (Penn, 1675), he championed English liberties of property, representation, and jury trial, and counselled magistrates to pursue a balanced policy toward the kingdom's religious communities. During the contentious Popish Plot years, Penn called for

Protestant unity amidst rumours of Jesuit conspiracies (*An Address to Protestants* (Penn, 1679a)), while arguing, in *One Project for the Good of England* (Penn, 1679b), that politically loyal Dissenters of all stripes ought to be guaranteed liberty of conscience. During the latter half of the 1680s, Penn assisted James II in his (ultimately ill-fated) campaign to bring toleration to England, offering his support in works like *A Perswasive to Moderation* (Penn, 1686) and his three *Letters from a Gentleman in the Country* (Penn, 1687a, 1687b, 1687c).[4]

## Restoration Political Argument and the Politics of Toleration

Restoration tolerationist arguments, which shaped William Penn's thinking and which he in turn helped to shape, drew upon their predecessors from the Civil War, Commonwealth and Protectorate, and came in several forms. *Christian (more specifically, Protestant) arguments* emphasized the sanctity of individual conscience, the right of conscience to be free from compulsion; and drew on Scriptural references like Jesus's claim that his kingdom was not of this world (John 18:36), the parable of the tares and wheat (Matthew 13), and St. Paul's exhortation that whatever is not of faith is sin (Romans 14). *Epistemological arguments* argued that belief was a faculty of the understanding and not the will, and was thus impervious to physical coercion. Attempts at coercion in matters of faith, quite simply put, were doomed to fail, because they attempted to dictate the impossible. *Historical or political arguments* invoked the ancient English constitution and Magna Carta, maintaining that religious dissent did not justify civil penalties or the deprivation of political liberties. Such arguments often presented catalogues of English and European public officials who endorsed principles of religious liberty, thus providing an historical pedigree for tolerationist claims. Nascent social contract theories also circulated, emphasizing the limited nature of government and its fundamental tasks of preserving property and maintaining civil peace. Civil governments, on this view, held the authority to control their subjects' bodies for the common civic good, but not to compel belief. Finally, *prudential or pragmatic arguments* stressed the prosperity and civil peace that toleration would yield, after years of religious strife. Such arguments often pointed to the example of tolerating polities like the Netherlands, and made the sociological point that Dissenters in England were not only numerous but also "industrious" members of society, whose persecution would wreak havoc on the nation's economic health.

But tolerationists always faced an uphill battle, since they struggled against often-vivid memories of numerous instances where political and religious unrest clearly *had* gone hand in hand, with tumultuous consequences for the nation. It is impossible to understand discourses of toleration without careful consideration of the contemporaneous discourses of orthodoxy and uniformity with which they did battle. *Historical arguments* drew on memories of the 1640s and 1650s, when religious dissent fired a civil war that resulted in a regicide. Advocates of uniformity sought to link tolerationists to Anabaptism, sectarianism, republicanism and rebellious Scottish Presbyterianism; each of which (to its critics, at least) elevated individual religious experience or religious authorities over established civil institutions. *Religious or ecclesiastical arguments* charged civil rulers with overseeing matters of worship within their borders, if not for the protection of pure religious doctrine, then at least for the preservation of peace. Anglican thinkers developed a doctrine of passive obedience that was only reluctantly discarded in 1688, and then only in the face of a frontal assault by a Catholic monarch (see Goldie, 1991). And *theological or epistemological arguments* held that, although coercion might not able to bring about a change in belief directly, it could nonetheless play a part in a larger approach that afforded individuals the opportunity to reconsider erroneous beliefs and thus come to accept true ones. No one epitomized the power of the antitolerationist position better than Samuel Parker, who became Archdeacon of Canterbury in 1670 and whose ferocious polemic *A Discourse of Ecclesiastical Politie* appeared that same year, bringing together existing arguments against religious dissent and setting the standard for the antitolerationist literature to come (Parker, 1670; Ashcraft, 1986, pp. 41–47).

Tolerationists and their opponents, then, drew on coherent and persuasive theoretical and ideological edifices during the Restoration years. Tolerationists were trying to convince a sceptical population – sceptical for many good reasons – that longstanding ties between church and state authority ought to be severed, or at least considerably attenuated. Their opponents defended the Restoration church-state settlement by highlighting the many risks associated with such a gamble.

## Toleration and Liberty of Conscience (I): Penn's Early Political Writing

The cornerstone of William Penn's political thought during the early years of his public career (1668–1671) was his dogged pursuit of liberty of conscience. During these years, agitators for liberty of conscience tied their arguments directly to concerns about the rights of free assembly as they opposed the Conventicle Act, which became law in spring 1670 and which forbade attendance at "any Assembly, Conventicle, or Meeting under colour or pretence of any Exercise of Religion in other manner than according to the Liturgy and practice of the Church of England."[5] The postscript to Penn's *Great Case of Liberty of Conscience* defined a religious assembly as "where persons are congregated with a real purpose of worshipping God, by prayer, or otherwise, let the persons be esteemed doctrinally orthodox or not" (1670a, p. 54). Thus, he and his tolerationist allies insisted that "conventicles" were not dark places filled with revolutionary plots, but sites where politically loyal, conscientious Christians met to work out their responsibilities to God.

*The Great Case of Liberty of Conscience*, published in 1670, was the closest thing to a systematic treatise on liberty of conscience that William Penn ever wrote, denouncing persecution as contrary to Christian principles, antithetical to nature and reason, imprudent, and false to the historical precedents laid down by enlightened rulers and public officials in English history and across time. It was a systematic treatise animated by a specific set of events: the public unrest and contention surrounding the passage of the Conventicle Act. Appended to each edition of the *Great Case* was a postscript that parsed the definition of conventicle offered in the law's text, and insisted that its terms were not properly applied to Quakers (Penn, 1670a).

The second edition of *Great Case* – which announced its intention to "serve the place of a general reply to such late discourses, as have opposed a toleration" – laid out, for the first time, Penn's definition of liberty of conscience, a definition that would remain relatively constant over the next forty-odd years:

> By *Liberty of Conscience*, we understand not only a meer *Liberty of the Mind*, in believing or disbelieving this or that Principle or Doctrine, *but the Exercise of ourselves in a visible Way of Worship, upon our believing it to be indispensibly required at our Hands*. . . . Yet we would be so understood to extend and justifie the Lawfulness of our so meeting to worship God, as not to contrive, or abet any Contrivance destructive of the Government and Laws of the Land, tending to Matters of an external Nature . . . but so far only, as it may refer to religious Matters, and a Life to come, and consequently wholly independent of . . . secular Affairs. . . .
>
> By Imposition, Restraint, and Persecution, we don't only mean, the strict Requiring of us to believe this to be true, or that to be false; and upon Refusal, to incur the Penalties enacted in such Cases; but by those Terms we mean thus much, any coercive Lett or Hindrance to us, from meeting together to perform those Religious Exercises which are according to our Faith and Perswasion.
>
> (Penn, 1670a, pp. 11–12)

Penn sought to expand the notion of liberty of conscience to include not only individual belief but also corporate worship; to assert not simply an individual but a collective right ("the exercise of ourselves in a visible way of worship"). He likewise sought to expand the category of imposition, or "coercive let," to include not merely political and legal sanctions for the exercise of conscience, but any hindrance to meeting for religious worship with like-minded others, since such meetings serve an integral purpose to the exercise of individual conscience.

This expansion of the range of behaviours that might be infused with conscientious justification (and thus off-limits to government interference) was precisely the approach that so incensed critics like Parker, who had claimed that

> to exempt religion and the consciences of men from the authority of the supreme power is but to expose the peace of kingdoms to every wild and fanatick pretender, who may, whenever he pleases, under pretences of Reformation thwart and unsettle government without control; seeing no one can have any power to restrain the perswasions of his Conscience.
>
> (1670, pp. 14–15)

As such, and to appreciate the way in which Penn's expansive definition grew out of and gave shape to the debates over conventicles, we must appreciate its many-sided nature.

At its most basic level, according to Penn, persecution represented human interference with God's sovereignty. It "directly invade[s] divine prerogative, and divest[s] the almighty of a due, proper to none besides himself. . . [and] enthrones man as king over conscience, the alone just claim and privilege of his creator" (Penn, 1670a, pp. 12–13). The Christian nature of the argument for toleration is also evident from Penn's reliance on Scripture and the example of Christ himself as key elements of his tolerationist rhetoric. The *Great Case* offers a range of Scriptural examples, from Jesus's parables and the Golden Rule to Paul's exhortations to bear meekly with others, and in making such references, Penn reflected broader tendencies in the tolerationist literature of the day (Penn, 1670a; Murphy, 2016, chap. 2).

But the religious argument for toleration in England was never simply about Christianity; it was always closely allied, more particularly, with Protestant identity, and thus also intertwined with longstanding English anti-Catholicism. In his first published work, *Truth Exalted*, Penn excoriated both Catholics, who (in his view) erected persecutory mechanisms with no foundation in Scripture and made ceremonies and human traditions the core of Christian doctrine; and Anglicans, who had abandoned the principles of the first Reformers and built their church on unscriptural grounds all too similar to the Catholics they displaced (Penn, 1668). (As Protestants, he insisted, Anglicans really ought to have known better.) Penn opened his *Seasonable Caveat against Popery* with a defence of the authority of Scripture and a denunciation of Catholic subordination of the scriptural text to the interpretations offered by church councils (Penn, 1670b, chap. 1). More generally, *A Seasonable Caveat* rehearsed a fairly standard litany of anti-Catholic views, attacking Catholic doctrine and

Catholic religious practice (including the Church's views on Scripture, the Trinity, the Eucharist, prayers in Latin, praying to saints, and so on). It also took aim at Catholics' political loyalty, accusing that church of violating the moral law, engrossing the wealth of Europe, and encouraging dissembling and disobedience to magistrates. And in the *Great Case*, Penn lamented that Protestants persecuting other Protestants "overturns the very ground of [their] retreat from Rome" and put them in the place formerly occupied by Catholic persecutors: "for doubtless the papists said the same to you, and all that you can say to us: Your best plea was, Conscience upon principles, the most evident and rational to you: Do we not the like?" (1670a, pp. 26, 32).

Denunciations of Roman Catholics were ubiquitous among English tolerationists, who remained virtually unanimous in the view that Catholics ought not to fall within the scope of any toleration scheme. Yet Penn distinguished between ordinary Catholics and their leaders, admitting that "a great number of Romanists may be abused zealots, through the idle voluminous traditions of their church" (1670b, p. 4) Indeed, he offered a kind of pre-emptive, defensive approach to the political implications of Catholicism: religious error alone was not sufficient to justify suppression (in this regard, "popery" was a political, and not a religious, category), and he always entertained the possibility that Catholics whose political loyalty could be guaranteed might be granted toleration. Penn favoured "a universal toleration of faith and worship" and insisted that he did not intend to pursue liberty for Quakers by encouraging the affliction of others ("nor would I take the burden off my own shoulder, to lay it on theirs" (Penn, 1670b, p. 32)). In fact, to be even more clear, he articulated his intentions in writing the *Seasonable Caveat* as an endeavour to safeguard English liberty against the threat of Catholic tyranny: "[I]t is not our purpose to bring them under persecution; but to present the people with such an information, as may prevent them from ever having power to persecute others" (1670b, p. 36). A year later, Penn admitted, in a letter to an English Catholic, that "I am, by my principle, to write as well for toleration for the Romanists" ("To Richard Langhorne", 1671, in Dunn and Dunn, 1981, pp. 209–211).

Since God created humans, Penn maintained, the very structure of human nature provided clear evidence of God's intentions for human conduct and argued in favour of religious liberty. God created humans, Penn insisted, and "has given them both senses corporeal and intellectual, to discern things and their differences, so as to assert or deny from evidences and reasons proper to each" (1670a, p. 19). And this process of judging involves religious judgments as well:

> As he that acts doubtfully is damned, so Faith in all acts of religion is necessary: now in order to believe, we must first will; to will, we

must first judge; to judge any thing, we must first understand; if then we cannot be said to understand any thing against our understanding; no more can we judge, will, and believe against our understanding. . . . In short, that man cannot be said to have any religion, that takes it by another man's choice, not his own.

(Penn, 1670a, p. 19)

For religion to be efficacious, it had to be the product of a mature understanding and deliberate consideration; thus "where any are religious for fear, and that of men, 'tis slavish; and the recompense of such religion is condemnation, not peace" (Penn, 1670a, pp. 16, 19). Thus, Penn's "religious" arguments are hardly distinct from his arguments about human nature; indeed, since Scripture is the source of Christian understandings of the nature of God and of God's creatures, one can reach the same conclusion from epistemological arguments as from citations to Job or the writings of Paul, as Penn does elsewhere in *The Great Case* (1670a, p. 16; quoting Job 32:8; and Paul's letter to the Romans). This emphasis on understanding and judgment, and the necessity of both for true belief, represents an ongoing commitment of advocates for religious liberty down through the seventeenth century.

Not only was persecution, then, an affront to Christianity, to Protestantism, and to a basic understanding of the functioning of the human mind, it was bound simply *not to work*. In other words, "the understanding can never be convinced, nor properly submit, but by such arguments, as are rational, persuasive, and suitable to its own nature. . . . Force may make an hypocrite, 'tis faith grounded upon knowledge, and consent, that makes a Christian" (Penn, 1670a, p. 22). Physical punishments delivered by punitive measures may induce behavioural changes, but they are powerless to effect the real inner change at the heart of true religion. And as a corollary of the argument that compulsion cannot produce true faith, Penn writes of the special cruelty of punishing people for not doing something they are unable to do. As the influential Nonconformist John Owen, whom Penn knew well from his student days at Christ Church College, Oxford Owen put it, "Neither can a man himself force himself, neither can all the men in the world force him, to understand more than he doth understand, or can do so" (1667, p. 15). This view of belief would later be put, most famously, by John Locke in his *Letter Concerning Toleration*:

Such is the nature of the understanding, that it cannot be compelled to the belief of anything by outward force. Confiscation of estate, imprisonment, torments, nothing of that nature can have any such efficacy as to make men change the inward judgement that they have framed of things.

(Locke, [1689], 2010, p. 13)

As in many other dimensions of the tolerationist movement, Locke here presented a pithy encapsulation of a much broader element of public discourse.

In addition to the polemical arguments that liberty of conscience was desirable, and that persecution was misguided and harmful, it was also important for Penn to argue that toleration would not undermine the social and political order. Toward that end, the final chapter of Penn's *Great Case* offered an extensive list of historical figures (including many Christian saints, but also pagan rulers from the ancient and medieval world) who tolerated Dissenters and reaped the benefits. Such a roster provided further evidence of the happy coincidence between the interest, properly understood, of magistrates and their people, and the way that granting liberty of conscience would assure both of those ends (Penn, 1670a, chap. 6).

## Toleration and Liberty of Conscience (II): Penn, Pennsylvania and James II

Regardless of how persuasive later audiences might find the standard arguments in favour of toleration, Pennsylvania only came into being because of the failure of the tolerationist cause in England, and of Penn and his allies' inability to convince their contemporaries that this policy was worth embracing. Perhaps this fact ought not surprise us. For almost the entire 1640s – the decade in which Penn was born – the realm had been mired in a civil war in which Parliamentary forces, supported by religious dissenters, took up arms against the King, whom they executed in 1649. This experience of religiously fired war and violence cast a long shadow over not only William Penn's childhood and youth, but also over the nation into which he grew as a political figure. (After the restoration of the monarchy in 1660, the tensions only became even more complex.) Reasonable people had plenty of reasons to be suspicious of calls for religious liberty during Penn's time, and it was only when prospects for such liberty seemed at their bleakest in England – in the aftermath of a severe political and constitutional crisis of late 1670s – that Penn turned his attention to America and envisioned his "holy experiment".

In his *Frame of Government* for Pennsylvania, published in spring 1682, Penn offered an elaborate theoretical preamble arguing that civil government is necessary due to the effects of human sin and the Fall. The Frame also distinguished between religion and government, as Penn had done previously in his career: "[religion] more free and mental, [government] more corporal and compulsive in its operations." That said, although this distinction was theoretically important, in practical terms he insisted that government was "a part of religion itself, a thing sacred in its institution and end". He went on to describe it as "capable of kindness, goodness and charity," and to suggest that seeing government as simply repressive and controlling fails to understand the positive role it has to play in the promotion of human happiness.

> They weakly err, that think there is no other use of government, than correction, which is the coarsest part of it: daily experience tells us, that the care and regulation of many other affairs, more soft, and daily necessary, make up much of the greatest part of government.
> (Penn, 1682, Preface)

Following on the theoretical distinction between the spiritual and the carnal (worldly) realms that thinkers like Penn (and, later, Locke) would articulate, subsequent liberal theorists would come to view the realms of church and state as dichotomous in nature and argue in favour of the institutional separation of the two as a necessary condition for true religious liberty. Penn's own view, as we see here, is more nuanced. Church and state each represent one aspect of communities' search for ways to facilitate their inhabitants living lives of conscientious integrity.

In practical terms, as we shall see in more detail, Penn never argued explicitly for the separation of church and state. Given the concrete political contexts within which he found himself in England, his main concern lay in ending persecution. Pennsylvania, it is true, had no legally established church, though Quakers exerted an outsize influence on its public life (much to the chagrin of many of the colony's non-Quakers). Though there is not space here to go into the details of Pennsylvania's founding and early history (see Murphy, 2013), it is worth pointing out that in one of the laws Law appended to the *Frame of Government*, Penn guaranteed liberty to all who confessed a belief in God, and opened office holding to all Christians. (Although these guarantees may seem rather more restrained than Penn had called for in England, it remained more expansive than prevailing practice in England; and the English government maintained veto power over all colonial legislation, making it nearly impossible for Penn to guarantee more extensive rights than existed at the time in the home country.) Such guarantees, of course, represented a major advance on what was open to Quakers and other Dissenters in England during the early 1680s.

Despite its guarantees of liberty of conscience for the colony's inhabitants, Pennsylvania's *Frame of Government* also included morals legislation, which evoked Penn's notion that one of government's proper duties was the suppression of moral vice. Law 37 laid out these concerns in great detail, forbidding

> all such offences against God, as swearing, cursing, lying, prophane talking, drunkenness, drinking of healths, obscene words, incest, sodomy, rapes, whoredom, fornication, and other uncleanness (not to be repeated) all treasons, misprisions, murders, duels, felony,

seditions, maims, forcible entries, and other violences, to the persons and estates of the inhabitants within this province; all prizes, stage-plays, cards, dice, May-games, gamesters, masques, revels, bull-battings, cock-fightings, bear-battings, and the like, which excite the people to rudeness, cruelty, looseness, and irreligion.

(Penn, 1682, p. 11)

It is not clear how energetically these restrictions were enforced, particularly after Penn left Pennsylvania to return to England in 1684. But these limitations envisioned by Penn reinforce an important observation; although restrictions on worship and religious assembly remained proscribed, the society that Penn envisioned was anything but a secular one in which a minimal government eschewed all attempts to shape the moral character of its citizens. The tension between liberty of conscience on the one hand, and the notion that government retains important functions with regard to the moral qualities of its citizenry, continues to animate liberal theorists around questions of "neutrality" down to our own day (see, most recently, Laborde, 2017).

After spending two years in Pennsylvania, setting up the colony's institutions and overseeing its early development, Penn returned to England in 1684. Shortly thereafter, James II, the new King, recruited him to serve as a key component in a grand plan to bring liberty of conscience to the realm. James's open Catholicism and autocratic tendencies, to say nothing of intense English anti-Catholicism, would doom him to a short reign and an unceremonious ejection in the "Glorious Revolution" of 1688. But during the early years of his reign, the campaign's prospects looked more promising, and Penn was the "most famous" of James's high-profile supporters, the King's "close friend and ally" and "an intellectual architect" of his toleration project (Sowerby, 2013, pp. 9, 24, 40). Among the many works he published in that cause, the most extensive was *A Perswasive to Moderation* (Penn, 1685, 1686). In it, Penn attempted to vindicate the *political* outcomes of toleration, against the claim by antitolerationists that granting liberty of conscience endangered the state. He also defended toleration from *religious* critiques, such as the claim that toleration abandoned erroneous individuals to their errors and perpetuated disunion.

At the heart of Penn's political argument in the *Perswasive to Moderation* is a prudential, pragmatic, interest-driven notion of balanced governance as mutually beneficial to both ruler and ruled. "Interest will not lie," Penn wrote on more than one occasion, repeating a widespread early modern trope and reviving an argument he made earlier about the primacy of civil interests in a religiously diverse community (Penn, 1686, p. 25, Preface; see also Gunn, 1968). Repealing penal laws would remove the chief complaints of Dissenters against the government since the passage of the Conventicle Act: the use of informers, upon whose testimony (however unscrupulous the informer) Dissenters' goods were liable to be seized, and themselves thrown in prison; and the abandonment of jury trials in many cases. Toleration would secure the rights of property, and ensure that "no man suffer[s] in his civil right for the sake of . . . dissent" (1686, p. 20).

The *Perswasive*'s political arguments represent yet another attempt to answer the chorus of critics who persistently linked religious dissent to rebellion and disloyalty, drawing heavily on their experience of the Civil Wars. In Penn's view, historical experience taken more broadly showed plainly that religious divisions had often coexisted with political stability, and that, in both the English and European Reformations, official religions had changed multiple times without any negative consequences to the state. Echoing his earlier presentation in *The Great Case*, Penn offered a variety of historical examples in which the two coexisted – from ancient Israel to the Roman Empire, from the King of Persia to the Kings of Poland and Denmark, and German princes. (And in an aside that Penn did not elaborate, he mentioned "the down-right toleration in most of his Majesties plantations abroad" as proof of the assertion that toleration may subsist with monarchy (1686, p. 15; more generally, pp. 4–15)). With regard to the English case, and particularly the Civil War, Penn acknowledged that Dissenters formed a key part of the alliance against Charles I, but argued that the war was fought over many issues unrelated to religion ("that unhappy controversie . . . began upon other topics than liberty for church-dissenters"), and that dissenters were not tolerated in those days (and thus the Civil War can hardly offer an argument against their toleration now). He also repeated his claim that persecution fosters disloyalty, that it alienates people from their rulers and breeds resentment, by arguing that "the war rather made the Dissenters, than the Dissenters made the war" (1686, pp. 19–20). If anything, the Civil Wars showed the likely outcome of persecuting dissenters, and not a strong argument against toleration.

Rulers benefited from a policy of toleration as well. Penn emphasized that indulgence to dissenters is not only the Christian and charitable way to proceed in a society characterized by religious diversity, but is also in the ruler's interest: "men embarked in the same vessel, seek the safety of the whole, in their own, whatever other differences they might have" (1686, Preface). In the 1685 preface, Penn argued that "severity . . . is [injurious] to the interest of the prince," that "in prudence as well as conscience, moderation is a desirable thing," and that "the interest of prince and people . . . conspire in the repeal" of penal legislation (Penn, 1685, Preface). Penn defended the King's prerogative as a vehicle for the protection of religious dissenters, for the exercise of clemency and Christian charity in a world where, though we might wish for unity in religious matters, we are unlikely to find it. After all, if Dissenters were mistaken, it was a mistake in their *understanding*, and the remedy for such mistakes must address itself to the understanding and not descend into the seizure of dissenters' liberty or property.

Under a regime of toleration, then, the people's affections and interests would align with those of the King, who would have his most skilled subjects at his command. "The King has the benefit of his whole people, and the reason of their safety is owing to their civil, and not ecclesiastical, obedience." Such a scenario, in which rulers have the choice of the ablest public servants available in the realm, would secure the government both at home and abroad, since "to be loved at home, is to be feared abroad". (Penn, 1686, pp. 22, 27)

This emphasis on the power of interest in politics – "all perswasions center with it" continued themes that we have seen raised in Penn's earlier work, and promised "a balance at home" among the kingdom's various religious parties, an improvement in the conditions for trade, and an encouragement to "those that are upon the wing for foreign parts, to pitch here again" (Penn, 1686, pp. 30, 32–33). Each party had something to gain from toleration, the Church of England no less than Catholics and Protestant Dissenters; thus a policy of toleration recommended itself both on principled and prudential grounds. Persecution, by contrast, presented Dissenters with the options of "be ruined, fly, or conform," and what a choice that was: forfeiting one's goods, leaving for other countries or British colonies, or engaging in hypocrisy by conforming to the established church without true belief in its doctrines (1686, p. 36). Neither did Penn neglect the standard arguments about trade and prosperity being advanced by tolerationists, arguing that

> as men, in times of danger, draw in their stock, and either transmit it to other banks, or bury their talent at home for security... (and either is fatal to a kingdom), so this mildness entreated, setting every man's heart at rest, every man will be at work, and the stock of the kingdom employed.
>
> (1686, p. 33)

With regard to the more particularly religious arguments – that toleration allows for the persistence of error and undermines the church – Penn offered familiar responses in support of the duty of toleration: that conscience cannot be forced, and thus persecution is ineffectual in planting true religion in human souls; that Christ forbade fire from heaven and taught forbearance in the parable of the tares and wheat; that as the Church of England declines to claim infallibility for its doctrines, to persecute in support of them is unreasonable.

In keeping with his basic definition of toleration ("an admission of dissenting worship, with impunity to the dissenters" [1686, p. 20]), Penn's argument always aimed for liberty of worship and participation in public life without hindrance. Although the logic of his position as it was laid out during the 1670s and 1680s, with its stark distinction between church and state, between spiritual and carnal things, seems to press toward disestablishment (and though many thinkers in the liberal tradition have assumed disestablishment to be a *sine qua non* of religious liberty), Penn never himself agitated for disestablishing the Church of England, nor did he attack the Church's landholdings or established positions of privilege in the universities or the government: "I would not be thought to plead for Dissenters' preferment; tis enough they keep what they have, and may live at their own charges". "That the Church of England is preferred," he wrote elsewhere in the same text,

> and has the fat of the earth, the authority of the magistrate, and the power of the sword in her son's hands, which comprehends all the honors, places, profits, and powers of the kingdom, must not be repined at: Let her have it, and keep it all. . . . But to ruin Dissenters to complete her happiness, is Calvinism in the worst sense.
>
> (1686, pp. 25, 42–43)

The bottom line for Penn during these debates, as had long been the case, was that English law provided plenty of opportunities for authorities to detect and punish treasonous and disloyal behavior without resorting to punishments for conscientious worship: "We have laws enough to catch and punish the offenders," he wrote, and offered a scheme by which Dissenters would certify their fidelity to the government, provide lists of their members, police their own ranks, and refrain from "nick-names. . . [and] terms of reproach" (1686, pp. 47–48).

## From Toleration to Liberty of Conscience

Whether we look at theory laid out in England or the practice of politics in Pennsylvania, we find Penn looking to use government to bolster the civic dimensions of religion – its fostering of charity, good works, and neighbourliness – and suppress disruptive social behavior, while restraining it from meddling with the details of individual and group beliefs. In this regard, as Christie L. Maloyed (2013) has argued, we might view Pennsylvania as embodying a "liberal civil religion". Penn's simultaneous insistence that government has no business enforcing religious doctrine and that government may, indeed must, uphold standards of general morality (and even "general and practical religion") complicates the standard story that the origins of secular, liberal modernity are to be found in a "privatizing" religious impulse (ascribed to Locke).

Of course, none of these concepts – toleration, liberty of conscience, religious freedom – are static entities; rather, they are part of broader historical developments with complex outcomes. George Washington's 1790 letter to the Hebrew Congregation of Newport, Rhode Island, illustrates that even just a century after Locke and Penn, the terms of debate had shifted radically: "It is now no more that toleration is spoken of,"

Washington wrote, "as if it were the indulgence of one class of people that another enjoyed the exercise of their inherent natural rights" (Washington, 1790). The notion of toleration as treatment offered at the discretion of a ruling party, subject to revocation at any time, seems a far cry from what Washington calls "the exercise of their inherent natural rights". That said, tolerationist arguments offered by theorists during the early modern era, and the concrete victories won over the course of the seventeenth century, were hardly minimal to those who engaged in them. They required protracted sacrifices and represented a hard-earned level of social acceptance for people who had long faced fines, corporal punishment and jail time simply for following the dictates of their consciences.

The relationship between ideas articulated in the seventeenth-century world of William Penn and John Locke and the broader tradition of institutions, principles and theories that go by the name of "liberalism" is by no means linear. What Penn sought, long before the term "liberalism" took on the meanings with which we associate it today, was a Christian society typified by Christian liberty, in which gathered congregations of many sorts could freely pursue their own understandings of what God required of them. His embrace of religious liberty went hand in hand with civil liberty: government based on consent, trial by jury, property rights, and so on. Toleration represented one piece of a broader puzzle, the ongoing struggle to build a world in which limited governments ensured that individuals and communities could live lives of conscientious integrity.

## Notes

1. Tate, "John Locke and the Foundations of Toleration", in this volume.
2. Locke himself would have apparently preferred a somewhat broader liberty than the Act provided, though he considered it a promising start: "Toleration has now been established by law. . . . Not perhaps so wide in scope as might be wished for. . . . Still, it is something to have progressed so far" (quoted in Hoppit, 2000, p. 33).
3. It is a myth that one would have thought finally demolished by Richard Ashcraft nearly thirty years ago (Ashcraft, 1986, pp. 514–20). The story has been cited by many Penn scholars, including Buranelli, 1962, p. 174; Illick, 1965, p. 137; Beatty, 1939, pp. 5–6, 10.
4. With the exception of *An Address to Protestants* and the three *Letters*, the works mentioned in this text are among those included in my forthcoming edition of Penn's political writings (Penn, 2021).
5. Charles II, "1670: An act to prevent and suppress seditious conventicles", text available at www.british-history.ac.uk/statutes-realm/vol5/pp648-651#s1

## References

Ashcraft, R. (1986). *Revolutionary Politics and Locke's Two Treatises of Government*. Princeton: Princeton University Press.

Beatty, E. C. O. (1939). *William Penn as Social Philosopher*. New York: Columbia University Press.

Buranelli, V. (1962). *The King and the Quaker*. Philadelphia: University of Pennsylvania Press.
Dunn, M. M. (1967). *William Penn: Politics and Conscience*. Princeton, NJ: Princeton University Press.
Dunn, M. M. and Dunn, R. S. (1981). *The Papers of William Penn*, vol. I. Philadelphia: University of Pennsylvania Press.
Goldie, M. (1991). The Political Thought of the Anglican Revolution. In: R. Beddard, ed., *The Revolutions of 1688: The Andrew Browning Lectures*. Oxford: Clarendon Press, pp. 102–136.
Gunn, J. A. W. (1968). 'Interest Will Not Lie': A Seventeenth-Century Political Maxim. *Journal of the History of Ideas*, 29, pp. 551–564.
Hoppit, J. (2000). *A Land of Liberty? England, 1689–1727*. Oxford: Clarendon Press.
Illick, J. E. (1965). *William Penn, the Politician: His Relations with the English Government*. Ithaca: Cornell University Press.
Laborde, C. (2017). *Liberalism's Religion*. Cambridge, MA: The Belknap Press of Harvard University Press.
Locke, John. (2010). *A Letter Concerning Toleration and Other Writings (1689)*. Ed. Mark Goldie. Indianapolis, IN: Liberty Fund.
Maloyed, C. L. (2013). A Liberal Civil Religion: William Penn's Holy Experiment. *Journal of Church and State*, 55, pp. 669–689.
Marshall, J. (2006). *John Locke, Toleration, and Early Enlightenment Culture*. New York: Cambridge University Press.
Miller, N. P. (2012). *The Religious Roots of the First Amendment: Dissenting Protestants and the Separation of Church and State*. New York: Oxford University Press.
Murphy, A. R. (2013). The Limits and Promise of Political Theorizing: William Penn and the Founding of Pennsylvania. *History of Political Thought*, 34, pp. 639–668.
Murphy, A. R. (2016). *Liberty, Conscience, and Toleration: The Political Thought of William Penn*. New York: Oxford University Press.
Murphy, A. R. (2019). *William Penn: A Life*. New York: Oxford University Press.
Owen, J. (1667). *Indulgence and Toleration Considered in a Letter unto a Person of Honour*. London.
Parker, S. (1670). *A Discourse of Ecclesiastical Politie*. London.
Penn, W. (1668). *Truth Exalted, in a Short but Sure Testimony . . .* London.
Penn, W. (1670a). *The Great Case of Liberty of Conscience*. London.
Penn, W. (1670b). *A Seasonable Caveat Against Popery, or, a Pamphlet Entitled, an Explanation of the Roman-Catholick [sic] Belief*. London.
Penn, W. (1670c). *The Peoples Ancient and Just Liberties Asserted in the Trial of William Penn and William Mead*. London.
Penn, W. (1675). *England's Present Interest Discover'd*. London.
Penn, W. (1679a). *An Address to Protestants upon the Present Conjuncture in II Parts*. London.
Penn, W. (1679b). *One Project for the Good of England*. London.
Penn, W. (1682). *The Frame of the Government of the Province of Pennsylvania in America Together with Certain Laws Agreed upon in England*. London.
Penn, W. (1685). *A Perswasive to Moderation to dissenting Christians*. London: Andrew Sowle.

Penn, W. (1686). *A Perswasive to Moderation to Church Dissenters*, 2nd ed. London.

Penn, W. (1687a). *A Letter from a Gentleman in the Country, to His Friends in London, upon the Subject of the Penal Laws and Tests*. London.

Penn, W. (1687b). *A Second Letter from a Gentleman in the Country to His Friends in London upon the Subject of the Penal Laws and Tests*. London.

Penn, W. (1687c). *A Third Letter from a Gentleman in the Country, to His Friends in London, upon the Subject of the Penal Laws and Tests*. London.

Penn, W. (2021). *William Penn: Political Writings*. Ed. Andrew R. Murphy. Cambridge: Cambridge University Press.

Robbins, C. (1967). Absolute Liberty: The Life and Thought of William Popple, 1638–1708. *William and Mary Quarterly*, 24, pp. 190–223.

Scott, J. (1991). *Algernon Sidney and the Restoration Crisis, 1677–1683*. New York: Cambridge University Press.

Sowerby, S. (2013). *Making Toleration: The Repealers and the Glorious Revolution*. Cambridge, MA: The Belknap Press of Harvard University Press.

Tate, J. (2020). John Locke and the 'Problem' of Toleration. This volume.

Washington, G. (1790). Letter to the Hebrew Congregation at Newport, 18 Aug. [online] Available at: http://teachingamericanhistory.org/library/document/letter-to-the-hebrew-congregation-at-newport/ [Accessed 28 Apr. 2020].

# 3 On Liberalism, Liberty of Conscience and Toleration

Some Historical and Theoretical Reflections*

*Mark A. Hutchinson and Timothy Stanton*

The relationship between toleration and liberalism continues to beguile. The two cannot be sundered no matter how often or how persistently it is tried: the pairing remains a focus of fascinated discussion. They are the Richard Burton and Elizabeth Taylor of political thought. Some years ago Jeffrey Collins (2009) ruminated upon fifteen or so substantial volumes, published during the previous decade, which offered direct or indirect commentary upon the history of the relationship, citing countless other productions along the way. The flood of publication has not abated since (compare Balint, 2017; Bejan, 2017; Cohen, 2018; Forst, 2013; Macedo, 2019; Parkin and Stanton, 2013). Liberal pundits pronounce that toleration is "one of the core values of liberalism" (Drerup and Kühler, 2019); that it is "central to the liberal tradition" (Murphy, 1997, pp. 593–594); that it is "of course an essential and inseparable part of the great tradition of liberalism" (Hayek, 1987, p. 46); that it is "the substantive heart of liberalism" (Hampton, 1989, p. 802), "a necessary constituent of a liberal society" (Galeotti, 2002, p. 39), "a constitutive part of liberal political practice" (Drerup and Kühler, 2019), the other side of this story being that the liberal state is merely the institutional expression of the mutual toleration of individual citizens (Jones, 2012). It has even been asserted, without pause or premeditation, that by definition "liberals are tolerant" (Kautz, 1995, p. 61).

Perhaps one reason why these pronouncements come so easily is that many pundits remain under the spell of some version of the grand historical narrative according to which the "great tradition of liberalism" delivered up the toleration of religious minorities that was a milestone in the creation of modern societies like their own and a marker of their superiority over every alternative form of social and political life, past and present (Mandelbrote, 2001, p. 93). This narrative has a long and venerable history. It started to take shape in Europe as early as the eighteenth century, when various French writers began describing their age as one in which *lumières* were spreading across the continent as never before (Mortier, 1969, pp. 13–31). At the same time their German counterparts were voicing the perception that a period of darkness and ignorance was giving way to an age of *Aufklärung* (Schmidt, 1996). Writers in English used equivalent locutions to depict their epoch likewise as one in which light was at last being diffused over the world, by which they meant, among other things, that where once "ignorance, superstition, and bigotry over-shadowed and disgraced the land" now "it [wa]s permitted us to think, to judge, to act for ourselves" (Kippis, 1788, pp. 9, 36) with all the happy consequences for peace, prosperity and progress that were perceived to follow (see Domínguez, 2017). This was a narrative that assumed in its general outlines that human societies "pass through stages of development" such that "the more advanced, or civilized, a society is, the greater the tolerance it will practice" (Kaplan, 2007, p. 5). Tacitly it subscribes to a "Whig" interpretation of liberty and of toleration, abiding still, in which Protestants are cast in the role of heroic and ultimately victorious victims of Roman Catholic tyranny and oppression. Their victory is the victory of reason over dogmatism, of freedom over slavery, of civility over barbarism, with religious toleration and liberty "advancing" in lockstep "towards the light" (Moots, 2020, p. 104; Zagorin, 2003; Grayling, 2007).

This story was passed down to the twentieth century by successive generations of nineteenth-century scholars who taught that religious toleration, or freedom of conscience, was a Protestant achievement and a natural attribute of a liberal society (Vaughan, 1840; Lecky, 1866). It is not an accident that the first wave of adulation John Locke enjoyed as a liberal icon reached its high watermark early in the century when he was appropriated by the Dissenting campaign to repeal the Test and Corporation Acts, allowing Dissenters to serve in parliament and public office, and receded with the achievement of that aim in 1828. Mementos of the campaign were Lord King's biography cum hagiography (1829) and Thomas Forster's edition of Locke's correspondence (1830). King stated that Locke was owed "veneration" by all "friends of freedom" (King, 1829, p. [v]). Forster called Locke the hero of "the great struggle for freedom of conscience [by] thinking men, who opposed themselves boldly to the tyranny of the Church of England [who were as apt to persecute as the papists] in those days of bigotry and oppression" (Forster, 1830, pp. viii–x; See Goldie, 2004). Locke was a crucial figure from the beginning because 1688 was a decisive crux, the Whig "Year Zero" in which practice joined hands with theory after the missed opportunities of the civil wars.

This line of thought again originated very early on. Writing in 1788, Andrew Kippis observed that the "flame of Freedom burnt as brightly and rose as high during the civil wars as it had ever been known to do"; but, "through an unfortunate concurrence of events, nothing was transacted that was solid, effectual and lasting" (Kippis, 1788, p. 31). So 1644, for instance, was a false dawn. It may have signified in theory as a turning point, when (as one recent historian has put it) the intellectual "consensus concerning persecution was irreparably fractured" with the publication of John Milton's *Areopagitica*, William Walwyn's *The Compassionate Samaritane*, Henry Robinson's *Liberty of Conscience* and Roger Williams's *The Bloudy Tenent of Persecution* (Coffey, 2000, p. 47), but in practice, persecution remained the default. This default was due not least to the "unfortunate concurrence" to which Kippis alluded, namely the combination of a ruler in Cromwell willing to erect "the edifice of slavery upon the very foundation of liberty" and a population whose minds had been "seized" by "madness" (Kippis, 1788, p. 31). By "madness", Kippis meant, in the vocabulary of his day, "enthusiasm".

Locke had added a chapter about enthusiasm (IV.xix) to the fourth edition of *An Essay concerning Human Understanding*, which appeared in 1700. He discussed it as the conceit that God imparted special revelations immediately and directly to the mind in a way that was at once irresistible, self-affirming, and compulsive: the recipient was impelled to follow its promptings (Locke, 1975, pp. 696–706). Locke had canvassed the opinion of his friend Molyneux about the addition. Molyneux replied that the matter could be addressed briefly, because enthusiasm was "no other than a Religious sort of Madnes", that is to say, opposition to reason, of which Locke had already written elsewhere (Locke, 1976, pp. v, 317, referring *inter alia* to Locke, 1975, pp. 161, 395). David Hume's essay of 1741, "Of Superstition and Enthusiasm", took up a similar line. Hume defined enthusiasm as kind of frenzy in which the imagination became overheated and "the deluded fanatic [was inspired] with the opinion of Divine illuminations" (Hume, 1965, p. 149). But he went on to say that "enthusiasm, being the infirmity of bold and ambitious tempers, is naturally accompanied with a spirit of liberty". The same point appeared in his *History of England*, where it was claimed that the spirit of enthusiasm, "bold, daring, and uncontroled; strongly disposed the minds [of those possessed by it] to arrogate, in their actions and conduct, the same liberty, which they assumed, in their rapturous flights and ecstasies" (Hume, 1983, v, p. 559). Hume's broader tale showed how, when placed in relation to each other, existing institutional forms, and events, the two together produced a "spirit of independency": "that spirit, partly fanatical, partly republican, which predominated in England" in the seventeenth century (Hume, 1983, vi, p. 83).

A paradox was that while Hume's rhetoric gave central place to the "noble" spirit of liberty, his underlying message was that the baser spirit of enthusiasm was the secret engine that had driven the course of events. In his words, the 1640s had been "ennobled by the spirit of liberty. . . [but] disgraced by . . . fanatical extravagances" the consequences of which, for good and ill, lived on into the Restoration until the Glorious Revolution cemented a new constitutional order in place. If, as Hume supposed, the spirit of independency had eventually triumphed in 1688, it was largely through the agency of "[the spirit of liberty's] religious associate, from which it reaped more advantage than honour", and which had been active in "the greater part of the kingdom" since the Reformation (Hume, 1983, v, p. 559). From the time of Elizabeth, Hume concluded,

> the precious spark of liberty had been kindled, and was preserved, by the puritans . . . and it was to this sect, whose principles appear so frivolous and habits so ridiculous, that the English owe[d] the whole freedom of their constitution.
> (Hume, 1983, iv, p. 145–146)

Inscrutably and, on the face of things, perversely, puritanism had been instrumental to outcomes that benefited both society and government.

The extravagances to which Hume referred might have been gathered at his leisure from Daniel Neal's *History of the Puritans* (Neal, 1732–38). These included (besides the ruthless, bloody proscription of the Roman Catholics of Ireland) the legal suppression of the Church of England, or, as its opponents then termed it, "prelacy" and attempts in the English Parliament, led by the Presbyterian faction, to impose their own version of Genevan discipline, enforced by threats of death, life imprisonment, and corporal punishment to anyone suspected of espousing Arminian, Antinomian, Baptist, Fifth-Monarchist, Papist, Quaker or other heretical doctrines of the types catalogued in Thomas Edwards' *Gangraena* (1646). As John Milton famously remarked, "New Presbyter" was become "Old Priest writ Large", just another "Forcer of Conscience". Leading Presbyterians in England and Scotland lined up to disclaim the principle of toleration: "My judgement in that much debated point, of Liberty of Religion, I have alwaies freely made known", wrote one of their "more liberal" ideologues, Richard Baxter (Lecky, 1866, ii, p, 75). "I abhor unlimited Liberty or Toleration of all, and think my self easily able to prove the wickedness of it" (Baxter, 1653, p. 246).

A consequence was that when prelacy and Prayer Book Anglicanism was re-established at the Restoration, the Presbyterians, suffering a swift and ignominious reversal of fortune, found themselves lumped in with Baptists, Fifth Monarchists, Quakers and the rest under their own despised category of "sectary" (see Dudley, 1912, p. 72). One of their number, John Corbet, protested in 1661 that they had "no fellowship with the spirit of enthusiastical . . . frenzy", and repudiated "sectarian anarchy" and "the gangrene of sects and schisms" (Corbet, 1661, pp. 34, 67, 69), urging mutual accommodation within a unified national church. But the boot was now firmly on the other foot. In 1662 many Presbyterian ministers were ejected from their livings and suffered thereafter, in varying degrees, under the penal laws collectively known as the Clarendon Code. The prosecutions, fines, sequestrations and imprisonments that followed led some twentieth-century historians to term the Restoration era "the period of the great persecution" (Cragg, 1957). A less charitable strand of contemporary opinion contrasted the imperiousness shown by the Presbyterians in imposing upon the consciences of their fellow Protestants when in the plenitude of their power with the underdog whimpering in which they were now indulging (Assheton, 1663, sig. A2–B; see Goldie, 2004). It might have been thought that the experience of persecution would generate a tolerant mentality in the persecuted. Evidently not always.

The more immediate point is that the association between puritanism and liberty upon which Hume insisted has never really gone away. Historians are still inclined to speak of religious liberty more in relation to those who were oppressed by the Elizabethan or early Stuart church, or those who resisted its Presbyterian or its Restoration successors – an inclination apparent in Coffey's textbook account of *Persecution and Toleration in Protestant England*, where "Anglicans" scarcely figure until the arrival of the so-called "latitudinarian" divines of the Restoration church who were willing to contemplate the kind of plea Corbet had made in 1661, albeit on their own terms (Coffey, 2000). An alternative but in some ways complementary account has stressed a sceptical, Erasmian approach among some "Anglican" elements with earlier roots, stretching from William Chillingworth via Jeremy Taylor to Restoration latitudinarians and ending up with Locke, whose thinking on toleration is linked to this fairly orthodox Anglican position. Here, again, seeds sown in the Victorian historiography of Vaughan, Lecky, and others, bore fruit in the twentieth-century scholarship (see e.g. Kamen, 1967, pp. 167–169, 231–240; Trevor-Roper, 1967; Marshall, 1994). This looks like an alternative account because the term puritanism, which retains the stigma of bigotry, has dropped out of sight. But puritanism remains, drained of its immoderation, converted into liberalism and yoked to a transformational climacteric that makes toleration, not persecution, the default: the Glorious Revolution of 1688 which saw the conquest of England by William of Orange and his allies.

The toleration that became official doctrine in England with the so-called "Toleration Act" of May 1689 was not the unlimited liberty of all that Baxter so deplored. Dissenting ministers were required to subscribe to some of the 39 Articles of the Church of England; all Dissenters had to swear loyalty to the King and deny the Catholic doctrine of transubstantiation; the civil disabilities established in the Clarendon Code by the Test and Corporation Acts still applied to them. The Toleration Act did permit Dissenters to worship in their own meetinghouses, so long as they were registered and kept the doors unlocked. For the first time, something like half a million citizens had legal protection – though Catholics remained outside the protection of the law (Jager, 2012, p. 570). Gilbert

Burnet, the latitudinarian divine who preached William's coronation sermon and would shortly become Bishop of Salisbury, wrote that the Act

> gave the King great content. He in his own opinion always thought, that Conscience was God's Province, and that it ought not be imposed on: and his experience in Holland made him look on Toleration, as one of the wisest measures of Government. He was much troubled to see so much ill humour spreading among the Clergy, and by their means over a great part of the Nation. He was so true to his Principle herein, that he restrained the heat of some, who were proposing severe Acts against Papists [and others].
> (Burnet, 1724–34, pp. ii, 212)

The equation between toleration and liberty of conscience that is present in Burnet's remarks is very important. It is still a commonplace of many scholarly works – too many to list in this place. It is a means by which early modern notions of religious toleration are converted into notions of religious autonomy to which every individual bearer of conscience has a right. This right to liberty of conscience implicates related freedoms of worship, association, speech and of the press (Forst, 2013, p. 179).

A further presupposition is that these freedoms too are construed as rights upheld (or denied) by civil authority; and in these terms only one jurisdiction besides the individual's jurisdiction over his own beliefs seems to be necessary to explain the provision and maintenance of right, namely state jurisdiction. These presuppositions, when combined, tend to produce a story in which right is invoked to set up claims about toleration. This is a right which belongs to "the individual", which cannot be ceded to the state, and which has a content that includes options about what to believe, how to act, and with whom to associate and so on that the state is brought into existence to enforce. Thus it is suggested that an individual option right to religious immunity from state action is what is primarily in view and that the unfolding story of religious toleration is best construed in something like these terms:

> that society and state should, as a matter of right, extend complete freedom of religious belief and expression to all their members and citizens, and should refrain from imposing any religious tests, doctrines, or forms of worship or religious association upon them.
> (Zagorin, 2003, p. 7)

So construed, the rise of toleration represents the paradigm case of the discourse "of political and individual sovereignty" which, Rainer Forst argues, "pressed for new forms of social and political life". "This [Forst continues] would become the central problem of the seventeenth century during which the [range] of justifications for toleration . . . took shape which informs reflection on toleration to the present day" (Forst, 2013, p. 169). In this way the older interpretative tradition linking puritanism and liberty lives on as the triumph of the "puritan" conscience. Liberty of conscience becomes a *synecdoche* for the entire liberal constellation of individual rights and limited government. The architectonic structure of the earlier narratives, in which "the progressive thought of learned elites triumphs over a relentless and ingrained popular instinct to persecute" (Walsham, 2006, p. 7) also remains in place. This goes some way to explaining why Locke continues to be cast so readily in the roles in which he was cast in King's adulatory biography: the personification of progressive thought, the theoretical mastermind of 1688, and the founder of liberalism (see Stanton 2018).

There are some people, wrote King,

> who would fain keep mankind in a state of perpetual pupilage, who, carrying their favourite doctrine of . . . obedience [to authority] into all our spiritual as well as temporal concerns, would willingly deliver us over in absolute subjection, for one to the rulers of the Church, and for the other to the rulers of the State.
>
> (King, 1829, p. vi)

Locke was not among them. The "important *effects produced* by his opinions and his writings in promoting the free exercise of reason" included a widespread embrace of "toleration . . . or freedom of conscience" on the one side and on the other side the preservation of the "just and natural rights" and "liberties" of the "people" under a "lawful government" to which they had given their "consent". None of this was possible without him. Standing between two ages, Locke was the filter by means of which puritanism was decontaminated and transmuted into liberalism. He was both the puritans' "most illustrious and enlightened disciple", and the avatar of a future they could not have imagined (King, 1829, pp. 276–277, emphasis added).

Even in King's day these were common enough tropes. In 1773 Kippis declared that the seventeenth-century puritans had "never entertained any just sentiments upon the subject" of toleration until they were exposed to the doctrines contained in Locke's *Letter Concerning Toleration* (Kippis, 1773, pp. 23–27, 41–43). This viewpoint was echoed by David Bogue and James Bennett in their *History of the Dissenters* (1808–12) which cited Locke on the separation of church and state and called the *Letter Concerning Toleration* the "best treatise on religious liberty" ever produced (Bogue and Bennett, 1833, I, p. 244; see Goldie, 2004). It may be significant that it was the English translation of the *Letter*, by William Popple, that drew their admiration. Popple, who felt the Toleration Act was too restrictive, wanted "*Absolute liberty*", and he took some of his own with Locke's text, introducing the claim that "liberty of conscience is every man's natural right" without any warrant from Locke's Latin (Locke, 1983, pp. 21, 51; compare Locke, 1968, pp. 134-135). This suppositious phrase consolidated the equation of toleration with liberty of conscience and supplied a Lockean proof.

Liberal political theorists of the present day tend to write in the same schematic vein: as one of the authors of this chapter noted elsewhere, with them Locke marks a boundary and a bond between the past and the present. The high road to modernity originates with him (Stanton, 2011, p. 8). Little wonder that many treatments of toleration and liberalism which purport to be historical fall into the same pattern, reducing arguments about toleration to "a face-off between inquisitorial persecutors and . . . Locke . . . quickly followed by either Kant or Mill" (Collins, 2009, p. 608). Within these terms, it even becomes possible to condense the whole history of the transition from a persecuting past to a liberal future into the confines of Locke's own life and intellectual biography via alleged shifts in his conception of freedom of conscience (Tate, 2016, 2020).

Johann Sommerville once wrote of two alternative views of conscience, one "Anglican" and one "puritan". In the Anglican model, individuals are morally obliged to obey the state, and must obey its laws in things indifferent such as religious ceremonies as a matter of conscience. It is in the nature of this conscience that it cannot be "forced" because it is God's province alone. In the puritan model, individuals are not morally obliged to obey human laws unless they are in conscience persuaded to do so. It is in the nature of this conscience that it should not be "forced" because the use of force against it is irreconcilable with its character as the voice of God in man (Sommerville, 2004, pp. 166–179). The "early" Locke, it is said, adopted the first position, the "later" Locke the second; and so we get the triumph of the puritan conscience all over again, with Locke the *fons et origo* of a liberal tradition which, from the beginning, has been pulled in two different directions.

In one direction it has exalted "liberation through reason from externally imposed authority" and "sustained rational examination of self, others and social practices" (Galston, 2002, pp. 21, 24), with autonomy its prime value. In another direction it has sought to regulate rival religious differences, mistrusted conscience, and wished to manage diversity for the sake of civil peace (Galston, 1995, pp. 525–527, 2002, pp. 21, 24–25), with concord the prime value. William Galston, for one, claims that the universalized principle of puritan conscience that Locke "placed at the core of liberalism" had the effect of "narrow[ing] the range of possibilities available within liberal societies. In the guise of protecting the capacity for diversity, the autonomy principle in fact exerts a kind of homogenizing pressure on ways of life that do not embrace autonomy" (Galston, 2002, p. 23; see also Galston, 1995, p. 523; Tate, 2013 for extended discussion). Jonathan Israel dismisses Locke for his "ungenerous, defective, and potentially menacing" account of toleration and blames it for the "semi-secular establishment doctrine of authorized government intolerance" (Israel, 2006, pp. 141–145). Edward Andrew argues that modernity is "the product of [unresolved] tensions between Protestant conscience and Enlightenment reason" (Andrew, 2001, p. 9); likewise Locke himself. Other writers suggest that, just as Locke succeeded in resolving the dialectic between these two principles in his own thinking, so liberalism may resolve them out of its own resources. Political theorists in the Rawlsian mode, we observe, are especially prone to inserting this conclusion into their premises (Tate, 2013, 2016).

Rawls himself located "the historical origin" of liberalism in "the Reformation and its aftermath, with the long controversies over religious toleration in the sixteenth and seventeenth centuries. Something like the modern understanding of liberty of conscience and freedom of thought [Rawls continued] began then", when "pluralism made religious liberty possible". In their turn, liberal institutions made it possible for pluralist societies to experience over time "the successful and peaceful practice of toleration" (Rawls, 2005, pp. xxiv–xxv). He presents his own theory of justice as fairness as the continuation and culmination of vectors of thought developed along this line. He makes the striking claim that

> were justice as fairness to make an overlapping consensus possible [then] it would complete and extend the movement of thought that began three centuries ago with the gradual acceptance of the principle of toleration and led to the nonconfessional state and equal liberty of conscience

leaving "citizens themselves to settle questions of religion, philosophy, and morals in accordance with views they freely affirm" (Rawls, 2005, p. 154).

Nothing remotely similar was possible under medieval Christianity, Rawls claimed, in consequence of its five defining characteristics: (1) It claimed an authority that was institutional, central, and nearly absolute, (2) It was a religion of salvation, and salvation required true belief as the Church taught it, (3) Hence, it was a doctrinal religion with a creed that was to be believed, (4) It was a religion of priests with the sole authority to dispense means of grace essential to salvation, and (5) it was an expansionist religion of conversion that recognized no territorial limits to its authority short of the world as a whole. His own position, in contradistinction, requires, he notes, something like the presuppositions that Locke's *Letter* put into currency: (1) That God has given no man authority over another, (2) That no-one can give up the care of his own salvation to another, (3) that true belief cannot be compelled, (4) that no one is required to belong to any particular church and (5) that churches are voluntary societies that people may enter or leave without civil penalty

(Rawls, 2005, p. 145). Rawls, in short, depends upon almost all of the assumptions the present reflections have attempted to expose to scrutiny, whether about the move from persecution to toleration, the equation of toleration with liberty of conscience, the assumption that liberty of conscience, when it is entire, implies a full civil liberty and vice versa, or the assumption that Locke is and must be the pivot on which the whole story turns, because the nonconfessional state and equal liberty of conscience begins with him.

These are claims about Rawls's thinking, but they are claims which have considerable importance for historical study. For the historian is as likely as the political theorist to absorb unreflectively the assumptions current in his or her world, and some of these may not help to illuminate the past as it really was. As the biblical scholar J. B. Lightfoot observed, "the idols of our cave never present themselves in a more alluring form than when they appear as the "spirit of the age". It is comparatively easy to resist the fallacies of past times, but it is most difficult to escape the infection of the intellectual atmosphere in which we live." (Lightfoot, 1893, p. 23, discussed by Harris, 2011, p. 2). "Infection" may be too strong a word, but nevertheless it captures the fact that the historian may not be sufficiently conscious that the present bears marks which are not always those of the past. It may be that he or she will allocate attention in a way that overlooks the importance of distinguishing between toleration and liberty of conscience, or is impatient with historical detail when discussing the grounds of that distinction, or misses its implications for thinking about civil liberty, or its relation to competing conceptions of grace and redemption then abroad. It may be beneficial to look again at the "Protestant conscience" without the distorting effects produced by the great gravitational pull Locke exerts upon it. These reflections lead on to the next part of this chapter, which deliberately puts aside the assumption that liberty of conscience is the seed of a "modern" toleration in which it finds completion. That "toleration", we have argued, is largely the product of preconceptions drawn from a body of historiography that has been rolling on like a snowball, gathering mass as it goes, for almost three centuries. What follows is a brief examination of liberty of conscience as it appeared to its proponents in the 1640s.

In their principal sense and reference, claims to "liberty of conscience" in this period were assertions of a freedom to search out knowledge of God for oneself. But disputes about the scope of that "liberty" raised pointed questions about other liberties in what we would today call the political sphere. A surpassing concern was the possibility that those who had not fully submitted their "wills" to God's will could not, properly speaking, be said to have true "liberty of conscience" at all, and were unlikely to make use of the liberty to act they enjoyed in the political sphere to the right ends, serving God and the common good (Davis, 1992). *Au fond* this was a question about the process of redemption and whether a freer searching-out of God offered any guarantees that "conscience" would discover Him and grasp His directions aright, providing an unimpeachable basis for the correct use of the wider set of liberties at issue. This was the context in which the language of toleration came into play. "Toleration" was a reluctant acknowledgment of the possibility of error. It was a practice associated with the structures of "the state", which regulated external action in a manner that recognized the existence of a plurality of beliefs and guarded against its potential destabilizing consequences. It was a secondary issue, as is clear from the relative paucity of references to it in the pamphlet literature of the early 1640s. The real issue remained "liberty of conscience" which in its "true" form should have brought all to know God and to act in unity for the common good, rendering toleration otiose.

When the civil wars first broke out, the bones of contention being gnawed by the contending parties were the "historic" rights and liberties of Englishmen. Recourse to the language of "conscience" was superfluous because grounds for discontent could be discovered in established law and practice which, it was claimed, were being disdained. The decision to take up arms against the king in 1642 presented a more formidable challenge, representing as it did the explicit repudiation of the rulers now on earth. John Goodwin's *Anti-Cavalierisme* (1642) attempted to bypass the problem of higher earthly powers by reaching for "conscience". In his defence of parliament's action, Goodwin spoke of acting "out of conscience of that obedience which we owe [God]", of "this liberty, or duty rather, of examining the commands of superiors . . . pressed upon the consciences of men" and of acting for our "lawfull liberty" (Goodwin, 1642, pp. 10–11; Coffey, 2006, pp. 85–96). Only near the end of his pamphlet did Goodwin elucidate the political implications of these remarks when speaking directly of "civill and politick libertie" (Goodwin, 1642, p. 38). Claims to "conscience" as the basis for action quickly proliferated in a burgeoning literature which justified militant resistance. That literature offers a sense of the nuances in Protestant opinion.

All Protestant parties on the parliamentary side accepted the validity of the claim to liberty of conscience in some form. Every subject and citizen, as a creature of God, had the liberty or right to search out knowledge of Him. The differences between their positions flowed from the different accounts of redemption with which they were operating and the inferences they drew from them when thinking of the wider claims made to liberty or liberties in the political sphere.

The orthodox Calvinist position, rejected by Goodwin, was that only the action of God's saving grace would turn "the will" away from sin and bring humanity's "will" into conformity with God's. It was on an individual's "conscience" that God's grace was thought to operate, via the intercession of the Holy Spirit. This presupposed the broader view that the understanding was determined by the considerations that came before it, whether through the senses or by the direct intervention of the Spirit. If it were the case that man was unlikely to sustain a proper faith through his own resources, he would need to be persuaded to that faith through the workings of the Spirit. This persuasion, delivered immediately by God, was not subject to the test of scripture or reason; rather it was subsequent to "the secret testimony of the Spirit", which revealed knowledge in which the mind could rest more firmly and securely than in any human judgement. As Calvin had put it, "the testimony of the Spirit is superior to reason". Calvin supposed that such persuasion would direct men to belief in the conventional teaching of scripture, by revealing its truth more perfectly. "Let it therefore be held as fixed", Calvin had added,

> that those who are inwardly taught by the Holy Spirit acquiesce implicitly in Scripture; that Scripture . . . owes the full conviction with which we ought to receive it to the testimony of the Spirit. Such . . . is a conviction which asks not for reasons. . . [but] which accords with the highest reason.
> (Calvin, 1953, pp. i, 71–73)

It is easy enough to see that this view of redemption meant that the "liberty" to seek out God would need to be tightly circumscribed. Only in the confines of a correctly reformed church, the model of which was exemplified in a Presbyterian church settlement, would the Spirit appear; and only in such a setting would the correct discipline and admonition be provided by the different godly members of the congregation, to ensure the godly grew in true knowledge of God while the unredeemed might be identified and restrained. Otherwise anarchy would ensue, especially if, as some were beginning to suggest, the Spirit was sent to reveal additional truths by which God wished people to try the authority of scripture and reason (and churches).

Others, not only Independents like Goodwin but also those involved with the rising Leveller movement, were inclined to give greater weight to reason. If Hooker had been right when he claimed that "God illuminateth every one who come into the world" with "the light of reason" (Hooker, 1868, p. 36), it followed that reason enjoyed divine authority and that man's rational capacities could be used to seek out knowledge of Him. It was not denied that "the will" remained corrupt and mired in sin, or that without grace "the will" could not turn away from sin; but it was nevertheless argued that humanity retained sufficient capacity to turn towards God and to accept or reject His offer of redemption. This more universalist theology did not see humanity in the binary terms of "elect" and "damned" – that division was beyond human judgement to determine, but other matters were not. Here the language of "liberty of conscience" was deployed with some force to denote the broader and freer liberty required to search out that knowledge of God He had fitted men with reason to acquire. From a more orthodox Calvinist perspective, this was a bogus account of redemption that opened the floodgates to a plurality of miscreants possessed of an unreformed "conscience", claiming the use of a wider set of liberties to pursue whatever ends they wished. In the absence of God's grace, which necessarily *was* absent, such persons would inevitably be ignorant of "the will" of God and of the common good. In a series of Fast sermons delivered by orthodox Calvinist ministers to Parliament from 1642 onwards, this point was underlined with passionate intensity.

An early example is John Brinsley's *The Healing of Israels Breaches* (1642). Brinsley was an orthodox Calvinist who upheld the authority of the civil magistrate and who had been prevented from preaching at different points through the 1620s and 30s (Cust, 2004). To dispel any doubts about the point he was making, in the first of six sermons Brinsley made reference early on to the Irish rebellion, which would later transform into the Irish Confederacy (the group of Gaelic Irish and Old English noblemen and gentry who would establish a government loyal to the king based in Kilkenny, which would openly practise Roman Catholicism). From Brinsley's perspective their claim to "liberty of conscience", which meant subjection to the Church of Rome, had formed the basis for a misappropriation of all other forms of liberty. As he put it,

> In the neighbour nation, the *Trumpet of rebellion* is sounded, the Kingdome divided . . . by the means of a seditious party of *Romish confederates*, who, under a pretence of vindicating the liberty of their own, seek and indeavour the extirpating, and rooting out the true Religion of God.
>
> (Brinsley, 1642, p. 22)

Turning next to Protestants, and the growing religious pluralism in England, Brinsley pointed to the interdependence of church, state, liberty and conscience which were now being pulled asunder: "*Breaches* [are] made both upon *Church*, and *state* among our selves. Breaches made upon the *estates* of men, upon the *liberties* of *subjects*, the *bodies*, nay the *souls* and *consciences* of *Christians*" (Brinsley, 1642, p. 23). This observation informed his understanding of current misdirected claims to liberty.

Brinsley chose to speak of the claims being made to "religion" and "liberty" because he observed a conjunction between the increasing plurality of religious factions and modish claims to liberty in the political sphere. He did not speak directly of "liberty of conscience", which from his perspective could only mean conformity with God's 'will' and so unity. Under the cover of a "new" claim to liberty, people had acted

> not out of *love to the Truth it selfe*, but rather out of *self-love* . . . led and carried . . . rather by the *examples* of others, whose *persons they*

> have in admiration . . . because of advantage . . . not in *love* to the truth, but to themselves, their own credits.
>
> (Brinsley, 1642, p. 40)

This point was further clarified when "the will" was discussed. Individuals should act according to "[God's] *own will*. . . as if it were indeed their *own selfe*. Whence it is sometimes so called; *If any man will come after me, let him deny himselfe, i.e. his owne will*"; but a loose call for "religion and liberty" made room for the self-willed: "in all, the great Breach-maker is *selfe*. That men are *selfe-willed* and s*elfe-conceited: Presumptuous are they, and selfe-willed*" (Brinsley, 1642, pp. 80–81). In summary, in the absence of true "liberty of conscience" and the submission of one's own "will" to God's, any claim to a wider set of "liberties" was a claim to exercise an unredeemed "will" bound by sin and directed towards self-interested ends. The claims to "religion and liberty", against which Brinsley was railing, would soon be rephrased as claims to "religious and civil liberty" (Worden, 2012). This semantic shift was grounded on an account of redemption he could not countenance, in which reason and "conscience" joined hands.

In arguing that humanity was owed the opportunity to seek out knowledge of God, and had to exercise reason in order to be assured in "conscience" of the truth of the Gospel, claims to "liberty of conscience" became less about the duty to build a united godly society and more about the liberty of thought and external action needed to pursue one's proper ends, to seek redemption and salvation. Hence the turn to a language of "religious and civil liberty", which implied negative checks on the actions of those in authority as against a set of "liberties" or "liberty" united by a notion of duty, this being the duty to build a united godly society. The latter became more difficult to sustain in a context of increasing plurality. The grounds of the shift became clearer as the new vocabulary gained traction. They were laid out with exemplary clarity in the writings of the Leveller William Walwyn.

Walwyn's *The Compassionate Samaritane* (1644) argued for the right of different protestant groups to separate from the established ecclesiastical order, as put forward by the Presbyterian platform, on the basis of this different account of redemption. Under the title "liberty of conscience asserted", Walwyn argued first that the exercise of "reason" played a crucial role in the process of redemption. As the reason of fallen man was not infallible, error was possible, which put question marks beside the claims of clerical authorities to impose a conformity of belief. Considering "[t]he uncertainly of knowledge in this life: no man, nor no sort of men can presume of an unerring spirit" (Walwyn, 1989, p. 104). Calvin would have blenched. Second, it was not simply God's saving grace, but "reason" which operated on an individual's "conscience" and since "conscience being subject only to reason (either that which is indeed, or seems to him which hears it to be so [true])", compulsion and the imposition of religious conformity would violate or curtail the natural operation and interplay of conscience and reason (Walwyn, 1989, p. 105). Third, for Walwyn, "whatsoever is not of faith is sin, and that every man ought to be fully perswaded of the trueness of that way wherein he serveth the Lord" (Walwyn, 1989, p. 114). Forcing anyone to conform and act against what their conscience judged true was to force them to act contrary to "faith", which was to force the citizen or subject to sin.

By the later 1640s, with parliamentary and Presbyterian attempts to come to a settlement with the king and institute a yet more restrictive Presbyterian discipline, the connections between conceptions of "liberty of conscience" and the reshaping of the political vocabulary of liberty were being explored by other writers too. The development of these connections under the banner of "liberty" was a self-defensive manoeuvre as much as it was an aggressive one, with particular weight being placed upon the political vocabulary as the details of the Leveller programme began to be worked out. In the 1647 *Remonstrance of Many Thousand Citizens*, attributed to Richard Overton, which sought to sketch out that programme, a call for equality was grounded in the claim that "where their assent is necessary and essentiall, they [the people] must be as Free as you, to assent, or dissent as their understandings and Consciences should guide them: and might as justly importune you, as yee them" (Overton, 1944, pp. 116–117; Foxley, 2013, pp. 130–143). The attack on equality implicit in the attempt to impose a new Presbyterian settlement, coupled with the lack of a voice in parliament and unequal property ownership, meant the "wills" and interests of one group were being forced upon others. This violated the sense in which conscience and reason should be freely exercised:

> [W]hereas now they [parliament] Act and Vote in our affaires but as intruders, or as thrust upon us by *Kings*, to make good their Interests, which to this day have been to bring us into a slavish subjection to their wills.
>
> (Overton, 1944, p. 117)

Now an explicit connection was drawn between "liberty of conscience" and the liberty of persons in the political sphere, with a warning posed as a rhetorical question:

> [W]hat will not a opprest, rich, and Religious People doe, to be delivered from all kinds of Oppression, both *Spirituall* and *Temporall*, and to be restored to *purity* and *freedome* in Religion, and to the just liberty of their *Persons* and *Estates*?
>
> (Overton, 1944, p. 118)

Conscience remained the touchstone throughout. Would not such liberty (freedom from "the will" of others) allow citizens or subjects to "enjoy the Peace of quiet Consciences"? (Overton, 1944, p. 119). Overton threw in the Norman yoke for good measure: it was in "the Writts, of the *Establishment* of *Religion*, [which] sheweth that in that particular, as many other, we remain under the *Norman* yoke of an *unlawfull Power*, from which wee ought to free our selves" (Overton, 1944, p. 123). His call for a liberty of the press was presented in concordant terms. Its absence would prevent subjects from seeking out "understanding" and thus exercising their "consciences": "let the imprisoned Presses at liberty, that all mens understandings may be more conveniently informed" (Overton, 1944, p. 128). But how far, in the end, did these undoubted shifts around "liberty of conscience" reshape the language of liberty in the political sphere? The changes are not as profound as they may first appear. We have said that the fundamental issue in dispute arose from two rival accounts of how one came to be in receipt of knowledge of God and God's grace, which would reform an individual's conscience and bring a corrupt and sinful will into line with God's will. Whilst the more "liberal" protestant position espoused by Walwyn and his friends on the surface implies greater individual agency and freedom, that freedom was a means, not an end in itself: liberty was an instrument that enabled the pursuit of higher ends. The emphasis laid on civil liberties or rights was not really about securing the freedom of the individual, but rather about securing the conditions under which the process of redemption was accessible to all, so that they could, finally, act in unity with God and for the common good. Both parties, "orthodox" and "liberal", viewed each other in identical terms: their bodged conceptions of "liberty of conscience" implied a bodged conception of redemption and so alienation from God. All claims to a wider set of liberties, in this setting, were to be dismissed as the offspring of a sinful and self-interested will.

Walwyn's *Compassionate Samaritane* condemned orthodox Calvinists in precisely these terms. The opposers of "liberty of conscience", namely the Presbyterians, were possessed of a "love which aimes only at it selfe; those endeavours which would procure liberty only to themselves, can at best be called but selfe love and selfe respects" (Walwyn, 1989, p. 102). His understanding of liberty in the political sphere, grounded on a "correctly" disposed conscience, meant that those who wished to deny such freedom to others were clearly not in possession of a reformed conscience or will—a point he laboured in a series of pamphlets. They might be compared fitly to "devouring Locusts, no lesse ravening then the Egyption ones"; they were "like the stiffe-necked and unwieldy Hebrewes, that wisht they were slaves in Egypt againe, where the much loved Flesh pots were, for that it was troublesome and dangerous passing through the Wildernesse into Canaan, a land

## Liberalism, Conscience and Toleration  69

of plenty and lasting liberty"; and they "becommeth [not] the gospel of Christ, but are carnall and walke as men, as vaine, fantastically, inconsiderate men" (Walwyn, 1989, pp. 65, 70, 83). John Lilburne followed a similar line. His writings placed great stock on equality before the law, popular sovereignty and full adult male suffrage. But at bottom equal liberty was about freeing humanity from its carnal passions (Scott, 2000, pp. 269–77). The provision of true liberty to all would remove the sinful impulses driven by self-interest, allowing conscience to attain true knowledge of God. Like Walwyn, Lilburne turned the presumption of sin back on those who, like the Presbyterians, rejected his preferred account of liberty. Their own lack of knowledge of God meant they appropriated the vocabulary of liberty to mask the pursuit of their own sinful ends.

The authors of the 1641 *Grand Remonstrance* had looked to "Gods grace still to persist in our duties. . . [to] the preservation of the Lawes and liberties of England". Without such action, "Religion, Lawes, liberties and Parliaments, will not long be lived after us" (Lilburne, 1647, p. 5). But the refusal to grant "liberty of religion", namely "liberty of conscience", to Independents and others, and to provide liberty and equality to all, arose from a lack of internal reform, of redemption, and a true understanding of the function and end of liberty. Lilburne quoted Christ's admonition of the Pharisees when admonishing the Presbyterian party – "yee make cleane the outside of the cup, and of the platter, but within they are full of extortion and excesse" (Lilburne, 1647, p. 5). In fact, Lilburne argued that the refusal to adopt a more expansive and inclusive idea of liberty in respect to the parliamentary franchise, supported as it was by the "orthodox" account of liberty espoused by Presbyterians, was a deliberate stratagem "to involve the generallity of the people in an everlasting case of confusion" which would allow those presently in power to make "their wills and lusts a law, their envy and malice a law, their coveteousnesse, and ambition a law" (Lilburne, 1647, p. 8). In the Leveller pamphlets it was only those "conscientious" men who had a claim to liberty – men who understood true "liberty of conscience" (Walwyn, 1989, pp. 156, 217, 300; Lilburne, 1648, p. 318. See Foxley, 2013 for discussion).

If not much has been said so far about toleration, it is because not much was said by the authors in view. Walwyn's own infrequent use of the term is indicative of how it was generally understood. As we have emphasized, what he and others sought was a true "liberty of conscience", which, duly perfected once all had attained true knowledge of God, implied virtuous citizenship and a society united in one will. Toleration was the practical expedient required when disagreements threatened to impede the progress of "conscience" to its true end. His 1645/6 pamphlet, *Tolleration Justified, and Persecution Condemned*, was plain that "toleration" was something established by the "Civil Magistrate" and its practice took on a specific civil form as countenanced by "the state". Walwyn went on say that

> those deserve least countenance of a State that would be Persecutors, not because of their consciences in the practice and exercise of their Religion, wherein the ground of Freedome consists; but because a persecuting spirit is the greatest enemy to humane society, the dissolver of love and brotherly affection, the cause of envyings, heart-burnings, divisions, yea, and of warres it selfe.
> (Walwyn, 1989, p. 162)

"Toleration", was something which was understood in terms of the unity of the state and civil society, where political bonds of friendship needed to be maintained, whereas "liberty of conscience" was the true ground of the "freedom" which only "reason" and "God's grace" could bring about. Civil authority could do nothing except create the conditions which would allow liberty of conscience to emerge and the work of God to take place.

Even at the height of discussion over "toleration" under the Commonwealth and then the Protectorate, the common and most referenced vocabulary remained that of "liberty of conscience" (Worden, 1984). Perhaps this is not surprising. "Liberty of conscience", the unity of the godly, and internal godly reform, remained the keystones of a wider understanding of liberty in the political sphere and of political virtue. Toleration was really a side issue, a necessary practical step which might be taken by "the state", and which would be unnecessary if all possessed true knowledge of God and thus true "liberty of conscience". At first glance we are world's away from the tales told by Rawls and his followers about liberty of conscience, the result of which is pluralism rather than unity, pluralism being the "natural outcome of the activities of human reason" under conditions of freedom (Rawls, 2005, p. xxiv). Yet it may be worth observing, by way of conclusion, that there is a side to Rawls's way of thinking which is in its origin and form theological. The "moral geometry" towards which he spoke of striving in his *Theory of Justice* (Rawls, 1999, p. 105) is the perfect realization of an abbreviated form of Christian morality, one in which good works are matched by faith in a minimal creed which, invoking the fundamental precepts of natural law, emphasizes the importance of our duties to ourselves and others in the economy of salvation. The pluralism he celebrates is a "reasonable" pluralism. In the *Theory* he launches a trenchant assault on the intuitionist doctrine of the "purely conscientious act", according to which the "highest moral motive is the desire to do what is right and just simply because it is right and just", a conviction, one might say, that asks not for reasons. This would mean that the desire to so act "lacks any apparent reason", which means in turn that there could be no assurance on the part of others that the bearer of that desire would voluntarily maintain and act from it" (Rawls, 1999, p. 418).

For the thinkers we have just been discussing, the appeal to reason was an appeal to an unimpeachable authority. They understood the dictates of reason to be the voice of God in man. These dictates were for practical purposes synonymous with the law of nature. Thus, natural law, reason and truth coincided. How, then, to explain the manifest failure of all individuals to converge upon truth? The answer, we have seen, is that the Fall of man diminished, but did not obliterate, the power of reason, and that fallen man required the assistance of divine grace if he were to reason rightly, grasp and follow God's dictates and live in truth. And grace, it was ordinarily assumed, could not be acquired through the autonomous action of individuals alone. It was a gift of God which flowed from Jesus through the office of the Holy Spirit via a corporate body – the church – which ameliorated the effects of sin.

For the young Rawls, we now know, in theology, ethics and politics alike, the problem remained "one of controlling and ridding the world of sin" (Rawls, 2009, pp. 7–8, 127–128). This has the effect of collapsing religion, morality and politics into one, with the result that the political community, even as it appears in his later writings, is modelled on a church; and this church organized around a moral religion itself orchestrated around a minimal creed to which all assent and by which all agree to live. Every individual rationally affirms, from the point of view of his or her own good, the two principles of justice at the heart of this creed as finally regulative. These principles specify the terms of co-operation between individuals and define what Rawls calls "a pact of reconciliation between diverse religions and moral beliefs, and the forms of culture to which they belong" (Rawls, 1999, p. 194). Rawls has no compunction about speaking of the "reasonable faith in the real possibility of a just constitutional regime" that all citizens must hold in common (Rawls, 1999, p. 448), or of the rational validity of all the laws they live under. The purifying grace of reflective equilibrium, by which individual judgements are brought into line with the demands of public justice, is available to all. The obverse of this view is that those who fail to recognize the validity of those demands are *eo ipso* unreasonable, indeed sinful. As Rawls puts it, "the propensity to commit acts" which violate just laws "is a mark of bad character" and punishment rightly falls on those who display "these faults" (Rawls, 1999, p. 277). Such persons may be legitimately coerced, because coercion is always a matter of enforcing reasonable standards of behaviour upon the irrational or unreasonable. All constitutional essentials and matters of basic justice are settled by reason, and the basis for social unity assured. Those who refuse to conform have to be defective, whether morally or intellectually.

If it is objected that things are altogether different in the Rawls of *Political Liberalism*, who acknowledges the possibility – indeed the inevitability – of reasonable disagreement between individuals, we respectfully demur from that view. When Rawls abandoned the aspiration for moral geometry and sought instead to ground constitutional essentials and matters of basic justice in popular political opinion, the implicit slide into the philosophy of Jacobinism was arrested by the invocation of a public doctrine, which he calls "public reason". Without the allegiance of all citizens to public reason, he announces, "divisions and hostilities between doctrines are bound in time to assert themselves". "[H]armony and concord among doctrines and a people's affirming public reason [he continues] are unhappily not a permanent condition of social life". They "depend upon the vitality of the public political culture and on citizens' being devoted to and realizing the ideal of public reason" (Rawls, 1999, pp. 484–485). How can this be assured? Only, Rawls indicates, by ensuring that those who run politics, whether the holders of, or candidates for, political office, or judges, espouse the doctrines of political liberalism and promulgate what they have learned to the masses.

In the preface to the paperback edition of *Political Liberalism* Rawls adduces the fate of the Weimar Republic to illustrate the consequences of failure by elites "to shape the underlying attitudes of the public culture" appropriately. "A *cause* of the fall of Weimar's constitutional regime", he writes there, was that the "*belief* that a decent liberal parliamentary regime was possible" was no longer widely shared, because the traditional German elites had given up on it and on their role in promulgating its values (Rawls, 2005, p. lxi, *emphasis added*). Its structure of beliefs had become dilapidated, and barbarism entered in. In short, the later Rawls, no less than the earlier, assumes that theory precedes practice, that correct doctrine is of the first importance, and that the theorists' role is to teach the principles without which a liberal order is impossible. We find ourselves back in the world of King's Locke, and closer to the world of Walwyn, Brinsley and Lilburne than the epigones of Rawls would find it comfortable to admit. This is just one unexpected result of reflecting historically and theoretically on liberalism, liberty of conscience, and toleration.

## Note

\* The authors would like to thank the Leverhulme Trust for funding the research programme from which this chapter develops: *Rethinking Civil Society: History, Theory, Critique* (RL-2016–044, Leverhulme Trust Research Leadership Award, http://rethinkingcivilsociety.org/).

## References

Andrew, E. (2001). *Conscience and Its Critics: Protestant Conscience, Enlightenment Reason, and Modern Subjectivity*. Toronto: University of Toronto Press.
Assheton, W. (1663). *Evangelium Armatum: Or, the Scripture Abus'd*. London.

Balint, P. (2017). *Respecting Toleration: Traditional Liberalism and Contemporary Diversity*. Oxford: Oxford University Press.
Baxter, R. (1653). *Plain Scripture Proof of Infants Church-Membership and Baptism*, 3rd ed. London.
Bejan, T. M. (2017). *Mere Civility: Disagreement and the Limits of Toleration*. Cambridge, MA: The Belknap Press of Harvard University Press.
Bogue, D. and Bennett, J. (1833). *The History of the Dissenters, from the Revolution to the Year 1808*, 2 vols. London: F Westley & A. H. Davies.
Brinsley, J. (1642). *The Healing of Israels Breaches*, 2nd ed. London.
Burnet, G. (1724–34). *From the Revolution to the Conclusion of the Treaty of Peace at Utrecht, in the Reign of Queen Anne, to Which Is Added, the Author's Life, by the Editor, vol. 2, Bishop Burnet's History of His Own Time*, 2 vols. London.
Calvin, J. (1953). *Institutes of the Christian Religion*, 2 vols. London: SCM Press.
Coffey, J. (2000). *Persecution and Toleration in Protestant England, 1558–1689*. Harlow: Pearson Education.
Coffey, J. (2006). *John Goodwin and the Puritan Revolution: Religion and Intellectual Change in 17th-Century England*. Woodbridge: Boydell & Brewer.
Cohen, A. J. (2018). *Toleration and Freedom from Harm: Liberalism Reconceived*. London: Routledge.
Collins, J. (2009). Redeeming the Enlightenment: New Histories of Religious Toleration. *The Journal of Modern History*, 81, pp. 607–636.
Corbet, J. (1661). *The Interest of England in the Matter of Religion*. London.
Cragg, G. R. (1957). *Puritanism in the Period of the Great Persecution 1660–1688*. Cambridge: Cambridge University Press.
Cust, Richard. (2004). Brinsley, John. In: *Oxford Dictionary of National Biography*. Available at: https://doi.org/10.1093/ref:odnb/3441.
Davis, J. C. (1992). Religion and the Struggle for Freedom in the English Revolution. *Historical Journal*, 35, pp. 507–530.
Domínguez, J. P. (2017). Introduction: Religious Toleration in the Age of Enlightenment. *History of European Ideas*, 43, pp. 273–287.
Drerup, J. and Kühler, M. (2019). Introduction: The Politics and Ethics of Toleration. *Critical Review of International Social and Political Philosophy*. Available at: www.tandfonline.com/doi/full/10.1080/13698230.2019.1616876.
Dudley, A. C. (1912). Nonconformity Under the 'Clarendon Code'. *The American Historical Review*, 18, pp. 65–78.
Forst, R. (2013). *Toleration in Conflict: Past and Present*. Cambridge: Cambridge University Press.
Forster, T. (1830). *Original Letters of Locke; Algernon Sidney; and Anthony Lord Shaftesbury*. London: J. B. Nichols & Son.
Foxley, R (2013). *The Levellers: Radical Political Thought in the English Revolution*. Manchester: Manchester University Press.
Galeotti, A. E. (2002). *Toleration as Recognition*. Cambridge: Cambridge University Press.
Galston, W. A. (1995). Two Concepts of Liberalism. *Ethics*, 105, pp. 516–534.
Galston, W. A. (2002). *Liberal Pluralism: The Implications of Value Pluralism for Political Theory and Practice*. Cambridge: Cambridge University Press.
Goldie, M. (2004). The Dissenters and Toleration: The Impact of Locke. Unpublished ms.

Goodwin, J. (1642). *Anti-Cavalierisme*. London.
Grayling, A. C. (2007). *Towards the Light: A Story of the Struggles for Liberty and Rights that Made the Modern West*. London: Bloomsbury.
Hampton, J. (1989). Should Political Philosophy Be Done Without Metaphysics? *Ethics*, 99, pp. 791–814.
Harris, I. (2011). 'And the Least Sceptical': Knowledge, Natural Theology and Liberty of Conscience in Bayle's *Commentaire Philosophique*. Unpublished ms.
Hayek, F. A. (1987). Individual and Collective Aims. In: S. Mendus and D. Edwards, eds., *On Toleration*. Oxford: Clarendon Press, pp. 35–47.
Hooker, R. (1868). *Book I of The Laws of Ecclesiastical Polity*. Ed. R. W. Church. Oxford: Clarendon Press.
Hume, D. (1965). *Of the Standard of Taste and Other Essays*. Ed. John. W. Lenz. New York: Library of the Liberal Arts.
Hume, D. (1983). *A History of England from the Invasion of Julius Caesar to the Revolution in 1688*, 6 vols. Indianapolis, IN: Liberty Fund.
Israel, J. I. (2006). *Enlightenment Contested: Philosophy, Modernity, and the Emancipation of Man, 1670–1752*. Oxford: Oxford University Press.
Jager, C. (2012). Common Quiet: Tolerance around 1688. *English Literary History*, 79, pp. 569–596.
Jones, P. (2012). Legalising Toleration: A Reply to Balint. *Res Publica*, 18, pp. 265–278.
Kamen, H. (1967). *The Rise of Toleration*. New York: McGraw-Hill.
Kaplan, B. J. (2007). *Divided by Faith: Religious Conflict and the Practice of Toleration in Early Modern Europe*. Cambridge, MA: The Belknap Press of Harvard University Press.
Kautz, S. (1995). *Liberalism and Community*. Ithaca and London: Cornell University Press.
King, P. (1829). *The Life of John Locke: with Extracts from his Correspondence, Journals, and Common-Place Books*. London: Henry Colburn.
Kippis, A. (1773). *A Vindication of the Protestant Dissenting Ministers*. London.
Kippis, A. (1788). *A Sermon Preached at the Old Jewry . . . Before the Society for Commemorating the Glorious Revolution*. London.
Lecky, W. E. H. (1866). *History of the Rise and Influence of the Spirit of Rationalism in Europe*, 2 vols., London: Longman, Green, & Co.
Lightfoot, J. B. (1893). *Essays on the Work Entitled 'Supernatural Religion'*, 2nd ed. London: Macmillan.
Lilburne, J. (1647). *The Out-Cryes of Oppressed Commons*. London.
Lilburne, J. (1648). *Several Proposals for Peace & Freedom*. In: Don Marion Wolfe, ed., *Leveller Manifestoes of the Puritan Revolution*. New York and London: T. Nelson, pp. 311–321.
Locke, J. (1968). *Epistola de Tolerantia/A Letter on Toleration*. Ed. R. Klibansky, trans. J. W. Gough. Oxford: Clarendon Press.
Locke, J. (1975). *An Essay Concerning Human Understanding*. Ed. P. H. Nidditch. Oxford: Clarendon Press.
Locke, J. (1976). *The Correspondence of John Locke*, 8 vols (to date). Ed. E. S. de Beer. Oxford: Clarendon Press.
Locke, J. (1983). *A Letter Concerning Toleration*. Ed. J. H. Tully. Indianapolis, IN: Hackett Publishing.

Macedo, S. (2019). Liberalism Beyond Toleration: Religious Exemptions, Civility and the Ideological Other. *Philosophy & Social Criticism*, 45, pp. 370–389.

Mandelbrote, S. (2001). Religious Belief and the Politics of Toleration in the Late Seventeenth Century. *Nederlands Archief voor Kerkgeschiedenis*, 81, pp. 93–114.

Marshall, J. (1994). *John Locke: Resistance, Religion and Responsibility*. Cambridge: Cambridge University Press.

Moots, G. A. (2020). Religious Exercise and Establishment in Early America. In: M. D. Breidenbach and O. Anderson, eds., *The Cambridge Companion to the First Amendment and Religious Liberty*. New York: Cambridge University Press, pp. 101–139.

Mortier, R. (1969). *Clartés et Ombres du Siècle des Lumières: Études sur le 18e Siècle Littéraire*. Geneva: Droz.

Murphy, A. R. (1997). Tolerance, Toleration, and the Liberal Tradition. *Polity*, 29, pp. 593–594.

Neal, D. (1732–38). *The History of the Puritans or Protestant Non-Conformists, from the Reformation to the Act of Toleration . . . in 1689*, 2 vols. London.

Overton, R. (1944). A Remonstrance of Many Thousand Citizens [1646]. In: Don Marion Wolfe, ed., *Leveller Manifestoes of the Puritan Revolution*. New York: T. Nelson, pp. 109–130.

Parkin, J. and Stanton, T. (eds.) (2013). *Natural Law and Toleration in the Early Enlightenment*. Oxford: Oxford University Press for the British Academy.

Rawls, J. (1999). *A Theory of Justice*, expanded ed. New York: Oxford University Press.

Rawls, J. (2005). *Political Liberalism*, paperback ed. New York: Columbia University Press.

Rawls, J. (2009). *A Brief Inquiry into the Meaning of Sin and Faith*. Ed. Thomas Nagel. Cambridge, MA: The Belknap Press of Harvard University Press.

Schmidt, J. (ed.) (1996). *What Is Enlightenment? Eighteenth-Century Answers and Twentieth-Century Questions*. Berkeley, CA: University of California Press.

Scott, J. (2000). *England's Troubles: Seventeenth-Century English Political Instability in European Context*. Cambridge: Cambridge University Press.

Sommerville, J. P. (2004). Conscience, Law and Things Indifferent: Arguments on Toleration from the Vestiarian Controversy to Hobbes and Locke. In: H. E. Braun and E. Vallance, eds., *Contexts of Conscience in Early Modern Europe, 1500–1700*. Houndmills: Palgrave Macmillan, pp. 166–179, and notes at 222–226.

Stanton, T. (2011). Authority and Freedom in the Interpretation of Locke's Political Theory. *Political Theory*, 39, pp. 6–30.

Stanton, T. (2018). John Locke and the Fable of Liberalism. *Historical Journal*, 61, pp. 597–622.

Tate, J. W. (2013). 'We Cannot Give One Millimetre'? Liberalism, Enlightenment and Diversity. *Political Studies*, 61, pp. 816–833.

Tate, J. W. (2016). *Liberty, Toleration and Equality: John Locke, Jonas Proast, and the Letters Concerning Toleration*. New York: Routledge.

Tate, J. W. (2020). John Locke and the 'Problem' of Toleration. This volume.

Trevor-Roper, H. R. (1967). *Religion, the Reformation, and Social Change*. London: Palgrave Macmillan.

Vaughan, R. (1840). *The History of England Under the House of Stuart . . . Part II: Commonwealth; Charles II; James II*. London: Baldwin and Cradock.

Walsham, A. (2006). *Charitable Hatred: Tolerance and Intolerance in England, 1500–1700*. Manchester: Manchester University Press.

Walwyn, W. (1989). *The Writings of William Walwyn*. Eds. Jack R. McMichael and Barbara Taft. Athens, GA: University of Georgia Press.

Worden, B. (1984). Toleration and the Cromwellian Protectorate. *Studies in Church History*, 21, pp. 199–233.

Worden, B. (2012). Civil and Religious Liberty. In: *God's Instruments: Political Conduct in the England of Oliver Cromwell*. Oxford: Oxford University Press.

Zagorin, P. (2003). *How the Idea of Religious Toleration Came to the West*. Princeton, NJ: Princeton University Press.

# Part II
# Toleration and the Challenges to Liberalism
## Conceptual and Justificatory Issues

# 4 The Mutual Independence of Liberalism and Toleration

*David Heyd*

## 1. From Non-liberal Toleration to Right-Based Liberalism

In their recent introduction to a special issue on the subject of toleration Johannes Drerup and Michael Kühler state at the very beginning that "toleration is widely considered as one of the core values of liberalism", and in an even more committed tone add that "toleration is usually regarded as . . . a *constitutive* part of liberal political practice" (Drerup and Kühler, 2019; my italics). This chapter wishes to challenge this conceptually strong association of toleration and liberalism and argue that there is no conceptual link between the two and that the relation between them is at most contingent or instrumental. The strong link between toleration and liberalism has definitely become the dominant view in both theories of toleration and those of liberalism. My aim will be to critically examine the historical and theoretical grounds of this allegedly conceptual relation and suggest that they should be dismissed for theoretical and normative reasons.

The issue regarding the relation between liberalism and toleration is obviously dependent on the way we understand the *concepts* of liberalism and toleration. The way the linguistic terms are ordinarily used cannot guide the debate and can easily miss the philosophical issue. It is useful to be reminded of the genealogy of the idea of toleration which demonstrates the gradual change in the use of the term and the development of the concept. Originally the term was understood pejoratively, as an unjustified attitude of indulgence towards bad behaviour or dangerous beliefs. But it was also associated with the privilege of kings and princes who could by an act of personal discretion avoid using their power to repress beliefs and practices that were considered wrong or dangerous. This was toleration as grace. Then, sometime in the 16th century, toleration was recommended as a more principled policy of pacifying religious strife and saving the integrity of a religious community by searching for a common denominator and reaching compromise (consider Erasmus and his idea of *adiaphora*). Later, with the rise of the idea of rights in the 17th-century toleration gained a non-prudential value as an independent principle (see typically Locke's political theory). But in the 18th century, tension between being tolerated and being respected due to one's rights has surfaced with the consequence of a dialectical shift back to a negative view of toleration as a paternalistic, even arrogant, attitude. Kant and Thomas Paine are well-known examples of this modern turn.

But in the pluralistic and multi-cultural societies of the 20th-century toleration has again gained a special positive status as the typical means of countering oppression and promoting civil equality of religious and cultural minorities. This was again an attempt to deal with religious discord by appealing to tolerant restraint, but this time backed by a fully developed system of individual rights, which is the core of modern liberal democracy. The theoretical challenge is now how to accommodate the virtue of toleration with right-based liberalism. Some philosophers suggest that the implementation of a regime of rights by the state amounts to what we consider as toleration (Peter Jones); others regard toleration as the necessary attitude of individual citizens in the social contract for the creation of a politically fair system of cooperation (Rawls); some argue that toleration is the recognition and full acceptance of cultural and religious minorities in a liberal pluralistic society (Galeotti); and there are philosophers who view toleration as a transitional value, an interim virtue, on the way from persecution to full acceptance (Williams). In what follows I will suggest another way of framing the relationship between toleration and liberalism which separates the two on the conceptual level without denying that they belong to the same political culture and are mutually supportive.

But in order to show that we need to fix the meaning of both the concept of toleration and that of liberalism.

## 2. The Concept of Toleration Strictly Speaking

Due to the vicissitudes in the history of toleration, its meaning is typically messy as both its dictionary entry and the varied philosophical usage throughout the ages prove. Consequently it is useful for philosophers to provide it with a more distinct meaning. The natural strategy to do so it to distinguish it from the meaning of close cognate terms with which it has often been conflated. Since I have undertaken this enterprise in a previous article (Heyd, 2020, forthcoming) I shall only briefly mention what in my view toleration is after distilling the concept from what toleration is not.

The semantic fields of the cognate concepts of toleration can be mapped into five semantic fields: the cognitive, the pragmatic, the psychological, the moral and the political. In the cognitive field, we want toleration to be distinguished from scepticism, agnosticism, relativism, "open-mindedness", epistemic laziness, and the Lockean proposition that beliefs cannot be forced on people. We equally wish to distinguish between toleration and the pragmatic avoidance of interfering with the beliefs and practices of others because of the wish to achieve peace (*concordia*), compromise (*modus vivendi*), coexistence and social stability. Toleration is rightly associated with certain psychological traits of character, like patience, restraint, indulgence, indifference, acquiescence, condonation and apathy; but we are reluctant to identify these personal qualities and character traits as toleration. Charity, magnanimity and grace are typically moral attitudes that have been closely connected with toleration but by no means capture what we intend – especially in modern times – by toleration. And even in the case of toleration regarding matters of taste and conventional norms, toleration demands more than just politeness, etiquette and civility. Finally, in the political semantic field, we want to avoid identifying toleration with both respect for rights and with state neutrality. This distinction in the political sphere will be the focus of the rest of this chapter.

Why is this theoretical purity in the isolation of a concept of toleration from all its afore-mentioned cognates important? Why not maintain the richness of the meanings of the idea of toleration as it was entertained by the history of the concept and by ordinary usage? The answer relates to the theoretical advantage in using a semi-technical concept for the framing of the current debates about the role of toleration in the political life of a democratic, pluralistic society. The normative questions like whether toleration amounts to recognition or whether toleration is a condescending, paternalistic attitude can be given persuasive answers only if we hold on to a specifically defined concept of toleration which is well-distinguished from kindred concepts. Michael Walzer's concept of toleration is intentionally wide in scope so as to include, for instance, the political attitude of the Roman (or Ottoman) Empire to the many ethnic and religious minorities living under its rule. But such an inclusive concept is helpful in a historical survey and the classification of different regimes of toleration but hardly of use in the *normative* disputes about the current relations of the state to homosexuals or to religious fundamentalists.

Theoretical terms should be judged for their usefulness in explaining phenomena or justifying normative positions and principles. I suggest that a strictly defined concept of toleration can serve us in pursuing those aims. This concept should consist of the traditional conditions associated with the attitude of toleration: (i) reasoned objection or opposition; (ii) urge and reason to intervene; (iii) power to intervene; (iv) a *principled* choice not to intervene; (v) burden or suffering (*tolerare*) from not intervening. With these conceptual clarifications we can now move to the discussion of the relationship between liberalism and toleration.[1]

## 3. Respect for Rights

The sharpest challenge to the idea of political toleration comes today from the idea of the rights of individuals (be they natural, human, legal or civil). Since modern liberalism is primarily based on the idea of rights and the duty of both individuals and the state to respect them (often serving as trumps in cases of conflict with other political values), the question is first whether there is a difference between tolerating people and respecting their rights, and secondly, if there is, what is the role of toleration in a right-based liberal regime. What makes the first question hard to answer is that both respect for rights and toleration basically involve the originally Augustinian distinction between the value of a practice or a belief on the one hand and the value or standing of the agent holding the belief or acting on it on the other. Strictly speaking we respect persons – not beliefs and practices, and we similarly tolerate persons rather than the propositions or actions. This distinction between action and agent is crucial to any kind of liberalism which provides the normative means for living in a pluralistic society in which identifying the value of persons with that of their practices and beliefs may lead to constant strife and persecution.

However, there are important differences between respect for rights and toleration. Toleration is by definition a judgemental attitude; it is not neutral regarding the value of the tolerated beliefs and practices. It calls not to intervene with them *despite* their negative value. It requires restraint because avoiding intervention involves pain. Respect for rights is on the other hand neutral with regards to the behaviour which is protected by the right. The protection is based on a formal principle which is independent of the substantive value of the belief or behaviour covered by it. Respecting one's right to free speech does not necessarily imply disapproval of the content of one's speech and the abstention from intervention with the speech does not necessarily involve pain or call for restraint by the respecting party.

Furthermore, as we have seen, toleration can be exercised only by the party which has the power to interfere in another's life; but respecting people's rights is not similarly hierarchical in nature. My boss can tolerate my rude language, although I cannot be said to tolerate his rude language (since I have no power to tell him how to behave). But both of us can respect the right of free speech of each other regardless of our respective positions.

Rights are impersonal and are distributed systematically among individuals. Toleration involves a personal attitude and hence is shown or exercised in more haphazard ways in society. Showing toleration in one case does not commit the tolerator to do so in similar cases or to other people. Rights create duties and in Nozick's terms serve as absolute side constraints on one's actions. These constraints are formal in the sense that the prohibition of interfering with the right holder's action is not grounded in our attitude towards the agent of this action. Toleration is not a duty and to be tolerated is not a right since it is discretionary and dependent on the attitude of the tolerator towards both the particular action and the particular agent of that action. It is differential in being exercised towards some people rather than others, or to some kinds of behaviour rather than others. Toleration is, as will be argued later, supererogatory.

So it seems that although the distinction between the agent and the action stands at the core of both respect for rights and toleration, the way the agent-perspective overrides the judgement of the action is different in the two cases. The idea of rights is universal (at least within a certain domain) and is binding independently of the attitude of the person respecting the right while toleration targets a specific individual or a particular group selected by the tolerator. Thus, human beings have universal human rights in virtue of being human but it would be strange to say that we tolerate human beings as human beings (unless perhaps if we are misanthropes!). We respect the civil rights of citizens as people who belong to the same polis. But individuals and states do not tolerate people simply as citizens. Toleration is directed either at an individual, qua individual, or at specific groups such as minorities or religious sects.

## 4. The Liberal State: Neutral or Perfectionist

Although individuals are encouraged to exercise toleration toward their fellow men and women, the state is the prominent agent in the political theory of toleration. This has been the case for centuries, since Locke's *Letters on Toleration*. But the question is now whether the modern liberal state still maintains this role and whether it is consistent with the current conception of liberalism, the rule of law and the respect for rights. Of course there are different conceptions of liberalism and the liberal state, but my argument will be that none of them is compatible with the idea of state toleration. I shall take two principal versions of the role of the liberal state in political life – one which holds to the ideal of moral neutrality of the state and one which is perfectionist – and claim that neither can be based on the principle of toleration, at least not in the strict sense which I have articulated.

John Rawls sees the state as having the double function of implementing the principles of distributive justice and respecting the political rights of its citizens. The state has no business in taking sides in the deep disagreements between citizens about moral and religious issues. More importantly, the state should remain neutral also with regard to value of moral pluralism and personal autonomy. It should not side with Millian views of the good life, since they are themselves contested. Rawls accordingly insists on a *thin* version of liberalism, which he calls "political".

But if the state is neutral in that sense, how can it exercise toleration? If it meets citizens' violations of the principles of justice or of the political rights of other citizens, it must respond by punitive or corrective measures according to its own laws. And if the citizens' behaviour is morally repugnant but does not infringe the justice-based laws, then the state must not interfere. Such behaviour lies beyond the scope of state action. The liberal state is based on permissiveness: whatever is not forbidden is permitted – not tolerated. The state is indifferent towards the realm of the permitted. What is permitted is not, from the point of view of the state, a "second best" or something we should live with or accommodate. Furthermore, the state cannot even be said to have to *restrain* itself from intervening in such cases since the state has no values on the basis of which it would want to oppose or constrain beliefs or behaviour of discordant value. Finally, the state acts according to the law (or the principles of justice) and consequently must apply it in a universal way, with no favouritism, concession, or partiality of the kind necessarily involved in toleration. The state permits but does not make concessions out of good will.

Nevertheless, Rawls does grant toleration an important place in his theory. But since the traditional concept of political toleration does not fit his thin, political liberalism, he refers to it as *philosophical* or epistemological toleration. In a pluralistic society reasonable people may disagree on moral values, without detracting from their reasonableness. The sources of these disagreements are "the burdens of judgement". These burdens mark the limits of what we can expect to be able to justify to others in the sphere of value. Now, according to Rawls, my commitment to my comprehensive moral doctrine does not exclude your different (even incompatible) comprehensive doctrine from the scope of reasonable doctrines, despite my belief that it is not true. For I maintain that you have the capacity – both theoretical and practical – to form a consistent, long standing, coherent and realistic system of values. In distinguishing between reasonableness and truth Rawls seems to adopt the afore-mentioned distinction between the subject and the belief or the agent and the act.[2] So it seems that the *philosophical* attitude towards reasonable doctrines which we do not hold to be true can indeed receive the title of toleration. We are called to tolerate all reasonable doctrines of our fellow citizens. We must not use state power to repress such doctrines.

But why? Rawls answers that "reasonable persons . . . endorse some form of liberty of conscience and freedom of thought" (Rawls, 1993, p. 61); and then "There is no reason . . . why any citizen or association of citizens, should have the *right* to use the state's power to decide constitutional essentials . . . that one's comprehensive doctrine directs" (p. 62, italics mine). But if that is the reason for not repressing other people's beliefs in a democratic society, then we are back at the respect for rights rather than the traditional argument of toleration.

The basis for the prohibition on using political power to intervene in the beliefs and practices of individuals who live according to their comprehensive doctrines is the contract of their representatives in the original position (Rawls, 1993, p. 62). Being under the veil of ignorance no one in the original position would agree to such state intervention. This of course makes perfect sense, but is that an agreement on toleration or rather a commitment to a system of political rights? And who is the tolerating party – the individuals or the state? Rawls says that the toleration he is talking about it *philosophical*: "political liberalism applies the principle of toleration to philosophy itself" (Rawls, 1993, p. 10). But this expression is unfortunate. The idea of political liberalism is not that of tolerating substantive moral doctrines ("philosophy") but to find – in Rawls's own terms – a *practical* solution to the unbridgeable disagreements regarding deep moral values. Political liberalism is grounded in the distinction between the political and the moral, between the conditions of fair social cooperation and moral and religious truth. The contract does not commit us to tolerate other moral conceptions of which we disapprove but only to refrain from using political power to repress these conceptions (Rawls, 1993, p. 62). It amounts to the agreement to establish a state that will prevent individuals from using power against moral views and practices which they oppose. For that purpose the state must itself be neural and act exclusively on the basis of the rule of law, the universal principles of justice and political rights. Therefore, it cannot be the state which exercises toleration because all that is expected of it is not to have any substantive values of its own. The state does not restrain itself from interfering in moral matters but just disregards them for being beyond its business.[3]

In what sense can individuals be the agents of toleration for Rawls? If we think about individuals as contractors in the original position, we cannot ascribe them with toleration since they do not know under the veil of ignorance what their comprehensive doctrines are and to what extent it would be rational for them to exercise toleration once they become aware of their deep moral commitments. All they can rationally consent to is the idea of political liberalism, namely the exclusion of private moral beliefs from the public sphere, or public reason. On the other hand, Rawls says that individual citizens in actual society can be expected to adopt the virtue of toleration since it is no different from other liberal virtues such as civility, reasonableness and the sense of fairness which are crucial in upholding a just society without leading to a perfectionist state (Rawls, 1993, p. 194). As we shall see, toleration may indeed be of value to a liberal political regime but it is still only instrumentally so rather than constitutive of liberalism.

My conclusion from the discussion of Rawls's view of the role of toleration in liberal society is that the state cannot be said to be strictly speaking an agent of toleration; that individuals in the hypothetical contract situation cannot be said to ground their political agreement on an attitude of toleration to each other; and that toleration – although not a constitutive element in the grounding of the authority of the state and the limits on its legitimate exercise of power – is a highly prized virtue in individual citizens wishing to implement the social contract. One may say that while tolerating a neighbour involves respecting her as a particular human being living close by, restraining oneself from violating her rights shows respect for her as a citizen. At least under this interpretation Rawls belongs to those who do not see toleration and liberalism as conceptually dependent.

Rawls's neutral state cannot display toleration. But can the state in perfectionist versions of liberalism be tolerant? Joseph Raz believes it can. According to his view the liberal state cannot and ought not to be neutral. Its prime function is to safeguard and promote personal autonomy and in order to do so must actively advance certain values and opportunities which would make people's lives valuable. Not all the citizens accept those values and may even feel that their interests and life styles are not sufficiently recognized by the state. However, such a state is still liberal in the sense that it both permits also life styles that are not within its priority and protects the right of the citizens to pursue them.

Without going into the philosophical debate between Rawls's thin political liberalism and perfectionist conceptions (like Joseph Raz's) which reject the idea of state neutrality, the question is whether the perfectionist state can be said (or expected) to be tolerant. I have dealt with Raz's view elsewhere (Heyd, 2020) but will add here that giving special weight to some forms of life or activities does not imply disapproving of all others. As we have seen, the concept of toleration should be distinguished from indifference. I may think highly of my neighbour's piano playing to which I am exposed, and disapprove of her playing the drums in the middle of the night, but I am completely indifferent to her playing no instrument. Thus I can be said to tolerate her only in the case she plays her hateful drums but not of her playing no instrument (despite believing that it would have been better for her had she played the piano). The same, a fortiori, applies to the perfectionist state: it may decide to promote and allocate money to sport organizations rather than to train spotting or (the proverbial Rawlsian example) counting grass blades, but without restricting the freedom of the latter activity.[4] The avoidance of restricting the activity does not involve any attitude of toleration since there is no opposition to the activity to begin with. And with regard to the drum playing or playing at midnight, the question is who the tolerating party is. Even if the individual neighbour can show toleration towards this behaviour, the state (assuming that there is a law against making noise at night) cannot and ought not to be tolerant to the violator of the law and that is the case regardless of its being a neutral state or a perfectionist state. In other words, the perfectionist state can have preference for some life projects and can be indifferent to others; but when it has reasons *against* certain activities it must prohibit them and enforce the prohibition; it cannot tolerate them.

Finally, we can say that liberalism (at least in its rich, moral sense) celebrates pluralism while toleration merely contains it.

## 5. Toleration-Based Liberalism: Peter Jones

Most liberal theories consider toleration as a major liberal value. But there are philosophers who even see it as the *core* principle of liberalism. A forceful argument for such a view is offered in a series of articles by Peter Jones. Unlike many theoreticians of toleration Jones is aware of the problem of ascribing toleration as an attitude to the state.[5] Instead, he suggests a more sophisticated account according to which strictly speaking it is the citizens who can be regarded as tolerant and the liberal state is merely the impersonal institutional expression of the mutual toleration of the individual citizens (Jones, 2012).[6] Jones' idea is that in a divided society, most typically on religious matters, there is no way to reach agreement but through a tolerant attitude, a commitment not to interfere with the beliefs and practices of others despite the disapproval with which they are held. For Jones toleration is not a kind of relation of ruler to his subjects but a political regime which is constituted by a system of laws, rules, rights and duties which manage those divides and unbridgeable disagreements (Jones, 2007).

Indeed, Jones is right in holding the state to be an impersonal agent, having no psychological or moral attitudes. But the question remains whether tolerant attitudes can be institutionalized in laws applying universally to all citizens at all times. Such institutionalization misses the *discretionary* element of the exercise of toleration and the personal choice which motivates it. As we shall see, once toleration takes the form of a law, it becomes obligatory, a matter of political or legal duty. And if institutions, such as the courts, government agencies or the taxman are expected to demonstrate toleration, their function as fair, impartial and egalitarian would be seriously undermined. For toleration, being a matter of choice is not equally and impartially exercised towards all.

Jones proposes to adopt an impersonal standpoint regarding toleration, that is to say, approach it neither from the point of view of the tolerator nor from that of the tolerated party. But even if such a concept of toleration which consists of an impersonal system of laws and rights is accepted, the question remains whether it adds anything to the concept of the liberal state based on exactly such system of rights and laws. Toleration under this impersonal and deontically fixed status (being obligatory) becomes redundant. Theoretically we lose the uniqueness of toleration as a personal and discretionary attitude without gaining any further basis for liberal democracy beyond the impartial rule of law, universal civil and human rights and the fair exercise of punitive or distributive measures.

Jones and Balint (2017) argue that in a democratic regime we can ascribe the state with a tolerant treatment of citizens whose beliefs and practices do not fit those of the state. This may be the case even when the state is supposed to be morally neutral, since there are some exceptions to this neutrality, primarily in the case of non-liberal and intolerant groups of people. Thus, the state can decide to what extent it wishes or is prepared to avoid interfering with such groups and by that display toleration. I am not sure that even in this context state toleration is a helpful concept. Liberals want to allow for illiberal comprehensive moral doctrines, at least as long as they do not actively undermine the liberal regime. The dividing line between the right to hold illiberal or even intolerant views and the right of the state to intervene in the freedom of those who hold them is admittedly fine. But this line can and should be anchored in a stable and consistent definition of the rights and duties of citizens, what they are allowed by law to do and what they are prohibited from doing. For that we do not need the concept of state toleration.[7]

Take for example the attitude of a European state to a minority of Muslim fundamentalists who believe that a *Shari'a* state should replace the current liberal regime. The way to treat such groups is a sensitive and complicated matter but the principles by which it should be decided pertain to the limits of human, civil and political rights. We are misled here by the term "intolerable" that characterizes such fundamentalist groups. "Intolerable" here means what the state has no *tolerance* for (rather than what should not be tolerated). Tolerance is closer in its meaning to the medical property of the capacity to *endure*. It is more of a natural, descriptive concept than a normative concept.[8] The liberal regime cannot survive fundamentalist attempts to establish its illiberal values and hence may prohibit them. This does not mean that when it allows fundamentalists to express in writing or in religious ritual their illiberal conceptions it shows toleration to them. It simply views such expressions as protected by basic political rights and liberties.[9]

Jones is aware of the possible objection to his conception of toleration as the institutionalization of non-interference in the lives of others in a pluralistic society. He offers two answers to the question why the language of rights does not suffice for the characterization of the liberal state. First, the language of rights is much wider than that of toleration and does not capture its uniqueness. Secondly, the language of toleration has a historical dimension. Indeed it is true that the respecting rights covers a wider range of cases of principled non-interference in the affairs of others; but it does all that is required for the liberal political order. The uniqueness of the attitude of toleration, i.e. what is not captured by the respect for rights, might even undermine some basic principles of a rights-based political regime: the personal attitude and the discretionary character of toleration are incompatible with the impersonal nature of state action. If toleration is defined as obligatory, all it can achieve is already covered by the language of rights and justice. And if we introduce the personal element into the operation of state agencies, we may lose the impartial and universal aspect of rights and justice which are constitutive of political liberalism.

Jones argues that toleration remains toleration even when it is legally required in the same way as restraint from interference remains restraint even when it is legally required. But there is a difference between the two: the law requires restraint but it is indifferent to the reasons and motives of this restraint. Toleration, in contrast, is not just a behavioural regime for controlling illegal behaviour. It is restraint based in a principled, morally motivated avoidance from interfering with the beliefs and actions of others. It is a matter of choice and maybe also of good will. And hence, unlike mere restraint, toleration cannot remain toleration if it is enforced by the law. Jones proposes that the motive of restraint is not fear of the law but rather a culture of toleration that the liberal regime represents (Jones, 2007). But then, toleration cannot be legally required. Furthermore, respecting the rights of fellow citizens can do the same job of a principled motive of restraint and hence make the idea of toleration redundant as a principle of political liberalism.

The main point of contention proves to be the deontic status of toleration. The question here is not semantic but theoretical and normative. Jones treats toleration as obligatory – legally required or a matter of justice. This implies that to be tolerated is a right of citizens, which sounds even more counter-intuitive than being under a duty to tolerate.[10] My own suggestion, shared – as far as I know – only by Glenn Newey, is to regard toleration as *supererogatory* (Heyd, 2008). Toleration is a morally valuable attitude that is not obligatory. Its particular worth lies in the good will that motivates it and more importantly in the personal discretion that is a condition for its exercise. I can force you to restrain yourself from intervening in the life of others but I (or the state) cannot force you to tolerate others. Jones, who explicitly objects to the supererogatory account of toleration (Jones, 2013, 2020), argues that if toleration lies beyond the call of duty then it cannot be "political". I believe that he is correct on that and accordingly argue that this is exactly the reason why toleration is not political, at least in the sense that it cannot be ascribed to the state.

To better understand the issue about the deontic nature of toleration, consider the practices of forgiveness and charity which are more naturally considered as supererogatory (Ben-baji and Heyd, 2001). Can the state be expected, or even allowed to be forgiving or charitable? Unlike a political entity governed by an individual ruler (King or Prince) who is above the law, a democratic state must govern by the rule of law and that includes institutions such as the courts and the ministry of welfare. The court should not act in a forgiving way because that would mean digressing from the instruction of the criminal law. For the same reason, the ministry of welfare should not act out of charity since it must distribute financial assistance according to strict criteria in an impartial and fair way. Forgiveness and charity are personal attitudes and are by definition exercised as a matter of discretion. My suggestion is to see toleration as analogical to forgiveness and charity. Although all three practices cannot serve as principles of state action this, as we shall see in the next section, does not mean that the state has no interest in them. It may want to inculcate them among its citizens, educate the young to adopt the respective virtues of free giving, considerateness and compassion; but the state itself does not have such personal virtues and its principles of operation must be different. The state cannot go beyond its duties, i.e. act supererogatorily, since by that it may violate the principles of justice and equality before the law. The state can give tax exemptions for charitable donations but cannot act directly as a charitable organization. Similarly, it can introduce classes about the value of interpersonal toleration in school curricula but it cannot tolerate people's deviation from the law of the land. The presidential power to grant legal pardon, which is typically discretionary and not obligatory, is just the exception which proves the rule. It is a remnant of the traditional royal power of a pre-democratic state.

Jones supports his argument for the obligatory nature of toleration by the claim that it is the best remedy or antidote to intolerance. But it seems that this claim is based on a conceptual misunderstanding, about which John Horton has warned long ago. The right way to fight white supremacist intolerance is not by making white supremacists tolerant, but hopefully instil in them respect of universal human rights and the equal moral standing of all human beings. Such respect is owed as a matter of *duty* to all people and is not a matter of discretionary choice or virtuous attitude (although these may be instrumental in advancing such respect and in the case of white supremacists a second-best strategy). Intolerance is usually understood as the willingness to persecute, to take active action against actions that one opposes. But there are many ways in which such active interference in the affairs of others may be prevented – compromise, respect for other's rights, inculcating indifference, boosting epistemic scepticism about the validity of one's own views, etc. Toleration is by no means the exclusive answer to intolerance. And in liberal regimes, respect for rights is a superior measure due to its impersonal and universally obligatory nature.

Thus, when two groups in a society – like let's say Muslims and Christians – are in conflict, both asking for state support on a contested matter, the state is not expected to exercise toleration, as Jones argues (Jones, 2007), but to make a morally neutral decision based on state law or the principles of justice underlying it (see also Newey, 2013). It would be nice if the two groups could reach an agreement based on toleration without appealing to the state's verdict, but such a method for conflict resolution cannot be stable and cannot be relied upon. It cannot replace a system of rights and duties nor can it serve as the basis of such a system. If we speak of toleration in the strict sense suggested earlier, we can say, contrary to Jones, that modern, right-based liberal regime does supersede the older liberal idea based on toleration. Jones cautions that if we do not ascribe toleration to the state with regards to non-liberal groups we will end up pushing toleration to the margins of democratic liberalism (Jones, 2012). I believe that this is exactly the place of toleration in the political theory of the liberal state: it does not lie at the core of the liberal state although it still plays an important role in the way *citizens* of the state relate to *each other*. This will be our concern in the next section.

## 6. The Relation of Toleration – Vertical or Horizontal?

It has become customary to refer to the toleration of the state (democratic, monarchical or otherwise) as vertical and to toleration of citizens or groups of citizens to other such groups as horizontal. On the vertical axis toleration is unidirectional since all power lies in the state and the powerless citizen does not have the opportunity to tolerate the state. On the horizontal level toleration may also be one-sided, typically in the relations between majorities and minorities or between the social and cultural mainstream and the marginal sectors in a society. But unlike the state, which by definition is the most powerful agent in society, the balance of power within social groups may always change and in that sense the call for toleration can apply to all groups. Furthermore, and again unlike the state toleration on the vertical level, one individual or group may have power over another on a certain matter and in certain circumstances while the other individual or group may have such leverage over the other under other circumstances. I can tolerate the noise from your midnight party because I have the power to call the police; but then, you can tolerate my children's playing hide and seek in your garden because you have the power to kick them out of your property. In that sense horizontal toleration is potentially mutual and this applies in a less trivial way to relations between social and religious groups in the way they manage their social co-existence.

Now if, as I have proposed, toleration cannot be exercised by the liberal state (though it could be shown by a monarch or a dictator), vertical toleration, at least on the political level, is incompatible with proper state functioning (Heyd, 2008). But that does not make toleration redundant in the general culture of liberal society which is based on an informal ethos of mutual respect, willingness to forgive, social solidarity, good will and personal relations. People are not merely law-abiding citizens respecting the rights of others and living by the principles of justice; they are also moral persons who can, and sometimes want, to show compassion, understanding and considerateness to their fellow citizens. Doing my duty and respecting the rights of others does not exhaust the good life in liberal society. Although such a society expects its government to implement just distributive principles and to protect citizens from the violation of their rights, individual citizens want to take certain social responsibilities which lie beyond those expected of the state. Tolerant practices are part of such behaviour in the public sphere which expresses personal concern that complements legally permitted behaviour. Good citizenship includes certain norms which are not and should not be enforced by the law.

Why should such virtue of toleration be also in the interest of the state? Take again the analogy of toleration and charity. The state should not operate on the grounds of charity since its function in the provision of goods is justice (and utility). But there are needs that cannot be provided by the state, such as unforeseen circumstances, cases of individual one-time crisis, or lacunae in the system of justice. In the case of toleration there are conflicts of ideological or religious nature which are hard to settle by general or neutral principles. The liberal state strives to be as minimal as possible, even if it is not minimal in Mill's or Nozick's terms and even if it takes some perfectionist responsibilities upon itself. The lesser the conflicts which call for arbitration or legislation, the better. Therefore, the state should inculcate toleration among its citizens through education as it encourages charitable giving by giving tax exemptions. Or take family courts: they have to make their verdicts in divorce cases according to the law. But that does not mean that often it is their prime concern or interest to let the couple sort the issue between themselves based on good will and a spirit of compromise. One of the most typical exercises of toleration by individual citizens is *not insisting on one's rights*. This supererogatory kind of inaction is not only in many cases good in itself (for both the tolerator and the tolerated party), but is also in the interest of the state which strives to the reduction of litigation and the need to enforce the law). There are of course limits to tolerant behaviour of its citizens towards each other, namely tolerating the intolerable. The state should not allow for example tolerant behaviour towards paedophiles. And this is similar to the limits on tax exemptions which are not granted to donations to violent sects or to pornographic libraries.

This means that even the most neutral or minimal state, which shuns any moral position, is perfectionist at least with regards to the promotion of the value of toleration (and maybe also of charity). Supererogatory behaviour strengthens social bonding and social solidarity to which even the most liberal state is not indifferent. Furthermore, even respect for rights, which is a constitutive core of liberal politics, can only be reinforced by the personal virtue of toleration, since, as we have mentioned earlier, the two are based on the distinction between judging the act (or belief) and judging the agent (or the subject). So although mutual toleration between groups and individuals in society cannot be relied upon as a principled universal method of conflict resolution, it is a highly instrumental means of promoting social cohesion and some relief from the need to appeal to state intervention as the arbiter of such conflicts.

It seems then that despite the fact that toleration and political (state) liberalism are conceptually independent, they are mutually reinforcing. It is possible to envision a liberal state based on justice and the universal application of the law with no toleration exercised by its citizens; and it is not only possible but also a historically confirmed fact that there can be undemocratic and illiberal political regimes in which toleration is shown by the ruler to the subjects or by people towards each other. But both options are unattractive to our vision of a well-managed political life. Liberalism must allow for and even encourage as a complement to the rule of law a culture of toleration in the same way that the morality of duty and rights is impoverished if no place is left for supererogatory action.

## Conclusion

This chapter argued that if we adopt a strict, narrow concept of toleration, it cannot serve as a constitutive element of political liberalism, i.e. the liberal state cannot and ought not be tolerant to its citizens and social groups. But then we are thrown back to the original methodological question: why adopt such a strict concept of toleration to begin with? Why not follow the history of the various uses of the concept from the early modern period (such as John Locke's)? Why not work with the ordinary meaning of the term in common liberal parlance (speaking for example about state toleration of religious minority practices)? My response was both theoretical and normative. Toleration should be taken as a theoretical term, that is to say serving a philosophical account of a political and moral relation. It is a thick concept which is far from being universal. Most societies till the modern age had no concept of toleration and applying it to regimes that did not have even a term for the concept risks anachronism. So in the philosophical discourse of toleration the concept must be well defined. Furthermore, it should be of value in *accounting* for the phenomenon to be explained and do so in line with other principles of the respective theory.

In the case of moral and political theory, the test of the way a concept is used is its contribution to the *normative* ends of the theory. And here I have tried to argue that there is moral and political value in distinguishing between the realm of rights and duties, justice and impartiality on the one hand and that of toleration and compromise, forgiveness and charity, on the other hand. The liberal regime is of paramount importance but it does not cover all aspects of social or even political life. Without the complementary sphere of interpersonal and inter-group relations the life of citizens under the rule of law and state neutrality is diminished. From the point of view of the liberal state such a complement is badly needed, although not as part of its own (state) order.

So we can conclude that from the point of view of the liberal state toleration is redundant. It adds nothing to the system of rights and duties and hence is a theoretically unhelpful concept as well as undermining the clarity of the right-based version of the liberal state. And from the point of view of the overall liberal moral point of view toleration is to be promoted and encouraged as a personal virtue. But conflating the two points of view may only muddy the attempt to understand what toleration is all about and undermine its normative justification.

## Notes

1. In articulating the strict, "negative", concept of toleration, I follow John Horton (2017) who does not believe that toleration as positive recognition can solve the conflicts which are inherent to modern pluralist societies. But I take issue with his claim that the state, which is not completely neutral, can be expected to *tolerate* citizens due to the need of reaching political compromises.
2. Although Rawls is not fully clear about this distinction since he also talks about the reasonableness of the belief system rather than just the subject forming the belief.
3. For an excellent articulation of this view and the separation of the public sphere and the private (in which toleration can be ascribed only to the latter), see Newey 2017. I fully agree with his claim that the state has no attitude and that unlike the state in pre-liberal times it is not a "second party" to social, moral and religious conflicts.
4. For a similar example see Laegard (2015), who argues that the fact that the state favours one religion without persecuting or restricting other religions may indicate that the state tolerates the other religions. For the same reasons, I do not think that this is the case in a liberal state based on the freedom of religion.
5. Sune Laegard (2015) also discusses this issue. He correctly points out that respect for rights – exactly like toleration – is an *attitude* and if we deny the state the ability to tolerate, we should equally deny that it can respect the rights of its citizens. But here again, it seems that the concept, like that of toleration, of respect can be understood either normatively or descriptively. Only citizens can respect other citizens as an attitude (involving recognition or appraisal); the state can only respect its citizens in the behavioural sense of applying impartially rules of non-interference. In any case, even under the descriptive, behavioural sense, toleration does not add anything not covered by the demand from the state to respect the rights of citizens.
6. For a very similar view, see Kok-Chor Tan (2019, p. 397), who also adopts an "institutional" concept of toleration. But my reservation about this proposal is that the fact that the system of the state respect for the rights of citizens is the product of the tolerant attitude of the citizens who wish to institutionalize it does not mean that the state itself can be tolerant. This is exactly the problem with Rawls's view that the impersonal system of justice is the product of the "philosophically tolerant" attitude of the individual contractors. Institutionalization means that the tolerant attitude of individuals is replaced by the

strict respect for rights by the state which makes toleration (on the state level) conceptually superfluous and morally wrong.
7. Admittedly, the liberal state might have reasons to avoid acting on its principles and laws, typically in cases in which full enforcement would endanger the public order. These reasons are pragmatic but although they are fully valid, I wish to argue – contrary to Kühler (2019) – that they do not make such non-interference a case of state toleration. On the contrary, these reasons may even demonstrate the lack of power of the state, i.e. the absence of one of the constitutive elements in the concept of toleration. And when the state is called to deal with a conflict between liberal values such as freedom of speech and the fight against racist demonstrations, the state is expected to make a principled solution of such a conflict, difficult as it may be, rather than show toleration. For the scope of each liberal principle should be set in a principled way. So both the pragmatic and the "political" reasons that the state may have for non-interference or non-enforcement do not seem to establish a concept of state toleration (as suggested by Kühler).
8. I think that this distinction between "tolerance" and "toleration" has some firm semantic evidence, confirmed by the Oxford English Dictionary. But beyond that it is theoretically superior to the way King (1998) draws the distinction. Jones (2013) says we can be tolerant to squeaking doors and barking dogs. But this is exactly where "tolerant" should be understood as having *tolerance* rather than toleration. We are simply able to endure these unpleasant sounds (rather than deciding not to interfere for a reason and with some good will with the door's hinges. Peter Balint (2017) explicitly prefers a descriptive concept of toleration over the normative because it better fits the practical use of the idea in politics. For Balint toleration, in this descriptive sense, is compatible with liberal neutrality since toleration does not consist of any commitment to substantive values. But that does go beyond the idea I have suggested of toleration "strictly speaking".
9. Consider the case of mass immigration: we can say that a liberal state can tolerate (in the descriptive sense of endure) up to a certain number of new immigrants. But once it lets them in, it ought to grant the rights rather than tolerate them in the normative sense which concerns us here.
10. Jones suggests that toleration is the product of a social contract in which people agree on mutual toleration in the sense of claim rights to liberty (Jones, unpublished). However, if that is the case, what does toleration add to the commitment to respect the rights of each citizen?

# References

Balint, P. (2017). *Respecting Toleration*. Oxford: Oxford University Press.
Ben-baji, H. and Heyd, D. (2001). The Charitable Perspective: Forgiveness and Toleration as Supererogatory. *Canadian Journal of Philosophy*, 31, pp. 567–586.
Drerup, J. and Kühler, M. (2019). The Politics and Ethics of Toleration: Introduction. Special issue on toleration of *Critical Review of International Social and Political Philosophy*, 22. [online] Available at: www.tandfonline.com/doi/full/10.1080/13698230.2019.1616876 [Accessed 30 Apr. 2020].
Heyd, D. (2008). Is Toleration a Political Virtue? In: M. Williams and J. Waldron, eds., *Toleration and Its Limit*, New York: NYU Press, Nomos series, 48, pp. 171–194.

Heyd, D. (2020, Forthcoming). What Toleration Is Not? In: M. Saroc, ed., *The Palgrave Handbook of Toleration*, 1st ed. London: Palgrave Macmillan.

Horton, J. (2017). Why the Traditional Concept of Toleration Still Matters? In: D. Endyvane and M. Matravers, eds., *Toleration Re-Examined*, 1st ed. London: Routledge.

Jones, P. (2007). Making Sense of Political Toleration. *British Journal of Political Science*, 37, pp. 383–402.

Jones, P. (2012). Legalising Toleration: A Reply to Balint. *Res Publica*, 18, pp. 265–278.

Jones, P. (2013). Toleration. In: G. Gaus and F. D'Agostino, eds., *The Routledge Companion to Political Philosophy*. New York: Routledge.

Jones, P. (2020, Forthcoming). Power, Liberty, and Rights: Preston King on Toleration. In: K. E. Jensen, ed., *Preston King: History, Toleration, and Friendship*, 1st ed. New York: Peter Lang.

Jones, P. Toleration, Supererogation, and Rights. Unpublished ms.

King, P. (1998). *Toleration*. London: Frank Cass.

Kühler, M. (2019). Can Value-Neutral Liberal State Still Be Tolerant? *Critical Review of International Social and Political Philosophy*, 22. [online] Available at: www.tandfonline.com/doi/abs/10.1080/13698230.2019.1616878 [Accessed 30 Apr. 2020].

Laegard, S. (2015). Attitudinal Analyses of Toleration and Respect and the Problem of Institutional Applicability. *European Journal of Philosophy*, 23, pp. 1064–1081.

Newey, G. (2013). *Toleration in Political Conflict*. Cambridge: Cambridge University Press.

Newey, G. (2017). Toleration as Sedition. In: D. Endyvane and M. Matravers, eds., *Toleration Re-Examined*, 1st ed. London: Routledge.

Rawls, J. (1993). *Political Liberalism*. New York: Columbia University Press.

# 5 Regimes of Toleration
## Liberal and Republican
*Cillian McBride*

## Introduction

Is it possible to formulate a republican challenge to liberal toleration? Toleration will strike many as an essentially liberal concern not readily shared by other political traditions. In contrast to the liberal emphasis on individual freedom of conscience, republicans are usually associated with the communitarian ideal of civic unity, exemplified by Rousseau's revival of the idea of a civic religion to bolster devotion to the common good and to the norms and institutions of the republic (Zurbuchen, 2002, p. 47). To be fair to Rousseau, his civic religion is supposed to confine itself to a few essentials relating to the requirements of good citizenship, after which "everyone may hold whatever opinion he pleases" (Rousseau, 1997, p. 150). What will not be tolerated is sectarian intolerance for that is destructive of the unity of the state: anyone proclaiming that there is no salvation outside the Church must be driven out! The contemporary French doctrine of *laïcité*, in no small part inspired by Rousseau, while still too communitarian for liberal tastes is similarly complex, combining ostensible state neutrality with respect to religion, and a perfectionist commitment to individual and political autonomy with an emphasis on civic unity (Laborde, 2018).

The communitarian strands of this sort of republicanism is readily contrasted with liberal toleration, for even where it is tolerant, it draws the limits of toleration at the point at which civic unity is apparently threatened, rather than at the point at which individual liberty is at risk of being undermined. The republicanism adopted here is instead the neo-Roman republicanism which centres on the notion of freedom as non-domination (Pettit, 1997). Rousseau helped to create a modern republicanism which was not simply communitarian, but also populist in the way it married the notion of sovereign power with democratic self-government, but neo-Roman republicanism is resolutely constitutionalist in orientation and defends the primacy of individual freedom from domination rather than Rousseauan positive freedom (Pettit, 1997, p. 8). To be free, on this view, is to be freedom from the possibility of arbitrary, or better, *uncontrolled*, interference in one's life (Pettit, 2012, p. 58). While Pettit insists that there remains clear blue water between this republicanism and contemporary liberalism (1997, p. 9), it is certainly arguable that the resulting view, which prizes individual freedom and the rule of law, if not negative liberty, is actually much closer to egalitarian liberalism than might at first appear (Rawls, 1996, p. 205).

This certainly complicates matters, for, unlike a communitarian, perfectionist, populist republicanism, it will be more difficult to formulate a challenge to liberal toleration on this basis. That this should be so is not really surprising, for in contrast to the popular self-image of the liberal tradition as sole defence of liberty against monarchical despotism in the modern era, the history of modern political thought is now understood to be a more complex affair in which republican ideas played a central role, from the Harringtonians, through Montesquieu to Rousseau and beyond. It is only in the aftermath of the French Revolution that republicanism is seriously challenged by a self-consciously liberal mode of thought which distinguished sharply between the collective liberties of the ancients and the individual liberties of the moderns (Constant, 1988). Subsequently, the republican tradition loses its definition, although it contributes to socialist ideas about wage slavery (Gourevitch, 2013), nationalist ideas about national political culture, and of course, 'liberal' ideas about the importance of constitutions and the rule of law as bulwarks to freedom (Montesquieu, 1989). While a sharp contrast can be drawn between republican and libertarian ideas about freedom and politics, it should be no surprise, that the lines between egalitarian liberalism and republicanism should be more blurred. That toleration must, however, continue to play an important role in guiding social relations in a world marked by deep and persistent ethical religious, and political differences, will not be disputed here. Toleration will not be rejected but *reframed* in republican terms. This primarily entails a challenge to how we think about different "regimes" of toleration, that is, how we think about the way relations between tolerator and tolerated, are situated in a context of social norms and institutions affecting their relative power and authority, rather than the moral grounding for toleration in some conception of equal respect, on which liberals and republicans may find common ground.

## 1. What Is Liberal Toleration?

There appears to be a special connection between the idea of toleration and that of liberalism. The historical emergence of liberalism is typically traced back to developments in the seventeenth century such as natural rights and social contract theory and the idea of state sovereignty and the regimes of toleration established following the conclusion of the wars of religion with the Treaty of Westphalia (Rawls, 1996, p. 26). For liberals and their critics alike, it seems that it is not too much to say that the history of toleration is the history of liberalism (Cohen, 2014, p. 1; Galeotti, 2002, p. 23).

In order to regain a critical perspective on the relation between liberalism and toleration it is necessary to revisit the history of the idea and to challenge the common assumption that toleration is the invention of liberalism. Forst notes that the term *tolerantia* makes its first appearance in Cicero, figuring in an account of stoic dignity as a capacity for endurance (2013, p. 37). While this is essentially a matter of one's relation to oneself, it takes the more familiar form of a cluster of norms and attitudes governing social relationships, particularly those between believers, heretics and members of rival religions in the Christian era. Toleration figures here not only as a political practice, but also as a sophisticated set of, primarily theological, reflections on that practice. Augustine, for example, argues for freedom of conscience as essential for authentic faith but later comes to argue that this is nonetheless consistent with a measure of coercion where this can help to render someone open to the gift of God's grace (Rohr, 1967; Forst, 2013, pp. 54–55). Locke's argument regarding the effectiveness of persecution is best situated within this long-standing debate, rather than seen as a radical departure from it (Forst, 2013, p. 224). The theological account of the value of freedom of conscience later gives way to modern, secular notions of autonomy, but along the way there is a long history of attempts to explore the theological bases for toleration, including those which focus on the distinction between essentials and *adiaphora*, or inessentials, echoed in Rousseau's notion of a minimalist civic religion. This strategy of seeking to uncover a basic unity which permits toleration of inessential differences remains popular into the Enlightenment era (Forst, 2013, p. 267). Even the briefest reflection on the history of toleration reveals that liberalism and toleration are not born twins, but rather that liberalism, is both shaped by and in turn appropriates key elements of these earlier debates about toleration and its permissibility.[1]

What distinguishes a modern, liberal, approach to toleration, from earlier approaches? The liberal conception appears to have two closely related features. Firstly, it appeals to secular grounds for toleration, i.e. for justifying restraint despite one's objection to the object of toleration. This is supplied by some account of the value of individual freedom, often autonomy (Raz, 1988; Forst, 2013, p. 9). The story of modern toleration is the story of the emerging autonomy of morality (Forst, 2013, p. 336). Secondly, and perhaps more controversially, liberal conceptions of toleration entail a shift from a vertical conception to a horizontal conception of toleration, that is, from toleration as practised by the sovereign towards his subjects (Heyd, 2008, p. 173) to toleration as a virtue or an attitude adopted by citizens with respect to one another. Forst characterizes this in terms of a shift from a "permission" conception to a "respect" conception of toleration (Forst, 2013, p. 6).

On the permission conception of toleration a minority enjoys a measure of freedom from persecution, albeit without enjoying the same rights and status of the majority. They enjoy this freedom with the permission of the ruler, that is, not as a right. This permission may be withdrawn at any time, however, so whatever toleration one enjoys is not secure. It does not necessarily rely on any principled self-restraint on the part of the ruler concerned but is rather a product of a modus vivendi. There is nothing distinctively liberal about this style of toleration – pre-modern Christian debates about toleration assumed that if toleration was permissible, then it would have this form. The Ottoman millet system similarly took the form of toleration as permission (Gray, 2000). The tendency to trace the roots of liberalism back into the seventeenth century tends to obscure this point, encouraging the idea that the sort of religious toleration established by the Peace of Westphalia marked a radical break with earlier ideas about toleration and overlooking the underlying continuity with them. This is bound up, no doubt with the larger liberal narrative of itself as the sole standard bearer for freedom in the modern era rather than as just one particular strand of thought about it.

The permission conception continues to attract support from perfectionists, value pluralists and "realists" some of whom identity as liberals (Gray, 2000; Williams, 2005; Smith, 2008) but it is clearly deeply problematic, even from a liberal perspective. Once citizens are to be regarded as having equal rights and dignity, the idea that some have the authority to grant permission to others to exercise their fundamental freedoms can only be regarded as a denial of that equal standing and as such, an insult. This is why Goethe believed that (permission) toleration could at best serve only as a way station on the road to recognition (Forst, 2007). Paine famously rejects this model of toleration, praising the French revolutionary government for affirming a general right to freedom of conscience and thereby rejecting both "toleration" and "intoleration" (Paine, 2000, p. 94). The significance of this move is that the state becomes a guarantor of equal rights, rather than an agent of toleration as such, because it now foregoes the role of enforcing religious orthodoxy on behalf of a church. Toleration survives now as a virtue practised by citizens with respect to one another, with the state merely overseeing these relations, ready to step in should the intolerance of some threaten to invade the rights of other citizens. The state itself refrains from making the sort of ethical judgments that might prompt it to act as a direct agent of toleration itself.

On the republican view adopted we can go further than this. If domination consists in being exposed to the possibility of arbitrary or uncontrolled interference in one's life, then permission toleration is a textbook case of domination (Honohan, 2013). The fact that one is presently free from persecution by the authorities is no doubt preferable to being actively persecuted, but one's freedom is not secure. One must not only live with the possibility that persecution may return, possibly without warning, but one's everyday social relations will be shaped by the need to keep one's head down in order to avoid drawing attention to oneself. This does not only threaten to damage one's self-esteem and self-respect, i.e. one's sense of self-worth and sense of entitlement to recognition as an equal, in doing so it compounds one's unequal status by fostering adaptive preferences that discourage one from taking up opportunities that might risk provoking the dominant party. Republicans must clearly reject permission toleration.

Republicans will share the liberal commitment to equal respect but they have reason to be wary of the appeal to respect for autonomy as a basis for the practice of toleration, at least on some interpretations of what this entails. This is not because autonomy has simply been replaced by freedom as non-domination in republican thought, although this is the view of some prominent republicans (Pettit, 1997, p. 82). In fact, as conceived here autonomy, recognition, and non-domination are inseparable. It is because respect for autonomy in the context of interpersonal relations will strike the republican as insufficient. While a principled commitment to toleration grounded in respect for autonomy is superior to permission toleration insofar as it will be more robust across a range of contexts, it still appears to afford considerable latitude to the tolerating agent to determine when and how to tolerate. To be secure from domination one must not be secured against the possibility of uncontrolled interference, and the while the respectful tolerator has more powerful reasons to refrain from interference, in the absence of these controls the possibility of domination remains. A republican account of toleration directs our attention then towards the problem of unequal power in social relations and the degree to which liberal toleration is sensitive to the way that the power to tolerate may be very unequally distributed. This, it will be suggested, is as true of liberal multiculturalism as it is of more traditional liberalism.

## 2. Regimes of Toleration

The republican emphasis on freedom from domination not only helps to clarify what is wrong with the permission conception of toleration, but it also complicates the neat picture of a historical switch from the vertical, state-centred, permission conception, to the horizontal respect conception in which toleration is practised by citizens towards one another. To focus on whether this picture is accurate is to focus not on moral foundations, but on the configuration of different "regimes" of toleration, that is, norms, practices, and institutions and the power relations that both shape them and are shaped by them (Walzer, 1997; Brown, 2009). While republicans have good reason to endorse the moral argument for toleration grounded in mutual respect, they also have good reason to dissent from the "liberal" conception of a regime of toleration in which the state has simply dropped into the background because it is no longer involved directly in the business of toleration to be replaced by a "flat", non-hierarchical regime of toleration in which, ideally, citizens practise toleration with respect to one another. This picture is at best an idealization of a much messier reality. It assumes a distinctively individualist model of social relations which represents the parties as similarly situated and endowed with roughly equal power to interfere with one another, as in the model of seventeenth-century social contract theories. As such, it relies on the questionable notion of a clean break between modern and pre-modern worlds, with hierarchy and equality, freedom and oppression. The reality of the contemporary regime of toleration is rather different and the republican tradition, with its insistence that we are not as distant from a world of masters and servants as we like to think, is well placed to cast a critical eye over it.

Liberalism's tendency to fall back on a simplistic, atomistic, social ontology has long been a target of critics (Hegel, 1991, p. 276; Honneth, 2014). To be sure, while libertarians continue to rely on this model, egalitarian liberals have distanced themselves from it, first by pointing to the way the basic structure of society situated us differently with respect to one another, and more recently, by adopting a new appreciation of the role of social groups in the social order. That said, liberal multiculturalism's discovery of the importance of groups has not prompted much reflection on the nature of social formations more generally, as evidenced by the way all social collectivities were readily assimilated to the idea of "cultural" groups, contributing to an unhelpful "culturalization" of politics (Honneth, 2003, p. 161). What is still missing from this picture is an appreciation of the role of powerful agents and institutions other than the state, and in particular of the way that powerful corporate actors, primarily in the form of private business corporations dominate the social and political world as much as they do the economy.

Just as liberalism's hegemonic narrative of itself as *the* political theory of modernity has been challenged by scholars of seventeenth- and eighteenth-century political thought who have recovered the persistence of republicanism in this era (Pocock, 1985; Robbins, 2004) the current neo-republican revival has in recent years begun to trace the survival of republican ideas well beyond the French Revolution into the nineteenth century and the arguments of early socialists against wage-slavery. Just as liberals appropriated republican constitutionalism, socialists were inspired by republicanism's expansive conception of social freedom to transform it into a radical critique of market relations and of corporate power (Gourevitch, 2013; O'Shea, 2019). This is instructive for the case at hand.

We cannot make sense of the contemporary regime of toleration without an appreciation of the place of private corporations within it. As Anderson has argued, they function in many ways as a form of "private government" wielding considerable power over their employees (2019). To be sure, they do not wield the legal authority held by actual governments, employees do have a right of exit, and they are constrained by laws regulating their freedom of action (Breen, 2015) but it remains the case that they retain extensive powers over their employees and beyond, to the extent that they have the power to dominate, even if this power is not unlimited. As Pettit notes, domination may be more or less intense (1997), and while corporations may vary in the intensity of the power they wield, they retain sufficient discretion to pose a problem from a republican point of view.

Socialist republicans have concentrated on the power of employers to control the organization of work within firms, but it can also be argued that the discretionary power wielded by corporations is also relevant to the question of toleration as it extends beyond the organization of work and into the sphere of regulating employees in their ethical, political and religious commitments. Take, for example, the case of the American woman who was fired by her boss for giving President Trump the finger as his motorcade drove past her (BBC, 2017). She was not at work and not wearing any uniform or insignia identifying her as an employee and yet she could be sacked because her boss was intolerant of her expression of her political beliefs. Where employers have the option of penalizing their employees' political beliefs in this way, we would be justified in concluding that permission toleration survives even if it is not obviously practised directly by constitutional democracies themselves. The Trump case is an extreme one, on account of the way the employer was free to extend his reach out into the public sphere, but there are many examples in recent years of employees even in countries with our robust employment rights than the US coming into conflict with employers over the issue of religious practice and the expression of their religious commitments in the workplace. What often remains in the background in debates about the rights of persons of faith to express their faith commitments 'in public' is the assumption that employers retain extensive discretion to regulate their employees within the workplace. Perhaps relatively few employers would choose to exercise their power like the boss in the Trump case, but while many may be relatively tolerant and forbear to interfere, if they have the discretion to intervene in this way then the relation is one of domination.

This power may extend beyond questions of political and religious difference to less well-defined ethical projects. Consider the way that contemporary workplaces have increasingly blurred the strict division between the private life of the employee and their "public" life as an employee in favour of more "flexible" network relations in which short-term projects play an ever larger role. Sociologists have argued that this entails a blurring of the public and private aspects of the employees' life as the growing importance of social networking brings our personal qualities and relations to the fore in the work environment (Boltanski and Chiapello, 2007, pp. 461–463). This sets the scene for the disciplinary power of the modern form to seek to mould their workers into "entreployees" (Rose, 1992). To view this simply through the lens of the sociology of work, or an exclusively Foucauldian focus on the ways in which selfhood is produced, would be to miss two important phenomena. Firstly, that of the discretion still afforded employers to discipline employees. Secondly, the way that contemporary ethical projects are not confined to religious doctrine or "cultural" identity, however defined, but extend to questions of the moulding of dispositions and the cultivation of virtues by organizations who increasingly reach into our "private" lives to advance their goals.

At this level, of course, there is a question about wider cultural imperatives and social power, reaching beyond individual corporate agents to encompass their relations to other corporate actors, competitors, lobby groups, management consultants, states, etc. It might be thought that once we leave identifiable agents of toleration/domination behind we are no longer directly concerned with questions of toleration and in a sense this is true. There is obviously a difference between the relatively intense personal domination as exercised by the boss in the Trump case, and the structural factors, the legal, political, economic, and cultural factors, both normative and institutional which structure the relations between agents, individual and corporate, and which enable more or less intense forms of personal domination (Gourevitch, 2013, p. 604). If we are concerned with developing a republican analysis of the wider regime of contemporary toleration, these background conditions must be regarded as of central importance, while they will drop out of the picture if our deliberations are framed solely by the ideal of dyadic mutual toleration.

This outline of the contemporary regime of toleration and the place of corporations as agents of toleration would not be complete without noting a further complication. As Mill noted, the state does not simply drop out of the picture once it apparently relinquishes its role as a direct tolerator (1989, p. 8). Ideally, it confines itself to upholding citizens' rights and refrains from making the sort of additional evaluative judgements required for toleration.[2] It does not directly tolerate itself but regulates the practice of toleration by its citizens. Of course, in doing so, it becomes the focus of attempts by groups of citizens to recruit its power to regulate others, for better or ill. Democratic states are themselves always open to the possibility of capture by the organized intolerant. To the extent that corporations have the legal and social power to regulate their employees' lives, they too can become a direct focus of social and political pressure by lobby groups (Young, 2011, p. 149). Historically this has typically served equality to the extent that unions etc. have lobbied against various discriminatory practices, etc. but it is not obvious that this must always be the case and we may see more controversial attempts to direct corporate power in the future by activists, for instance, the efforts of the US right to police the academy. In addition to this dispersed focus of activism, there is the issue of corporations, and social media corporations in particular, taking on a quasi-governmental role in the regulation of toleration in social media, by now central to the contemporary public sphere. To the extent that states do not closely regulate the actions of social media corporations, they are afforded the discretion to become second order tolerators, enjoying considerable discretion to determine what is and is not tolerable on their platforms, that is, in what has become our shared public space. Their libertarian rhetoric cannot disguise the fact that they dominate public space in ways inconsistent with freedom from domination. In all of these ways, the disciplinary power of contemporary corporate agents to mould and tolerate or not, the lives of their employees, and to act as arbiters of toleration for the public sphere, is sufficiently significant to challenge the idea that we have left permission toleration, just because states, arguably, do not practise it.

## 3. Recognition: Authority and Conditionality

Liberals and republicans can agree that the permission conception assumes that the tolerators and tolerated are not recognized as equals. Their unequal legal status reflects a more fundamental moral inequality: the tolerated do not "count" as equals in the eyes of the tolerating party. One significant challenge to the liberal interpretation of the contemporary regime of toleration focuses on the role of social recognition in reflecting and sustaining this status difference. Evidently, informal social norms and attitudes must form a central part of any regime of toleration. Liberal multiculturalism has argued that problematic forms of social recognition have persisted even if formal legal norms are ostensibly committed to equality (Galeotti, 2002). Some even argue that egalitarian ideas about equality, respect and dignity, can themselves reflect a fundamental intolerance of cultural difference (Taylor, 1994). In view of this last, the liberal multiculturalist proponents of "recognition" have argued not for equal respect, but rather for a form of "inclusion" rooted in the "positive acceptance" of minority cultural practices and identities.

This is typically understood to pose a challenge to the notion of toleration per se, to the extent that toleration must always contain an "objection component", that is, a reasoned, or unreasoned objection to another, which is then denied practical force, without being eliminated, by some ground for acceptance (King, 1976). "Recognition" holds out the prospect of replacing objection and the attitude of forbearance that follows from it with positive "acceptance". Understood in this way, "recognition" features as an alternative to toleration rather than a form of it, as is sometimes suggested (Galeotti, 2002; Walzer, 1997). In popular parlance, toleration of differences is to be replaced with the "celebration" of these differences.

This is typically understood to involve a revaluation of minority cultural practices and identities. Given the way our relations to ourselves are bound up with social attitudes to culture and identity, positive evaluation of these becomes a form of positive social recognition for the members of the culture in question (Taylor, 1994, pp. 25–26). To view minority cultures in a negative light is to withhold recognition from their members. One obvious problem with such a move is most cultures and social identities are deeply shaped by problematic social norms and attitudes, sexist, racist, sectarian etc. Indeed, given the way social identities are usually interrelated, there may be no way to extend social esteem to one without necessarily withholding it from another, something often overlooked in these debates, which typically assume "cultures" to be so tightly bounded that they can be judged in isolation from one another. This poses an insurmountable challenge to the hope of simply replacing toleration. Taylor suggests that, at most, there may be some presumption that other cultures may turn out to have real value, in effect, a plea for greater openness in our attitudes to minority cultures (1994, pp. 66–67). Galeotti rejects the idea of blanket endorsement of cultures on the grounds that it would violate liberal neutrality (2002, p. 104). As she rejects the idea of the state engaging in direct ethical evaluations of cultural practices but is also critical of the idea that equal rights are sufficient to ensure "inclusion" it is not clear what sort of "positive acceptance" she has in mind. It cannot be equal respect for the simple reason that she thinks that not every group is entitled to it, but only those who have suffered historical injustices (Galeotti, 2002, p. 112).

In the end, the "recognition" challenge to toleration turns out to be much more limited than talk of the celebration of differences suggested. Not all differences can be judged worthy of "recognition" and unless these are simply to be eliminated, there would seem to be room for retaining toleration as an appropriate response to some of these differences. While we might have good reason to re-evaluate our attitudes to cultural differences in general, and to resist assuming that assimilation and homogenization are to be preferred to diversity, we must still judge differences on a case-by-case basis and revision to our evaluations cannot always be positive.

Republican toleration, it has been suggested, entails a form of social recognition (Honohan, 2013). If the regime of toleration is composed of both formal institutions and informal norms and attitudes, then a concern to ensure that toleration is not dominating must include an account of social recognition. It must, however, take a different form to that of liberal multiculturalism (Laborde, 2008, pp. 21–23). The first point to note is that recognition of the worth of particular identities and practices, one application of recognition as social esteem (Honneth, 2003) may be positive and even "inclusive" without being equal. The standard assumption is that minority cultures are simply undervalued and even stigmatized so that the remedy must involve rectifying this recognition deficit (McBride, 2013). This is indeed, often the case, but it doesn't follow that social esteem is itself unproblematic. Marginalized people are not simply excluded, but included in unequal ways, and even where their cultures and identities are seen as worthy of esteem, they can be esteemed in ways that do not alter their subordinate place in the social hierarchy. The condescension involved in orientalism, for example relies on prizing the exotic, while at the same time holding the "oriental" at arms' length (Fanon, 2008, p. 98). Just as the educated Greek slave can be esteemed by his Roman owner while remaining a slave, positive acceptance in the form of esteem recognition does not necessarily deliver inclusion as an equal (Pettit, 1997, pp. 22–23).

Franz Fanon in his account of the recognition struggle between the white master and black slave identifies the underlying problem – the failure to address the unequal power relations between the parties concerned and the way that the desire for the recognition of the other can in fact cement relations of domination by failing to place in question the authority of the master to extend or withhold recognition (Fanon, 2008, p. 3) On this view, the problem is not whether one lacks the master's esteem, but rather that one continues desire it, even when one opts to affirm one's "difference". While liberal multiculturalism is motivated to address inequalities rooted in the recognition order of contemporary societies, the limited nature of their analysis of social recognition prevents them from seeing that a call for dominant groups to revalue different others is an inadequate response to this problem. Esteem recognition is not an alternative to the insult offered by permission toleration, but essentially just another version of it to the extent that the power of dominant groups to recognize or not is not placed in question.

Treating recognition as a good which can simply be redistributed, thereby remedying the recognition deficit experienced by the marginalized is the wrong way to think about recognition (Honneth, 2003). As Fanon's more Hegelian account of recognition as a complex struggle reveals, it is not possible to think about social recognition without understanding it in terms of authority relations, the authority to recognize or not, and to be recognized in turn as an authoritative interpreter of the relevant social norm. To claim social recognition is already to recognize another as having the authority to grant this recognition. In the case of social esteem, claims to the recognition of the worth of one's practices, identity, contribution or achievements requires one to recognize the other as an authoritative judge of these things, but it does not entail that the dominant party must recognize the claimant as having equal authority to make these judgments and to interpret the criteria used to make them. This sort of recognition exchange, then, has the same conditional structure as permission toleration. It may be good to enjoy the positive social esteem of the dominant but it is not secure and it does not mean that one now counts as an equal: the underlying difference in social authority remains.

Closely related to this basic inequality in social, i.e. normative authority is the fact that esteem recognition is fundamentally *conditional*. It lies in the gift of the master to dispense it or not as he sees fit and it must be earned by those who seek it (Fanon, 2008, p. 171). They must show that they have exhibited the traits valued by the dominant party, made the sorts of contributions that he values, and will continue to do so if they are to retain the esteem of the dominant. In interpersonal relations this aspect of esteem is a valuable source of social regulation (Brennan and Pettit, 2006) but when applied outside the realm to whole classes or groups of people, it is more problematic, cementing, rather than challenging their subordinate status. Consider, Booker T. Washington's attempts to present freed slaves, as worthy of white America's esteem in virtue of the industry and good characters and his conviction that their merits will, in due course, be recognized (1995, p. 20). We see the same pattern at work with respect to immigrants, who must earn their place in society through their contribution, a contribution which can readily be overlooked or dismissed. The conditionality of esteem recognition and the unquestioned authority of socially dominant groups to dispense it, means that it has essentially the same structure as permission toleration and is just as insecure. The liberal multiculturalism regime of toleration must strike republicans as inadequate for the very same reasons then.

## 4. Respect Recognition and Republican Toleration

If esteem recognition for cultural minorities is deeply flawed, this does not mean that social recognition does not have an important role to play in republican toleration. The form of recognition involved, however, is that of equal respect, rather than that of unequal esteem. The fundamental distinction between these two modes of recognition is often overlooked in debates about the "politics of recognition" and while Taylor acknowledges that recognition of human dignity is an important mode of social recognition he appears to offer a caricature of it as requiring social homogeneity (Honneth, 2003, pp. 122–123). While the function of esteem recognition is always to distinguish its object from others, whether positively or negatively (McBride, 2013), respect recognition is something every person is entitled to simply in virtue of being a person (Darwall, 1977, p. 38) and is, in principle, enjoyed by all, to the same degree. It serves to assert one's unconditional entitlement to be regarded as an equal in the face of distinctions of esteem, deserved or otherwise. While positive esteem must be earned, equal respect is an entitlement which may be *demanded* of others, and these demands cannot reasonably be rejected. As such it forms the basis of equal citizenship, liberal and republican and provides the only secure basis for toleration, that is, acceptance in the face of objection, grounded in recognition of the other's equal status, rather than one's esteem for them.

Equality is often relegated simply to the legal sphere by those who argue for cultural recognition (Galeotti, 2002, p. 96). This overlooks the way that a public system of rights is itself an embodiment of recognition respect (Honneth, 1995, pp. 118–121). That said, there is still a sense in which the recognition afforded by the legal order may be insufficient, e.g. if the law is in effect a dead letter through biased or ineffective enforcement and especially if the equal status supposedly guaranteed by it is not reliably recognized by one's fellow citizens. What is needed here is not conditional esteem, however, which would only grant good treatment to the currently favoured, but rather recognition of one's entitlement to be regarded and treated as an equal. Respect recognition must have primacy over esteem if one's status and freedoms are to be secured against the whims of others. Respect can be demanded as of right from another, regardless of their private attitudes towards me. While authority relations in the case of esteem are always unequal, in the case of respect, each member of the community of equals enjoys the same normative authority to control the attitudes of others, and to be controlled in turn (Feinberg, 1980).

Some argue that it doesn't matter why people tolerate each other as long as they do in fact tolerate one another (Williams, 2005). This argument is motivated by the perceived difficulty of finding a public basis for acceptance. It is surprising, however, to see this view presented as a "realistic" view. From the republican perspective, respect recognition is not something merely symbolic, but rather is fundamentally practical insofar as it is central to structuring our relations to others and determining the sorts of consideration and treatment for which we are eligible. As such, its absence is of great practical consequence. In this case, bare toleration would be deeply unsatisfactory because it would afford its objects the security to live their lives openly as equals if they were unable to count on most of their fellow citizens practising the appropriate self-restraint with respect to them, restraint grounded in equal respect. To be thrown back on relying solely on the legal order, with a policeman on every corner, would clearly be inadequate as a protection against domination, to say nothing of the way that order would in turn be shaped over time by citizens unmoved by considerations of equal respect.

One might imagine an alternative objection. This would point to the way that even on the respect conception of toleration, individual citizens in practice exercise discretion over whether or not to respect, and/ or over how to interpret the demands of respect in particular cases. Any account of toleration must include not only objection and acceptance components, after all, but also some account of the limits of toleration

(Forst, 2013, p. 24) and citizens would enjoy considerable discretion on each of these issues. If republican freedom is essentially a matter of freedom from the possibility of arbitrary or uncontrolled interference, then the practice of toleration, even respect toleration, appears to permit the exercise of precisely this sort of dominating discretion. Would it not be better to focus on eliminating such lacunae from the republican social and political order, that is, for the state to devote itself to combatting domination rather as Paine seems to suggest? In contrast to the liberal regime of toleration, however, this republican order would aim to eliminate the sort of discretionary judgment involved in toleration.

This is not a plausible, or attractive, picture. It would entail an order in which freedom of thought and action would be severely constrained. Eliminating the sorts of judgment involved in toleration, a combination of (negative) esteem and respect, would rob us of the regulatory power of esteem judgment in not only in personal relations, but also constrain our evaluative judgments in the sphere of personal and political deliberations. As noted earlier, in democratic states the practice of toleration has both interpersonal and political aspects. In interpersonal relations one must consider whether some sort of response is called for, and if so, what sort of response, that is, should one bite one's tongue, express disapproval or seek to intervene? In the political sphere one must consider whether or not the practice in question breaches the limits of toleration such that one must initiate and/or support campaigns for legal regulation? It would be impossible to imagine a democratic republic which did not only allow but also protect the freedom of citizens to make these sorts of judgments for, if nothing else, they would be unable to exercise the sort of democratic control over their government that would ensure that its power was not dominating, because inadequately controlled.

Republicans must insist on the fundamental freedom to make these sorts of judgments and must, therefore defend the idea that citizens should practise respect toleration with respect to one another. They must also, however, be vigilant against the possibility that this discretionary authority might become dominating. A republican regime of toleration will attend closely not only to the way the power to tolerate, directly and indirectly, is distributed across different sorts of agents, corporate and otherwise, but also to the way social norms themselves afford greater social authority to some to make these judgments. Republican vigilance cannot simply be a matter of relying on formal institutional mechanisms to ensure that no one enjoys uncontrolled discretion to tolerate or not, although this is of great importance: no one should enjoy absolute, i.e. unconstrained, authority to make these sorts of judgements. As the social authority to make and express these sorts of judgments is typically unevenly distributed and more subtly so than the notion of multicultural recognition allows, if republican citizens are to ensure that the practice of toleration in their daily lives is not dominating, they must, in consequence be highly reflective about the relevant social norms and attitudes shaping these judgements. This sort of critical reflection, of course, must involve self-reflection as much as scrutiny of others.

This account of republican toleration suggests that there are differences in the way that (even egalitarian) liberals and republicans think about the regime of toleration, even if they do not differ significantly on the question of the moral foundations of toleration. Some republicans will, of course, dispute this, suggesting that the ideal of non-domination can replace notions of respect and autonomy as a foundation. Pettit, is well known for the claim that autonomy, for example, is not a political value (1997) and while equal recognition is connected to non-domination it is not wholly clear what role it plays here, whether as a means or simply a heuristic in the form of the "eyeball test" (Pettit, 2014, p. 26). The account presented here suggests an alternative view in which the interest in equal recognition grounds the interest in freedom from domination. Autonomy, however, also plays a central role here, both in relation to respect recognition and the realization of non-domination. In the case of recognition it is intimately connected to the idea of respecting another as an equal where this is taken to require a norm of mutual justification as an implication of respecting other's capacity for autonomy. It also figures as essential to realizing non-domination in practice, for the sorts of control required over formal political institutions and over informal social norms and attitudes requires citizens to adopt the sorts of critical reflection essential to autonomy.

All of this would require further argument, however. It is sufficient to note here that even if republicans share similar moral foundations to egalitarian liberals, as one might expect given their complex history, there are reasons to think that there is, nonetheless, a distinctively republican view of toleration and its place in our lives.

## Notes

1. Forst rejects the claim that traditional toleration is too focused on doctrine and private belief (Galeotti, 2002, p. 86) as religious toleration was historically concerned with communal practices and doctrines that are inseparable from the personal and collective identities of the faithful (Forst, 2013, p. 172).
2. "Ideally" for even if the state relinquishes its role in monitoring its citizens' religious or ethical projects, it may still tolerate in a more limited way even on this view. Even when it confines itself to vigilance with respect to rights violations it may find itself "tolerating" extremist groups in the sense that it may refrain from banning and or charging members simply in order to better monitor their activities, however controversial this policy may be from a rule of law perspective.

# References

Anderson, E. (2019). *Private Government*. Princeton, NJ: Princeton University Press.
BBC.com, (2017). *Woman Fired for Showing Trump Motorcade the Middle Finger*. [online] Available at: www.bbc.co.uk/news/world-us-canada-41892544 [Accessed 4 Apr. 2020].
Boltanski, L. and Chiapello, E. (2007). *The New Spirit of Capitalism*. London: Verso.
Breen, K. (2015). Freedom, Republicanism, and Workplace Democracy. *Critical Review of International Social and Political Philosophy*, 18, pp. 470–485.
Brennan, G. and Pettit, P. (2006). *The Economy of Esteem*. Oxford: Oxford University Press.
Brown, W. (2009). *Regulating Aversion: Tolerance in the Age of Identity and Empire*. Princeton, NJ: Princeton University Press.
Cohen, A. (2014). *Toleration*. Cambridge: Polity Press.
Constant, B. (1988). The Liberty of the Ancients Compared with That of the Moderns (1819). In: B. Fontana, ed., *Benjamin Constant: Political Writings*. Cambridge: Cambridge University Press, pp. 307–328.
Darwall, S. L. (1977). Two Kinds of Respect. *Ethics*, 88, pp. 36–49.
Fanon, F. (2008). *Black Skin White Masks*. London: Pluto Press.
Feinberg, J. (1980). The Nature and Value of Rights. In: J. Feinberg, ed., *Rights, Justice and the Bounds of Liberty*. Princeton, NJ: Princeton University Press, pp. 143–158.
Forst, R. (2007). 'To Tolerate Means to Insult' Toleration, Recognition, and Emancipation. In: D. Owen and B. van den Brink, eds., *Recognition and Power*. Cambridge: Cambridge University Press, pp. 215–237.
Forst, R. (2013). *Toleration in Conflict*. Cambridge University Press.
Galeotti, A.-E. (2002). *Toleration as Recognition*. Oxford: Oxford University Press.
Gourevitch, A. (2013). Labor Republicanism and the Transformation of Work. *Political Theory*, 41, pp. 591–617.
Gray, J. (2000). *The Two Faces of Liberalism*. Cambridge: Polity Press.
Hegel, G. W. F. (1991). *Elements of the Philosophy of Right*. Cambridge: Cambridge University Press.
Heyd, D. (2008). Is Toleration a Political Virtue? In: M. Williams and J. Waldron, eds., *Toleration and Its Limits*. New York: New York University Press, pp. 171–194.
Honneth, A. (1995). *The Struggle for Recognition*. Cambridge: Polity Press.
Honneth, A. (2003). Redistribution as Recognition: A Response to Nancy Fraser. In: N. Fraser and A. Honneth, eds., *Redistribution or Recognition?* London: Verso, pp. 110–197.
Honneth, A. (2014). *Freedom's Right*. Cambridge: Polity Press.
Honohan, I. (2013). Toleration and Non-domination. In: J. Dobbernack and T. Modood, eds., *Tolerance, Intolerance and Respect*. London: Palgrave Macmillan, pp. 77–100.
King, P. (1976). *Toleration*. London: St. Martin's Press.
Laborde, C. (2008). *Critical Republicanism*. Oxford: Oxford University Press.

Laborde, C. (2018). Toleration and laïcité. In: C. McKinnon and D. Castiglione, eds., *The Culture of Toleration in Diverse Societies*. Manchester: Manchester University Press, pp. 161–178.
McBride, C. (2013). *Recognition*. Cambridge: Polity Press.
Mill, J. S. (1989). On Liberty. In: S. Collini, ed., *On Liberty and Other Writings*. Cambridge: Cambridge University Press.
Montesquieu. (1989). *The Spirit of the Laws*. Cambridge: Cambridge University Press.
O'Shea, T. (2019). Socialist Republicanism. *Political Theory*. Available at: https://doi.org/10.1177/0090591719876889 [Accessed 6 Apr. 2020].
Paine, T. (2000). The Rights of Man. (1791–12). In: B. Kuklick, ed., *Paine: Political Writings*. Cambridge: Cambridge University Press.
Pettit, P. (1997). *Republicanism*. Oxford: Oxford University Press.
Pettit, P. (2012). *On the People's Terms*. Cambridge: Cambridge University Press.
Pettit, P. (2014). *Just Freedom*. New York: W.W. Norton.
Pocock, J. G. A. (1985). *Virtue, Commerce, and History*. Cambridge: Cambridge University Press.
Rawls, J. (1996). *Political Liberalism*, 2nd ed. New York: Columbia University Press.
Raz, J. (1988). Autonomy, Toleration, and the Harm Principle. In: S. Mendus, ed., *Justifying Toleration*. Cambridge: Cambridge University Press, pp. 155–175.
Robbins, C. (2004). *The Eighteenth Century Commonwealthman (1959)*. Indianapolis, IN: Liberty Fund.
Rohr, J. A. (1967). Religious Toleration in St. Augustine. *Journal of Church and State*, 9, pp. 51–70.
Rose, N. (1992). Governing the Enterprising Self. In: P. Heelas and P. Morris, eds., *The Values of the Enterprise Culture: The Moral Debate*. London: Routledge, pp. 141–164.
Rousseau, J. J. (1997). The Social Contract. In: V. Gourevitch, ed., *Rousseau: The Social Contract and Other Later Political Writings*. Cambridge: Cambridge University Press.
Smith, S. D. (2008). Toleration and Liberal Commitments. In: M. Williams and J. Waldron, eds., *Toleration and Its Limits*. NOMOS XLVII. New York: New York University Press, pp. 243–280.
Taylor, C. (1994). The Politics of Recognition. In: A. Gutmann, ed., *Multiculturalism*. Princeton, NJ: Princeton University Press, pp. 25–74.
Walzer, M. (1997). *On Toleration*. New Haven, CT: Yale University Press.
Washington, B. T. (1995). *Up From Slavery*. New York: Dover.
Williams, B. (2005). Toleration, a Political or Moral Question? In: G. Hawthorne, ed., *In the Beginning Was the Deed*. Princeton, NJ: Princeton University Press, pp. 128–138.
Young, I. M. (2011). *Responsibility for Justice*. Oxford: Oxford University Press.
Zurbuchen, S. (2002). Republicanism and Toleration. In: M. van Gelderen and Q. Skinner, eds., *Republicanism: A Shared European Heritage*, vol. 2. Cambridge: Cambridge University Press, pp. 47–71.

# 6 Liberalism and Toleration

*Jon Mahoney*

## Introduction

Toleration is fundamental to liberalism. Yet liberal political philosophers do not agree about the justification for toleration, the limits of toleration or whether every society is obligated to adopt a liberal conception of toleration. Does toleration depend on the harm principle (Mill, 1978)? Does liberal toleration depend on a basic right to justification (Forst, 2013)? Does a principle of toleration apply to political philosophy itself (Rawls, 1996)? Does liberal toleration require accommodating illiberal practices within liberal states? Is liberal toleration compatible with gender-egalitarian policies designed to make it harder for certain marriage and family practices to persist (Schouten, 2019)? What is the relation between toleration and neutrality (Balint, 2017)? Do those who affirm a collectivistic conception of political morality have an obligation to meet the requirements of a liberal conception of toleration? These and other questions generate disagreement about liberal toleration. Liberals continue to debate these and related topics about the basis for toleration, and how we should treat one another within and across diverse societies. In some ways debates about toleration are similar to debates about liberty and equality: shared concepts do not entail shared conceptions.

Some ideas unite competing conceptions of toleration (Forst, 2017). One is that to tolerate is to be willing to permit something one opposes. Another is that political liberty is a moral basis for toleration. The first agreement point – that to tolerate is to be willing to permit some things one finds objectionable – is central to the very idea of toleration. The second agreement point – that political liberty requires toleration – is central to liberalism. Putting the two together, we can characterize, in abstract, the fundamental idea behind liberal conceptions of toleration as follows: citizens and government should affirm a right to liberty and in doing so respect the diversity and pluralism that respect for liberty permits. There are important debates about which conception of liberty is most appropriate, whether political values such as equality should inform liberal toleration or whether the individualism that informs liberal political morality is a bias that reflects dominant western religious and cultural identities. Yet common ground – liberty is a primary basis for toleration – and the disputed ground – applications, universalism and limits – can be stated in this way.

This chapter will consider liberalism and toleration with three issues in focus: liberal and non-liberal conceptions of toleration, toleration and equality, and toleration and pluralism. First, it adapts ideas from Rainer Forst's taxonomy (2013, 2017) of conceptions of toleration. Non-liberal conceptions of toleration will be briefly considered as well. Second, it examines some ways that equality in status is relevant to liberal toleration. Being a Muslim American and being a Protestant American correlate with different social statuses, irrespective of an official state policy of religious equality. This is relevant to questions about liberal toleration. Third, it considers pluralism as a challenge to liberal toleration. When considering toleration from the standpoint of comparative or global philosophy some traditional liberal convictions about political morality may be harder to maintain. Finally, I conclude with a proposal to explore new ways that liberal political philosophers can approach toleration.

## 1. Varieties of Toleration: Conceptions and Practices

Toleration does not depend on liberal political values. Liberty as a moral basis for toleration is something that distinguishes liberal from non-liberal conceptions of toleration. A conception of toleration that does not rest upon the idea of a fundamental right to liberty is non-liberal. Two examples of non-liberal conceptions of toleration are coexistence and permission (Forst, 2013, pp. 27–29).

*Illiberal Toleration.* Religious, ethnic or cultural groups might accept a principle of toleration because they believe that coexistence is preferable to violence. The Hobbesian principle, "seek peace if others are willing to seek peace" can serve as the basis for a coexistence practice of toleration. In some contexts, this might be the most feasible alternative to significant hostilities. For example, following a long and protracted conflict, members of different religious, ethnic or cultural groups who are unwilling to affirm a principle of liberty might be willing to accept a kind of *modus vivendi* as preferable to open hostilities and conflict.

Some authoritarian states enact another kind of non-liberal toleration. For example, a hegemonic state might grant minority groups permission to practise a religion, speak a minority language or maintain a cultural practice conditioned on loyalty to the state and acceptance of official status inequalities. The Ottoman state policy of imposing lower tax burdens on Muslims while permitting Greek and Armenian Christian religious practices is an example of the permission conception of toleration. The Ottoman millet system also granted individual millets the authority to adopt their own marriage and family law along with limited autonomy in some other areas of life. Official inequality in status between privileged subjects and other groups is one way that this permission model of toleration differs from a liberal model. As with coexistence, the permission conception does not presuppose political liberty. Nevertheless, the permission conception does represent a form of toleration as can be shown by contrasting it with the oppression and intolerance within other kinds of authoritarian regimes.

By contrast with the Ottoman millet system, current Chinese policy in contemporary Xinjiang province is designed to force-assimilate Uighurs into an imagined national identity (Jacobs, 2017). This is just oppression. State policy directed at the language, culture, or religion of its own population, with the aim to radically reshape the group's identity, is a kind of internal colonialism. Forced-assimilation was not the aim of the Ottoman millet system. In that respect treatment of Greek Orthodox and other groups is an example the permission conception of toleration.

Coexistence and permission count as a form of toleration without liberty in the sense that groups of religious or cultural minorities are accommodated, but not on the basis of fundamental political rights. A regime based on one of these conceptions of toleration will be deficient according to a liberal perspective on toleration.

Some liberal states treat religious minorities in ways that violate standard norms of liberal tolerance. Sometimes minority groups face persecution within liberal states to a greater extent than in non-liberal states. Liberal states founded by settler colonists, such as the US and Australia, treated indigenous minority groups with extreme intolerance. Internal colonialism is not unique to illiberal states. Both policies and treatment of Native Americans in the nineteenth century were genocidal; the Ottoman millet system was not. Sometimes liberal states adopt intolerant policies towards some groups, and sometimes citizens in liberal states are not prevented from harming unpopular groups. Mormons in the nineteenth century, and Jehovah's Witness in the early twentieth century, were subject to significant hostilities by both citizens and state actors in the US. Violence against Jehovah's Witness in early-twentieth-century America involved mobs who attacked a religious minority they believed were disloyal Americans and whose understanding of Christianity differed from the mainline Protestant identity reflected in the majority religious identity (Smith, 2015, pp. 119–150). An account of toleration should be able to reckon with these and many other kinds of cases.

*Liberal Toleration.* A liberal conception of toleration will affirm liberty as a fundamental value. On a liberal view, toleration is required by liberty. Peter Balint expresses the basic idea behind a liberal position on toleration that is endorsed by liberals ranging from Mill to Rawls and many others: "I take it as a fundamental tenet of liberalism that it is interference, rather than non-interference that must be justified" (Balint, 2017, p. 11). On this view toleration is required by political liberty, including freedom of religion, expression and association. Liberty is the basis for the respect conception of toleration (Forst, 2013, pp. 29–30). Forst calls this the respect conception and by doing so refers to a set of views on liberal toleration according to which affirming individual liberties, such as freedom of thought or liberty of conscience, is an important moral basis for toleration.

To illustrate the respect conception, let's consider an example from American case law. In *West VA v Barnette* (1943) the Court ruled on whether children in a public school can be compelled to affirm a pledge to the American flag. Even today many American citizens support a practice of requiring children in public schools to recite a pledge to the civic and political values widely believed to be central to American national identity (Rasmussen Reports, 2013). On this view, a mandatory pledge of allegiance does not violate neutrality. By contrast, were a public school to require students to participate in a religious ritual, or to affirm a religious viewpoint, many citizens would agree that this violates neutrality, and also the liberty of conscience affirmed by the First Amendment. The main idea is this: whereas a mandatory religious service for children in public schools would compel a citizen to endorse a religious viewpoint in violation of religious neutrality, a political or civic ritual affirming the shared bases for citizenship does not violate neutrality in the relevant sense. It matters that *Barnette* was decided in 1943, before the phrase "one nation under God" was added to the pledge of allegiance. That phrase was added in 1954 (Shiffrin and Blasi, 2009). We can refer to the pre-1954 version as a secular-political pledge.

Is it intolerant for a liberal state to compel students in a public school to assert a secular-political pledge of the sort challenged in *Barnette*? In the early twentieth century, some Jehovah's Witness opposed the mandatory pledge in public schools claiming the policy requires their children to engage in a kind of idolatry. Since the prohibition on idolatry is a religious obligation, the mandatory secular-pledge, according to this view, requires children to disavow a core principle of their religious faith. Whereas an oath to God is a matter of religious duty, the mandatory pledge is compelled by a secular state, and so it constitutes a pledge to a political not religious authority. We can imagine other, similar claims. For example, suppose a Muslim parent objected to the pledge on grounds that Islam requires Muslims to affirm a principle of monotheism according to which, "there is no God but God". Suppose the Muslim parent insisted that a mandatory pledge puts the state and its education policy between her child and God, forcing a student to choose between a religious obligation and an official state policy. We can also imagine a secular citizen claiming it is a violation of liberty to compel citizens to participate in a mandatory loyalty ritual. In addition to the social stigma of non-conformity to a mass loyalty ritual, the injury to liberty of conscience, whether religious or secular, is a serious consideration this case.

Although in *Barnette* the Court did not consider the hypothetical cases of a Muslim or a non-religious opponent to the mandatory pledge in public schools, both the real and hypothetical examples show how a mandatory pledge of this sort might be objectionable to some citizens. Since liberty is the basis for a respect conception of toleration, we need to unpack the idea of liberty to see how a liberal conception of toleration might handle cases like this one.

Seanna Shiffrin's "thinker-based approach" (Shiffrin, 2011) to liberty of thought offers a perspicuous account of why a case like *Barnette* is not a debate over trifles. In an insightful passage, Shiffrin summarizes some of the moral dimensions to liberty of thought, with *WV v. Barnette* in view:

> What seems most troubling about the compelled pledge is that the motive behind the regulation, and the possible effect, is to interfere with the autonomous thought processes of the compelled speaker. Significantly, the compelled speaker is also a compelled listener and is compelled to adopt postures that typically connote identification with her message. The aim, and I believe the potential effect, is to try to influence the speaker to associate herself with the message and implicitly to accept it, but through means that bypass the deliberative faculties of the agent. Compelled speech of this kind threatens (or at least aims) to interfere with free thinking processes of the speaker/listener and to influence mental content in ways and through methods that are illicit: nontransparent, via repetition, and through coercive manipulation of a character virtue, namely that of sincerity, that itself is closely connected to commitments of freedom of speech.
>
> (Shiffrin, 2011, p. 302)

On this view, the mandatory pledge is a violation of freedom of thought. The practice cannot be reconciled to the idea of respect for liberty at the heart of a liberal regime that professes a commitment to toleration.

The thinker-based approach to freedom of expression provides a compelling illustration of why liberty of thought is important to individuals. In doing so it highlights something that is fundamental to the liberty that a conception of liberal toleration is supposed to protect: freedom of thought, a fundamental interest that persons have to express their agency without coercive interference. Liberty on this view is inclusive of freedom of association and freedom of religion, among other freedoms.

Whether aligned with a thinker-based approach or some other liberal conception of liberty, a respect conception of toleration can side with those who oppose a mandatory pledge, like the one in dispute in *Barnette*. That kind of compelled loyalty oath in the face of a religious or other value-based objection, is a form of intolerance. It denies someone the liberty of thought that is at the base of liberal political morality. It is a harder question to decide which forms of political loyalty are legitimately enforceable and by what means such loyalty may be enforced. For example, judges or politicians take an oath as a condition for serving in an official capacity. In the US citizens cannot be compelled to take an oath on the basis of a religious doctrine, because the Constitution prohibits a religious test as a condition for public office. Yet public servants can be required to take a political oath.

Is it unreasonable from the standpoint of toleration to require police and many other agents of the state to take an oath to comply with norms governing their professional obligations as agents of the state? An agent of the state has a different status, legally and morally, than a subject of a state. Legally, because the state authorizes their power; morally, because their legally authorized power is exercised on citizens. Agents of the state are still citizens of course, so policies that govern this area must serve multiple aims. One is to guarantee that the policing authority of government reflects legitimate political values, rather than the private judgment of the public servant. Another is to refrain from curtailing the liberty of public servants in their official capacities beyond what is necessary to maintain the first aim. If we grant this perspective, we can say that as an agent of the state one's role is defined by the political authority the agent represents. The liberty at the root of toleration applies foremost to citizens exercising their own judgments on behalf of their own views.

The respect conception of toleration is well suited to handle conflicts between expressions of liberty and state policy. In *Liberty of Conscience* Nussbaum construes the conflict between piety and secular law as an *Antigone Dilemma* (Nussbaum, 2008, pp. 116–120). That framing is apt, because the conflict is a result of perceived irreconcilable demands on a person's conscience. There can be non-religious versions of this dilemma too. A non-religious citizen might object to mandatory flag salutes on grounds that mass loyalty oaths compelled by the state are an affront to freedom of thought. A respect conception of toleration will favour minimizing *Antigone Dilemmas* either by eliminating policies that create them, or by granting exemptions to accommodate those with conscientious objections to legitimate state policy. There are hard questions about limits. Yet as a matter of framing liberal toleration, Nussbaum's position as well as Shiffrin's thinker-based approach to freedom of thought represent examples of how liberty is a basis for the respect conception of toleration.

Stated as a general view that ranges across conceptions of liberalism the respect conception, "proceeds from a morally grounded form of mutual respect on the part of the individuals or groups who exercise toleration" (Forst, 2013, p. 29). Citizens and government are tolerant when they permit activities protected by political liberties such as religious freedom, freedom of association, freedom of thought, and freedom of expression. Some liberals will put more emphasis on non-interference as the basis for political liberty; others will emphasize a principle of equal liberty of all compatible with liberty for each; some will invoke the idea of a right to justification; yet all liberal positions on toleration will place political liberty at the centre.

## 2. Toleration and Equality

Some forms of identity standout because they correlate highly with inequality. Though not an exhaustive list, the following are familiar examples: culture, religion, ethnicity and class. Inequalities that correlate with these forms of identity may be material, symbolic, social or political. For members of some groups, inequalities will be manifest in more than one or even all of these forms. Some liberal political philosophers claim that a liberal view on toleration should take status inequalities seriously (Galeotti, 2002.

In an early defence of multicultural liberalism Charles Taylor (1994) once advanced the claim that recognition is the appropriate attitude towards diversity, partly on grounds that every culture is centred on some intrinsic values that are unique to that culture. Respect for the value of diversity is another consideration. On Anna Galeotti's view, "toleration as recognition does not imply taking sides" (Galeotti, 2019, p. 6). Rather it offers "a public declaration that a given practice . . . is a legitimate option among others" (Galeotti, 2019, p. 6). A third consideration that has been develped in greater detail by those defending multicultural liberalism emphasizes ways that cultural and other identities matter to those who affirm such identities. For example, Alan Patten's equal recognition approach is based on the principle that persons should have a fair opportunity to pursue meaningful conceptions of the good life (Patten, 2014).

Some status inequalities might be judged to correlate with choices under fair background conditions, such as choosing membership in a reclusive religious community when other options are open. A citizen who elects to remain a committed Old Order Amish in the US will in doing so give up a number of opportunities ranging from university education, a lucrative career in cybersecurity, among other pursuits that in principle are open to everyone. She will also be seen as a kind of outsider by many members of the majority culture. Provided this affiliation is chosen, it might seem that all things considered her material and political status is not objectionable.

However, the politics of tolerating minority groups is often far more complicated. When status inequalities correlate with patterns of discrimination emphasizing a liberty right to choose membership in the group whose members have "opted out" of options is disrespectful. Consider those who insist that sexual orientation "is a choice", not because they celebrate liberty and toleration, but because they want to discriminate. Religious bigotry is sometimes expressed on a similar basis. A person might be convinced that their anti-Muslim bias is motivated by a judgment that, since someone chooses to be a Muslim, it is acceptable to express anti-Muslim views. If an "anti-Muslim" judgment is about a religious doctrine and not a person's identity in any fundamental sense, so the person reasons, this is not a form of objectionable prejudice. An appropriate reply to this is "not so fast!" Reasons to challenge that view include that the colour of a person's skin will often determine whether a judgment of anti-Muslim bias is made; whether a Muslim is a woman and if so whether she wears a headscarf may trigger a judgment of anti-Muslim bias; and many other factors ranging from nationality to language can influence the anti-Muslim bias expressed by those who claim they are simply making a judgment about a doctrine and not a person. In actuality intolerance of persons is often conflated with value judgments about a doctrine.

An American Muslim has a place in the collective imaginary of American national identity that is very different from that of a Protestant Christian. Despite an official state policy prohibiting religious discrimination many opportunities will be more difficult to realize for an American Muslim. If she wears a hijab, has dark skin or is a recent immigrant, these factors will affect her status. If she is outspoken or critical of state policy, her loyalty may well be questioned. There is a clear double standard here: white Protestant citizens can engage in far more forms of dissent without their loyalty being called into question. Many Americans believe the proposition, "we are a Christian nation". This belief is often expressed in a way that equivocates between a merely demographic statement and a normative claim about equality in status. This obfuscation is sometimes intentional: "we are a Christian nation" is a familiar way to mark those who do not squarely fit into the imagined national identity with a kind of outsider status, regardless of nationality. From a purely legal standpoint, citizenship might confer equal status, but politics and culture often deviate from that legal standpoint. The toleration as recognition approach may be better able to address this issue than a traditional respect conception.

Political discourse in the service of a majoritarian identity, real or imagined, usually downplays the many effects of unequal status. Unequal status can undermine what Rawls termed, "the social bases for self-respect" (Rawls, 1996). Whether the idea of liberal neutrality associated with the respect conception of toleration is objectionably difference-blind is one issue taken up by proponents of a recognition approach to toleration.

According to Galeotti the standard liberal view on toleration, "makes it impossible to recognize the issue of unequal membership" and thus, "all differences become equally invisible from a political standpoint" (Galeotti, 2002, p. 67). Toleration as recognition is motivated in part to address status inequalities. Another version of the toleration as recognition approach combines ideas about fairness, such equality of opportunity, and liberty. For example, Patten defends an equal recognition approach (Patten, 2014). On his view, each member of a liberal society should have an equal opportunity for self-determination. The site of recognition on Patten's conception is the liberty to pursue conceptions of value or the good under background conditions of fair equality of opportunity.

Proponents of the recognition approach do not reject the idea that liberty is essential to toleration. The tolerant open society will protect the one from the many by standing behind the liberty right to be different. Yet a central question is, how so? Will a tolerant open society remain neutral towards status inequalities, except in clear cases of coercion that violate a non-interference criterion? Or will a tolerant open society also commit to mitigating effects of inequalities in status? There is a morally relevant difference between an effort by a Christian majority to prevent the construction of a mosque – all liberals concur that a tolerant open society will oppose that effort – and the asymmetrical statuses that correlate with majority and minority religious statuses, not just in private but also public domains. Should a liberal conception of toleration focus only on the former?

Oftentimes there are no easy answers to questions about cases, in part because there are almost always multiple factors in play. For example, past discrimination against a religious minority can be salient to contemporary politics; intergenerational effects of bias can be reflected in state policy; status privileged citizens often resist calls to recognize inequalities in status, and resist efforts to address them even more so; and proxies for bias often serve as tools that permit messaging strategies that affirm a form of bigotry under the guise of something else. Status anxiety among members of a dominant group whose effort to maintain dominance can inspire various forms of intolerance. Any person judged to be a threat to status dominance is a possible target of resentment. White racial resentment in the American context is a paradigm case. Richard Hofstadter (1964) offered a classic formulation of this idea when discussing the American Civil Rights Movement. Moreover, when members of a group that has been subject to intolerance demand better treatment, resentment on the part of those who favour the intolerance, most especially from those who benefit from it in the form of status privilege, is a common response.

Institutions may or may not be complicit in objectionable unequal statuses. Yet even when they are not, equality in status matters across a range of contexts from interpersonal relations, employment opportunities for high status positions and access to political office. A main focus of classical liberal theory is on questions about political authority and the state's role in protecting citizens' political liberty. Yet the power conferred by privileged status benefits some in formal and informal contexts, sometimes irrespective of state policy. Offices and opportunities, ranging from official positions in government to opportunities to pursue various careers, may be more or less open to a citizen in virtue of her religious identity. Should a tolerant society seek means to ensure that if persons pursue a permissible conception of the good this does not correlate with status inequalities? And if so, by what means?

Critics of the recognition approach sometimes argue that a liberal conception of toleration should not compromise on the idea that liberty is the primary basis for toleration. Those who defend a recognition approach to toleration can respond by pointing out that one ought not to have a diminished status in the political community merely because of one's membership in a cultural or religious group.

Patten's equal recognition approach is one way to take on the challenges posed to the toleration as recognition approach that emphasize an individual right to liberty. On his view, liberty is affirmed in the idea of an equal right to opportunities for self-determination (Patten, 2014). Equality is affirmed in the idea of an equal treatment standard that can measure whether opportunities for self-determination are fairly maintained. There is room for debate about adopting a distributive model for toleration, one that integrates the idea of fair equality of opportunity with the idea of liberty rights to religious freedom, freedom of association, and freedom of expression (Jones, 2017). Yet if we grant the principle of fair equality of opportunity for self-determination, we can see how it supports an idea of toleration that meets what would otherwise be the competing desideratum of the respect and recognition conceptions of toleration.

## 3. Ethical Pluralism and Toleration

Most work by liberal political philosophers focuses on value pluralism within a western religious, political, and cultural context. Classical liberals such as Locke and Mill framed questions about toleration in order to address that perspective. Some recent developments in comparative philosophy or what is sometimes called global philosophy point to a different set of issues for a liberal view on toleration (Hashemi, 2009). Some of this work highlights pluralism across traditions, for example traditions that affirm an individualistic view of political morality and traditions that affirm collectivistic conceptions of political morality (Buchanan, 2013; Kim, 2014). This raises a number of challenging questions, including, are there reasonable yet incompatible conceptions of political morality, some of which are collectivistic and non-liberal?

Those with expertise in Islamic political philosophy (March, 2019), Chinese political philosophy (Angle, 2012), or collectivistic conceptions of political morality that inform ideas about human rights (Buchanan, 2013), have offered interesting proposals on the prospects for liberal political values in these contexts. I draw on some of their work here not to add to their scholarship to but to examine questions for liberal toleration in comparative perspective.

In his recent book on ideas about political authority and sovereignty within modern Islamic political thought Andrew March (2019) notes that within Sunni Islam an influential view holds that God authorizes the Muslim community – *Umma* – to form an Islamic democracy. In a formulation of the relation between religious and political authority that resembles a Lockean view one of the intellectuals who informed Kemalism in the early Turkish Republic, Ziya Gokalp, proclaimed, "God's representative (on earth) is the people. . . . Authority belongs to the people and not to the Sultan. . . . To it belongs all power – legislative, judicial, and executive" (March, 2019, p. 38). Nader Hashemi (2009) examines contemporary debates among Shia political thinkers who stake out positions ranging from a defence of secular government, Islamic democracy, and theocracy. For example, Hashemi considers an interesting parallel between the Locke-Filmer debate on political authority and contemporary Iranian political thinkers (Hashemi, 2009, pp. 67–102). Those who advocate a secular conception of political authority are more likely to favour toleration for Baha'i and others who face discrimination. Stephen Angle (2012) explores ways that within Confucian thought leadership is conferred by characteristics of a virtuous ruler whose moral authority to rule depends on having the right characteristics.

Pluralism across states raises a different set of questions for liberal toleration than does pluralism within states. For example, Canada and the US have minority cultures and religions that embrace collectivistic and non-liberal values, yet the dominant political cultures reflect a broadly liberal perspective on individual liberty. There are significant differences between the minority status of someone who affirms liberalism in a non-liberal society and someone who affirms an illiberal view in a liberal society. A Lockean liberal living in the Chinese Republic does not have the same status under law as an Old Order Amish living in the USA. One obvious difference is that in one case a person might be exercising religious liberty, whereas in the other, a person is denied such liberty.

In an interesting examination of Protestant and Hindu religious doctrine and practice Spinner-Halev (2005) notes that for most practising Hindus belonging to a practice is far more central than belief. Ritual is primary. Religious conscience is secondary. Liberal ideas about liberty and respect for conscience largely reflect the legacy of the impact of Protestant Christianity on early liberal thought.

Belonging precedes belief for many religious persons, whatever the religious tradition and wherever it is practised. It is better to refer to degrees of individualism and degrees of collectivism in religious self-understanding. However, as a matter of doctrine, the priority of inner conviction over outward ritual plays a special role in Protestant Christianity. There is a clear connection between this Protestant conception of religious doctrine and the classical liberal liberty and toleration. A "thinker-based" approach to liberty, for example, places emphasize on inner conviction and individual agency. By contrast rituals at the heart of a collective identity, religious or non-religious, may be understood as more basic, and a more important source of values and human identity.

Many liberals will bristle at the thought of a communal "ritual-based" alternative to the thinker-based approach of Shiffrin. Yet that there are so many examples of collectivistic conceptions of value, including political morality, at odds with the value individualism central to liberalism raises an interesting challenge for liberal positions on toleration. It is one thing to ask, what is the most appropriate conception of toleration for citizens in a diverse society who agree that every citizen is free and equal? That question is challenging enough even when diverse citizens whose views are mutually intelligible to one another struggle to find shared bases for a liberal conception of toleration. Pluralism within and pluralism across traditions raise different kinds of challenges. One example of pluralism within a tradition is competing conceptions of liberal values, including debates over how to understand liberty and equality. Pluralism across traditions includes individualistic and collective conceptions of political morality that divide those who mostly agree with liberal political morality and those who do not. Of course, there are illiberal doctrines defended within the context of dominant liberal traditions as well as liberal doctrines defended in the context of dominant illiberal traditions.

Open mindedness about conceptions of toleration need not entail affirming toleration without limits. Yet open mindedness about practices of toleration should be at the centre of liberal theories of toleration. Judgements about the basic moral convictions deemed essential to liberty and equality are frequently negotiated by people who disagree on some fundamental points. Taking the widely discussed options on pluralism within liberal societies and rethinking them in comparative perspective is one way to develop this idea. Another is to consider conceptions of toleration from within non-western traditions of political morality. The pursuit of these and other options should be embraced rather than resisted by liberal political philosophers.

Lastly, an important issue that needs to be considered in this context is how dialogue across traditions is framed. There can be a chauvinism on the part of liberal political philosophers who assume that productive dialogue will result in a Chinese political philosopher embracing liberal values without mutual influence across traditions. Yet why should the influence be one-way? It is likely that there are forms of liberal toleration yet to be imagined, including those that reflect mutual influence across traditions.

## Conclusion

The perspectives on toleration considered in this chapter highlight illiberal and liberal practices of toleration, cases where liberal states are sometimes more intolerant than non-liberal states, as well as different formulations of toleration within liberal political philosophy. Having a taxonomy of conceptions of toleration can clarify a wide range of practices within both liberal and non-liberal states. This is helpful for at least two reasons. First, whether the best conceptions of toleration will be adapted to liberal political morality is a separate question from which practices qualify as a form of toleration. Second, the paradigm cases that liberal political philosophers examine are important, yet also limited. There are both global and historical perspectives on toleration that can inform how we think about toleration. Why limit cases and examples of toleration to modern or to western states unless we are offering a proposal for toleration that applies to just those contexts?

Whether theories of toleration offer helpful perspective on moral progress, reform or diffusing political conflicts will depend in part on open mindedness about how states and persons can realize practices of toleration. A selection bias informs many liberal accounts of toleration: these accounts focus on cases in the American or European context. The headscarf debates in Europe or the religious exemptions debate in the US are important cases for thinking about toleration. Thinking about political and moral dimensions of toleration from just these perspectives comes at the risk of introducing a parochial bias in liberal views on toleration. It also encourages political philosophers to overlook biases in how they think about the political values that inform their understanding of toleration. Consideration of non-liberal practices of toleration and the pluralist challenge can help us appreciate the limitations of standard positions.

To conclude, a consideration of various forms of pluralism and their implications for toleration might lead to more or less radical positions. Chandran Kukathas (2017) has recently argued for a conception of toleration without limits, a conception informed by skepticism about attempts to justify limits to toleration with the harm principle, a basic right to justification, or some other standard. That is one possible outcome. Another option is to defend a kind of moral minimalism as a basis for toleration. Forst defends such a view when he claims, "No other values or norms except *the principle of justification itself* can provide the foundation of . . . toleration" (Forst, 2013, p. 400). A comparative or global philosophy approach might lead to third outcome, one that affirms value pluralism in a way that supports multiple conceptions of toleration. The main focus of this chapter has been on liberalism and toleration, yet the central ideas are presented with the recognition that there are many more questions to examine than have hitherto been adequately addressed.

## References

Angle, S. (2012). *Contemporary Confucian Political Philosophy*. Cambridge: Polity Press.
Balint, P. (2017). *Respecting Toleration: Traditional Liberalism and Contemporary Diversity*. New York: Oxford University Press.

Buchanan, A. (2013). *The Heart of Human Rights*. New York: Oxford University Press.
Forst, R. (2013). *Toleration in Conflict: Past and Present*. Trans C. Cronin. Cambridge: Cambridge University Press.
Forst, R. (2017). Toleration. In: *Stanford Encyclopedia of Philosophy*. Edward N. Zalta (ed.), Available at: https://plato.stanford.edu/archives/fall2017/entries/toleration/ [Accessed 28 Apr. 2020].
Galeotti, A. (2002). *Toleration as Recognition*. Cambridge: Cambridge University Press.
Galeotti, A. (2019). Rescuing Toleration. *Critical Review of International Social and Political Philosophy*, pp. 1–22. [online] Available at: https://doi.org/10.1080/13698230.2019.1616882 [Accessed 28 Apr. 2020].
Hashemi, N. (2009). *Islam, Secularism, and Liberal Democracy: Toward a Democratic Theory of Muslim Societies*. New York: Oxford University Press.
Hofstadter, R. (1964). The Paranoid Style of American Politics. *Harper's Magazine*, Nov.
Jacobs, J. (2017). *Xinjiang and the Modern Chinese State*. Seattle, WA: University of Washington Press.
Jones, P. (2017). Religious Exemption and Distributive Justice. In: C. Laborde and A. Bardon, eds., *Religion in Liberal Political Philosophy*. Oxford: Oxford University Press, pp. 163–176.
Kim, S. (2014). *Confucian Democracy in East Asia: Theory and Practice*. Cambridge: Cambridge University Press.
Kukathas, C. (2017). Toleration Without Limits: A Reconstruction and Defense of Pierre Bayle's *Philosophical Commentary*. In: C. Laborde and A. Bardon, eds., *Religion in Liberal Political Philosophy*, Oxford: Oxford University Press, pp. 262–274.
March, A. (2019). *The Caliphate of Man: Popular Sovereignty in Modern Islamic Thought*. Cambridge, MA: The Belknap Press of Harvard University Press.
Mill, J. S. (1978). *On Liberty*, 8th ed. Indianapolis, IN: Hackett Publishing.
Nussbaum, M. (2008). *Liberty of Conscience: In Defense of America's Tradition of Religious Equality*. New York: Basic Books.
Patten, A. (2014). *Equal Recognition Equal Recognition: The Moral Foundations of Minority Rights*. Princeton, NJ: Princeton University Press.
Rasmussen Reports. (2013). 68% Think School Children Should Say Pledge Allegiance Every Morning. Available at: www.rasmussenreports.com/public_content/lifestyle/general_lifestyle/september_2013/68_think_school_children_should_say_pledge_of_allegiance_every_morning [Accessed 28 Apr. 2020].
Rawls, J. (1996). *Political Liberalism*, expanded ed. New York: Columbia University Press.
Schouten, G. (2019). *Liberalism, Neutrality, and the Gendered Division of Labor*. Cambridge: Cambridge University Press.
Shiffrin, S. (2011). A Thinker-Based Approach to Freedom of Speech. *Constitutional Commentary*, 21, pp. 283–307.
Shiffrin, S. and Blasi, V. (2009). The Story of West Virginia Board of Education v. Barnette. In: M. Dorf, ed., *Constitutional Law Stories*, 2nd ed. St Paul, MN: Foundation Press, pp. 409–453.
Smith, D. (2015). *Religious Persecution and Political Order in the United States*. Cambridge: Cambridge University Press.

Spinner-Haley, J. (2005). Hinduism, Christianity, and Liberal Religious Toleration. *Political Theory*, 33(1), pp. 28–57.
Taylor, C. (1994). The Politics of Recognition. In: A. Guttman, ed., *Multiculturalism*. Princeton, NJ: Princeton University Press, pp. 25–75.
*West Virginia State Board of Education v Barnette*. (1943). 319 US 624.

# 7 Public Reason and the Burdens of Citizenship
## A Case for Toleration
*Andrea Baumeister*

## Introduction

While toleration is generally viewed as a core liberal value, recent debates have been marked by scepticism regarding the relevance and role of traditional notions of political toleration in a modern, value-neutral liberal polity. Toleration is widely taken to entail an intentional decision not to prohibit or hinder conduct viewed as objectionable, despite having the power to do so.[1] Thus, in the paradigmatic case of political toleration, traditional sovereigns, who permit religions other than their own, are said to practise toleration. However, in contrast to the traditional sovereign, who has both grounds to object and the power to intervene in religious practices, the modern liberal state is neutral vis-à-vis citizens' diverse, yet reasonable, conceptions of the good. While such a state may prohibit conduct that violates the principles of justice, it has no grounds to object to the wide array of justice-respecting ways of life citizens may choose to pursue. Indeed, in a modern liberal polity, citizens' religious or moral commitments are "private" and as such not the state's concern. Thus, for critics of political toleration, in as far as the modern liberal state is value neutral, it cannot be tolerant.[2]

In the face of this challenge to the practice of political toleration in a modern liberal polity, this chapter argues that, far from being incompatible, the liberal commitment to justificatory neutrality provides distinctive grounds for acts of toleration, conceived as legal exemptions from generally applicable laws. Contemporary liberal notions of justificatory neutrality centre on the idea of public reason, that is to say the notion that the exercise of coercive state power can only be justified by an appeal to reasons that are shared, accessible or acceptable to all. While the exclusionary character of public reason aims to safeguard the equal standing of all citizens in the public political realm, it also gives rise to a distinctive picture of the burdens of citizenship. Although mainstream conceptions of public reason are less vulnerable than critics frequently assume to the charge of undermining citizens' personal integrity by compelling them to split their identity, attempts to separate out public reasons from the complex web of reasons citizens bring to any given political question can lead to the exclusion of considerations that some citizens view as genuinely morally significant. While not discriminatory, these exclusions can curtail the extent to which such citizens can view themselves as politically autonomous and may lead citizens to feel alienated from the common life of the polity.

Given the foundational liberal commitment to equality of respect, these burdens can provide good grounds for exemptions from generally applicable laws for citizens whose sincere conscientious commitments are at odds with public laws. This chapter will argue that such exemptions are best viewed as acts of toleration grounded in respect for freedom of conscience and the worth inherent in our fellow citizens' capacity for moral and spiritual agency. Although it is the state which secures toleration by granting legal exemptions, such acts of toleration are ultimately grounded in the relationship between free and equal citizens committed to the practice of justifying political power to one another. Toleration, therefore, assumes a distinctive political role. By offering redress for the difficulties and limitation inherent in the search for a common evaluative standard, toleration affirms the equal standing of citizens and helps to facilitate continued political engagement among citizens in the face of the plurality of conscientious commitments that characterize the modern liberal polity. Conceived in these terms, political toleration is not merely compatible with the liberal commitment to justificatory neutrality, but is central to the idea of public reason as a regulative ideal that guides deliberation among free and equal citizens.

To develop this argument for political toleration the following section will clarify the burdens of citizenship associated with the liberal commitment to justificatory neutrality. The subsequent section will argue that given the intricate link between the idea of public reason and a commitment to citizenship as a shared political project, these burdens are best addressed not by abandoning the search for a common evaluative standard, but by granting citizens legal exemptions from generally applicable laws at odds with their sincerely held conscientious commitments. Such exemptions can be shown to meet the classical hallmarks of toleration, and the last section will consider some of the implication for the limits of toleration inherent in such a conception of toleration.

## 1. Public Reason and the Burdens of Citizenship

While liberalism aims to protect the freedom of individuals to pursue their personal life plan and conception of the good, citizens in a liberal polity also have a common life and participate in a shared political project grounded in a commitment to live together on the basis of fair terms of social cooperation. In the face of the plurality of conflicting, yet reasonable, worldviews and ways of life characteristic of modern liberal societies, political liberalism seeks to ground this common project in an appeal to a distinctive political conception of justice, which separates key moral and political values from more comprehensive religious and secular ideas. While this political conception reflects fundamental moral ideals latent in the public political culture of a democratic regime, it does not entail any particular comprehensive metaphysical or religious ideas. Political liberals content that this political conception of justice can, therefore, be endorsed by citizens who subscribe to a diverse array of reasonable religious or secular worldviews and ways of life. The Rawlsian notion of an overlapping consensus constitutes probably the best-known expression of this picture of the common life of citizens in a modern liberal polity.

While this political conception of justice aims to safeguard the freedom and equal standing of citizens in a liberal polity, it also gives rise to a distinctive picture of the legitimate burdens of citizenship. To respect fellow citizens as free and equal implies that citizens aim to justify the use of coercive political power to one another. Indeed, such justifications must be public, that is to say they must be based on reasons that all citizens can, at least in principle, endorse.[3] While precise definitions vary, mainstream political liberals take this to imply that legal coercion must be justified in terms of reasons that are shared, accessible or acceptable to all.[4] After all, in the face of a plurality of worldviews and ways of life, only reasons that are in some sense shared, accessible or acceptable to all can hope to gain the endorsement of all citizens. Public reason is therefore exclusionary – only an appeal to particular types of reasons can justify the exercise of coercive state power. Thus, for example, for Rawls only the narrow subset of reasons that reflects the core political values and ideals of a liberal democratic society can be classed as public reasons.

The use of public reason, therefore, requires an element of restraint. To adopt the language of public reason implies that we forgo any appeal to reasons grounded solely in our particular, sectarian perspectives. Citizens, therefore, should only support laws that meet the constraints of public reason and should be ready to demonstrate their commitment to the norm of reciprocity by being willing to provide reasons for the political decisions they advocate that free and equal fellow citizens could at least in principle endorse. To do so, citizens must align their political conception of justice and their comprehensive moral commitments. Where conflicts between these two sets of commitments arise, reasonable citizens either revise their moral commitments in the light of the demands of political justice or accept that these aspects of their comprehensive conception of the good must be "privatized" and thus cannot provide the basis of public political justifications of coercive state power.[5]

Public reason, therefore, places substantial demands on citizens. Even though, it is important not to overstate the burdens inherent in this picture of public justification. While elected officials and office holders immediately engaged in shaping public law and policy must justify legal coercion exclusively in terms of public reason, for citizens at large a commitment to public reason merely entails a requirement to do "what they can to hold government officials to it" (Rawls, 1997, p. 769). Indeed, even on Rawls's (1997, p. 783) demanding conception of public reason, arguments grounded in reasonable comprehensive doctrines "may be introduced in public political discussion at any time, provided" these are translated "in due course" into "proper political reasons". A commitment to public reason, therefore, does not require citizens at large engaged in political debate in the informal public political sphere to "bracket" or "set aside" their most important personal beliefs and moral convictions.

For example, while religious reasons are typically cited as the paradigmatic example of the types of reasons excluded by an appeal to public reason, a commitment to public reason does not imply that religious citizens cannot express themselves in a religious idiom in public political debate or that public reason is hostile to the moral insights that religious traditions and discourses may offer. While such contributions will have to be translated into the language of public reason if they are to influence formal political decision-making, these burdens of translation need not necessarily fall exclusively on religious citizens themselves. Habermas (2008), for instance, argues that such translation should be conceived as a cooperative effort involving both secular and religious citizens. Moreover, while religious citizens must accept the priority of public reason in the formal public political sphere, Habermas recognizes that in the informal public political sphere a liberal state committed to freedom of religion cannot reasonably expect citizens to justify their political statements independently from their religious convictions. Indeed, not only do advocates of public reason such as Habermas recognize that religious discourses can be a vehicle for conveying important moral insights and intuitions,[6] arguments which deploy religious references or imagery to convey universal moral insights do not necessarily violate the constraints of public reason (March, 2013). Catholic writings on human dignity, for example, may well be accessible to and can be appreciated by even the most ardent secularists. Thus, religious conservative arguments regarding issues such as "the public good of social order", "the good of the institution of marriage" or "the right to life" that are publicly accessible and not grounded in an appeal to scripture or transcendental authority, "cannot be ruled out as incompatible with public reason" (Laborde, 2017, p. 123). Finally, while the demands of public reason imply that "reasonable citizens only affirm religious and moral views that can be made consistent with a political conception of justice" (Hertzberg, 2019, p. 36), reasonable political conceptions of justice can take many forms ranging from John Finnis's account of natural law to Jürgen Habermas's discourse ethics (Rawls, 1997).

As this example illustrates, stated carefully mainstream conceptions of public reason do not prevent citizens at large from engaging in political advocacy on the basis of their comprehensive moral doctrines and worldviews. This suggests that such conceptions of public reason are less vulnerable than critics frequently assume to the charge of undermining citizens' sense of personal integrity by compelling them to split their identity.[7] However, the principles of liberty and equality at the heart of the liberal commitment to justificatory neutrality not only seek to protect citizens' capacity to pursue a diverse array of well-integrated ways of life, but are also indicative of the idea of citizenship as a common project. The modern liberal polity marks the sphere where citizens committed to living together on the basis of fair terms of social cooperation come together on an equal footing to collectively will the rights and norms that are to govern their polity (Watson and Hartley, 2018). Justificatory neutrality is, therefore, intricately linked to notions of political autonomy, civic equality, popular sovereignty and democratic self-limitation. It is in this regard that the exclusionary character of public reason poses particular challenges.

Political decisions typically require us to weigh a variety of considerations. In this context, public reason demands that we privilege reasons that are shared, accessible or acceptable to all and set aside reasons grounded solely in our particular sectarian perspectives. Yet, as Jeremy Waldron (2007, p. 117) notes, the strength of reasons in favour of a particular decision will always depend upon "how their strengths line up in relation to the strength of the reasons opposing the decision". Moreover, the relative weight of arguments for or against a decision is often influenced by the range and type of reasons regarded as legitimate or worthy of consideration within a given setting. Here it is important to bear in mind that the reasons people advance typically do not constitute a discrete list of independent concerns, but form complex and structured systems. Indeed, the weight or significance people attach to particular reasons often reflects "the internal structuring of the whole array of reasons that the citizen brings to the matter" (Waldron, 2015, p. 127). Public reason, however, focuses on a particular subset of reasons and seeks to detach these from the wider web of reasons citizens may hold. If this attempt to separate out public reasons leads to the exclusion of considerations that some citizens view as genuinely morally significant, the exclusionary character of public reason may constrain the extent to which such citizen can view themselves as politically autonomous, that is to say as authors as well as subjects of the law.

Religious reasons, again, provide an apt example here. If, for instance, we "believe that neglecting to help the poor is a way of turning one's back on the Son of God", we have a "staggeringly important reason in favour of a duty to help the poor" (Waldron, 2007, pp. 117–118). Such a belief would, for example, provide a decisive reason for opposing proposals to abolish all welfare assistance for the poor so as to deter irresponsible choices. Yet, the very thing that makes this reason so overwhelmingly significant for religious believers – the appeal to the divine – cannot be captured in the language of secular public reason. While it is precisely the association with transcendental authority which leads religious citizens to view certain reasons as particularly weighty, it is at best difficult to explain to someone who is not part of a particular religious tradition what is entailed in an appeal to revealed truth and such reasons are liable to prove highly resistant to "translation" (Habermas, 2011). Moreover, even if we can identify secular public political reasons which echo religious moral intuitions, these could not capture the special significance or weight that attaches to these reasons from a religious standpoint and the role they play within the structured array of reasons that informs this perspective. While such secular public political reasons may well be accessible to religious citizens, they will, from a religious perspective, miss the most pertinent point. Even if religious citizens can recognize the validity of a particular set of secular public political reasons, there simply is no guarantee that what constitutes the right sort of action by an appeal to "otherworldly" sources of validity will necessarily coincide with those based on an appeal to strictly secular "innerworldly" sources.

For example, although secular conceptions of human rights and Christian writings on human dignity share considerable common ground, secular conceptions cannot capture the significance and weight Christian accounts attach to the "obligation to humanity and to the creator that is imposed by a theistic conception of the human person as created in the image of God" (Areshidze, 2017, p. 733).[8] These differences can impact on what citizens regard as the right course of action. For instance, while religious citizens may well be able to recognize and endorse the validity of secular arguments against the use of torture, to view torture as a "crime against high heaven and the holy spirit of man . . . for which there can be no forgiveness", is to have an overwhelmingly strong reason to view the prohibition against torture as an absolute ban (Seymour Cocks cited in Waldron, 2015, p. 131). Yet, in the absence of an appeal to the force of such a religious absolute, purely secular moral considerations regarding respect for personhood or a suspect's dignity may be more readily overridden by countervailing considerations such as the need to protect large numbers of people from the imminent threat of a terrorist attack (Waldron, 2015).

Where in the construction of public reasons religious considerations regarded by believers as morally significant are "lost in translation", subsequent decisions may, from a religious perspective, "sell people short" by excluding or marginalizing those interests that these considerations draw attention to. The decision may, for instance, pay insufficient attention to our duty to help the poor or may fail to recognize the absolute sanctity of human dignity. This may constrain the extent to which religious citizens can independently endorse particular laws and political decisions as legitimate for reason they themselves can recognize as rationally acceptable and may, in turn, curtail the extent to which such citizens can view themselves as politically autonomous.[9] Where the language of public reason fails to properly take account of reasons religious citizens regard as morally highly significant, such citizens are liable to struggle to view themselves as the authors as well as the subjects of such laws. Furthermore, the inability to persuade fellow citizens of the evidential basis of one's beliefs for the purposes of public political justification does not necessarily diminish the sense of conviction with which individuals experience their beliefs at a personal level.[10] Indeed, beliefs grounded in revealed truth and a search for salvation are often held with a particularly strong sense of personal conviction. Even if religious citizens recognize that a commitment to public reason requires that for the purposes of public political justification "otherworldly" considerations are effectively blocked, this will not necessarily lessen the 'pull' of religiously grounded obligations at a personal level.

As this example illustrates, although the full constraints of public reason do not apply to public political debate among citizens in the informal public sphere, for some citizens the demands associated with public reason justifications may none the less be significantly more burdensome than for others. Where the language of public reason cannot properly account for considerations central to the internal structuring of the complex array of reasons that citizens bring to a particular matter, the demand to "privatize" reasons that cannot form the basis of public political justifications may impose considerable moral costs on such citizens. Such costs make it more difficult for such citizens to accommodate themselves to the restraints inherent in a commitment to public reason. Of course, the mere fact that the burdens associated with public reason justifications are distributed unequally does not necessarily imply that such demands are inequitable or discriminatory. As Rawls (1993, p. 193) notes, while political liberalism is neutral in its aims vis-à-vis particular conceptions of the good, "this is not to be confused with neutrality of effect and influence". Although the constraints associated with political liberalism may make some forms of life more difficult than others, to be legitimate law need not be neutral in terms of the costs it imposes on citizens. After all, political liberalism's political conception of justice is not value neutral, but is grounded in a substantive commitment to the principles of liberty, equality and mutual respect. Moreover, while some citizens may find public reason justifications particularly burdensome, the foundational values that underpin these justifications also safeguard the space within which citizens can exercise their personal autonomy in pursuit of their own life plans and conception of the good. For instance, with reference to religious conceptions of the good, it could be argued that the freedom of religion enjoyed by citizens within a liberal democratic polity is itself underpinned by the same foundational commitment to liberty, equality and mutual respect as public reason justifications.[11] Finally, although some citizens may struggle to give public reason justifications their "full throated support" (Waldron, 2015, p. 125), this does not imply that such justifications are inaccessible to such citizens or that such citizens cannot grasp the values that motivate the search for common evaluative standards.

## 2. Addressing the Burdens of Citizenship: A Case for Toleration

Although not necessarily discriminatory per se, the fact that the demands of citizenship are liable to be significantly more onerous for some citizens rather than others is nonetheless troubling for political liberals committed to a conception of citizens as free and equal. Indeed, Habermas (2008) explicitly acknowledges that even in the absence of discrimination an unequal distribution of the burdens of citizenship gives rise to legitimate concerns. After all, an unequal distribution of the burdens associated with citizenship may well impact on the extent to which citizens will be able to view themselves as full members of the body of free and equal citizens engaged in the shared political project that marks the public life of a liberal polity. In essence, in the face of an unequal distribution of the burdens of citizenship there is a danger that some citizens will feel alienated from the common life of the polity. This is particularly worrying where the exclusionary character of public reason places constraints on the extent to which some citizens can class themselves as politically autonomous. In the face of such worries political liberals may adopt one of two strategies: (a) abandon the search for a common evaluative standard in favour of a less exclusionary conception of public reason or (b) alleviate the burdens associated with the exclusionary character of public reason in instances where these are particularly onerous for a specific group of citizens.

Kevin Vallier's (2014) intelligible reason requirement constitutes a prominent example of the first strategy. Rather than search for a common evaluative standard, Vallier (2016, p. 614) argues that to count as a justificatory reason for coercive law it is sufficient that reasons are intelligible; that is to say fellow citizens can see that the person who offers the reason is "entitled to affirm it given that person's own evaluative standards". On this account, legal coercion is justified not via an agreement on shared or generally accessible or acceptable reasons, but through the convergence of the particular intelligible private reasons that citizens have to support a given law. While citizens may invoke very different reasons, a law is publicly justified if each citizen has some conclusive reason to accept the law. Public justification, therefore, does not entail an appeal to a common evaluative standard, but arises from the network of different intelligible private reasons that lead diverse citizens to endorse a particular law. For example, for a law stipulating an increase in welfare provisions to be convergence justified, it is of no consequence that some citizens support this law solely because they believe that to fail to do so would be to "turn one's back on the Son of God", while other citizens endorse these provisions due to their commitment to the idea of fair terms of social cooperation. Rather than insist that citizens only support laws that are justified in terms of reason that can in principle be endorsed by all, citizens should merely refrain from supporting laws that are not convergence justified. Indeed, given well-designed political institutions that ensure that only laws that are convergence justified can be enacted, there is no need to place restraints on the kind of laws that citizens can advocate or the reasons they may cite in support of their proposals (Gaus and Vallier, 2009).

However, while Vallier's intelligible reason requirement may well ease some of the burdens associated with public reason justifications, this "inclusivism" comes at considerable cost. Indeed, it is not clear that such a thin conception of public justification can capture the idea of citizenship as a shared political project, which motivates the very appeal to public reasons and is pivotal to the fundamental principles that underpin political liberalism. As Hartley (2016, p. 18) notes, for political liberals public reason justifications play a vital role in enabling citizens to "find shared terms of social cooperation" that citizens can "collectively will" on terms that are "consistent with the status of all persons as free and equal". The picture of public justification inherent in the convergence liberalism championed by inclusivists such as Vallier cannot capture this facet of citizenship in a liberal polity. While every citizen may have sufficient reasons to endorse a particular law, "there is no collective will in the sense that law is justified to persons with a common project" (Hartley, 2016, p. 318). There is, therefore, no sense of citizens adopting a public perspective to dialogically justify their polity's vision of the public good (Hertzberg, 2019) Moreover, there is no guarantee that the sufficient reasons citizens have for accepting a particular law are consistent with the principle of equality of respect. For example, while some may believe that women should be permitted to wear a burka in public places because they respect women's autonomous choices, others may support such a position because they believe the presence of women in public places is problematic and in need of constraint and control. Such a picture of public justification does not sit well with the foundational commitments that motivate political liberalism and fails to account for the "beliefs and commitments necessary for democratic citizens to cooperate on just terms with each other" (Hertzberg, 2019, p. 55).

Instead of offering an attractive alternative, the difficulties inherent in Vallier's intelligible reasons requirement point to the intricate link between the search for a common standard of evaluation and the idea of citizenship as a shared project in pursuit of public purposes. This suggests that rather than abandon the search for a common evaluative standard, political liberals should seek other avenues to redress the difficulties associated with the exclusionary character of public reason. Granting citizens legal exemptions from generally applicable laws which would otherwise "compel them to betray their beliefs or bear a burden not born by others" (Jones, 2015, p. 544) can provide such redress. Such exemptions do not imply that the burdens associated with public reason are to be regarded as discriminatory. While legal exemptions are frequently conceptualized in terms of balancing competing claims of discrimination (Vickers, 2015), exemptions designed to redress the burdens of citizenship in a liberal polity are best viewed as acts of toleration grounded in respect for freedom of conscience and the worth inherent in our fellow citizens' capacity for moral and spiritual agency (Jones, 2015). After all, generally applicable laws that meet the formal criteria of public reason are legitimate. Indeed, given the link between public justification and the search for shared terms for social cooperation, there are good reasons to presume that citizens should comply with such laws. Moreover, while the exclusionary character of public reason may constrain the extent to which some citizens can independently endorse particular laws, such citizens may nonetheless be able to accept that, in the absence of reasons grounded in their particular conscientious commitments, the law in question is entirely justified.[12] In this context to grant a legal exemption to citizens for whom – for conscientious reasons – compliance with a given law would be particularly burdensome, is to allow respect for such citizens' beliefs to override the public reasons that justify the law. As Jones (2015) notes, such 'overrides' echo the classical characteristics of toleration – power plus objection – and are therefore best conceived as acts of toleration.

Although it is the state which secures toleration by granting the exemption (Jones, 2015), such acts of toleration are ultimately grounded in the relationship between free and equal citizens committed to the practice of justifying the use of coercive political power to one another. Here it is important to bear in mind the intricate link between the idea of public justification and the political autonomy of citizens in a liberal polity. While as subjects to the law individual citizens in a liberal polity are clearly not free to choose whether or not to tolerate one another, as co-authors of the law citizens have both good reasons to expect others to comply with the law and the power to seek compliance. Yet, in the light of the inevitable limitations and constraints inherent in the search for a common evaluative standard, citizens as a self-governing collective tolerate the conscientious commitments of fellow members of the polity for whom compliance with publicly justified laws would be particularly burdensome. Legal exemptions designed to redress the unequal distribution of the burdens of citizenship are, therefore, not instances of preferential treatment imposed by the state upon a reluctant citizenry, but are themselves publically justified in terms of reasons that citizens can at least in principle endorse. Toleration thus marks a relationship amongst equals who recognize the intrinsic worth inherent in the capacity of their fellow citizens for moral and spiritual agency.[13] While statutory exemptions typically seek to safeguard options that law would otherwise remove, the primary good of toleration thus conceived does not lie in securing freedom from interference, but stems from a commitment to non-domination, grounded in a relationship of mutual respect that sets limits to what we may impose on one another.[14] On this account, the granting of exemptions by the state is best seen as the institutional expression of a settled practice of toleration among free and equal citizens.

Seeking to redress the difficulties associated with the exclusionary character of public reasons by granting citizens legal exceptions may give rise to the worry that such an approach is liable to undermine the notion of citizenship as a shared project in pursuit of public purposes and thus is open to objections akin to those levelled against Vallier's convergence conception of public reason. In his critique of legal exceptions Leiter (2013), for example, argues that exemptions from generally applicable laws pose a threat to the promotion of the "common good" and the search for shared terms for social cooperation. Yet, it is not clear that this is indeed the case. To give fellow citizens "a break" by accommodating their sincerely held conscientious commitments can constitute an acknowledgement that the inevitable burdens associated with pursuing the 'common good' within a liberal polity may at times be particularly heavy for some and as such can be seen as an affirmation of our commitment to recognize one another as free and equal – a commitment central to the very conception of the 'common good' in a liberal polity.

Conceptualized in these terms, toleration assumes a distinctive political role. By offering redress for the difficulties and limitation inherent in the search for a common evaluative standard, toleration affirms the equal standing of citizens and helps to facilitate continued political engagement among citizens in the face of the plurality of conscientious commitments that characterize the modern liberal polity. Here it is important to bear in mind that public reason not only refers to criteria to assess the legitimacy of laws and formal political decisions, but also constitutes a regulative ideal that guides and orients deliberation among free and equal citizens in a liberal polity. Indeed, perfect justificatory neutrality is an idea that in practice is rarely, if ever, fully realized. By redressing the dangers of alienation from the common life of the polity, legal exemptions as acts of political toleration encourage citizens who feel particularly burdened by the demands of citizenship in a liberal polity to continue to participate in the ongoing, yet difficult and often incomplete, search for shared evaluative standards that can guide citizens towards the realization of their common political project.

## 3. Legal Exemptions and the Limits of Toleration

Conceiving of legal exemptions as acts of toleration in the face of the challenges inherent in the search for a common evaluative standard not only highlights the distinctive role of political toleration in a liberal polity, but also helps to shed light on the limits of such acts of toleration. Given the goals, values and characteristics of the conception of political toleration advanced in the previous section, political toleration encompasses only citizens who in principle endorse the idea of public justification; must not give rise to undue burden shifting; and should not undermine the inclusive and egalitarian ethos of a liberal polity.

Just like justificatory neutrality, political toleration in a liberal polity entails substantive normative commitments, which delimit the scope of acts of political toleration. While the liberal state is neutral vis-à-vis the wide array of justice-respecting ways of life that citizens may choose to pursue, political liberalism's political conception of justice is not value neutral, but is grounded in a substantive commitment to the principles of liberty, equality and mutual respect. The liberal commitment to justificatory neutrality, therefore, does not extend to ways of life that are "in direct conflict with the principles of justice" (Rawls, 1993, p. 196). In the same vein, a liberal commitment to political toleration grounded in mutual respect and a commitment to non-domination does not extend to life-styles and doctrines that reject the foundational values that underpin the political conception of justice. For example, racists' desire to actively discriminate against fellow citizens whom they view as not worthy of equal standing and respect, does not provide legitimate grounds for legal exemptions from anti-discrimination legislation. While the legal framework of a liberal polity constrains the capacity of racists to act on their discriminatory views, these constraints are not the product of the inevitable limitations and difficulties inherent in the search for a common evaluative standard by citizens committed to living together on the basis of fair terms of social cooperation. On the contrary, the racist rejects the legitimacy of this political project and the principle of public justification it entails.

Political toleration motivated by a desire to redress the difficulties associated with the exclusionary character of public reason encompasses only broadly reasonable, justice respecting ways of life committed to the search for fair terms of social cooperation. On the basis of the account of toleration developed in the preceding section, questions of political toleration, therefore, only arise in respect of citizens who in principle endorse the idea of public justification, but for whom – for conscientious reasons – compliance with a given law would be particularly burdensome. While a liberal polity may on occasions have good prudential reasons for not prohibiting lifestyles and doctrines that reject the principles of justice, such prudential non-intervention does not exhibit the goals, values and commitments definitive of an act of political toleration. For example, when in the aftermath of the 2005 London bombings, the British government stepped back from its original decision to ban Hizb ut Tahrir, because it feared that diving the organization underground would backfire, this decision was not motivated by a commitment to toleration, but by security considerations. After all, this decision was not informed by a principled commitment to permit the organization in the face of strong objections, but reflected a desire to identify the most effective means of neutralizing the organization by frustrating its goals and objectives.[15]

While on this account the reasonableness of conceptions of the good delimits the scope of political toleration, within this range a liberal polity must also ensure that acts of toleration as legal exemptions do not give rise to undue burden shifting. If legal exemptions do indeed constitute acts of toleration designed to redress the distribution of the burdens of citizenship associated with the exclusionary character of public reason, it will be important to ensure that exemptions do not simply shift particularly onerous burdens from one group of citizens onto another. While some legal exemptions (e.g. the right to be exempt from certain dress codes because of one's religious beliefs) arguably do not impose significant burdens on fellow citizens or society at large, other claims of conscience (e.g. exemptions from mandatory military service) require "people to make a sacrifice or bear a cost or endure an inconvenience for the sake of beliefs they do not share" (Leiter, 2013; Jones, 2015, p. 549). Indeed some exemptions do not impose burdens on the state or the public at large, but place the costs on specific members of civil society, such as employers or the providers of particular goods or services (Jones, 2015). Adjudicating such claims inevitably entails careful and at times quite complex assessments of the costs and burdens on both sides. Given that it is not unreasonable to hold individuals at least partially responsible for the costs associated with their beliefs, such balancing does not imply that burdens should be distributed equally. Legal exemptions are most readily justified in cases where costs for believers are great, but the burdens on those who accommodate are comparatively modest (Jones, 2016).

Since some aspects of individual's conscientious commitments can only be fully expressed and vindicated in association with others, political toleration motivated by a desire to redress the difficulties associated with the exclusionary character of public reason can provide good grounds for legal exemptions, not just for individuals, but also for civil society associations. Provided such associations are grounded in broadly reasonable, justice-respecting conceptions of the good and can credibly claim to represent and cater for their members' interests, claims for legal exemptions by civil society associations will be subject to the same "burden shifting" tests as exemptions designed to cater for the conscientious claims of individuals.

Legal exemptions for civil society associations, however, also raise some more specific concerns. At least some civil society associations do not merely seek to cater for the needs of their members, but also aim to provide a service to the "public at large". For example, many religious organizations are engaged not only in the pursuit of direct religious purposes central to core religious practices, but also perform a wide variety of public welfare functions within wider society, such as education, healthcare provisions, adoption services and care for the elderly. Indeed many of these provisions are not merely "public facing", but are designed to support the state in the provision of public services. Engagement in such public roles raises particular concerns regarding the legitimate limits of acts of toleration conceived as legal exemptions from generally applicable laws. The campaign by the Catholic Church for Catholic Adoption Agencies to be exempt from the requirements under the UK Equality Act (Sexual Orientation) Regulations 2007 to offer adoption services to gay and lesbian couples highlights some of the difficulties in this regard. Access to public services, such as adoption agencies, is typically a marker of membership of the polity and signifies a citizen's status and standing. Indeed, what public services are provided, how and for whom shapes the ethos of civil society and is indicative of the civil identity of a political community. This ethos provides the setting within which citizen collectively shape their shared political project. As in most contemporary liberal societies, the ethos of public service provision in the UK embodies a strong commitment to inclusivity and equality. To have granted Catholic Adoption Agencies an exception from the requirement to provide adoption services for gay and lesbian couples would have undermined this general ethos of public service provision and would have detracted from wider policy objectives regarding non-discrimination and the equal public standing of traditionally marginalized groups in society. These considerations were indeed pivotal to the ruling by the Upper Tribunal against Catholic Care Leeds ([2012] UKUT 395(TCC)). As this example illustrates, while a due regard for citizens freedom of association can provide good grounds for legal exemptions, the need to safeguard the inclusive and egalitarian character of a liberal polity sets firm limits to the legitimate scope for such acts of toleration with regard to civil society organizations engaged in the provision of public services.

## Conclusion

Despite recent scepticism regarding the continued relevance of traditional conceptions of political toleration, acts of toleration conceived as legal exemptions from generally applicable laws continue to play an important role in a modern, value neutral liberal polity. By offering redress for the difficulties associated with the exclusionary character of public reason, toleration helps to affirm the equal standing of citizens and facilitates continued political engagement among citizens in the face of the plurality of conscientious commitments that characterize the modern liberal polity. Conceived in these terms political toleration is not merely compatible with the liberal commitment to justificatory neutrality, but is central to the idea of public reason as a regulative ideal that guides the common life of citizens committed to the idea of citizenship as a shared political project. The normative commitments central to this account of political toleration not only highlight the distinctive contribution of political toleration to the shared political project that defines the modern liberal polity, but also sheds light on the limits of political toleration. Questions of political toleration only arise in respect of citizens who in principle endorse the idea of public justification, but for whom – for conscientious reasons – compliance with a given law would be particularly burdensome. Moreover, acts of political toleration must not give rise to undue burden shifting and must be mindful of the need to protect the civil identity of the political community.

This case for political toleration has been supported throughout by reference to examples of religious conscientious commitments. This, indeed, is not purely coincidental. If questions of political toleration arise because the language of public reason cannot properly account for considerations central to the complex array of morally significant reasons that some justice-respecting citizens bring to a particular matter, religious conscientious commitments are liable to feature prominently in debates regarding political toleration. Not only does the appeal to transcendental authority play a central role in many religious discourses, but religions typically also have long-standing, deep and often complex traditions of thinking about moral concerns that can be difficult to fully capture within the language of public reason. While this does not imply that religion occupies a unique place in a liberal polity, it does suggest that religious conscientious commitments will continue to be central to debates regarding political toleration in a liberal polity.

## Notes

1. This definition of toleration draws on Horton (1996)
2. See for example Gray (1995), Newey (1999), Meckled-Garcia (2003), and Heyd (2008).
3. Political liberals frequently rely on a degree of idealization here (e.g. public reasons are those that citizens conceived as perfectly rational would endorse).
4. This characterization of public reason draws on Vallier (2014).
5. Public reason, thus, acts as an epistemic filter, which guides citizens as to which aspects of their comprehensive moral commitments are appropriate to bring into the political sphere and which are to remain private (Hertzberg, 2019).
6. The recognition that religious discourses can offer important moral insights in part motivates Habermas's call for a cooperative effort at translation.

7. For a discussion of this line of critique of mainstream conceptions of public reason see Vallier (2014).
8. While even ardent secularists can appreciate and learn from Catholic writings on human dignity, these writings are embedded within a wider discursive tradition with a "distinctive understanding of humanity's role in the created order" that is resistant to translation (Areshidze, 2017, p. 732).
9. For Rawls (1993, p. 216) in a democracy political power "is the power of the public that is of free and equal citizens as a collective body". Political autonomy is, thus, intricately linked to the liberal principle of legitimacy, which stipulates that to subject citizens to coercive political power they themselves cannot recognize as rationally acceptable violates the principle of equal respect.
10. For an insightful discussion of why a lack of external validation need not give rise to scepticism per se see Mendus (2000).
11. See Habermas (2008).
12. For example even Sikhs, who wish to be exempt from legislation that makes it compulsory to wear a crash helmet when riding a motorbike, can recognize that in the absence of the reasons grounded in their own religious convictions, the general law is all things considered justified. (Jones, 2015).
13. While outside the scope of this chapter, this conception of toleration also offers a response to what Balint (2017) terms the despotism challenge, which links the practice of toleration to unequal power relations.
14. For the importance of toleration as an aspect of freedom of as non-domination see Ceva (2020). Conceiving of the good of toleration in these terms, poses a challenge to conceptions such as Balint's (2017), which locates the primary good of toleration in securing freedom from interference so that citizens can lead their lives as they see fit.
15. This example draws on Balint's (2017) discussion of this case. In contrast to the argument developed here, Balint seeks to defend a purely descriptive account of toleration and therefore argues that regardless of the motivations, this case should still be classed as an instance of toleration.

# References

Areshidze, G. (2017). Taking Religion Seriously? Habermas on Religious Translation and Cooperative Learning in Post-Secular Society. *American Political Science Review*, 111(4), pp. 724–737.

Balint, P. (2017). *Respecting Toleration Traditional Liberalism and Contemporary Diversity*. Oxford: Oxford University Press.

Ceva, E. (2020). The Good of Toleration: Changing Social Relations or Maximising Individual Freedom. *Critical Review of International Social and Political Philosophy*, 23(2), pp. 197–202.

Gaus, G. and Vallier, K. (2009). The Roles of Religious Convictions in a Publicly Justified Polity: The Implications of Convergence, Asymmetry, and Political Institutions. *Philosophy & Social Criticism*, 35(1), pp. 51–76.

Gray, J. (1995). *Enlightenments Wake*. London: Routledge.

Habermas, J. (2008). *Between Naturalism and Religion*. Trans. C. Cronin. Cambridge: Polity Press.

Habermas, J. (2011). 'The Political' The Rational Meaning of a Questionable Inheritance of Political Theology. In: J. Mendieta and J. Van Antwerpen, eds.,

*The Power of Religion in the Public Sphere*. New York: Columbia University Press, pp. 15–33.

Hartley, C. (2016). Book Review of Vallier, Kevin. *Liberal Politics and Public Faith: Beyond Separation*. Ethics, 127(1), pp. 315–319.

Hertzberg, B. R. (2019). *Chains of Persuasion: A Framework for Religion in Democracy*. Oxford: Oxford University Press.

Heyd, D. (2008). Is Toleration a Political Virtue? In: M. S. Williams and J. Waldron, eds., *Toleration and Its Limits*. NOMOS 48. New York: New York University Press, pp. 171–194.

Horton, J (1996). Toleration as a Virtue. In: D. Heyd, ed., *Toleration: An Elusive Virtue*. Princeton, NJ: Princeton University Press, pp. 28–43.

Jones, P. (2015). Toleration, Religion and Accommodation. *European Journal of Philosophy*, 23(3), pp. 542–563.

Jones, P. (2016). Accommodating Religion and Shifting Burdens. *Criminal Law and Philosophy*, 10(3), pp. 516–536.

Laborde, C. (2017). *Liberalism's Religion*. Cambridge, MA: The Belknap Press of Harvard University Press.

Leiter, B. (2013). *Why Tolerate Religion?* Princeton, NJ: Princeton University Press.

March, A. (2013). Rethinking Religious Reasons in Public Justification. *American Political Science Review*, 107(3), pp. 523–539.

Meckled-Garcia, S. (2003). Toleration and Neutrality: Incompatible Ideals? In: D. Castiglione and C. McKinnon, eds., *Toleration, Neutrality and Democracy*. Dordrecht: Kluwer Academic Publishers.

Mendus, S. (2000). Pluralism and Scepticism in a Disenchanted World. In: M. Baghramian and A. Ingram, eds., *Pluralism: The Philosophy and Politics of Diversity*. London: Routledge.

Newey, G. (1999). *Virtue, Reason and Toleration*. Edinburgh: Edinburgh University Press.

Rawls, J. (1993). *Political Liberalism*. New York: Columbia University Press.

Rawls, J. (1997). The Idea of Public Reason Revisited. *University of Chicago Law Review*, 64, Summer, pp. 765–807.

Vallier, K. (2014). *Liberal Politics and Public Faith Beyond Separation*. New York and London: Routledge.

Vallier, K. (2016). In Defence of Intelligible Reasons in Public Justification. *The Philosophical Quarterly*, 66(264), pp. 596–616.

Vickers, L. (2015). Religion in the Workplace. *The Equal Rights Review*, 14, pp. 106–118.

Waldron, J. (2007). Public Reason and 'Justification' in the Courtroom. *Journal of Law, Philosophy and Culture*, 1(1), pp. 107–134.

Waldron, J. (2015). Isolating Public Reasons. In: T. Brooks and M. C. Nussbaum, eds., *Rawls's Political Liberalism*. New York: Columbia University Press, pp. 113–137.

Watson, L. and Hartley, C. (2018). *Equal Citizenship and Public Reason: A Feminist Political Liberalism*. Oxford: Oxford University Press.

# 8 Modus Vivendi Beyond Toleration

*Roberta Sala*

## Introduction

This chapter will focus on the relationship between toleration and modus vivendi. The overall aim is to defend an idea of modus vivendi as a strategy for the political inclusion of people who are not tolerant, without betraying the fundamentals of liberal democracies. To do that, (1) some introductory notes about modus vivendi and toleration are required in light of Rawlsian criticism and of the following debate. After spelling out the essential meanings of both notions, (2) it will be shown how they go in parallel when they are both adopted in the political frame: a) modus vivendi can be the name for negative toleration as mere non-interference; b) modus vivendi can be the name for toleration as forbearance, hence it presupposes a negative even intolerant attitude towards the "tolerated"; c) modus vivendi can entail a positive idea of toleration as a moderate recognition; that is, modus vivendi can be here a strategy for non-tolerant people to be included into citizenry albeit under certain conditions. The expression "non-tolerant people" resonates the one used to indicate "unreasonable people", whom Rawls refers to in *Political Liberalism*: those who do not fall within the area of the overlapping consensus. As "unreasonable people" should be renamed as "non-reasonable people" for some reasons that will be displayed later, "intolerant people" should be renamed as "non-tolerant" people as well. Such different formulations are claimed to correspond to differentiated forms of political engagement within liberal democracy, more or less tolerant. (3) According to c), modus vivendi is thus propounded as a way for "non-tolerant people" to take active part into liberal democracy; despite the fact that they do not subscribe to the moral value of toleration, they may be counted as citizens, although under certain conditions. It entails that they may be compliant to institutions: they comply with the equal terms of cooperation demanded by a liberal democracy although they do not subscribe to them wholeheartedly. Such "non-tolerant people" still hold intolerant doctrines without exhibiting intolerant conduct. There is no paradox in this: their experiences of participating in shared social and political practices provide sources of motivation for "non-tolerant people" to support liberal institutions. (4) To conclude: modus vivendi proves to be a realistic way for "non-tolerant people" to join society. By integrating a practical perspective of social actors into the reasons to adhere to liberal institutions, modus vivendi turns to be a fruitful development of a liberal theorizing on realist grounds.

## 1. Modus Vivendi and Toleration: Meanings and Functions

### 1.1 Rawlsian Modus Vivendi and Toleration

Modus vivendi is an ambivalent notion: on the one hand, it suggests a negative approach to disagreement or even conflict, following the Hobbesian idea of modus vivendi, in which people agree not to make war one another. On the other hand, modus vivendi may be construed as a way to cope with disagreement or even conflict in a peaceful way. According to the former meaning, modus vivendi is not valuable or desirable in itself. Instead, it is understandable as only an extremely unstable equilibrium in which people try to find a way to coexist since better alternatives are unavailable. "Trying to balance" does not sound as the preferable style of life, as people would happen to live at the mercy – if it exists – of a Leviathan. Instead, according to the latter meaning of modus vivendi, the same balance may be labelled as a realistic solution for different people to find a way to cohabit in a non-belligerent way. If in the first sense a modus vivendi is a sort of truce, in the second one modus vivendi can be almost appreciated as a sort of peace: the result is probably the same but it is backed by different reasons and motivations. The suggestion, here, is that people seem to look for a sort of agreement in spite of their fundamental disagreement: they can agree on not interfering with respective ends at least to a certain extend. In the end, it seems that modus vivendi may be conceived of as an equivocal notion: it may resemble a war without bloodshed, and, by contrast, it may resemble a peace albeit armed. Be modus vivendi a bloodless war or an armed peace, it is a highly disputable arrangement for people to live in.

In contemporary political theory the term "modus vivendi" has been resumed by John Rawls, although he mentioned of it rarely and hastily. Indeed, Rawls has spoken about modus vivendi with the purpose of rejecting it, in order to defend his idea of an overlapping consensus (Rawls, 2005). Modus vivendi has been recalled by Rawls with the aim of explaining what it is not (Neal, 1990). In fact, to Rawls modus vivendi should be rebutted as unstable and somehow immoral. In opposition to Rawls, some views about modus vivendi focus on various reasons other than the ones that Rawls refers to modus vivendi. Indeed, Rawls rejects modus vivendi as backed by "wrong reasons", essentially immoral reasons.

In details, to Rawls modus vivendi appears as a precarious equilibrium depending on "circumstances remaining such as not to upset the fortunate convergence of interests" (Rawls, 2005, p. 147).[1] Modus vivendi is understood as a 'mere' Hobbesian equilibrium: it is deemed negatively because of its provisionality, given that people are likely to join a modus vivendi for 'unstable' reasons, with the tendency to change them according to contingent interests or opportunities. Here no "right reasons" lead people to seek peace, only wrong ones; those reasons are just prudential, not moral. With a slogan, it may be said that to Rawls modus vivendi represents a truce, but truce – again – is not peace. Such a modus vivendi condemns society to instability anyway: by contrast a fair society – as the Rawlsian one – cannot be stable for wrong reasons, namely, opportunity or fear. Its stability should be guaranteed by a generalized endorsement of values such as freedom, toleration and equal respect, which can be shared in spite of more-or-less deep moral disagreement. This is the goal of the so-called overlapping consensus: it is because people can share moral political values in spite of their moral substantive disagreement that a liberal democracy may obtain and persist over time. Rawls means that no society can be called fair if it is not "rightly" stable; no stability can be "rightly" reached if people are not willing to share moral political values, and do it autonomously. Having established such a negative interpretation of modus vivendi as a "mere" unstable equilibrium, Rawls seems to concede that another kind of modus vivendi can be conceived of, the one in which people who are initially unwilling to share such values, may turn to be willing to do it. Hoping so, Rawls shows to admit two instantiations of modus vivendi: precisely the Hobbesian one, and a second one that may be called a transitional modus vivendi, developing over time into an overlapping consensus.[2] With the first instantiation of modus vivendi Rawls thinks of the way of living within a society of the so-called "unreasonable", the ones who do not share the moral political values of a liberal democracy and that remain within it for "wrong reasons", the "immoral" reasons of prudence, fear and self-interest.[3] Modus vivendi is itself "immoral" hence unstable, because there are no moral values upon which it can rest. Its relying on people's self-interests, reasons of opportunity and fear, shows that there are no moral reasons as needed to attain a "just" cohabitation. Here modus vivendi is inevitably unstable as people make no mutual promise and, even if they do, they are not willing to keep any promise at all. People are not available to share costs, for instance, of a cooperation; they are ready to break any alliance if it turns to benefit themselves.[4] Such people are deemed as unreasonable or even irrational; they are the ones whom Rawls is worried about, as they represent to him a threat to social and political unity. He fears that, should they gain enough power, they would interfere and impose their views on others. Thus, a sort of toleration as forbearance should be adopted towards them as long as they do not menace the social order, and when they threaten to do so, coercion should be adopted to restrict their freedom (Forst, 2017). In such cases, says Rawls, "the problem is to contain them so that they do not undermine the unity and justice of society" (Rawls, 2005, pp. xvi–xvii). Liberal institutions have "the practical task of containing them – like war and disease – so that they do not overturn political justice" (Rawls, 2005, p. 64, n. 19). Incidentally, toleration appears here in correspondence to modus vivendi in its negative meaning: toleration is negative itself, here, and it appears as mere toleration, entailing forbearance and control.

The second instantiation of modus vivendi is more promising than the first one. As anticipated, it is a sort of transitional modus vivendi: having experienced the benefit from living according to the essentials of a fair society – freedom, toleration, equal respect, and so forth – even "unreasonable" people may become able to comply with liberal institutions freely and convincingly (Rawls, 2005, pp. 158–164). However, Rawls concludes this argument by saying that there is no guarantee for such an occurrence. Although it is unlikely that in a fair society such views would be strong enough to undermine it, there is no assurance; "that is the hope; there can be no guarantee" (Rawls, 2005, p. 172).

To summarize: Rawls depicts modus vivendi negatively, as the way for "unreasonable" people to inhabit a fair society. Those people can be unreasonable in different ways: they can be "moderately" unreasonable as they are available to become "full citizens" over time, transforming themselves into "reasonable" people, ready to uphold institutions from which they are benefiting. But those people can be "insuperably" unreasonable, irrational and disrespectful, totally unwilling to join society fairly, but ready to overturn institutions should they become powerful enough. Toward them, only negative toleration, control or even coercion should be granted for the sake of society.

## 1.2 Rescuing Modus Vivendi From Rawls Idealism

Having recapitulated the Rawlsian view of modus vivendi, several critics have deemed it as too narrow and pessimistic. The same critics have deemed the entire Rawlsian political theory as too unrealistic and even moralistic, since his account of liberal society does rest on unrealistic and moralistic consensus.[5] It is unlikely that people are realistically motivated to cooperate backed by same moral values or gaining a moral consensus on them *via* an overlapping of their respective moral positions. In criticizing liberal moralism as envisaged by Rawls and others[6] for ignoring actual practices of politics, they offer a defence of modus vivendi as a reminder of the gap between abstract theorizing and real political life. On the side of realism, modus vivendi can win over liberal moralism: the idea is that, notwithstanding Rawls, modus vivendi can be a normative not moralistic framework although it relies on moral reasons (McCabe, 2019). Modus vivendi is thus revaluated as a realistic way to politics. Modus vivendi plays here a vital role in maintaining conditions of peaceful coexistence among people who disagree strongly over ultimate values, practices, conceptions of justice, and so on. Such coexistence is indeed the primary goal of politics, away the moral criteria by which political regimes should be evaluated. Following Horton, modus vivendi is no longer only a Latin word to signal a free play of brute political power, as presumed by Rawls (Horton, 2007). It is neither a form of immoralism nor a licence for injustice. And, last but not least, it is not an instrument of tolerating any political regime, as long as they bring peace and security. Positively, modus vivendi may represent a chance for different people to settle a fair or a quasi-fair society in spite of their excluding ends. Moreover it can offer a chance of inclusion into the citizenry of people who deeply disagree on those moral political values on which political stability as idealized by Rawls should be reached and preserved.

Among the realist defenders of modus vivendi, John Gray deserves a special mention. Generally speaking, Gray is an intransigent critic of Rawlsian liberalism as nothing but a moral theory applied naïvely to politics, since politics seems 'forced' to embody moral principles such as toleration (here interpreted as a moral virtue). Such principles should act as a common moral ground upon which conflicts could be managed and finally overcome. Gray rejects a similar idea of liberalism and, about toleration, writes: "from the one side, toleration is the pursuit of an ideal form of life. From the other, it is the search for terms of peace among different ways of life" (Gray, 2000, p. 2).

The latter meaning of toleration – toleration as a search for peaceful cohabitation – is related to modus vivendi: "*modus vivendi* expresses the belief that there are many forms of life in which humans can thrive. . . . Where such ways of life are rivals, there is no one of them that is best" (Gray, 2000, p. 5). To Gray modus vivendi is not a form of political accommodation ordered to eliminate conflicts of value but, quite the contrary, it represents an accommodation of conflict as a matter of fact. In the background there is a pluralist theory of values: a value-pluralism is not merely a view that there is a diversity of ends that cannot all be realized simultaneously, but also that some of these ends cannot be compared or ranked. Since they are all valuable, and none of them is superior to the other, there is no compelling reason why people should pursue one rather than another. Such a pluralism is not an impediment of coexistence.

Gray inspired a notable group of critics: John Horton is perhaps one of the most notorious. Horton's idea of modus vivendi is somehow lighter than the one upheld by Gray. According to Horton, modus vivendi is a sort of device meant to assure a cohabitation, no matter whether it is backed by a theory of value-pluralism or not (Horton, 2007; see also Horton,

2010, 2011, 2019). Modus vivendi is a political arrangement conceived of as the practical outcome of processes of negotiation, bargaining and compromise prompted by conflict and disagreement as permanent features of a society. It could also be called a "pragmatic" approach to a political settlement. Spelt out in this way, modus vivendi may appear as an *anything goes* politics, that is, whatever political arrangement that can be appreciated for its ability to attain peace and security.[7] But it is not: to Horton modus vivendi is not an *anything goes* politics at all. What he declares is that that peace and security are not super-goods: in certain circumstances, people may decide to bracket peace and security if what they perceive to be their fundamental aims should conflict with them. Said that, peace and security are to be appreciated as *at least* instrumental values as they are a precondition for the achievement of almost any other goods. In being such a precondition peace and security are values for all. This point is central: it would be wrong to understand modus vivendi as lacking any moral dimension for those involved in it (Horton, 2007, p. 53). Such a belief is a prejudice due to the prejudicial idea that any moral commitment should be based on a "thick" moral consensus such as the Rawlsian overlapping consensus. On the opposite, it is reasonable to regard ourselves and others as having a moral commitment in circumstances in which no moral substantive content be shared. People may feel obliged (in a moral sense not only on a legal one) to do something politically although they do not share moral contents (Raz, 1985).

To conclude: such a reappraisal of modus vivendi makes one with a revival of political realism in a normative frame. Being realist entails taking reality seriously, not resigning to matters of facts when such a resignation should delete personal interests and neglect moral values. The challenge here is to conceive of modus vivendi as a way to coexist backed by a variety of reasons, moral and non-moral, as the last part of the chapter will attempt to do.

### 1.3 What About Toleration?

The foregoing section focused on the notion of modus vivendi. The word "toleration" occurred somewhere, with regard to the traditional idea of Hobbesian modus vivendi, in a negative sense. As already observed, a "mere" modus vivendi is the one in which reasonable and "unreasonable" people – to cite Rawls – find an equilibrium to coexist. "Unreasonable" people should be granted a kind of negative toleration as the necessary means of controlling their behaviour as they may represent a menace for the "right" stability, as grounded in liberal values such as toleration.

Traditionally, toleration is the principle that allows for the peaceful coexistence of individuals and groups who hold different views of life within the same society.[8] The problem of toleration arises in front of diversity – beliefs, actions or practices – which are disliked or even disapproved.[9] Dislike or disapproval create the "objection" condition without which one does not speak of toleration but of indifference. Said that way, tolerating seems to be in some way wrong, as toleration seems in fact to imply a negative judgement about what one decides to tolerate. In fact, one says to tolerate something or somebody not absolutely but at certain conditions; toleration refers to the conditional acceptance of something or somebody backed by a decision not to interfere with beliefs, actions or practices that one considers to be wrong but still "tolerable", so that they should not be prohibited or constrained. The adjective "conditional" qualifies the acceptance entailed by toleration. The context will decide how to balance the "objection component" and the "acceptance component" of toleration: the latter does not remove the negative judgement but offers positive reasons that trump the negative ones (Forst, 2017; see also Heyd, 1996, p. 11). In this way, the limits of toleration lie at the point where reasons for rejection become stronger than reasons for acceptance. It is salient here to underline how reasons for objection are not necessarily reasons for rejection, insofar as the "harm principle" is not infringed. The "harm principle" works exactly as the limit to toleration. The overall idea is that the differences regarded as issues of toleration are disagreeable but not totally wrong; they are objectionable but non-condemnable – in which case they would be not tolerable at all (Galeotti, 2006, pp. 565–566). This question is known as the "paradox of toleration" because to tolerate what one maintains as wrong or evil appears to imply renouncing one's own moral integrity (Raphael, 1988, p. 139). The paradox seems to be surmountable by recognizing the right of others to be granted respect. Respect works as the moral reason for toleration.

The paradox of toleration helps clarify both aspects of toleration: negative and positive. Negative toleration equates non-interference: it entails the decision not to interfere with differences that are disliked or disapproved. Positive toleration appears when positive reasons to tolerate have been provided. Among such reasons the principle of equal respect plays a central role. It is by virtue of it that one may decide not to interfere with the decisions of others although they are disputable if not completely wrong, or harmful. Toleration itself is a moral virtue insofar as one makes an effort to set aside one's own convictions in favour of the higher principle of respect. To put it differently: the two components of toleration – objection and acceptance, as corresponding to the negative and positive motivations to be tolerant – reveal the twofold aspect of toleration: toleration as mere non-interference, generally backed by prudential and pragmatic reasons; and toleration as implying a positive attitude toward the "tolerated", something like an acceptance of them – partial rather than full – in spite of the fact that such people are holders of traits or differences that the "tolerators" dislike or disapprove. In this case one tolerates others on the basis of positive (generally moral) reasons, first of all by the principle of respect.

In light of this brief overview of the notion of toleration, the next step consists in trying to make a parallel between toleration and modus vivendi. Many similarities catch the eye, as, for instance, the ambiguous meanings of both, negative and positive at the same time. But upon a careful perusal, modus vivendi could guarantee a better treatment of the ones who are involved in it. Indeed, in a revised modus vivendi – alternative to the "scrawny" one according to Rawls – people are not just "tolerated" in a negative sense or even with resentment; they are rather possible candidate for a partial inclusion into society or an inclusion at certain conditions. Inclusion involves much more than a "passive" coexistence; it involves the possibility to take part into political life actively, as it will be detailed shortly.

## 2. Modus Vivendi Beyond Toleration: A Way to Inclusion of the "Non-tolerant" People

### 2.1 Modus Vivendi and Toleration

So far, the notions of modus vivendi and toleration respectively have been briefly unpacked. We started by recalling the negative idea of modus vivendi rejected by Rawls, as that unstable equilibrium among parts contending public space. Rawls insists that such an equilibrium cannot be counted as stability for the "right reasons"; in fact, it is not stability at all but, again, a sort of adherence to institutions for prudential, not moral reasons. Modus vivendi is thus the only chance for the "unreasonable" (in Rawls's terms) to support institutions, as they may not sustain the political conception of justice – as the terrain underlying any fair society – as a moral political conception because they reject its fundamentals. Towards them a sort of toleration as forbearance should be adopted as long as they do not menace the social order, and when they threaten to do so, coercion should be adopted to restrict their freedom. Indeed, modus vivendi and toleration are strictly intertwined in Rawls's understanding of a plural society in which "unreasonable" people do exist as a matter of fact. *Tolerating the unreasonable* turns to be a sort of political necessity as dictated by their adhering to institutions through a modus vivendi. Again, toleration does not look like a virtue in such a context; rather it seems to be a strategy or a simple devise, pragmatically adopted for prudential reasons with the purpose to contain possible risks of instability.

After Rawls, various efforts of revitalizing modus vivendi have been made in the wake of the realist turn in normative political theory. Gray and Horton's thoughts – synthesized in the previous section – are excellent examples of such a turn. Both these authors put modus vivendi in relation to toleration. If Gray understands modus vivendi as expression of toleration interpreted as an accommodation of conflict as a matter of fact, Horton refers modus vivendi to a "traditional conception of toleration", to use his words. That is, modus vivendi is understandable as both the political order that its citizens can live with, given their differences and disagreements, and the search for that order itself. With a slogan, modus vivendi is here both a process and the result of it, encouraged by a variety of reasons, be they moral and non-moral. This point is quite important, and it needs to be explained better.

Interestingly, Horton propounds a revival also of traditional toleration by enlarging its meanings and functions (Horton, 2011).[10] On his view, toleration can be presented first as part of a politics of modus vivendi, to which negotiation and bargaining are as integral as forms of moral reasoning, and in which toleration itself has an important place as a viable form of accommodation between groups. Such groups may have their own reasons for favouring toleration, rather than coercion or repression, although others may not. Notwithstanding their differences, such groups may share enough to find a common ground on which to base the case for toleration, such as a desire for peace, security and prosperity. In brief, to Horton's mind modus vivendi and toleration are related insofar as toleration (traditionally conceived as primarily non-interference) is part of a politics of modus vivendi: the traditional conception of toleration offers the important form of a viable political settlement that a modus vivendi may take, without expecting that such a settlement will last over time. Modus vivendi is real politics; it may be stable for a long time and suddenly change. It relies on a complex interweaving of interests, ideals, prudence and morality: not only a set of reasons, in fact, but different kinds of reasons are suggesting modus vivendi. Modus vivendi aims to exploit whatever moral, pragmatic, intellectual and other resources are available in any particular set of circumstances to produce a political accommodation.

Having recalled the ideas of modus vivendi – and the correspondent notions of toleration – as propounded by Rawls and critics, the remainder of this chapter will focus on a different idea of modus vivendi and correspondently of toleration, ordered to arrange differently disagreement and conflicts as affecting present societies. To do that, some clarifications are needed about the adjective "unreasonable" targeting a specific group of people (in Rawlsian sense) with the aim to substitute "non-tolerant" for it. It is not just a play on words: instead, it is the attempt to cast a new light on such people in spite of their differences when they were cause of concern, hoping that they could be included into a society albeit at certain conditions, first of all at the condition of a loyal – partial if not full – compliance with institutions.

### 2.2 Modus Vivendi as a Form of Inclusion

In this section an alternative take of modus vivendi – a stable one – will be propounded. To use here again the Rawlsian word "unreasonable", modus vivendi can be "tolerable" (and, *pace* Rawls, truly reasonable) when it represents both the process through which "unreasonable" people turn to be part of a fair society and the result of such a process, when such "unreasonable" people have become "reasonable" hence they come to take part in that society itself. But this is not enough: notwithstanding Rawls, modus vivendi may be defended positively as a way of inclusion into citizenry of people who are and do remain somehow "unreasonable" (again to use Rawls's term). The argument will develop as follows: first, a revision of the Rawlsian idea of modus vivendi will be detailed, with regard to "non-tolerant" people (echoing the "unreasonable" ones). Second, a revision of toleration will be defended by including affirmative elements such as positive acceptance and respect, even a form of recognition. Such elements can be classified into two sets: the first regards institutions as inclusive of non-tolerant people, at least partially; the second regards such people and their motives to ask for a conditional inclusion into citizenry.

Let us recall how a "mere" modus vivendi has been thought of as the way for "unreasonable people" to be counted in a fair society. *Pace* Rawls, those people whom he is speaking of as 'unreasonable' are not necessarily unreasonable in his own terms; that is, they are not necessarily irrational or even crazy for not believing in the fundamentals of such society.[11] If being unreasonable implies not being properly motivated to support institutions, that is, not being able to share the political values of a liberal democracy (freedom, toleration, equal respect, etc.), it does not necessarily mean being a menace to society. To put it differently: although "unreasonable people" are unlikely to become "reasonable" in the Rawlsian sense – as they will not endorse necessarily the values that form the overlapping consensus – they can be ready to support liberal institutions, albeit for reasons that are not the "right ones", as Rawls would put it. Those persons may support the liberal-democratic order for their own reasons, which fall outside the domain of public reason.

By way of drawing a parallel with what has been discussed, unreasonableness may be now rephrased as intolerance, rather, as non-tolerance. The matter now is double-faced: what being non-tolerant does mean and how to deal with non-tolerant people as those who do not share the fundamentals of liberal society while not representing a menace to the stability of it. Stability does not seem to be threatened by the mere fact that shared institutions are supported also by people who are somehow unable to find any "continuity" between their beliefs and the liberal values, but who are nonetheless ready to engage in cooperation with the others. Of course, non-tolerance has to be spelt out better: it does not entail the will to coerce others by imposing on them alternative beliefs; indeed, the expression "non-tolerant people" indicates the ones who are professing intolerant views but who are sincerely able to join society in a tolerant way, that is, without interfering with others' freedom. As remarked before, renaming intolerance as non-tolerance is not just a trick: on the contrary, it would disclose the sincere attempt to distinguish beliefs and behaviour, ideas and actions, not to celebrate an odd incoherence of those who think in one way and act in the other, but to consider realistically human beings and their multiple belongings, as it happens to those true-believers who see themselves as members of a church and loyal citizens as well (Horton, 2000, p. 17). Indeed, even non-tolerant persons – those who do not share the moral reason for toleration (the principle of respect for autonomy first) but able to behave in a tolerant way – may recognize liberal-democratic society as the place to pursue their ends without being interfered with by others and without interfering with them. An example of non-tolerant people is a cultural community within a liberal state, being such culture quite distant from the liberal one. Members of a cultural community are likely to conform their lives to cultural habits and traditions, sometimes tacitly and unconsciously. But nothing prevents them from feeling a parallel sense of belonging to citizenry: they live with fellow-citizens in a peaceful way, and do that for *their* reasons, no matter if moral or non-moral, cultural or prudential or whatever else, surely not the same reasons grounding a liberal democracy, recognized earlier as the moral political values on which the members of a fair society do agree. Again, non-tolerant people's reasons are unlikely to be the "right" ones, to use again the Rawlsian terms, as the respect for autonomy: in fact, that respect is a moral reason that often they are not granted at all. Thus, going back to the way of cohabitation among tolerant and non-tolerant people, it may be remarked that, despite their non-tolerant beliefs, non-tolerant people may behave cooperatively on the basis of motivations which, albeit non-tolerant, are "compatible" with living under liberal institutions. Their participation in a liberal-democratic society may assume the form of a special and stable modus vivendi. A stable modus vivendi is here again the way in which non-tolerant people may permanently inhabit a liberal society, their political conduct being inspired by reasons that do not subscribe to liberal morality and shared liberal values as embodied in such society. Non-tolerant people comply with liberal-democratic institutions neither reluctantly nor as a mere form of negative toleration; they are ready to abide by the terms of cooperation for their own reasons – cultural, religious, moral or non-moral reasons or, even, simple motives that perhaps they are not totally aware of. That is, they comply with liberal-democratic institutions although they do not share the moral values in which such institutions are grounded.[12]

To sum up: modus vivendi is a way to coexist peacefully in spite of even deep disagreement, as forms of cultural gap among people, or as a distance among liberal and illiberal ones. On the one side, those people are non-tolerant as they nurture intolerant beliefs (as distant from classic liberal values such as toleration as moral virtue based on respect). But these people may behave tolerantly, that is, in a non-intolerant way: they show the capacity to join society backed by a variety of reasons, not necessarily immoral. On the other side, that is, on the side of institutions, modus vivendi is the way to include those people on the ground of a special toleration as recognition (Galeotti, 2002). That is a positive toleration as attitude to accept individuals not in spite of their beliefs but as *their* beliefs-holders, no matter what those beliefs are, with the only restraint that they never transform themselves in reasons for intolerant actions, maybe harmful, oppressive or violent. Of course, this kind of a stable modus vivendi is not backed by scepticism towards the notion that a wholehearted enforcement of institutions should be based on moral reasons. It is rather urgent to recognize realistically that a moral consensus is too idealistic to be reached by all people in a plural society, inhabited not only by tolerant, but also by non-tolerant persons. Similarly, modus vivendi is valuable insofar as people choose it as a way to stay "within" society differently, without holding that living peacefully with others in a stable way is attainable only through sharing liberal values, and eventually renouncing one's own values and morals.

There is something more to add. Until now modus vivendi has been sustained *via* the reasons that may support it.[13] As has often been said before, modus vivendi is generally valuable for being a precondition – as any peaceful arrangement is – of the pursuit of one's idea of good. After that, it may valuably express a shared commitment to social order. Social order in turn represents the "good" that people are pursuing when they reach a modus vivendi. Social order represents both a good for some people – tolerant people have moral reasons to comply with a political settlement, for example, interpreting social order as peace – and a shared goal as embodied in the social rules for all, be they tolerant and non-tolerant. It is possible to refer to a sharing of social rules that people are accustomed to follow: those rules are such as to enable people to apply them to one another, in virtue of their being socially recognized (Vallier, 2015, p. 213). When these rules are socially recognized, they become the object of general compliance. To be compliant with social rules does not imply endorsing them; it entails only the readiness to follow them. People are generally inclined to do that, given that generalized adherence to these rules allows the cultivation of a set of mutual stable expectations, becoming a sort of reciprocal guarantee of stability and order. These rules function as a precondition for social order: the latter requires such rules if societies are to exist stably and if any individual is to be able to pursue his own "good" with any hope of success (Sala, 2019, p. 75).

Returning to non-tolerant people: they pursue social order because they need a stable framework in which to fulfil their personal self-realization. Non-tolerant people agree to rules without agreeing with them; in other words, they are ready to comply with rules without being obliged to share the values embodied by rules. Agreement among reasonable and non-reasonable people is thus achieved as they agree that people may coexist peacefully in spite of deep disagreement. In light of this, modus vivendi is found again as the process and the outcome of it. People who deeply disagree share it as a way towards self-realization or even towards the realization of a possible shared aim. Conceived so, modus vivendi is a way in so far as it is a process of a mutual accommodation of different claims. But it is also the aim of the process itself, that is, a dynamic political settlement pursuing peaceful cohabitation among people at odds with each other.

## Conclusion

This chapter aimed at perusing possible relationships between toleration and modus vivendi. It tried to do it by starting with a recall of the Rawlsian idea of modus vivendi and of the following critical debate. Indeed, such a recall has been motivated by the large echo that Rawlsian modus vivendi obtained, as a wrong way to cohabit in a public space. Modus vivendi has been stigmatized as the form of stability pursued for the "wrong" reasons, as Rawls says, the ones dictated by opportunity, self-interest, fear. In the end, such a stability turns into an unstable and risky settlement far from being liberal and democratic. Against Rawls, some authors belonging to the multifaceted family of realists, such as Gray and Horton, defended modus vivendi as a realistic way to live together. Interestingly, all the authors show how modus vivendi is intertwined with toleration, albeit in a variety of meanings. Some room has been left to disentangle their reciprocal interweaving. Then, a new understanding of modus vivendi has been approached, *via* a revision of the aforementioned notion of Rawlsian modus vivendi with the integration of a positive notion of toleration. Modus vivendi finds finally a defence as an arrangement implying toleration as recognition, on the side of institutions, and requiring a compliance to them on the side of non-tolerant people, on the ground of their own reasons and beliefs. What has been said throughout the chapter should be compatible with a realist approach to politics: indeed, pluralism as a fact of contemporary society has to be taken seriously, that is, with regard to actual differences, not just the ones somehow compatible with the morals of liberalism, whatever meaning such morals have assumed over time.[14]

## Notes

1. In Larmore's terms, modus vivendi is "hostage to the shifting distribution of power . . . individuals will lose their reason to uphold the agreement if their relative power or bargaining strength increases significantly" (Larmore, 1990, p. 346).
2. For a deepening about this point: Sala, 2013.
3. Reasonableness and unreasonableness are central notion in Political Liberalism (Rawls, 2005). In a nutshell, reasonableness has two aspects – the willingness to propose and honour fair terms of cooperation and the

willingness to recognize the burdens of judgement and the consequent fact of pluralism. Reasonable citizens accept the pluralism of reasonable comprehensive doctrines as a normal product of free reasoning and hence would never repress views different from their own. Unreasonableness means the opposite, and unreasonable people are the ones who do not satisfy both aspects of reasonableness. Unreasonable people may be can be equated with denying a liberal conception of justice.

4. Of course, the so-called wrong reasons – prudence, fear, opportunity and self-interest – should be much more detailed; Rawls is dismissing them as wrong or even immoral, as they are far from mirroring the political values on which an overlapping consensus can be reached.
5. Realism or even neo-realism as the trend of criticism against the Rawlsian account of political liberalism contains many positions. A common trait is the accusation of idealism or utopianism launched toward political liberalism, notwithstanding Rawls's intention to offer a realist account of a pluralist society in opposition of the 'monistic' one as drawn in *A Theory of Justice* (Rawls, 2005, p. xvii). See among others: Gray, 2000; Galston, 2010; Geuss, 2002; Horton, 2010; Newey, 2010; Sleat, 2011; Rossi, 2012; Rossi and Sleat, 2014.
6. For example, Larmore, 1990; Dworkin, 1996.
7. About this point: McCabe, 2010; Wendt, 2016. Modus vivendi arrangements have to satisfy certain moral criteria. Some institutions will not qualify as modus vivendi arrangements because they are too unfair or because they involve a violation of basic moral rights of some persons.
8. Literature on toleration is huge. Here some suggestions to approach the topic: Horton and Mendus, 1985; Mendus and Edwards, 1987; Mendus, 1988, 1989; Horton and Nicholson, 1992; Heyd, 1996; Walzer, 1997; Newey, 1999; Horton and Mendus, 1999; Galeotti, 2002; Forst, 2008, 2013; Balint, 2016.
9. For the following notes about toleration: Sala, 2010.
10. Horton defends the traditional idea of toleration against the so-called proponents of a 'new toleration': they call for a move beyond the traditional concept of toleration as 'reluctant acceptance' or mere forbearance to a form of toleration which is more welcoming and accepting. See, among others: Oberdiek, 2001; Galeotti, 2002. About the relationship between modus vivendi and toleration, see also Horton, 2019b.
11. For a deeper criticism to the Rawlsian idea of unreasonableness, see Sala, 2013.
12. For an alternative discussion of the relationship between toleration and modus vivendi, see: Kühler, 2019.
13. For a more detailed articulation of reasons to join a modus vivendi – namely, first-person reasons and second-person reason, or an intersection of the two – see: Sala, 2019.
14. Interesting accounts of liberal modus vivendi as a moralized one are offered by: McCabe, 2010; Wall, 2019.

# References

Balint, P. (2016). *Respecting Toleration: Traditional Liberalism & Contemporary Diversity*. Oxford: Oxford University Press.

Dworkin, R. (1996). *Freedom's Law*. Cambridge, MA: The Belknap Press of Harvard University Press.

Forst, R. (2008). The Limits of Toleration. In: I. Creppell, R. Hardin and S. Macedo, eds., *Toleration on Trial*, 1st ed. Lanham: Rowman & Littlefield, pp. 17–30.
Forst, R. (2013). *Toleration in Conflict: Past and Present*. Cambridge: Cambridge University Press.
Forst, R. (2017). Toleration. *The Stanford Encyclopedia of Philosophy*, fall 2017 ed. [online] Available at: https://plato.stanford.edu/archives/fall2017/entries/toleration/ [Accessed 11 May 2020].
Galeotti, A. E. (2002). *Tolerance as Recognition*. Cambridge: Cambridge University Press.
Galeotti, A. E. (2006). Difference, Identity and Toleration. In: J. Dryzeck, B. Honig and A. Phillips, eds., *The Oxford Handbook of Political Theory*, 1st ed. Oxford: Oxford University Press, pp. 564–580.
Galston, W. (2010). Realism in Political Theory. *European Journal of Political Theory*, 9(4), pp. 385–411.
Geuss, R. (2002). Liberalism and Its Discontents. *Political Theory*, 30(3), pp. 320–338.
Gray, J. (2000). *Two Faces of Liberalism*. New York: New Press.
Heyd, D. (1996). Introduction. In: D. Heyd, ed., *Toleration. An Elusive Virtue*, 1st ed. Princeton, NJ: Princeton University Press, pp. 3–17.
Horton, J. (2000). *Political Obligation*. London: Palgrave Macmillan.
Horton, J. (2007). John Gray and the Political Theory of *Modus Vivendi*. In: J. Horton and G. Newey, eds., *The Political Theory of John Gray*, 1st ed. Abingdon: Routledge, pp. 43–57.
Horton, J. (2010). Realism, Liberal Moralism and a Political Theory of Modus Vivendi. *European Journal of Political Theory*, 9(4), pp. 431–448.
Horton, J. (2011). Why the Traditional Conception of Toleration Still Matters. *Critical Review of International Social & Political Philosophy*, 14(3), pp. 289–305.
Horton, J. (2019a). Modus Vivendi and Political Legitimacy. In: J. Horton, M. Westphal and U. Willems, eds., *The Political Theory of Modus Vivendi*, 1st ed. Dordrecht: Springer, pp. 131–148.
Horton, J. (2019b). Toleration and Modus Vivendi. *Critical Review of International Social and Political Philosophy*, pp. 1–19. [online] Available at: https://doi.org/10.1080/13698230.2019.1616879 [Accessed 11 May 2020].
Horton, J. and Mendus, S. (1985). *Aspects of Toleration*. London: Methuen.
Horton, J. and Mendus, S. (1999). *Toleration, Identity & Difference*. London: Palgrave Macmillan.
Horton, J. and Nicholson, P. (1992). *Toleration: Philosophy & Practice*. Avebury: Aldershot.
Kühler, M. (2019). Modus Vivendi and Toleration. In: J. Horton, M. Westphal and U. Willems, eds., *The Political Theory of Modus Vivendi*, 1st ed. Dordrecht: Springer, pp. 235–253.
Larmore, C. (1990). Political Liberalism. *Political Theory*, 18(3), pp. 339–360.
McCabe, D. (2010). *Modus Vivendi Liberalism: Theory & Practice*. Cambridge: Cambridge University Press.
McCabe, D. (2019). Modus Vivendi as a Global Political Morality. In: J. Horton, M. Westphal and U. Willems, eds., *The Political Theory of Modus Vivendi*, 1st ed. Dordrecht: Springer, pp. 149–167.

Mendus, S. (ed.) (1988). *Justifying Toleration*. London: Methuen.
Mendus, S. (1989). *Toleration & the Limits of Liberalism*. Atlantic Highlands: Humanities Press.
Mendus, S. and Edwards, D. (1987). *On Toleration*. Oxford: Oxford University Press.
Neal, P. (1990). Justice as Fairness: Political or Metaphysical? *Political Theory*, 18(1), pp. 24–50.
Newey, G. (1999). *Virtue, Reason & Toleration: The Place of Toleration in Ethical & Political Philosophy*. Edinburgh: Edinburgh University Press.
Newey, G. (2010). *After Politics: The Rejection of Politics in Contemporary Liberal Philosophy*. London: Palgrave Macmillan.
Oberdiek, H. (2001). *Tolerance: Between Forbearance & Acceptance*. Lanham: Rowman & Littlefield.
Raphael, D. D. (1988). The Intolerable. In: S. Mendus, ed., *Justifying Toleration: Conceptual & Historical Perspectives*, 1st ed. Cambridge: Cambridge University Press, pp. 137–153.
Rawls, J. (2005). *Political Liberalism*, expanded ed. New York: Columbia University Press.
Raz, J. (1985). Authority and Justification. *Philosophy & Public Affairs*, 14(1), Winter, pp. 3–29.
Rossi, E. (2012). Justice, Legitimacy and (Normative) Authority for Political Realists. *Critical Review of International Social & Political Philosophy*, 15(2), pp. 149–164.
Rossi, E. and Sleat, M. (2014). Realism in Normative Political Theory. *Philosophy Compass*, 9–10, pp. 689–701.
Sala, R. (2010). Toleration and Respect in a Multicultural Society. *Notizie di Politeia*, 26(99), pp. 23–43.
Sala, R. (2013). The Place of 'Unreasonable' People Beyond Rawls. *European Journal of Political Theory*, 12(3), pp. 253–270.
Sala, R. (2019). Modus Vivendi and the Motivations for Compliance. In: J. Horton, M. Westphal and U. Willems, eds., *The Political Theory of Modus Vivendi*, 1st ed. Dordrecht: Springer, pp. 67–82.
Sleat, M. (2011). Liberal Realism: A Liberal Response to the Realist Critique. *The Review of Politics*, 73(3), pp. 469–496.
Vallier, K. (2015). On Distinguishing Publicly Justified Polities from Modus Vivendi Regimes. *Social Theory and Practice*, 41(2), pp. 207–229.
Wall, S. (2019). Liberal Moralism and Modus Vivendi Politics. In: J. Horton, M. Westphal and U. Willems, eds., *The Political Theory of Modus Vivendi*, 1st ed. Dordrecht: Springer, pp. 49–66.
Walzer, M. (1997). *On Toleration*. New Haven, CT: Yale University Press.
Wendt, F. (2016). The Moral Standing of Modus Vivendi Arrangement. *Public Affairs Quarterly*, 30(4), pp. 351–370.

# 9 Toleration, Liberal Democracy and the Problem of Intolerant Doctrines
## The Example of Right-Wing Populism

*Anniina Leiviskä*

### Introduction

In recent years, the electoral support of right-wing populist parties in many democratic societies has made discussions concerning the limits of toleration in liberal democracy increasingly topical. Contemporary European democracies have responded in different ways to the "threat" that right-wing populist parties and their potentially anti-democratic ideologies present to core democratic values and ideals. Some countries, including Italy, Austria, Denmark and Finland have taken somewhat tolerant and inclusive approaches toward these parties while other countries have adopted more repressive and intolerant strategies to protect formal decision-making institutions from anti-democratic or intolerant attitudes expressed by right-wing populists (e.g. Abts and Rummens, 2010). There is no unanimous view on how exactly democratic societies should address and deal with these doctrines which, while operating within democratic societies and their central institutions, express views and ideologies contradicting the most deeply held democratic values and principles, such as tolerance and respect for others as well as freedom and equality of citizens.

This chapter addresses right-wing populism as an example of "intolerant" doctrines from the perspective of the limits of toleration as they are drawn in three contemporary theories of democracy. By "intolerant" doctrines, I refer to ideologies that cross the "threshold" of toleration in a liberal democratic society by refusing to adhere to its central values and norms and denying basic forms of respect for others (e.g. Forst, 2004; Habermas, 1996; Rawls, 2005). The theories of democracy discussed in this chapter are John Rawls's political liberalism, Jürgen Habermas's deliberative theory of democracy and Chantal Mouffe's agonistic pluralism. In all three theories, the limits of toleration are associated with the constitutional democratic regime and the core values and norms embodied by it. The central difference between these theories is that while Rawls's and Habermas's theories rest on what Rainer Forst

## The Problem of Intolerant Doctrines   163

(2004) defines as the "respect conception" (p. 316) of toleration, which draws its justification from the idea of justification itself, in Mouffe's (2000, 2005) agonistic pluralism, the limits of toleration are seen as a result of purely political decisions and thus lacking moral or rational justification. The conclusion that Rawls (2005) and Habermas (1996) draw concerning intolerant doctrines is that they cannot be included in formal decision-making institutions because of their rejection of the respect conception of toleration and the associated idea of reciprocal justification. In contrast to this, Mouffe (2000, 2005) argues that envisaging the limits of the liberal democratic regime in the register of morality or rationality in the way exemplified by Rawls and Habermas – that is, excluding right-wing populists and other "intolerant" doctrines as morally "evil" (Mouffe, 2005, p. 75) or "unreasonable" (Mouffe, 2000, p. 24) – only contributes to the escalation of political conflicts between the included and excluded. Accordingly, Mouffe (2005) argues that the appropriate way to accommodate right-wing populists and similar doctrines is to include them in democratic politics as legitimate adversaries and to give up the attempt to justify the limits of toleration in moral or rational terms.

In this chapter, I examine the philosophical and political plausibility of the solutions that the three theories mentioned earlier provide for the issue of addressing right-wing populism in contemporary democracies. I particularly challenge the plausibility of Mouffe's suggestion that right-wing populists should be included in democratic politics as legitimate adversaries. I argue that this suggestion is in contrast with the way Mouffe (2000) herself delineates the limits of the liberal democratic regime and thus the limits of toleration associated with this regime. According to this delineation, doctrines that do not endorse the symbolic space of liberal democracy, constituted by the principles of equality and liberty, should be excluded as "enemies" (2000, p. 13) of the democratic regime. Consequently, Mouffe is unable to provide any more satisfactory response to the issue of accommodating these doctrines than Rawls and Habermas, according to whom intolerant doctrines should be excluded from formal political institutions. I also argue that Mouffe's hegemonic view of politics is normatively problematic as it relativizes the moral "core" of liberal democracy: the "unconditioned moral respect" (Forst, 2004, p. 321), which underlies the "respect conception" (p. 316) of toleration supported by Rawls's and Habermas's theories of democracy. By relativizing this core, Mouffe loses the possibility to present philosophically grounded normative critique towards doctrines that violate the democratic values of equality and liberty. Moreover, I suggest that while Rawls's and Habermas's theories of democracy are significant particularly for providing a normative framework for addressing the issue of intolerant doctrines in contemporary democracies, new forms of democratic intervention, which are rooted in the understanding of the causes of right-wing populism, must be developed in order to address this issue on the level of political practises.

The chapter is structured as follows: in the next section, I provide a brief introduction to the way the limits of toleration are drawn in Rawls's and Habermas's theories of democracy by using Rainer Forst's (2004) influential definition of the "respect conception" (p. 316) of toleration as my point of departure. I will then discuss Mouffe's critique of Rawls's and Habermas's theories from the perspective of her agonistic pluralism and its "hegemonic" (Mouffe, 2000, p. 56) understanding of the liberal democratic regime. After that, I move on to discussing right-wing populism as an example of "intolerant" doctrines. My aim is to demonstrate that the contemporary European forms of right-wing populism involve a varying degree of "proto-totalitarian" (Abts and Rummens, 2007, p. 414) or extremist features (Jamin, 2012) and thus these doctrines cross the liberal democratic threshold of toleration. Then, I will discuss the suggestions that the three theories of democracy provide for dealing with 'intolerant' doctrines – especially right-wing populism – in liberal democratic societies. The final section presents my concluding remarks.

## The Respect Conception of Toleration in Rawls's and Habermas's Theories of Democracy

In his influential definition of toleration, Rainer Forst (2004) refers to a "respect conception" (p. 316) of toleration, which is based on the idea of the reciprocal recognition of the tolerating parties. According to the respect conception, the tolerating parties recognize that while they may hold different, even incompatible ethical views, they respect each other as moral-political equals in the sense that they see that their common framework of social life should be guided by norms that all parties can equally accept. What follows from the respect conception of toleration is the demand to "tolerate those beliefs and practices with which one disagrees but which themselves do not violate the criteria or the 'threshold' of reciprocity and generality" (Forst, 2004, p. 317). As Forst (2004) points out, the limits of toleration are reached when one party tries to dominate others by making its rejectable views the general norm and thus violates others' right to justification. This represents a form of intolerance that cannot be tolerated. However, as Forst (2004) further argues, not tolerating such intolerance is not simply another form of ethical intolerance because it does not absolutize one controversial ethical view but, rather, is justified by the notion of justification itself. Hence, the respect conception of toleration cannot be refuted without rejecting the entire idea of justification. Moreover, Forst (2004) highlights that the determination of the limits of toleration must be reflexive and open to questioning by those who are excluded by these limits because a unilateral drawing of these limits would constitute another form of unacceptable ethical intolerance.

This respect conception of toleration underlies Rawls's and Habermas's theories of democracy. Both theories are motivated by the question of how citizens can legitimately regulate their common life by means of positive law in societies where people significantly differ in their views on how to organize their society together (Habermas, 1996; Rawls, 2005). Rawls's solution to this question is based on the idea of a public, political conception of justice – justice as fairness[1] – that is "free-standing" (Rawls, 2005, pp. 10, 12–13) in the sense that it does not derive from any comprehensive doctrine of society. Rawls initially defines and justifies this conception of justice in his earlier work, *Theory of Justice* (1999), through the well-known concepts of the "original position" (p. 11) and "veil of ignorance" (p. 11). In *Political Liberalism* (2005), Rawls reintroduces this conception of justice in the framework of democratic pluralism, arguing that it is supported by an "overlapping consensus" (p. xvii, 385) among different comprehensive doctrines and should thus be understood as a "module" (p. 145) that fits into and is compatible with a variety of different doctrines.

Importantly, Rawls's theory depends on a presupposition of "reasonableness" (Rawls, 2005, p. 58), which sets limits to what can be tolerated within a liberal democratic society. The central value inherent in the concept of reasonableness is reciprocity, referring to the idea that citizens' exercise of political power is justified only if they sincerely believe that the reasons they offer for their political action may reasonably be accepted by other citizens as a justification of these actions (Rawls, 2005, p. xliv). Hence, when acting in the political forum of society, citizens should be prepared to justify their actions through reasons that are not only acceptable to the representatives of their own comprehensive doctrine but to members of all reasonable doctrines. According to Rawls (2005), given its status as the locus of an "overlapping consensus" (p. xvii, 385) between reasonable doctrines, the political conception of justice can provide a common ground of justification for citizens. Hence, when fundamental issues of justice are at stake, reasonable citizens should appeal to the values and norms inherent in this conception when justifying their views to others. The political conception of justice thus gives content to the idea of "public reason" (Rawls, 2005, p. xvii) and draws the limits of toleration in a liberal democratic society. Correspondingly, doctrines and citizens rejecting the idea of reciprocal justification and the notion of public reason cannot be tolerated in liberal democracies. As Rawls (2005) points out, "Political liberalism does not engage those who think this way. The zeal to embody the whole truth in politics is incompatible with an idea of public reason that belongs with democratic citizenship" (p. 442).

The idea of toleration inherent in Habermas's theory of democracy is similar to the one expressed by Rawls and based on parallel ideas of public reasoning and reciprocal justification.[2] However, Habermas adopts a more strongly procedural approach in his theory of democracy, focusing on the issue of the institutionalization of procedures of rational deliberation through what he refers to as a "system of rights"[3] (Habermas, 1996, p. 82) that results "from the application of the discourse principle to the medium of law" (p. 122). The discourse principle is a metanorm, developed by Habermas (1990, 1993) in the context of his discourse ethics and based on his understanding of communicative rationality, which defines the communicative preconditions under which the validity of a disputed norm of action can be resolved in an impartial way. The principle states that "only those norms of action are valid to which all possibly affected persons could assent as participants in rational discourses" (Habermas, 1996, p. 459). By Institutionalizing this norm, the system of rights, which involves the basic individual and political rights embodied by the constitution, seeks to ensure that "legislative processes are regulated in such a way and take place in forms of communication such that everyone can presume that the regulations enacted in that way deserve general and rationally motivated assent" (Habermas, 1998, p. 215). In other words, the system of rights delineates the necessary conditions for institutionalizing democratic processes in the medium of law and politics.

The system of rights, and the basic individual and political rights articulated by it, are particularly important considering the idea of toleration because this system determines how citizens must understand each other and their mutual political relations in a democratic polity. More specifically, the system or rights requires that citizens must recognize each other as bearers of an equal set of basic individual and political rights and treat each other accordingly in their role as participants in democratic processes (Habermas, 1996). This means that they must carry out their political discussions within the normative conversational constraints delineated by basic individual and political rights, thus refraining from political claims and actions that violate the presupposition of equal rights of other citizens. By demanding this, the system of rights establishes the idea of reciprocity as the limit of toleration. Accordingly, the conclusion that Habermas draws concerning what *cannot* be tolerated in legitimate democratic processes is quite similar to Rawls's. Namely, Habermas (1998) argues that fundamentalisms, which "claim exclusiveness for a privileged way of life" (p. 224) and lack understanding of the fallibility of their claims, are incompatible with constitutional democracy and the associated idea of equal rights of citizens. Therefore, these doctrines cannot be engaged with as legitimate participants in democratic deliberation. As Habermas points out, "each act of toleration must circumscribe the range of behaviour everybody must accept, thereby drawing a line for what cannot be tolerated. There can be no inclusion without exclusion" (Habermas, 2004, p. 7).

However, Habermas's stresses that the limits of toleration cannot be drawn unilaterally by a single tolerating party but everyone who are affected by these limits must voluntarily agree on the conditions under which they wish to exercise mutual toleration (Habermas, 2004, p. 8; see also Thomassen, 2006). This leads to an understanding of the system of rights, and the constitution as the embodiment of this system, as "a project" (Habermas, 1998, p. 70), which needs to be legitimated through democratic processes in each historical situation and from the viewpoint of the diverse ethical doctrines existing in society. This idea of the constitution as a "project" is similar to the one expressed by Rawls in his essay *The Idea of Public Reason Revisited* (Rawls, 2005, pp. 440–490; from now on *Revisited*), which was initially published in 1997 and later included in the expanded edition of *Political Liberalism*. In this essay, Rawls (2005) develops his view of toleration further by making it significantly more reflexive and inclusive. Instead of placing a single political conception of justice (justice as fairness) at the core of public reasoning, he suggests that the content of public reason is constituted by a *family* of liberal political conceptions of justice. Hence, according to this understanding, a liberal democratic polity practices toleration regarding doctrines and citizens who refer to the values and norms included in *one* of the political conceptions of justice inherent in the family of available conceptions; one, which citizens sincerely believe provides the best answers to the questions concerning constitutional essentials and matters of basic justice. As Rawls (2005) points out, his intention is not to "fix public reason once and for all in the form of one favoured political conception of justice" (p. 451) and he emphasizes the need to allow for the existence and emergence of different and new interpretations of the content of public reason.

Moreover, it is noteworthy that for both Rawls and Habermas the requirement of reciprocity applies mostly to the formal public sphere of society, such as the courts and judges, government officials and candidates for public office (Rawls, 2005) and formal decision-making institutions (Habermas, 1996). Rawls (2005) also restricts the content of public reason by suggesting that it concerns the so-called "constitutional essentials" (p. 214), that is, basic rights and liberties included in a written constitution and fundamental issues of justice, which are related to the basic structure of society. Correspondingly, the legal demand of public justification does not extend to the so-called background culture of society (Rawls, 2005) or the civil society (Habermas, 1996), which is not guided by any single principle or value toleration.[4] Habermas (1996) suggests that the civil society as "an open and inclusive network of overlapping, subcultural publics having fluid temporal, social, and substantive boundaries" (p. 307) should remain relatively free from regulations. However, whereas the civil society is more "tolerant" concerning the forms of political discussion it permits, it is also much more vulnerable to "the repressive and exclusionary effects of unequally distributed social power, structural violence, and systematically distorted communication" (Habermas, 1996, p. 307).

## Mouffe's Agonistic Pluralism and the De(con)struction of the Concept of Toleration

Chantal Mouffe is one of the most well-known authors challenging Rawls's and Habermas's theories of democracy and the idea of toleration inherent in these theories.[5] To use Forst's (2004) terminology, Mouffe's theory of agonistic pluralism represents a "radical de(con)struction of the concept of toleration" (p. 314) in the sense that it labels the attempt to draw the limits of the liberal democratic regime in an impartial or rational manner as merely another, more or less effectively veiled form of intolerance. Mouffe's understanding of the limits of toleration as purely political (rather than rational or moral) is rooted in her "hegemonic" (Mouffe, 2000, p. 56) understanding of politics. According to this understanding, every political order constitutes a "regime" (Mouffe, 2000, p. 26), which reflects the existing relations of power in society and excludes those who do not adhere to the "grammar" (p. 26) of this regime. Importantly, in Mouffe's (2000, 2005) view, hegemonic political orders are historically contingent and politically constituted and thus there is no reason to perceive any order as more legitimate or rational than any other.

Another central feature of Mouffe's political theory is her notion of "the political" (Mouffe, 2000, p. 101, 2005, p. 9), which she adopts from Carl Schmitt's political philosophy. At the centre of this notion is the view that the affirmation of difference – the recognition of something as "other" – is a precondition for the existence of a collective political identity. Political identification thus involves drawing a line between the inside and "the constitutive outside" (Mouffe, 2005, p. 15) of a political community. From this "identification-through-differentiation" arises the view of the political as an antagonistic friend/enemy relation and the attendant idea of every political order as being constituted by the exclusion of those who are not accepted as a part of the uniform political community. Moreover, Mouffe (2000, 2005) sees this logic of the political as the constitutive logic of social relations in general, which is why she argues that antagonism can never be fully dispelled through the establishment of a "neutral" political order.

From these starting-points, Mouffe (2000) argues that Habermas's and Rawls's theories, especially their understandings of a neutral, impartial public sphere, are based on a fundamentally mistaken view of the political. Concerning the concept of toleration and the exclusion of intolerant citizens and doctrines from democratic participation, Mouffe (2000) argues that Rawls and Habermas merely disguise purely political decisions as moral or rational exigencies in order to justify these exclusions. In other words, Mouffe (2000, p. 24) suggests that instead of recognizing that the exclusion of some groups or citizens is based on purely political reasons, Rawls and Habermas label the excluded as "unreasonable" (p. 28) with the result of framing political debates as moral controversies.

According to Mouffe (2005), on the practical level, this ultimately leads to the escalation of politics into hostile conflicts between "good" and "evil". Consequently, she suggests that the attempt to envisage the limits of the democratic regime in moral or rational terms only contributes to the destructive consequences of political exclusion.

In *On the Political* (2005), Mouffe demonstrates further the practical consequences of the type of consensus-oriented politics that she sees as being theoretically exemplified by Rawls and Habermas. Mouffe's (2005) argument is that consensus-oriented politics does not abolish people's fundamental social need to belong to identity-based collectives but merely suppresses this need. Therefore, if the prevailing political order does not offer sufficiently opposing political identities for people to channel their political passions to, people will find channels of political identification from the outside of this order. Mouffe (2005) argues that the rise of right-wing populism and nationalism in Europe is an example of this type of development: through constructing oppositional political identities (between "the people" and "the elite"), these movements have provided the longed-for channels of passionate political identification that were missing in the consensual political culture.

As an alternative to the consensus-oriented models of democracy, Mouffe (2000, 2005) outlines her theory of agonistic pluralism, which aims to channel and tame the antagonistic dimension of the political in a way that is compatible with democratic pluralism. Mouffe (2000) suggests that the proper task of democratic politics is to enable the transition from violent political conflict between enemies into a respectful conflict between political "adversaries" (pp. 114–117) and thus from political antagonism into democratic "agonism" (p. 117). According to Mouffe (2000, p. 102), this transition is enabled by citizens' joint adhesion to the central ethico-political principles of liberal democracy, liberty and equality, which are embodied by the constitution of liberal democracy. According to Mouffe, these principles constitute a common symbolic space to which all citizens adhere although they might disagree on the interpretation and implementation of these principles. Democratic politics thus establishes a "conflictual consensus" (Mouffe, 1999, p. 4) among these interpretations, thus providing both, sufficiently diverse political identities to satisfy the basic human need of political identification *and* a shared symbolic space to provide a sense of unity between different groups.

Importantly, also in Mouffe's agonistic pluralism there are limits of toleration, which are drawn by the symbolic space of liberal democracy and its constitutive values of equality and liberty. As Mouffe (2005, p. 120) herself points out,

> I do not believe that a democratic pluralist politics should consider as legitimate all the demands formulated in a given society. The pluralism

that I advocate requires discriminating between demands which are to be accepted as part of the agonistic debate and those which are to be excluded. A democratic society cannot treat those who put its basic institutions into question as legitimate adversaries.

However, as pointed out, the central difference between Mouffe's and Rawls's and Habermas's approaches is that in Mouffe's agonistic pluralism the limits of toleration are drawn politically and lack rational or moral justification. As Mouffe points out,

> some demands are excluded, not because they are declared to be "evil", but because they challenge the institutions constitutive of the democratic political association. To be sure, the very nature of those institutions is also a part of the agonistic debate, but for such a debate to take place, the existence of a shared symbolic space is necessary.
> (Mouffe, 2005, pp. 120–121)

In the following sections of this chapter, I will discuss the consequences of Mouffe's hegemonic understanding of politics for the normative enterprise of liberal democracy and for addressing the issue of right-wing populism. First, however, I will address the topic of right-wing populism from the viewpoint of the limits of toleration, paying particular attention to the features based on which right-wing populism should be considered as an "intolerant" doctrine.

## Right-Wing Populism as an "Intolerant" Doctrine

Defining populism is not an easy task, because populism is a multifaceted political movement and its definition is a widely debated matter. For the sake of clarity, the type of populism I refer to in this chapter is the right-wing populism represented by many anti-immigration parties in contemporary European democracies in distinction to, for example, Latin American left-wing populism. Perhaps the most common way to define populism is through the antagonistic relation between the "pure people" and the "corrupted elite" (Canovan, 1999; Laclau, 1979, 2005; Mény and Surel, 2002; Mudde, 2004; Stavrakakis, 2004; Taggart, 2000). However, considering the focus of this chapter, the most significant feature of populism is the conceptualization of "a people" as a homogenous unity and the associated exclusion of those who are seen as "other" and not belonging to "us" (Canovan, 1999; Taggart, 2000; Abts and Rummens, 2007; Mudde, 2004). As Abts and Rummens (2007) point out, this logic of populism is "paradigmatically exemplified" (p. 406) by Carl Schmitt's understanding of "the political", which also underlies Mouffe's political theory. Abts and Rummens further define the logic of populism as "prototototalitarian" (p. 414) because it is characteristic of populist movements to suppress diversity in society and thus disregard the logic of otherness that is central to democracy. This proto-totalitarian and homogenizing logic is particularly important for defining right-wing populism as an "intolerant" doctrine, which crosses the threshold of toleration in a liberal democratic society by questioning others' equal rights for different ethical-cultural identities (e.g. Forst, 2004; Habermas, 1996; Rawls, 2005).

The proto-totalitarian features of right-wing populism are especially apparent in such cases where the party or group in question could be defined as "extreme right" (Jamin, 2012, p. 38) in distinction to more modest forms of right-wing populism. As Jamin (2012) points out, the distinction between populism and extremism is important because populism is not always connected with the extreme right and thus does not necessarily embody a threat to liberal values. Jamin (2012) explains that whereas the defining feature of populism is the distinction between the hard-working people and the corrupted political elite, right-wing extremism typically involves the features of racial inegalitarianism, nationalism and extremism. Racial inegalitarianism (i.e. racism) refers to an understanding of race as the defining feature through which racialized people are marked as "inferior" to the white population according to an alleged "natural order" (Jamin, 2012). Nationalism is typically associated with the idea of a homogenous ethnonational community whose well-being and unity is being threatened by enemies and forces, which penetrate the nation from the outside, such as immigrants and ethnic minorities. In addition to a radical way of acting and thinking, extremism is associated with similar features that Abts and Rummens (2007) define as "proto-totalitarian" (p. 414): the rejection of pluralism, difference, political negotiations and ambivalence in politics. Right-wing extremism is thus often characterized by a sort of 'monism' and philosophical, political and ideological simplism (Lipset and Raab, 1973, pp. 6–8).

However, despite the distinction between populism and extremism described earlier, drawing a line between these ideologies is particularly difficult in the case of contemporary European right-wing populist parties. Namely, many of them refer to themselves by the notion of 'populism' while exemplifying many of the aforementioned features of right-wing extremism. These parties include the *Vlaams Belang* in Belgium, the *National Rally* in France, *The Finns Party* in Finland, *The Freedom Party* of Austria, and *Alternative for Germany* to mention a few. As Jamin (2012) and Betz (1998) point out, while these and similar right-wing populist parties do not openly describe themselves as anti-democratic, they nevertheless express anti-system attitudes and the culture emerging from internal publications, the leaders' discourse and propaganda and the worldviews of the executives and activists can be considered to be anti-egalitarian, anti-pluralist and fundamentally opposed to the principles of the democratic system (see also Eatwell, 2000; Mudde, 1996). Based on these remarks, I use the notion of right-wing populism to refer to "intolerant" doctrines, involving a varying degree of the aforementioned proto-totalitarian or extremist features and thus crossing the threshold of toleration of liberal democratic societies.

## Addressing Right-Wing Populism from the Perspective of Three Theories of Democracy

From the viewpoint of Rawls's political liberalism, the homogenizing or proto-totalitarian logic of populism is irreconcilable with the idea of public reason and the value of reciprocity. Populism precisely expresses the "zeal to embody the whole truth in politics" (Rawls, 2005, p. 442) and, due to its homogenizing tendencies, does not adhere to the demand of reciprocal justification. In addition to the remarks included in *Political Liberalism* (2005), Rawls (1999) addresses the question of "toleration of the intolerant" (p. 190) in his *Theory of Justice* where he suggests that while tolerant citizens have no duty to tolerate the intolerant sects of society, suppressing these doctrines is advisable only in situations where they pose a direct threat to the constitution. In other cases, Rawls (1999) has a strong belief in the "psychological principle" (p. 192) that arises with the functioning of a well-ordered society. That is, Rawls suggests that "those whose liberties are protected by and who benefit from a just constitution will, other things equal, acquire an allegiance to it over a period of time" (Rawls, 1999, p. 192). Rawls thus claims that by treating the intolerant as equals, the institutions of a well-ordered society will gradually transform the intolerance of these citizens into tolerance thus making the suppression of their freedoms unnecessary. However, considering Rawls's strong emphasis on the need to protect the constitution, the inclusion of the intolerant into the public political forum of society would be questionable. Namely, having intolerant citizens as government officials would present a direct threat to the constitutional regime. Hence, Rawls's position indicates that right-wing populists should be tolerated as long as they do not pursue positions in the public political forum.

Habermas (2004) addresses the issue of tolerating the intolerant most extensively in his essay on religious toleration where he characterizes intolerant citizens as "enemies of the constitution" (p. 9) and argues that a liberal state must "resort to intolerance" (p. 8) toward such enemies, either through political criminal law or by prohibiting particular political parties. Habermas points out, however, that by practising intolerance, a liberal state encounters a difficult paradox: while it must protect itself against "existential enemies" (p. 8) it must also avoid the betrayal of its own key principles, including the equal right of political association and participation. Therefore, as noted earlier, the liberal state must seek to ensure that the limits of toleration are drawn reciprocally because drawing these limits unilaterally by the state would itself constitute a violation of the principle of toleration. However, referring to Forst's work,

Habermas (2004) argues that the possibility of tolerating others arises only when there are "legitimate justifications for the rejection of competing validity claims" (p. 10). What Habermas means by this is that it is possible to tolerate others only when one recognizes that although one can reject others' views as mistaken from an ethical viewpoint of one's own doctrine, one cannot reject these views from the impartial viewpoint of morality (see also Forst, 2004). Accordingly, Habermas (2004) uses the example of racist views to argue that they are not something to be tolerated, because then we would accept the racist's prejudice as an ethical judgment similar to the rejection of a different religion. Hence, if a right-wing populist holds inegalitarian, nationalist or racist views, these views cannot be *tolerated* but they must rather be countered through a struggle against discrimination.

Both Rawls's and Habermas's theories thus lead to the conclusion that right-wing populist parties embodying proto-totalitarian or extremist features cannot be legitimately included in the formal decision-making institutions of a democratic polity. In contrast to this view, Mouffe (2005) argues that right-wing populists should be treated as legitimate adversaries in the democratic regime. She claims that their exclusion from democratic politics as morally "evil" will only result in the further marginalization of these parties and thus to the creation of hostile political antagonisms. However, Abts and Rummens (2007) argue that the proto-totalitarian logic of populism itself, which is much like the logic of "the political" that Mouffe adopts from Schmitt, precisely *prevents* the possibility of seeing one's political rivals as legitimate adversaries in Mouffe's sense. The constitution of the people as a homogenous unity, which is at the core of the populist logic, requires treating those not belonging to this unity as enemies and threats to one's existence. Mudde (2004) and Galston (2018) make a similar remark stating that populism centres on conflict between friends and foes where opponents are not seen simply as people with different values and convictions but as *evil*, and this perception renders any compromise between the opposing parties impossible.

Accordingly, from the viewpoint of the definition of right-wing populism employed in this chapter, it seems unlikely that the inclusion of right-wing populist parties would lead them to accept the shared symbolic space of liberal democracy in the way Mouffe (2005) expects. Rather, it appears to be in the very logic of populism to construct political relations as antagonistic friend/enemy relations, which prevents populist parties from treating others as legitimate rivals. Mouffe's (2005) suggestion that right-wing populists should be treated as legitimate adversaries in liberal-democratic societies is thus either based on a very different understanding of the nature and features of right-wing populism than the definition employed in this chapter or, alternatively, Mouffe contradicts some of the fundamental assumptions of her agonistic pluralism by making this claim. As Mathias Thaler (2010, p. 790) argues, by introducing a measure to hold legitimate forms of contestation apart from illegitimate ones – the symbolic space constituted by equality and liberty – Mouffe also sets limits to toleration that cannot be disregarded without jeopardizing the democratic regime. While the goal of agonistic pluralism is to 'tame' the antagonism inherent in the political by including political enemies in the shared agonistic space, when this taming does not succeed – which is likely the case with right-wing populism – the democratic polity will have to exclude its enemies because their inclusion threatens its existence. Mouffe is thus drawn into the same dilemma as Rawls and Habermas: either to exclude right-wing populists and face the potential risk of escalating political conflicts or include them with the consequence of jeopardizing the democratic regime.

Mouffe's understanding of the limits of toleration as politically constituted also gives rise to significant philosophical and normative problems. First, as Forst (2004) points out, at least in principle, demonstrating that the limits of toleration are derived from the concept of justification itself has the benefit of depriving right-wing populists and other intolerant doctrines from the right to protest against their unfair treatment if they refuse to accept the demand of reciprocal justification. Namely, by protesting, they would be drawn into self-contradiction. Whether this makes any difference on the level of political reality evidently depends on the intolerant doctrine and its receptivity to reasons. However, perhaps more importantly, the significance of rationally justifying the limits of toleration has to do with what Forst (2004) sees as the incontrovertible moral core of democracy: the "unconditioned moral respect" (Forst, 2004, p. 321) that underlies the respect conception of toleration and constitutes a "democratic *Sittlichkeit*" (p. 321; *italics* in original). As Forst (2004) points out, while this *Sittlichkeit* is historically and culturally situated and "grows out of a plurality of sources and experiences that are by necessity particular" (p. 321) what has grown out of these particular experiences and sources is the deep and fundamental recognition of a non-relativizable idea "that a human being is a person who is to be respected *without* requiring any additional reasons" (p. 321; *italics* in original). This moral core of liberal democracy underlying the idea of reciprocal justification gives us reason to think of the limits of toleration as rationally rather than politically drawn. Namely, to see the limits of toleration as purely political decisions results in the relativization of the aforementioned moral principle and, ultimately, leads to the loss of the possibility to exercise philosophically grounded, normative critique of ideologies and doctrines that violate this principle.[6]

Accordingly, a hegemonic account of political power such as the one represented by Mouffe cannot take a critical normative stance when the liberal democratic regime is replaced by a populist one. It should simply consider such transition as a replacement of one hegemonic order by another. Mouffe's position in her latest book, *For a Left Populism*

(2018), reflects this hegemonic view. Namely, Mouffe has moved on from the protection of a liberal democratic order into a defence of a form of left populism, which she sees as a possible alternative to the authoritarian right-wing populism in the prevailing political landscape, which she defines as "the populist moment" (p. 1). Mouffe (2018) defines populism as a movement that brings together various forms of resistance to the long-prevailed neoliberal hegemony the crisis and collapse of which has created conditions for the emergence of a new hegemonic order. According to Mouffe (2018) the new left populism should be understood as a heterogeneous "chain of equivalence" (p. 21) – a concept adopted from Ernesto Laclau – among different democratic demands. These demands, presented by the workers, the immigrants and the precarious middle class, among others, give rise to the category of the "people" as opposed to the establishment, the 'oligarchy' (Mouffe, 2018, p. 21), and the authoritarian variant of populism.

While Mouffe's (2018) analysis of the genesis of right-wing populism and especially its roots in the resistance of neoliberal hegemony is convincing, the troubling part of Mouffe's position is her suggestion that right-wing populism should be responded to with more populism. Namely, the threat with this response is the fundamental instabilization of politics, resulting from the subordination of democratic institutions to the rapid changes in the power relations of society. This might result in the inability to protect the continuance of legitimate democratic processes and institutions. As Mouffe (2018) points out, in the new populist moment, there is no guarantee that the new hegemonic order will bring about significant democratic advances because the new order might be an authoritarian one. Hence, in my view, in order to prevent this authoritarian outcome, what is needed is the re-enforcement of the liberal democratic regime that is capable of protecting citizens from the instability resulting from the polarization of the political culture.

From the viewpoint of Rawls's and Habermas's theories of democracy, one of the major mistakes of contemporary democratic societies has been their insufficient protection of the limits of toleration, which has led to the inclusion and normalization of extremist discourses in both informal and formal political spheres of society. Accordingly, from the perspective of these theories, stronger means of containment, including legal forms of repression, administrative measures or even party prohibition, should have been exercised especially concerning the formal political institutions of society (e.g. Habermas, 2004; Abts and Rummens, 2010). However, Mouffe (2005, 2018) is correct in arguing that the neoliberal hegemony has in many ways incapacitated the liberal-democratic form of government with the result of citizens' loss of faith in democratic institutions. Accordingly, it may no longer be adequate or sufficient to rely on the "psychological principle" (Rawls, 1999, p. 192) in the containment of intolerant doctrines. The political landscape has transformed drastically as a consequence of the electoral support of right-wing populism and therefore the idea of "containing" marginal or growing anti-democratic voices seems outdated. Accordingly, strong measures such as party prohibition might even seem anti-democratic or authoritarian to the large part of the public that supports right-wing populism. As Alessandro Ferrara (2018) argues, addressing the problem of right-wing populism in contemporary democracies thus requires more than merely entrenching constitutionalism as we know it. In this sense, while Mouffe's response to the issue of right-wing populism is problematic from a normative viewpoint, also Rawls's and Habermas's theories seem somewhat inadequate to responding to the challenges arising from the current political reality of liberal democratic societies.

A genuine transformation of the democratic culture, and an effective response to the issue of right-wing populism, requires more than simply excluding or condemning these parties as intolerable. Primarily, it requires looking into the reasons underlying the rise of right-wing populism, especially the reasons associated with the functioning of the global market economy, which has led to the impoverishment of social and economic conditions of large groups of citizens in many liberal democracies (e.g. Salmela and von Scheve, 2017). Ferrara (2018) primarily associates the emergence of populist movements with the increase of economic inequality and the new absolute power that disembodied financial markets employ on democratic legislatures. Accordingly, he argues that one of the possible responses to populism is to intervene with these phenomena through legislation and government-funded class actions, which are directed at reclaiming democracy and equality in the market by holding commercial actors accountable for their actions and compensating unduly damaged citizens. For me, it seems that these type of interventions, which combine the rationally justified defence of liberal democracy with the awareness and resistance of the almost absolute power of global market economy, are among the most promising ways to respond to the issue of right-wing populism and the broader social, economic and political developments underlying this phenomenon.

Evidently, examining the causes underlying populism and developing novel ways of democratic intervention does not diminish the normative value of drawing and justifying the limits of toleration in liberal democracies. Rather, the idea of reciprocal justification and the underlying value of unconditioned moral respect (Forst, 2004) provide the normative foundation for these new forms of intervention. Accordingly, Rawls's and Habermas's theories of democracy are relevant for contesting the idea that liberal democracy is a thing of the past and also for demonstrating why the normative project of liberal democracy should be reinforced in the current political landscape. As Ferrara (2018) points out, the growth of indigenous unreasonability, including right-wing populism, has not yet called the democratic horizon in question; rather, it has destabilized important aspects of it and therefore "constitutes a *new inhospitable condition* with which democratic regimes must reckon in our historical context" (p. 475; *italics* in original).

## Conclusions

In this chapter, I have discussed the question of how right-wing populism should be addressed in contemporary democratic societies from the perspective of three theories of democracy and the conceptions of toleration inherent in them. My aim has particularly been to demonstrate some of the deficiencies of Mouffe's agonistic pluralism and thus to indicate that her response to the issue of right-wing populism may not be as plausible as she argues. Namely, in a similar way as Rawls and Habermas, Mouffe also draws limits of toleration in her agonistic pluralism and thus her theory leads to the conclusion that doctrines violating these limits, including contemporary right-wing populist parties, cannot be legitimately included in democratic politics. Moreover, I also indicated that as compared to Rawls's and Habermas's theories, Mouffe's agonistic pluralism faces the additional problem of not being able to provide a normative foundation for practising philosophically grounded critique of doctrines that violate central democratic values and principles. In this sense, at least from a philosophical or normative perspective, Rawls's and Habermas's theories can be seen as providing a more satisfactory response to the issue of right-wing populism than Mouffe's agonistic pluralism.

However, while Rawls's and Habermas's theories of democracy remain important for justifying and defending the limits of toleration in liberal democratic societies, the solutions that these theories provide for the practical problem of containing intolerant doctrines may no longer be adequate because of the significant transformations in the political culture of today's democracies. Accordingly, new forms of democratic intervention are required. While drawing from the normative ideals exemplified by Rawls's and Habermas's theories, these forms of intervention also need to be based on the awareness of the challenges faced by contemporary liberal democracies, especially those associated with the global market economy and its influence on democratic politics.

## Notes

1. For the definition of "justice as fairness", see Rawls, 1999, part 1, chap. 1, especially pp. 52–53.
2. There are certain philosophical differences between Habermas's and Rawls's theories of democracy concerning, for instance, procedural versus substantive justice and the adequacy of Rawls's notion of overlapping consensus. For these differences, see Habermas, 1998, part II and Rawls, 2005, "Reply to Habermas", pp. 373–434.

3. The rights included in the system of rights fall into five broad categories. The first three are the basic negative liberties, membership rights and due-process rights that together guarantee individual freedom and private autonomy. The fourth, rights of political participation, guarantees public autonomy. For a more extensive description of the system of rights, see Habermas, 1996, pp. 122–123.
4. Rawls suggests that the notion of public reason should apply as a *moral duty* to all citizens, which means that when engaging in the public forum, also citizens who are not government officials should think of themselves "as if they were legislators" (Rawls, 2005, p. 444). Rawls refers to this characteristic as "the duty of civility" (p. 444).
5. Mouffe herself uses the concept of tolerance or toleration only occasionally (e.g. Mouffe, 2000, p. 102). Typically she refers to the idea of toleration by referring to the limits of the liberal democratic regime or public sphere (e.g. Mouffe, 2000, p. 93).
6. Ben Cross (2017) has addressed the problem of normativity in Mouffe's agonistic pluralism by demonstrating that the normative conclusions that Mouffe draws from the descriptive claims inherent in her agonistic pluralism are in contrast with her initial descriptive claims, thus rendering her normative suggestions problematic.

## References

Abts, K. and Rummens, S. (2007). Populism Versus Democracy. *Political Studies*, 55(2), pp. 405–424.
Abts, K. and Rummens, S. (2010). Defending Democracy: The Concentric Containment of Political Extremism. *Political Studies*, 58(4), pp. 649–665.
Betz, H.-G. (1998). *The New Politics of the Right*. New York: St Martin's Press.
Canovan, M. (1999). Trust the People! Populism and the Two Faces of Democracy. *Political Studies*, 47(1), pp. 2–16.
Cross, B. (2017). Normativity in Chantal Mouffe's Political Realism. *Constellations*, 24(2), pp. 180–191.
Eatwell, R. (2000). The Rebirth of the 'Extreme Right' in Western Europe? *Parliamentary Affairs*, 53(3), pp. 407–425.
Ferrara, A. (2018). Can Political Liberalism Help Us Rescue 'the People' from Populism? *Philosophy & Social Criticism*, 44(4), pp. 463–477.
Forst, R. (2004). The Limits of Toleration. *Constellations*, 11(3), pp. 312–325.
Galston, W. A. (2018). The Populist Challenge to Liberal Democracy. *Journal of Democracy*, 29(2), pp. 5–19.
Habermas, J. (1990). *Moral Consciousness and Communicative Action*. Trans. C. Lenhardt and S. Weber Nicholson. Cambridge: Polity Press.
Habermas, J. (1993). *Justification and Application: Remarks of Discourse Ethics*. Trans. C. Cronin. Cambridge: Polity Press.
Habermas, J. (1996). *Between Facts and Norms: Contributions to a Discourse Theory of Law and Democracy*. Trans. W. Rehg. Cambridge, MA: The MIT Press.
Habermas, J. (1998). *The Inclusion of the Other: Studies in Political Theory*. Trans. C. Cronin. Cambridge, MA: The MIT Press.
Habermas, J. (2004). Religious Tolerance: The Pacemaker for Cultural Rights. *Philosophy*, 79(1), pp. 5–18.

Jamin, J. (2012). Two Different Realities: Notes on Populism and the Extreme Right. In: A. Mammone et al., eds., *Right-Wing Extremism in Europe*, 1st ed. New York and London: Routledge, pp. 38–52.

Laclau, E. (1979). *Politics and Ideology in Marxist Theory*. London: Verso Books.

Laclau, E. (2005). *On Populist Reason*. London: Verso Books.

Lipset, S. and Raab, E. (1973). *The Politics of Unreason: Right-Wing Extremism in America, 1790–1970*. New York: Harper Torchbooks.

Mény, Y. and Surel, Y. (2002). The Constitutive Ambiguity of Populism. In: Y. Mény and Y. Surel, eds., *Democracies and the Populist Challenge*, 1st ed. New York: Palgrave Macmillan, pp. 1–24.

Mouffe, C. (1999). Introduction: Schmitt's Challenge. In: C. Mouffe, ed., *The Challenge of Carl Schmitt*, 1st ed. London: Verso Books, pp. 1–6.

Mouffe, C. (2000). *The Democratic Paradox*. London: Verso Books.

Mouffe, C. (2005). *On the Political*. London and New York: Routledge.

Mouffe, C. (2018). *For a Left Populism*. London: Verso Books.

Mudde, C. (1996). The War of Words: Defining the Extreme Right Party Family. *West European Politics*, 19(2), pp. 225–248.

Mudde, C. (2004). The Populist Zeitgeist. *Government and Opposition*, 39(4), pp. 541–563.

Rawls, J. (1999). *A Theory of Justice*, revised ed. Cambridge, MA: The Belknap Press of Harvard University Press.

Rawls, J. (2005). *Political Liberalism*, expanded ed. New York and Chichester, West Sussex: Columbia University Press.

Salmela, M. and von Scheve, C. (2017). Emotional Roots of Right-Wing Political Populism. *Social Science Information*, 56(4), pp. 567–595.

Stavrakakis, Y. (2004). Antinomies of Formalism: Laclau's Theory of Populism and the Lessons from Religious Populism in Greece. *Journal of Political Ideologies*, 9(3), pp. 253–267.

Taggart, P. (2000). *Populism*. Buckingham: Open University Press.

Thaler, M. (2010). The Illusion of Purity: Chantal Mouffe's Realist Critique of Cosmopolitanism. *Philosophy and Social Criticism*, 36(7), pp. 785–800.

Thomassen, L. (2006). The Inclusion of the Other? Habermas and the Paradox of Tolerance. *Political Theory*, 34(4), pp. 439–462.

# Part III
# Toleration and Liberalism in Context
## Cases and Controversies

# 10 Religious Toleration, Education and the Headscarf Dispute

*Johannes Drerup*

## Introduction

In the present chapter I will reconstruct and discuss different, conflicting positions in the public controversy over a ban on headscarves in kindergartens and public schools. The wearing of headscarves in public institutions belongs to the classical topics and objects of debates about (religious) toleration and its limits (see, for instance: Galeotti, 2000; Laborde, 2006; Forst, 2013; Lacorne, 2019).[1] The topic (again) has become increasingly politically contentious in recent years, largely due the ban on the wearing of headscarves in kindergartens and primary schools in Austria and political proposals for corresponding bans in Germany. Opponents of headscarves in kindergartens and public schools appeal in part to a specific interpretation of the state requirement of neutrality. For example, they assume that the headscarf cannot be reconciled with the free and self-confident development of children and that it is an expression of religious coercion. Headscarf advocates, on the other hand, interpret the proposed ban as an expression of antireligious, intolerant and specifically antimuslim symbolic politics, and argue that it would amount to a restriction of the fundamental rights of parents and children (including their freedom of religion). I will begin by clarifying the relevant principles of secularism as aspects of the more general ideal of state neutrality (1). Then I will go on to discuss the most important arguments put forward by the opponents of headscarves and argue that a corresponding state "unveiling decree" would be incompatible with basic principles of liberal politics and education, suitably interpreted (2).

## 1. Principles of Secularism and Religious Pluralism: Problems and Controversies

Public school systems in liberal democracies have become the venues of ongoing debates and conflicts over toleration[2] that in many cases turn on the legitimate role and function of religion, that is of religious practices, beliefs and symbols, within a state, that is supposed to be neutral with respect to different conceptions of the good, be they religious, ethical or cultural. These controversies are prompted by the question of how pluralistic societies should deal with diverging values, which in many cases can give rise to value conflicts over the definition, harmonization and implementation of the tasks, rights and duties of the liberal state, of parents and religious communities and of children (see, for instance, Mahoney, 2014). Because of the "fact of reasonable pluralism" (Rawls, 2005) of religious and philosophical worldviews, that cannot be easily arranged in a binding way in a hierarchy of legitimacy or superiority within the framework of an objective order of values (or what Rawls called the "limits of reason"), liberal societies must rely on an inclusive overlapping consensus on basic public values. Public education in liberal states, nevertheless cannot remain neutral all the way down in the sense that it could be based on no normative and justificatory basis at all (see on the controversy over the question whether a neutral liberal state could – due to the objection component – be a tolerant state: Balint, 2017; Kühler, 2019). It rests on fundamental values and guiding principles (including the rights of the individual, personal autonomy and equal respect as educational goals), which are constitutive for democratic and liberal regimes, because "they provide these systems with their foundations and aims. Although these values are not neutral, they are legitimate, because it is they that allow citizens espousing very different conceptions of the good to live together in peace" (Maclure and Taylor, 2011, p. 11). However, it remains notoriously controversial in this context what state neutrality exactly requires as a postulate in the education system: How should liberal-democratic basic values be interpreted in concrete terms in relation to the public education system? How can they be justified and implemented vis-à-vis different conceptions of the good? And what concrete implications does this have when it comes to establishing pedagogical arrangements?

Maclure and Taylor (2011) discuss the associated questions concerning the neutrality of the state in terms of the concept of secularism, which refers to "one of the modalities of the system of governance allowing democratic and liberal states to grant equal respect to individuals with different worldviews and sets of values" (p. 19). Their assumption is that secularism should be understood as being "composed of a set of values *and* of means or 'operative modes'" (ibid.). According to this view, secularism is based on a plurality of principles, each of which fulfils certain tasks and can be realized through a variety of concrete means or operative modes. On the other hand, the failure to distinguish between values and means (or, in other words, between rationales and practices; see Drerup, 2013), regularly leads to confusion, such as when specific *means* for realizing secularism are accorded the same status as *goals* of secularism. According to Maclure and Taylor, the fact that the relevant goals and means can be realized in multiple ways and admit of different interpretations and arrangements is also one of the reasons why secularism cannot be reduced to simple formulas such as the "separation of church and state" or the "exclusion of religion from the public sphere," which only cover one aspect of secularism.

Secularism, Maclure and Taylor argue, is based on two principles – equality of respect and freedom of conscience – and two operative modes, namely the separation of church and state and the neutrality of the state toward religions, which are open to different interpretations and can "prove to be relatively permissive or rather restrictive with respect to religious practice" (Maclure and Taylor, 2011, p. 20). The principle of equal respect requires a liberal state to accord all of its citizens equal value or equal dignity, from which it follows that the state must not identify with a particular religion or belief, so that it must be ideologically neutral and must adopt a neutral stance toward different religions and belief systems. This also means that it must be able to justify its decisions toward all of its citizens, "which it will be unable to do if it favors one particular conception of the world and of the good" (ibid., p. 21).[3] The principle of freedom of conscience requires the secular state to show itself to be "'agnostic' on the questions of the aims of human existence", so that it "recognizes the sovereignty of the person in his or her choices of conscience" (ibid.). Among the central problems and dilemmas of liberal states is that the basic principles of secularism and the corresponding operative modes can come into conflict, for example when the principle of equal respect clashes with the principle of freedom of conscience. This can become relevant in the case of children or teachers wearing headscarves if the principle of equal respect is interpreted in such a way that religious symbols are not supposed to have any legitimate place in public institutions and hence should not be tolerated. However, this amounts to a restriction of the freedom of religion and conscience of the persons concerned.

According to Taylor and Maclure, these and other conflicts are interpreted and evaluated differently in the context of different "regimes of secularism". They distinguish between republican and liberal-pluralist regimes of secularism respectively. While the latter can be understood as "a mode of governance whose function is to find the optimal balance between respect for moral equality and respect for freedom of conscience," the republican model

> attributes to secularism the mission of favoring, in addition to respect for moral equality and freedom of conscience, the emancipation of individuals and the growth of a common civic identity, which requires marginalizing religious affiliations and forcing them back into the private sphere.
>
> (ibid., p. 34)

Therefore, variants of the republican model argue for a ban in the context of the debate over the wearing of headscarves in primary schools and kindergartens. In the following section, I will subject the arguments put forward in this debate to critical examination.

## 2. The Headscarf Dispute: Religious toleration and "Unveiling Decrees"

The arguments offered by opponents of the wearing of headscarves in kindergartens and primary schools can be classified into two types. *Firstly*, arguments are put forward that assume that the headscarf is a symbol of religious oppression, intolerance and of indoctrination and that it is therefore incompatible with respect for the developing personal autonomy of children (see Section 2.1). *Secondly*, it is assumed that the headscarf as a religious symbol does not have any legitimate place within the framework of a public school system, since this is not compatible with the principle of state neutrality (see Section 2.2).

Before reconstructing and discussing these two arguments, however, it is advisable to consider the political context of the different versions of the headscarf dispute. It has been noted, probably correctly, that the headscarf dispute (Galeotti, 2000) as well as some of the similar debates, such as those over the Burqa (Fateh-Moghadam, 2013) and the circumcision of children (Fateh-Moghadam, 2010; Brumlik, 2015; Voloj Dessauer, 2017), should be understood primarily as forms of symbolic politics.[4] The assumption is that these debates – also because of their rather low factual social relevance, for example in the case of the Burqa – turned and continue to turn less on questions of state neutrality or the like than on a politically orchestrated discourse of denigration and distrust that feeds off fears and intolerance toward a specific religion (e.g. toward Islam; Said, 1997; Nussbaum, 2014; Schiffauer, 2015; Thränhardt and Weiss, 2016).[5] This interpretation also acquires a certain plausibility due to the often rather one-sided focus on an essentialistic conception of "Islam" as the object and trigger of debates over toleration (Brown, 2006) and the associated political interests and strategies of right-wing populist parties and movements. Besides, this seems the only plausible explanation for the sometimes fierce reactions, such as in the debate concerning circumcision and the dispute over teachers wearing the hijab, in which courts have at times become "stages on which cultural conflicts are played out" (Graf, 2013, p. 36). Why, for example, should a teacher wearing a headscarf be per se more inclined to indoctrinate her pupils than a teacher who does not wear one? Why does a practice that is thousands of years old more or less suddenly become the focus of a public controversy over child welfare? Taking the example of child welfare, one can easily imagine a series of far more relevant topics, such as questions of nutrition or child poverty, about which people are much less preoccupied. When analyzing the relevant lines of argument, therefore, one should always bear in mind how "debates over religion" are embedded in historically evolved hierarchies and power relations and how these debates are used to construct enemy images in order to foment religious conflicts. Such an analysis is indispensable, of course, in order to counter the corresponding arguments, which, as the examples of Austria, Germany, France and other countries show, are not merely of academic relevance.[6]

### 2.1 What's Going on Under the Headscarf? Personal Autonomy, Equal Respect and Symbolic Politics

The question of whether children should or should not be allowed to wear headscarves in public educational institutions is inseparable from how the headscarf is interpreted as a symbol. Should it be interpreted primarily as a religious symbol, as a political symbol and/or as a symbol of the oppression of women? If one assumes that the headscarf *per se* is a symbol of the oppression of women or an expression of a political, and in all likelihood fundamentalist version of Islam, it could be argued that it is incompatible with basic liberal educational goals, personal autonomy and equal respect for persons. However, such an essentialist interpretation will be met with skepticism especially if one takes into account the history of critiques of Islam, for example in colonialist and neo-colonialist contexts, which were only superficially concerned with women's emancipation, but much more with legitimizing "Western" claims to superiority (Castro Varela and Dhawan, 2015). Therefore, it makes sense to recall the historical mutability not only of religious symbols in politically motivated debates and the fact that they are open to multiple interpretations. Heins summarizes the relevant point:

> The role played today on the European continent by the headdresses of Muslim women or the suddenly scandalous Jewish and Muslim practice of circumcising boys was played in New York a hundred years ago by the gherkins and other pickled foods beloved of Eastern European Jews, which patriotic social reformers and health inspectors believed would turn those who consumed him into "nervous, unstable" subjects and ultimately "bad Americans".
> (Heins, 2013, p. 11)

So when the headscarf was and is interpreted as a sign of "collective backwardness or a moral threat to the community" (ibid., p. 11), we would do well to refrain from rash judgments and generalizations.

The "true" meaning of a symbol such as the headscarf depends not only on processes of historical change, but also on the respective sociopolitical contexts and power constellations in which certain interpretations are propagated (Merry, 2007; Pink, 2018). In Saudi Arabia wearing the headscarf certainly does not mean the same thing as in the European Union, just as how the headscarf is worn and the motives for wearing it or dressing children in headscarves also vary in liberal democracies depending on the context and on the individuals concerned (Steinberg, 2015).[7] This is of course first and foremost an empirical question. At least when it comes to adults in Germany, it is true that "the overwhelming majority of women who wear headscarves are self-motivated, whereas the expectations of those people and their social environment merely accounts for around 12 percent of cases" (ibid., p. 214). Of course, the concrete meaning of the headscarf also varies between different Islamic religious communities. Thus it is often interpreted in such a way that children are only supposed to wear it after the onset of puberty, but not before, which has in turn prompted the claim that in the case of prepubescent children it should not be interpreted as a religious symbol (and that, unlike a prohibition of the kippah, for instance, its prohibition would therefore not conflict with the state's requirement of neutrality vis-à-vis different religions; see Section 2.2).

One of the most plausible arguments for a headscarf ban is without doubt that the decision in favour of smaller children, that is children of kindergarten and primary school age, wearing headscarves tends to be promoted by religious groups which, it is assumed, adhere to more traditional, if not fundamentalist, interpretations of Islam. The political and empirical assumption is that a ban sends a political signal to fundamentalists and ideally simultaneously protects the child from religious indoctrination (Toprak, 2019; Nettesheim, 2019)[8]. One has to conceded that there obviously *are* cases where the development of personal autonomy of children is restrained on the basis of religious reasons and rationales and where these children are *also* forced to wear a hijab:[9]

> Here, if necessary, the citizenry as a whole must speak out in support of a *minority within the minority* which is subordinate – in this case, under-age girls – wherever such practices exist. This is difficult to achieve in practice because it calls for extensive controlling and interventionary mechanisms which may entail a range of undesirable paternalistic side-effects. However, the proposal to draw such limits of toleration first in the *symbolic* domain by placing the wearing of the hijab under general suspicion not only misses the problem of *real* suppression. It incorrectly infers from the fact that some girls *might* be forced to wear a head covering that the latter *is* a symbol of an oppressive practice as such.
> (Forst, 2013, p. 557; emphasis added in original)

Against this backdrop, Taylor and Maclure observe:

> The question to be raised here is obviously what logical connection exists between the ban on wearing conspicuous religious symbols

in the public schools and the protection of girls subject to undue pressures. In what ways does the law protect girls who are victims of harassment in their communities? How is that law likely to put an end to the unreasonable demands for accommodation in public institutions? What we know, in any event, is that the ban restricts the freedom of religion of Muslim, Jewish, and Sikh students who voluntarily wear visible religious symbols.

(2011, pp. 33–34)

In the first place, therefore, one can question whether a ban really helps the affected children, especially when one considers that it seems to have counterproductive side effects (e.g. that in response to bans children are enrolled in private religious schools, although in France such effects have only occurred to a limited extent: Steinberg, 2015; Joeres, 2018; for a fundamental treatment of this topic see: Merry, 2007). In France, for example, the primary concern is with the "political costs" of the headscarf ban:

The cordial relations between the minister of the interior *Nicolas Sarcozy* and the Muslim associations, whose most visible expression was the founding of the *Conseil français du culte muselman* (FFCM) . . . were destroyed and the authority of the Council among Muslims was damaged, which led to an increased influx especially of young Muslims to the radical groupings.

(Steinberg, 2015, p. 61)

Since the specific relationship of the headscarf to certain pedagogical practices or to practices of religious indoctrination is not always obvious and it can be assumed that the main problem, assuming there is one, is the indoctrination and *not* the corresponding symbol, it remains unclear whether the means favoured by the republican model (banning headscarves) in fact represents a sensible way of achieving the desired goals (e.g. personal autonomy as an educational goal). After all, it is neither the task of the liberal state to speculate about the true, theologically appropriate meaning of religious symbols (Maclure and Taylor, 2011), nor to impose on all of its citizens the liberal *ideal of an autonomous conduct of life*, as opposed to *personal autonomy as an educational goal*, which is compatible with the autonomous choice of a non-autonomous way of life (Laborde, 2006, p. 360; Nussbaum, 2014). Against this it can be objected that, whereas in the case of older children the headscarf is certainly often freely chosen, it is equally certain that smaller children in particular, for example those under the age of 14, have not chosen it voluntarily, and therefore it is also unclear whether in such cases, strictly speaking, a prohibition can amount a restriction of "freedom of conscience," since such small children have not yet developed a stable conception of the good. But this also applies to many other decisions, of course, not just to those of a religious nature.

However, the central question of *pedagogical* and *political relevance* seems to be not so much whether children should wear religious symbols as whether these symbols contribute to undermining the development of their personal autonomy (see the position of: Nettesheim, 2019).

As long as children are not oppressed in their families and communities and can cultivate the abilities and basic values constitutive for liberal democracy (e.g. tolerance), and as long as it remains possible for them in principle to choose other forms of life (Gutmann, 1999), there is little to be said in favour of a ban from a strictly liberal-democratic perspective. With or without a headscarf, one can learn to respect others equally as persons regardless of their religious affiliation; with or without a headscarf, one can learn something about other ways and choices of life; and one can learn – likewise with or without a headscarf – to deal critically and reflexively with traditional religious guidelines (see also: Merry, 2007). These examples already demonstrate that the question of whether someone wears a headscarf or not must be distinguished from questions of education and training in public institutions of liberal democracies. Finally, how this question is answered has no bearing whatsoever on the central pedagogical issues, such as those of the content of the curriculum, which should be based on basic liberal-democratic values. In modern societies it is virtually impossible not to encounter people with different values, and therefore there is also no right to be insulated from other conceptions of good (Kreß, 2015, p. 398). Religious parents therefore also have to accept that, regardless of the religious community to which they belong,[10] their children are going to be confronted with other views of the good, for example that they will learn that there is such a thing as homosexuality and that homosexuals should be treated with equal respect (on this issue in the case of Christian fundamentalists see Brennan and Macleod, 2017). They must also accept, for example, that Christian or Islamic religious instruction is only acceptable in the context of liberal democracy if the way in which it is delivered is not likely to block the choice of other forms of life in principle (Gutmann, 1999) or to devalue them (Khorchide, 2017).[11] When it comes to the question of the headscarf and its interpretation, what is of primary relevance from an *educational* perspective within the public school system of liberal democracies is in any case whether and to what extent wearing a headscarf can be regarded as incompatible with central liberal-democratic educational goals. However, there is little to be said in favour of that view. In the case of the headscarf, the following ultimately holds: "What is decisive . . . is probably less *what* someone believes than *how* he or she believes – for example, whether his or her beliefs are able to accommodate elements of reflexive self-limitation" (Graf, 2013, p. 40). To reiterate, this works just as well with a headscarf as without. Hence the empirical and normative assumption that wearing religious symbols, like a hijab, would undermine education for personal autonomy as an aim of schooling (Nettesheim, 2019) is not plausible.

While a pedagogical contextualization of the debate about the headscarf *in* schools can rebut some of the most important reservations at least in part, it makes sense to re-examine the social and political context in which the headscarf discussion is conducted (for comparative analyses of hijab debates in different sociopolitical contexts and climates see: Mendus, 2011; Lacorne, 2019)[12]. As already indicated, it is open to question whether opponents of the headscarf are in fact concerned about the autonomy or even the emancipation of children, or whether there may not be other political reasons that contribute to repeatedly focusing attention on this example. Since it is unclear as an empirical matter how many children would actually be affected by a ban on wearing headscarves (Gökkaya and Sadigh, 2018), it also remains unclear to what extent it is a politically motivated phantom debate and a one-sided outcry, and to what extent it is a "really" relevant political and pedagogical problem. Especially in view of the decidedly one-sided focus that one also finds in academic debates on potential conflicts between a religious upbringing, associated religious symbols and personal autonomy (rather than, for example, on conflicts between personal autonomy and the potential effects of a capitalist consumer culture – see the critiques of Brown, 2006; Brighouse, 2007; Schinkel, 2010; Nussbaum, 2014), the debate shows how serious is the danger of assuming double standards grounded in an ethics of autonomy when it comes to determining the legitimate limits of tolerance in the liberal state. Then members of traditional communities suffer stigmatization and discrimination by being deprived of autonomy on paternalistic grounds. Attempts to determine the tolerability of decisions, attitudes and practices by appeal to the criteria of an ethics of autonomy present a range of epistemological and normative problems (on the following see Galeotti, 2015; Drerup, 2017). Just the problem of comprehending the psychology of others often means that it is virtually impossible to infer from a decision or behavior that the agent lacks autonomy. Judgments on the existence of autonomy therefore often stand on shaky ground: "on the basis of the same view of autonomy, the very same outward conduct in the same context can lead to different judgments about the agent's autonomy depending on a variance in the agent's responsiveness to her environment" (Galeotti, 2015, p. 280). The paternalistic justification of the instrumentalization of the denial of autonomy can lead to certain practices (such as piercing, cosmetic surgery and the like) being regarded as a perfectly normal part of a liberal culture, while other practices (for example wearing a hijab) are selectively deemed on the basis of double standards to be problematic and placed under general suspicion as incompatible with an ethics of autonomy: "It seems that the only relevant difference between them and hijab wearing is that the former are familiar practices of *our* culture;

although they may well signal the absence of autonomy, they are simply taken for granted" (ibid., p. 290; emphasis in original).

A distinction is made between those who *have* culture and those who are *shaped* by their culture (Brown, 2006), in order to perpetuate and consolidate claims to superiority and relations of domination. The headscarf as a visible symbol and an object of special laws thereby becomes a symbol of discrimination (Schiffauer, 2015) and a vehicle of the identity politics of the social majority, which amounts to an advocatory imposition of identity from above by the state (wearing the headscarf = expression of a deficient relationship to self and to the state; Steinberg, 2015, p. 213 referring to Forst, 2003).[13] As Forst puts it: "In this way, an ambiguous symbol is lent a negative moral interpretation which is in danger of disrespecting ethical-religious identities. This represents a further, very familiar dialectic of toleration: the attempt to combat intolerance itself becomes a form of intolerance" (2013, p. 557). A signal is sent to members of Islamic religious communities that they are not welcome, and the headscarf may become an object of shame from the children's perspective:

> The headscarf often functions like a projection screen onto which images of foreignness and danger are projected, images that clash with one's own identity-based national and ethical sensitivities. But this view of the headscarf also has an effect on those who wear it, for whom the headscarf question can quickly become a test of their level of emancipation.
> (Steinberg, 2015, p. 236)

In this way, children learn that how they and their parents exercise their religion and individuality is per se not tolerable and that they are different in a problematic way. This kind of fear-driven prohibitionist policy is certainly no way to foster the self-determination, emancipation and certainly not the tolerance of the children or the integration of Muslims (Gökkaya and Sadigh, 2018). If an emancipatory republican regime of secularism is really concerned about the basic values of autonomy and equal respect, then there is much to be said for implementing these values *without* recourse to a state unveiling decree. Reemtsma's reflection on the debate on female teachers wearing headscarves can therefore also be applied to children: "The school authorities should treat headscarves as a question of fashion. Symbols only become symbols through actions and appropriate contexts" (2008, p. 40). As long as wearing a headscarf is not incompatible with the basic values of a liberal democracy and a corresponding upbringing and education, it should be accepted as a legitimate aspect and expression of religious pluralism.

## 2.2 State Neutrality and the Political Value of Pluralism

A further argument put forward by advocates of bans on children wearing headscarves in public schools assumes that in this context religious symbols are not compatible with the state requirement of neutrality. Whereas from a pluralistic, liberal point of view this prohibition is interpreted in such a way that the public space of the school should accommodate a plurality of different concepts of the good and their associated symbols, practices, celebrations, and so forth, proponents of a republican regime of secularism assume that these belong in the private and not in the public domain. This was justified in France also with the argument that the headscarf was even "a statement of hostility against the republic and its essential institution of laïcité" (Taylor, 2011, p. 43). From this perspective, all religious symbols would have to be eliminated from public space, as is the case in French public schools. From this point of view, a specific privileging of a particular religion based on its supposed special place in Western culture, as was propagated in the case of the "crucifix controversy" in Germany, cannot be reconciled with the requirement of neutrality. This may also be why in the Austrian debate it was argued that in the case of children the headscarf is not even a religious symbol, since, according to the usual interpretation, it should only be worn after the onset of puberty. The primary motive driving this argument is clearly to strengthen the case for the crucifix (see on the crucifix-controversy in Germany: Forst, 2013). One could with equal justification argue that the crucifix is not really a religious symbol, because it is manifestly not used and interpreted as a genuine religious symbol (for example in pop-culture contexts). Such selective attempts to single out the headscarf are themselves one of the reasons why it should have a place in the classroom.

The central problem of a republican regime of secularism is that it confuses state neutrality with radical secularization imposed by the state from above, which can reasonably be interpreted from a religious perspective as an expression of intolerance. It makes more sense to assume that "the secular state ... stands in an equidistant relationship, and not in an oppositional stance, to all religious and ideological positions" (Dreier, 2018, p. 12). From the point of view of a liberal-pluralistic understanding of secularism, this is in principle compatible with allowing religious symbols and practices and their inclusion in the public sphere of the school system. This can be seen as a form of *symbolic legitimation of* the respective orientations and identity profiles (Galeotti, 2002), which is geared to ensuring that all children feel welcome as members of a liberal and genuinely pluralistic society.[14]

The prohibitionist view of religious symbols such as the headscarf propagated by proponents of republican regimes of secularism, on the other hand, falls prey to a *double fetishization*: firstly, a fetishization of the regulatory arrangements (Taylor, 2011) regarded as necessary to achieve the objectives of secularism (that headscarf ban) and, secondly, a fetishization of the object these arrangements are aimed at (the headscarf). However, this double fetishization proves to be counterproductive when it comes to achieving the central goals of secularism. It can be argued against it that pluralism and the manifestation of symbols and practices associated with it are central political values: "Pluralism is an important political value insofar as social diversity enriches our lives by expanding our understanding of differing ways of life. To reap the benefits of social diversity, children must be exposed to ways of life different from their parents and – in the course of their exposure – must embrace certain values, such as mutual respect among citizens, that make social diversity both possible and desirable" (Gutmann, 1999, p. 33). The justified hope in this case is that the habituation to plurality contributes to breaking down prejudices and also makes it possible to change the views of people of different faiths through direct social interaction (Warnick, 2012; on the contact hypothesis see Rapp, 2014). In this way, living and learning together can contribute to a de-dramatization of supposedly large differences, which are often transformed into antagonisms for political motives (Heins, 2013, p. 11). Taylor and Maclure note accordingly that

> young people who are exposed at an early age to the diversity they will encounter outside of school may more easily be able to sort out the differences and will consequently be less quick to apprehend them as threats. Peaceful coexistence in a diverse society requires that we learn to find normal a range of identity-related differences.
> (Maclure and Taylor, 2011, pp. 46–47)

On the other hand, a headscarf ban not only undermines the right of schoolgirls to equality and freedom of conscience,[15] but also "would likely deprive them of a unique opportunity for socialization with pupils and teachers from all origins and backgrounds" (ibid., p. 59, with reference to the conclusions of a committee set up in Quebec to address this issue).

This is also why the two guiding values of secularism, namely freedom of conscience and equal respect, are better served by being politically secured and pedagogically promoted at the organizational level (e.g. through the composition of the student body and teaching staff), at the curricular level (e.g. through forms of democratic education in corresponding subject areas that provide information about different concepts of the good; see ibid., p. 137) and at the interpersonal level (through respectful interaction and familiarization with different identity profiles). The result need not be that different conceptions of the good must be appreciated and valued,[16] which may be going too far for many people (Balint, 2017). But it does at a minimum call for equal respect for persons who have a claim to equal rights and a basic acceptance of the fact and also the value of pluralism. It can find expression in the *assumption* that the orientation of the other, however this is adjusted, is of equal worth (Taylor, 1994), as a starting point for developing ethical sensitivity to different points of view in the context of an ethics of dialogue (Maclure and Taylor, 2011, pp. 107–108). This, of course, does not exclude criticism of oppressive practices and attitudes that are incompatible with the basic values of liberal democracy, any more than it excludes the possibility that "in certain circumstances" the requirements of "an education in tolerance and pluralism" can justify restrictions on parental rights or on parents' requests for exemptions for their children (ibid., p. 102, for example in the case of conflicts over the contents of the curriculum of specific school subjects).

## Conclusion

The debate over the wearing of headscarves in the public school system is always also a proxy debate in which value conflicts in liberal democracies are (re)constructed and played out. This is bound up with the twofold problem that in many cases the focus on the headscarf, as a proxy for supposed "cultural or religious conflicts", distracts from problems of far greater political and pedagogical relevance and that the headscarf debate itself simultaneously serves as an instrument of discrimination. However, this instrumentalization of the debate is difficult to reconcile with basic liberal democratic values, whose defence is supposed to be the focus of the debates in question. These basic values, such as equal respect for the person and his or her rights and religious and political tolerance, can be politically implemented and fostered through education without headscarf bans. The fetishization of an item of clothing and associated decrees by the state banning headscarves in public schools will be of no help in this regard. On the contrary, they are more likely to exacerbate the problems they claim to solve.

## Notes

1. This chapter is a revised, translated version of Drerup 2019. The translation was done by *Ciaran Cronin*. I would like to thank Michael Kienecker from Mentis for the permission to use the material.
2. In the philosophical debate over toleration, a distinction is usually made between tolerance as a private and political or democratic virtue – that is, tolerance in direct social interactions, and tolerance between citizens or different groups. Tolerance as a virtue must in turn be distinguished from toleration as a political principle and as a regulating principle of social arrangements and practices that concern the relationship between the state and its citizens. Furthermore, participants in the German debate in particular often follow Forst's lead (Forst, 2013) in distinguishing between a basic or core concept of toleration and different normative conceptions of toleration (e.g. a so-called

respect conception), each of which claims to represent an appropriate way of spelling out this core concept. According to Forst, the core concept of toleration is characterized, among other things, by the interplay between an objection and an acceptance component:

(A) A distinguishing feature of toleration is that it is directed at features regarded as objectionable on moral or other grounds (*objection component*).
(B) At the same time, the objection component is trumped by certain positive reasons, without thereby invalidating the reasons for the objection (*acceptance component*).

Moreover, Forst distinguishes between different conceptions of toleration, for instance a permission or a respect conception. Depending on the conception of toleration, this basic conceptual structure will be filled in different ways, that is differing answers will be provided to the paradoxes of toleration (such as, the paradox of drawing the limits) as well as conflicts of toleration will be interpreted and evaluated in different way. According to a permission conception of toleration, for instance, the relation between the two parties involved in a conflict is asymmetrical and the more powerful agent tolerates the weaker agent only on the condition that the latter does accept its inferior status and does not demands equal political rights. A neo-Baylean respect conception, which is the one defended by Forst (2013), assumes that just relations of toleration should be structured according to the principles of reciprocity and generality. According to this conception it would, for instance, be unjust to accept the presence of a particular religious symbol in public schools, such as a cross, but not to tolerate other religious symbols such as a hijab worn by a teacher or children, because such a policy could not be reciprocally justified with respect to all the relevant individuals as free and equal citizens. This is also conceded by some defenders of a headscarf ban (Nettesheim, 2019), who are willing to apply such a ban also to other religious symbols.

3. In the debate about state neutrality one usually distinguishes between neutrality of intent, consequences or justificatory neutrality, while the last meaning is typically regarded as most relevant.
4. Concerning the notion of symbolic politics, Meyer observes: "Symbols always fulfill a vicarious function. They stand for a context that is not itself present, but which becomes present insofar as they are perceived.... The symbols of symbolic politics are real symbols, although what they appear to symbolize is not real. They render the fictitious context really present. They cannot be made accountable for the real status of the conceptions of which they are the vehicles. They are only responsible for the transport, not for the quality of what is delivered" (Meyer, 1992, pp. 54–55).
5. The accusation of racism frequently raised in this context should nevertheless be treated with caution, because often it is not only a hindrance to an objective debate, but in many cases an expression of illiberal attitudes. It is often specifically aimed at the limitation of the exercise of the right to free speech and free discussion, as is shown by the attempts to disavow and boycott a recent conference on the headscarf in 2019 (on this, see Thiel, 2019).
6. Despite the relevance of the context, the following analysis claims to be valid not only for a particular "Western" society but for all liberal democracies.
7. Rather, the problem seems to reside in a problem shift that results from concentrating on the headscarf instead of on forms of religious fundamentalism

and authoritarianism as propagated and exported by countries like Saudi Arabia. Accordingly, the focus on the headscarf tends to obscure the relevant problems instead of focusing attention on them.
8. I agree with major parts of the analysis of Nettesheim (2019) when it comes to his perfectionist interpretation of the *normative and legal framework* he adopts in his defence of a headscarf ban. I disagree, however, when it comes to the conclusions he draws from this framework, which assume that a ban of wearing the headscarf in schools would be an effective means to safeguard the developing autonomy of children.
9. The debate about a hijab ban in kindergartens and public schools is also instrumentalized by fundamentalist groups as a propaganda tool (see: Schmitt, 2019).
10. Skepticism is called for in this context concerning arguments that result in one-sided allocations and negative or positive revaluations of religions and religious communities, such as that Islam is supposedly incompatible with democracy or that Christianity has a special affinity with democracy (Khorchide, 2016; see also Graf, 2013; Kreß, 2015; Hidalgo, 2017). Concerning the concept of dignity, Fateh-Moghadam observes: "Dignity in the Christian sense was always a duty-generating construction that was opposed to releasing the individual from heteronomous bonds. The Christian concept of dignity never managed to conceive of dignity, as the German legal system does today, as the 'basic norm of personal autonomy.' Above all, the Christian conception of human dignity never went so far as to guarantee the inviolability of the individual also as regards his earthly legal protected rights" (Fateh-Moghadam et al., 2015, p. 75).
11. A form of liberal-democratic upbringing and education committed to a corresponding ethos of discontinuity between the parental home, school and society (Brighouse, 2007) can and should contribute to counteracting traditional patriarchal forms of upbringing in the parental home, which exist among followers of all religions, and to undermining them in the longer term.
12. It is interesting to note the huge differences between dealing with the hijab in France, where it became very much the object of identity politics (questions concerning "French identity") and hence also was constructed as a central educational and political problem, and, for instance, in the US, where this did not happen.
13. On a strict interpretation of the criteria employed, one would also have to prohibit other symbols and garments that could potentially be interpreted as expressions of political extremism (bomber jackets, Mohawk haircuts, etc.; see Würfel, 2019).
14. The argument put forward by Toprak (2019) that the headscarf should be banned because children could be bullied on account of it is based on questionable premises. Of course, children are bullied in schools for all sorts of reasons. But forbidding what provides the pretext for bullying, instead of doing something about the underlying attitudes, cannot be seriously proposed as the solution to the problem of bullying.
15. It will not be possible to discuss some of the relevant special problems in the present context. These include problems with defining the concept of religion (Dreier, 2018), "religious" toleration (Spinner-Halev, 2005), and questions about whether religious and non-religious beliefs and decisions of conscience should be treated similarly or differently (Maclure and Taylor, 2011; Laborde, 2017).
16. On the more general question concerning the appropriate attitude towards religion (toleration, different notions of respect etc., see Leiter 2009; Jones 2012; Bird 2013).

# References

Balint, P. (2017). *Respecting Toleration*. Oxford: Oxford University Press.
Bird, C. (2013). Does Religion Deserve Our Respect? *Journal of Applied Philosophy*, 30(3). [online] Available at: https://doi.org/10.1111/japp.12023 [Accessed 27 Apr. 2020].
Brennan, S. and Macleod, C. (2017). Fundamentally Incompetent: Homophobia, Religion, and the Right to Parent. In: J. Ahlberg and M. Cholbi, eds., *Procreation, Parenthood, and Educational Rights*, 1st ed. New York, Oxon: Routledge, pp. 230–245.
Brighouse, H. (2007). Channel One, the Anti-Commercial Principle, and the Discontinuous Ethos. In: R. Curren, ed., *Philosophy of Education: An Anthology*, 1st ed. Malden: Blackwell, pp. 208–220.
Brown, W. (2006). *Regulating Aversion: Tolerance in the Age of Identity and Empire*. Princeton, NJ: Princeton University Press.
Brumlik, M. (2015). Die Beschneidungsdebatte: Grenz- und Bewährungsfall einer advokatorischen Ethik. In: S. Andresen, C. Koch and J. König, eds., *Vulnerable Kinder*, 1st ed. Wiesbaden: Springer VS, pp. 223–241.
Castro Varela, M. and Dhawan, N. (2015). *Postkoloniale Theorie*. Bielefeld: Transcript.
Dreier, H. (2018). *Staat ohne Gott*. München: C.H. Beck.
Drerup, J. (2013). *Paternalismus, Perfektionismus und die Grenzen der Freiheit*. Paderborn: Schöningh.
Drerup, J. (2017). Compelle Intrare? Anmerkungen zur Grundlegungsparadoxie der Toleranz. In: J. Drerup and C. Schickhardt, eds., *Kinderethik. Aktuelle Perspektiven – Klassische Problemvorgaben*, 1st ed. Münster: Mentis, pp. 151–186.
Drerup, J. (2019). Regime der Laizität, religiöser Pluralismus und der Streit um das Kopftuch. In: N. Balzer, J. Beljan and J. Drerup, eds., *Charles Taylor: Perspektiven der Erziehungs- und Bildungsphilosophie*, 1st ed. Münster: Mentis, pp. 111–128.
Fateh-Moghadam, B. (2010). Religiöse Rechtfertigung? Die Beschneidung von Knaben zwischen Strafrecht, Religionsfreiheit und elterlichem Sorgerecht. *Rechtswissenschaft*, 2, pp. 115–142.
Fateh-Moghadam, B. (2013). Religiös-weltanschauliche Neutralität und Geschlechterordnung: Strafrechtliche Burka-Verbote zwischen Paternalismus und Moralismus. *Reprints and Working Papers of the Center for Religion and Modernity*. [online] Available at: www.uni-muenster.de/imperia/md/content/religion_und_moderne/preprints/crm_working_paper_2013_02_fatehmoghadam.pdf [Accessed 27 Oct. 2013].
Fateh-Moghadam, B., Gutmann, T., Neumann, M. and Weitin, T. (2015). *Säkulare Tabus*. Berlin: Matthes & Seitz.
Forst, R. (2003). *Toleranz im Konflikt: Geschichte, Gehalt und Gegenwart eines umstrittenen Begriffs*. Frankfurt am Main: Suhrkamp.
Forst, R. (2013). *Toleration in Conflict: Past and Present*. Cambridge: Cambridge University Press.
Galeotti, E. (2000). Zu einer Neubegründung liberaler Toleranz. Eine Analyse der 'Affaire du foulard'. In: R. Forst, ed., *Toleranz. Philosophische Grundlagen*

*und gesellschaftliche Praxis einer umstrittenen Tugend*, 1st ed. Frankfurt am Main and New York: Campus Verlag, pp. 231–256.

Galeotti, E. (2002). *Toleration as Recognition*. Cambridge: Cambridge University Press.

Galeotti, E. (2015). Autonomy and Cultural Practices: The Risk of Double Standards. *European Journal of Political Theory*, 14, pp. 277–296.

Gökkaya, H. and Sadigh, P. (2018). Das Kopftuch für Kinder ist kein Trend. *Die Zeit*. [online] Available at: www.zeit.de/gesellschaft/familie/2018-04/nordrhein-westfalen-kopftuchverbot-maedchen-debatte-meinungen [Accessed 16 May 2019].

Graf, F. W. (2013). Einleitung. In: F. W. Graf and H. Meier, eds., *Politik und Religion*. München: C-H. Beck, pp. 7–45.

Gutmann, A. (1999). *Democratic Education*. Princeton, NJ: Princeton University Press.

Heins, V. (2013). *Der Skandal der Vielfalt*. Frankfurt am Main: Campus.

Hidalgo, O. (2017). Religion und Politik – Über Komplexität, Besonderheiten und Fragestellungen einer interaktiven Beziehung aus politikwissenschaftlicher Perspektive. *Zeitschrift für Religion, Gesellschaft und Politik*, 1, pp. 111–132.

Joeres, A. (2018). Der Schleier in der Schultasche. *Die Zeit*. [online] Available at: www.zeit.de/gesellschaft/2018-04/kopftuchdebatte-frankreich-schulen-religioese-symbole [Accessed 16 May 2019].

Jones, P. (2012). Toleration, Religion and Accommodation. *European Journal of Philosophy*, 23(3), pp. 542–563.

Khorchide, M. (2016). Staat und Religion im Islam. In: U. Hunger and N. Schröder, eds., *Staat und Islam*, 1st ed. Wiesbaden: Springer VS, pp. 71–87.

Khorchide, M. (2017). *Islam ist Barmherzigkeit*. Bpb: Bonn.

Kreß, H. (2015). Weltanschaulicher Pluralismus und Wertekonsens. Gesellschaftliche Koexistenz von Christen, Muslimen und Angehörigen anderer Religionen oder Weltanschauungen im säkularen Rechtsstaat. In: M. Rohe, H. Engin, M. Khorchide, Ö. Özsoy and H. Schmid, eds., *Christentum und Islam in Deutschland*, 1st ed. Bonn: BpB, pp. 333–360.

Kühler, M. (2019). Can a Value-Neutral State Still Be Tolerant? *Critical Review of International Social and Political Philosophy*. [online] Available at: https://doi.org/10.1080/13698230.2019.1616878 [Accessed 30 Apr. 2020].

Laborde, C. (2006). Female Autonomy, Education and the Hijab. *Critical Review of International Social and Political Philosophy*, 9, pp. 351–377.

Laborde, C. (2017). *Liberalism's Religion*. Cambridge, MA and London: The Belknap Press of Harvard University Press.

Lacorne, D. (2019). *The Limits of Tolerance*. New York: Columbia University Press.

Leiter, B. (2009). Foundations of Religious Liberty: Toleration or Respect. [online] Available at: https://papers.ssrn.com/sol3/papers.cfm?abstract_id=1474324 [Accessed 23 Mar. 2019].

Maclure, J. and Taylor, C. (2011). *Secularism and Freedom of Conscience*. Cambridge, MA: The Belknap Press of Harvard University Press.

Mahoney, J. (2014). Justice in Education and Religious Freedom. *Social Philosophy and Policy*, 31(1), pp. 276–294.

Mendus, S. (2011). Religion and Education: More on God v John Rawls. In: E. Burns Coleman and K. White, eds., *Religious Tolerance, Education and the Curriculum*, 1st ed. Rotterdam: Sense Publishers, pp. 1–9.

Merry, M. (2007). *Culture, Identity and Islamic Schooling*. New York: Palgrave Macmillan.

Meyer, T. (1992). *Die Inszenierung des Scheins*. Frankfurt am Main: Suhrkamp.

Nettesheim, M. (2019). *Grundgesetz und Verbot eines 'Kinderkopftuchs': Zur Diskussion über Kopftuchverbote für Schülerinnen*. [online] Available at: www.frauenrechte.de/images/downloads/presse/kinderkopftuch/Nettesheim-Gutachten-Kinderkopftuch-Endfassung.pdf [Accessed 23 Mar. 2020].

Nussbaum, M. (2014). *Die neue religiöse Intoleranz: Ein Ausweg aus der Politik der Angst*. Darmstadt: WBG.

Pink, J. (2018). Islam? Welcher Islam? In: A. Nassehi and P. Felixberger, eds., *Kursbuch 196: Religion, zum Teufel!*, 1st ed. Hamburg: Kursbuch Kulturstiftung GmbH, pp. 128–144.

Rapp, V. (2014). *Toleranz gegenüber Immigranten in der Schweiz und in Europa*. Wiesbaden: Springer VS.

Rawls, J. (2005). *Political Liberalism*. New York: Columbia University Press.

Reemtsma, J. (2008). Muss man Religiösität respektieren? Über Glaubensfragen und den Stolz einer säkularen Gesellschaft. In: K. Liessmann, ed., *Die Gretchenfrage*, 1st ed. Wien: Paul Zsolnay Verlag, pp. 19–44.

Said, E. (1997). *Covering Islam*. London: Vintage.

Schiffauer, W. (2015). *Schule, Moschee, Elternhaus. Eine ethnologische Intervention*. Berlin: Suhrkamp.

Schinkel, A. (2010). Compulsory Autonomy-Promoting Education. *Educational Theory*, 60, pp. 97–116.

Schmitt, J. (2019). Antimuslimischer Rassismus als islamistisches Mobilisierungsthema. *Bundeszentrale für politische Bildung*. [online] Available at: www.bpb.de/politik/extremismus/radikalisierungspraevention/295951/antimuslimischer-rassismus-als-islamistisches-mobilisierungsthema [Accessed 23 Mar. 2019].

Spinner-Halev, J. (2005). Hinduism, Christianity, and Liberal Religious Toleration. *Political Theory*, 33(1), pp. 28–57.

Steinberg, R. (2015). *Kopftuch und Burka*. Baden-Baden: Nomos.

Taylor, C. (1994). *Multiculturalism: Examining the Politics of Recognition*. Ed. Amy Gutmann. Princeton, NJ: Princeton University Press.

Taylor, C. (2011). Why We Need a Radical Reform of Secularism. In: E. Mendieta and J. Van Antwerpen, eds., *The Power of Religion in the Public Sphere*, 1st ed. Berlin: Suhrkamp, pp. 34–59.

Thiel, T. (2019). Wider den Opferkult. *Frankfurter Allgemeine Zeitung*. [online] Available at: www.faz.net/aktuell/feuilleton/debatten/wende-in-frankfurter-kopftuchkonferenz-raum-fuer-freie-debatte-16179391.html [Accessed 16 May 2019].

Thränhardt, D. and Weiss, K. (2016). Die Einbeziehung des Islams in Deutschland zwischen Integrations- und Religionspolitik. In: U. Hunger and N. Schröder, eds., *Staat und Islam*, 1st ed. Wiesbaden: Springer VS, pp. 23–42.

Toprak, A. (2019). Ein Kopftuch erst ab der Religionsmündigkeit. *Die Zeit*. [online] Available at: www.zeit.de/gesellschaft/2019-05/kopftuchverbot-debatte-grundschule-kinder-identitaet-religion [Accessed 28 May 2019].

Voloj Dessauer, A. (2017). Religionsfreiheit und Kindeswohl – Rechtsvergleichende Überlegungen zur Beschneidungsdebatte vom Sommer 2012. In: J. Drerup and C. Schickhardt, eds., *Kinderethik. Aktuelle Perspektiven – Klassische Problemvorgaben*, 1st ed. Münster: Mentis, pp. 201–218.

Warnick, B. (2012). Students Rights to Religious Expression and the Special Characteristics of Schools. *Educational Theory*, 62(1), pp. 59–74.

Würfel, C. (2019). Krisengebiet auf dem Kopf. *Die Zeit*. [online] Available at: www.zeit.de/zeit-magazin/leben/2019-05/kopftuchverbot-oesterreich-frauen-maenner-kopftuch-kippa-feminismus [Accessed 28 May 2019].

# 11 The Harm Principle and Corporations

*Andrew Jason Cohen*

## Introduction[1]

In this chapter, I defend what may seem a surprising view: that John Stuart Mill's famous harm principle would, if taken to be what justifies government action, disallow the existence of corporations. My claim is not that harmful activities of currently existing corporations warrant *their* losing corporate status according to the harm principle. The claim, rather, is that taken strictly, the harm principle and the legal possibility of incorporation are mutually exclusive. This view *may* be surprising – and I do not at all mean to attribute it to Mill – but if I am right, it *should* be obvious. It should also encourage us to think more about the nature of the markets within which business occurs.

In the first section, I layout the view that follows from accepting the harm principle. In the second section, I explain the basic nature of legal incorporation. In the third section, I lay out the brief, but I think decisive, argument that the endorsement of the harm principle (as understood in the first section) is necessarily opposed to legal incorporation. I consider objections in the final section.

The basic argument presented is simple: if the only justification for state action is rectification or prevention of harm, there is no justification for the corpus of corporate law as that law is state instituted for reasons not having to do with harm. This is not to deny that the corporate model of the firm provides great benefit – by reducing costs that make goods and services less expensive for everyone (while also enriching a small group). Much of this benefit, however, could be established without state intervention. Importantly, though, the failure to make that benefit possible is not a harm as that term is used in the harm principle.

## 1. What Follows from the Harm Principle[2]

John Stuart Mill's harm principle reads:

> The sole end for which mankind are warranted, individually or collectively, in interfering with the liberty of action of any of their

number is self-protection . . . the only purpose for which power can be rightfully exercised over any member of a civilized community, against his will, is to prevent harm to others.

(Mill, 1859, p. 9)

Importantly, this is not the principle *primum non nocere* – first, do no harm. It does not merely mandate that we not harm others, but indicates that doing harm to others *is (the only) warrant for interference*. In other words, it sets a normative limit to toleration such that all *must* be tolerated *except* that which is harmful. While Mill ends up allowing interferences for other reasons, we can (and, I think, should) take the harm principle more seriously than he does himself.[3] We can take it as a necessary condition for interference. Doing so means endorsing the claim that harm and only harm justifies ending toleration by any agent, state or otherwise, and *pro tanto* permits interference. This allows the most extensive liberty that should be provided in society. No one denies that harm is *prima facie* good reason for interference. As no one wants to be harmed, we all want this limit to others' liberty and should accept it on our own activities.

It is important that the limit just specified is determined by *harm* and not mere hurts. To clarify: harms, for our purposes, are *wrongful setbacks to interests* – not *mere hurts*, which are setbacks to interests but not wrongful. (In his magnum opus, Joel Feinberg argues that this is the way harm is best understood in the harm principle.)[4] Jack's tripping on a stone in his path and thus skinning his knee is, in the ordinary case, a hurt, but not a harm. While Jack surely has an interest in not skinning his knee, if we assume – what is reasonable – that no one wronged Jack but that the stone just happened to be in the wrong place causing him to fall, with no one at fault, there is no wrongfulness and thus no harm understood as a wrongful setback to interests. With no harm, there is no reason for interference. Put simply, we don't think Jack has a justified complaint against anyone with whom we could or should interfere. By contrast, if you take Jill's laptop computer without her permission and claim it as your own, you wrongfully set back her interests in the computer, she is justified in complaining, and interference with you to rectify the situation is likely warranted. Similarly, if Albert stabs Charles in order to satisfy his (Albert's) desire to see blood, Charles is justified in complaining and interference with Albert is warranted to rectify the situation. Jack is hurt but not harmed. Jill and Charles are both harmed. According to the harm principle, interference is permitted in the latter cases but not the former.[5]

Many, of course, want the government to interfere in more instances than would be permitted if the harm principle were taken as providing the sole warrant for interference. They would allow that interference is permissible for reasons other than (i.e., in addition to) the prevention and rectification of harm. I do not here defend (but assume) the insistence that it is *harm alone* that justifies interference (and the corresponding extensive liberty that insistence would allow) – that is a task for another time.[6] I agree, of course, that the desire to be generous and help others is notable and to be encouraged, but am not inclined to think it can be part of public policy.[7] In any case, to assume requiring aid is permissible where no harm is present is to beg the question against the view I am discussing here, according to which, only harm provides warrant for interference[8] – indeed, for *any government actions*. Even the mere instituting of laws requires interference – for the funds necessary to determine, record or promulgate the laws.[9]

If the only justification for government action is the prevention or rectification of harm, the only acceptable laws are those that are needed to prevent or rectify harm. In a regime accepting this, there would be no laws regarding prostitution, pornography, homosexuality, same-sex marriage, smoking, stem cell research, assisted suicide or euthanasia. These would all be tolerated. (If any particular instance of these causes harm,[10] interference would be warranted – but that is true of bike riding, driving a car and everything else.) Of course, for any state to have the ability to prevent or rectify a harm, it likely must have a taxation program to pay for police and military to prevent harms where possible and to rectify harms that are not prevented.[11] Indeed, courts and other institutional means of harm prevention and rectification also may be used. Criminals in such a society – those who commit serious harms[12] – must be interfered with in order to prevent them from committing further harms and to provide rectification of harms done. Courts would also be necessary for cases where it is unclear whether a harm has been committed or if it is unclear who is responsible for the harm. Two parties may each think themselves harmed by the other and we need an impartial party to determine which, if either (or both), is correct. Overall, this sort of state has a government limited to certain minimal activities, a government that might be considered libertarian in nature. It may be ever-present to ensure justice, but constrained in that role to act only to prevent or rectify harm.

To be clear: the harm principle indicates when interference with individual behavior is warranted, but not when it is required – nor what sort of interference should be used. The warrant is something more than mere permission. When X is warranted, it is permitted and there is reason to X, but X is not required. X being warranted means there is *pro tanto* reason for X. Absent any (weighty enough) countervailing reasons, when X is warranted, X should occur. But there are often countervailing reasons. To take a simple example, if I caused you a minor harm – say I slap you across the face – it may not be that I should be arrested or even approached if, for example, I flew to another country immediately after slapping you. What I did would have been a harm and interference is thus permitted, but not required. The costs of interference can reasonably be taken into account by the authorities. Often, we ignore *de minimis* harms though we recognize them as harms.[13]

## 2. Legal Incorporation

There are a variety of types of business firms. The most simple is sole proprietorship. Sole proprietorship firms (and partnerships) have owners who are fully responsible for the firm's activities. Legally incorporating a firm allows an owner to limit her liability for the firm's activities. If an incorporated firm is sued, for example, its owners are responsible for nothing more than their investment in the firm. To take a simple example, imagine that Bill is the majority stockholder in ABC Corporation but takes no part in running ABC. If ABC Corporation is found guilty of dumping toxic waste and ordered by a court to pay $10 million, Bill's assets are unlikely to be used to settle that debt, even if ABC Corporation has only $3 million in assets and Bill has $200 million and all of that is due to his accumulation of stock dividends from ABC Corporation.[14]

"Limited liability" is a major benefit to owners. It is not, though, the only advantage of the corporate model. Whereas limited liability relieves individual investors of liability for the debts of the corporation, it is "entity shielding" that prevents the corporation from being liable for the debts of its investors.[15] Take an example similar to that just used. Jay is the majority (say 51 percent) shareholder in DEF Corporation and is the CEO of DEF. If Jay gambles and loses so that he has a debt of $10 million, DEF Corporation's funds will not be attached to any settlement against Jay even if he has no savings and DEF Corporation has cash reserves of $200 million.[16]

To be clear, there are variations in the ways firms are incorporated. Limited liability and entity shielding, though, are basic and normal elements of incorporation.

The corporate model is generally thought valuable as it promotes business activity. Legal incorporation (government granting of corporate charters),[17] allows individuals to work together with limited liability and entity shielding, thus allowing for the collection of capital needed for long-term projects. The main justification for such a system is that it significantly reduces transaction costs, making business more efficient so that more goods and services are produced than otherwise would be possible.[18] With more production, more people can lead good lives.

There are often, of course, economies of scale in business. Firms A and B might each be able to produce 1,000 widgets per day at $3/per unit, but a single firm producing 10,000 widgets per day may get discounts on the purchase of the raw materials needed to produce those widgets and may be able to invest in machinery that produces widgets faster and with less waste than either A or B could afford, thus getting the cost of production down to $2/per unit. The owner of firm A might dream of producing 10,000 widgets a day. As a sole proprietor, he can borrow money to buy the machinery, he can take on a partner with money to invest or he can incorporate and sell shares of his firm. Selling shares of the firm without limited liability laws would be difficult, as investors would not want to risk their other assets. (Similarly, without entity shielding, he would risk having to pay the debts of those investors.)

The owner of A could, without a legal system of incorporation, set up all contracts to limit the liability of investors, but this would require that all contracts include verbiage such that those signing the contracts – presumably customers, suppliers and employees of the firm – agree not to hold the investors liable for the firm's failures. The owner may not have used any contracts before, or may have used simpler contracts. A lawyer would have to be paid. Some potential customers, suppliers, and employees, might balk at signing the contracts. Put simply, without legal incorporation, limiting the liability of investors becomes more expensive for any firm and without limiting that liability, attracting investment becomes less likely.[19] Much of what is said here about limited liability may hold for entity shielding,[20] which would also involve the investor renegotiating contracts she had with others prior to her investment in firm A (unless she had the foresight to include the necessary clauses in her previous contracts). Hence, a legal system of incorporation reduces transactions costs and allows firms to produce more with lower costs by not requiring them to develop sophisticated and detailed contracts limiting the liability of investors and protecting them from debts incurred by those investors. The contractual verbiage is rendered unnecessary because, essentially, it is written into the law.

## 3. The Argument

Systems of legal incorporation have benefits: they allow less expensive production of goods and services that benefit everyone. They are not always harmless. To see this, consider cases of involuntary creditors. Say I am injured by the activity of a corporation (perhaps hit by a corporate-owned truck or made sick by corporate-produced pollution).[21] If the corporation's assets are not sufficient to compensate me for the injury, I would likely remain uncompensated.[22] This holds even if the corporation's stocks are 100 percent owned by a single individual who has assets far greater than the cost of my health care but is not responsible for the management of the firm.

The point in this chapter, though, is not about harms that corporations might cause. I take it as given that if the Hurter Corporation is guilty of some activity that results in my becoming incapacitated, it can be made to compensate me; if Hurter does not have the requisite assets, it may be forced into bankruptcy. The same is true if an individual does me harm. That Hurter may not be able to fully compensate me for my injury is not significantly different from Joe's not being able to fully compensate me for my injury. (Except of course that Hurter, unlike Joe, may have owners with deep pockets.)

## The Harm Principle and Corporations 207

The argument here is *not* about the harms corporations might do and that would justify interference. The argument here is, rather about the justification for the very existence of corporations. The argument is simple. Recall from the first section that according to the harm principle, the only justification for government action – including the institution of laws – is the prevention or rectification of harms. Here is the argument:

1. The only justification for government action – including the institution of laws – is the prevention or rectification of harms, understood as wrongful setbacks to interests.
2. Corporate law does not prevent or rectify harms.
3. There is no justification for corporate law.
4. With no corporate law, there could be no corporations.
5. There ought to be no corporations.

Let us look at this a bit further. Some will, of course, challenge the veracity of premise 1, but as already indicated, I do not defend it here; it is the point of this chapter to show that it is incompatible with the existence of corporate law, not to show that we should accept it.[23] So I move to premise 2.

Premise 2 seems clear; while corporate law might – as indicated in the previous section – provide benefits, it does not (and is not intended to) prevent or rectify harms. Considering a firm a legal (corporate) person is to confer upon its owners the benefit of dealing with others (persons and firms) as a person rather than as a set of people with a nexus of relations.[24] Founders of, investors in, and employees of, corporations fare better (at least potentially) because of corporate law; indeed, anyone who purchases the goods or services provided by the corporation potentially does better since the costs of production – and hence, the costs of the product – are lowered. But none of this is a matter of preventing or rectifying harms – wrongful setbacks of interests.

Premise 3 follows directly from premises 1 and 2, and the conclusion (5) follows directly from premises 3 and 4. That leaves premise 4.

As indicated in the previous section, much of the benefit of limited liability could be duplicated without a specific body of law instituted by a government. When I speak of corporations, however, I am referring to business entities that are incorporated by law, not by a network of contractual arrangements executed without a pre-established separate legal framework. Without a separate legal framework for corporate law, there are – analytically – no corporations. Premise 4 stands. Of course, this leaves the possibility of large firms that build clauses into all of their contractual arrangements so as to limit the liability of investors and shield the firm from the debts of those investors.[25] That is not a problem. The problem with corporations, if we take the harm principle as seriously as suggested here, is neither their size nor their attempts to limit liability or shield themselves from debts. The problem is with government action to make that easier; it is government provision of aid to some that is unjustified by the harm principle. Of course, it may well be that as a contingent matter, without corporate law, we would have only firms significantly smaller than those currently in existence. The argument stands nonetheless.

## 4. Worries

### 4.1 No Corporate Law, No Contract Law

The first objection that is worth considering is that if adhering strictly to the harm principle rules out the possibility of a corpus of corporate law, it also rules out contract law – which we surely want to maintain. Instituting contract law is not, the claim goes, responding to a harm. It is, we are meant to think, merely a benefit to those who are in position to enter contracts. The problem with this view is that everyone (of age) is in a position to enter contracts and, moreover, that in its simplest form, contract law *is* a matter of protection, that is, it is a means of preventing harm.[26]

That everyone is in a position to enter a contract is clear when we recognize that employees as well as employers, renters as well as landlords, consumers as well as producers, and so on, enter contracts. It is, of course, true that in our society contracts are written in such a way that most cannot be expected to understand them, but that is an objection to the existing legal system, not to having a system of contract law.[27] Contracts should be understandable to anyone that is party to them. This is necessary for the consent given to be fully voluntary.

Contract law accords with the harm principle. Interfering to enforce compliance with a voluntarily accepted contract protects both parties to the contract from harm – and provides no other benefit with any necessity. If, for example, Cody voluntarily agrees to rent an apartment from Maria for $1,000/month (signing a lease to that effect), but then refuses to pay Maria, she would have her interests wrongly set back – she would be harmed. Legal enforcement of the contract thus serves to prevent harm (or rectify it if Cody leaves but is later made to compensate Maria). Similarly, should Maria try to have Cody removed for reasons not specified in their contract, it would protect Cody – who would otherwise have *his* interests wrongfully set back by Maria refusing to honour the contract. Neither Maria nor Cody is given any benefit – other than protection from harm – by contract law. Contract law – again, in simple form – accords with the harm principle.

### 4.2 Reduced Welfare Without Corporations

Though the argument presented in the previous section is valid, some may take it to be a sort of *reductio* of the view that the only justification for state action is the prevention and rectification of harm as the view expressed in premise 1 requires.[28] As already hinted, they might suggest that absent corporate law (and corporations), we would lack the accumulation of capital that makes large-scale investment and production possible and that this means a society endorsing this view would be unable to sustain a population of any significant size.[29] This may be the most significant objection to the view presented here.

It may well be that a society wherein the government takes no actions that are not justified by the harm principle strictly understood will be one with only small scale markets. In such a society,[30] there would be small communities within which individuals can walk to each other and bring labour, capital, goods and services. A society of such small communities would allow for trade with those near enough to one another and as individuals accumulate wealth, they would be free to decide – individually or with neighbours – to improve the nearby infrastructure and extend their market. Perhaps, over time, this could grow enough for a mass economy. I do not know if this is the case, but it's not clear we should be concerned.

On the one hand, we might simply accept polities with small-scale communities, recognizing that in local markets with limited numbers of participants, limited goods and services bought and sold, and limited profits, accumulations of capital are unlikely to be sufficient to fund extensive infrastructure. If the sort of accumulations of capital present without government encouragement via corporate law would allow for national growth, it plausibly would be slow. On the other hand, though, it may be that government intervention to provide corporate law is unnecessary for a large-scale economy. The New York Stock Exchange, after all, began as a voluntary organization,[31] without government aid, and could *possibly* have sustained a national capital market without legal interventions. This may or may not be likely, but we need not be concerned about it either way. If it could work, we allow for the efficient benefit of large and efficient firms without government assistance to create them. I suspect the bigger worry centres on being *unable* to have mass production that creates efficiencies benefitting everyone.

How worrisome is the prospect of only small-scale economies? It is perhaps true that in such a system, people would remain poor longer than they have in our world (with corporate law). Still, we should note that this would be accompanied by fewer harms. We would have conditions vastly different from what we have historically seen.[32] Consider that if the Dalit in India (i.e., the so-called "untouchable" class) had always been allowed to trade as they pleased, their situation would undoubtedly be better than it actually was. They might not have attained great wealth (without the ability to use corporate law), but their plight would be better nonetheless. That is, strict adherence to the harm principle might mean lower levels of welfare because of less production of consumer goods due to the lack of benefits corporations provide, but may nonetheless be better for many – likely including the least well off. Moreover, even with a less extensive economic system, greater economic freedom might be beneficial for the poor as they would be free to seek to improve their income without intervention and as private charity might thrive given the lower taxes (and possibly stronger communal bonds) that would be present when government activity is limited to what is justified by the harm principle. Thus, we might have more egalitarian distributions of income and wealth even if without *large accumulations* of wealth.

So far, the objection has centred around the idea that the first premise in the argument *must be wrong* because corporations are too valuable, but has not provided a better claim about what justifies government action. The most likely proposal, I think, is something like a weak "benefit to others principle,"[33] allowing for government action when doing so can benefit individuals, without setting back the interests of others. That is, some would claim that government activity that is Pareto optimal is permissible even when no harm is prevented or rectified.[34] (Those making this suggestion would likely accept a modified harm principle that allows that while harm justifies interference, it is not alone in doing so.)

One response to this objection invites recognition that law is coercive and so cannot be Pareto optimal – as the presence of coercion means someone is made worse off. But whether law must be coercive is a difficult question we do better to avoid here.[35] So assume some law need not be coercive. In particular, assume corporate law is not coercive. Indeed, some would suggest everyone wants (perhaps because everyone benefits from) corporate law. If that were the case, instituting corporate law would plausibly be a Pareto optimal move: at least some would be made better off and none would be made worse off. My interlocutor here might, then, accept corporate law by rejecting the harm principle in its strict form – presumably still accepting that preventing and rectifying harm provides warrant for interference, but insisting that some benefit does as well. The problem with this move is that it opens the door to significantly more government activity than some of us, perhaps the same thinkers who seek to defend corporate law, are happy with. (Those happy with extensive government activity might rest their case here; perhaps oddly then, welfare liberals ought to endorse our system of corporate law or something like it while libertarians ought to reject it.)

Accepting that benefiting others is a justification for government instituting corporate law requires accepting that it is justification for other institutions that benefit others – a universal demogrant comes to mind, for example – unless it can be shown that those other institutions, unlike corporate law, are not Pareto improvements. Endorsing corporate law because it creates tremendous benefit, or does so efficiently, is accepting a particular consequentialist justification for government interference (a justification contingent upon empirical facts rather than principle). To maintain consistency, then, advocates of this move would either need also to approve of government aid to individuals *or* show that such aid would *not* have a similar benefit. There is at least some evidence, though, that providing everyone a basic income guarantee (also called an unconditional or universal basic income, or a guaranteed annual income) to all individuals is an efficient way to create tremendous benefit.[36]

Given that taxation would be necessary to provide a basic income guarantee, it may seem obvious that this cannot be Pareto optimal even if it does provide extensive benefit. (This is not the reply, mentioned earlier, that *all law is coercive*.) Taxation, after all, leaves some prima facie worse off than they were. Things are not as clear here as it may seem. We must realize that (a) even instituting bodies of law (like corporate law) will involve some taxation and (b) whether anyone is really made worse off will depend on what the baseline is. Some argue that government activity improves everyone's life; Liam Murphy and Thomas Nagel, for example, suggest that "if literally all government benefits were taken into account . . . we would notice that almost no one suffers a net burden from government."[37] On their view, though, far more government activity would be allowed than just the instantiation of corporate law.

The theoretical quandary for someone who wants to limit government activity to providing corporate law but not other things people like Murphy and Nagel think should be provided is to offer a principled explanation for the difference. One way to try to answer this quandary is to show that the former is Pareto optimal while the latter is not. As already indicated, I am sceptical that this will work. I know of no other way to defend the one while rejecting the other and so conclude that given commitment to the harm principle as strictly as suggested here, we ought to reject, rather than accept, both. I recognize that some would prefer to approve of a weak benefit-to-others principle in addition to a less strict version of the harm principle.

## 4.3 The Argument Proves Too Much

A different worry is that the argument presented proves too much – or rather, that it can be generalized too far. Government does a lot – like provide schools – that is not obviously about harm prevention or rectification. All such activity may seem to be ruled out on the view I discuss. The obvious response here is that this is an objection to taking the harm principle as strictly as I have suggested and not an objection to the argument that takes that principle as its first assumption. This chapter is not intended to offer a defence of that assumption; it is intended to show only that accepting it means rejecting corporate law and hence corporations. A second response here has also been noted; this is to argue that schools (and other goods that government might be thought justified in providing) do help prevent or rectify harms – perhaps by helping those who have been wrongfully disadvantaged to attain a better life. I will not, though, seek to defend that claim.[38]

### 4.4 Extremes Lead to Extremes

One final worry is straightforward. Some may wonder why they should be at all concerned about the argument I present since I begin with an undefended and extreme premise. That is, few would accept the harm principle in completely unadorned fashion as I suggest here, so providing a valid argument from that premise to a rejection of corporate law and corporations will not seem like an important accomplishment. There are three responses to this objection. First, if one had any antecedent reason to think there was something wrong with the corporate model, they now have some reason to take on the harm principle as the only principle justifying government action. This strikes me as significant. Secondly, and perhaps more importantly, I do think the harm principle can be defended as the only principle justifying government action. I have not provided that defence here, but see my 2014 and 2018. Finally, in many discussions of business ethics, there is an overly simple assumption that the business world must be taken as it is; my intention is to challenge that. Put differently, while it is important that business ethicists talk about any number of particular issues *within* business – and especially corporate – ethics, we can and should do more. We should seek to defend best practices within businesses and, just as importantly, how law should structure the markets within which business occurs.[39] An understanding of what corporations are and alternative structures that might be possible would be extremely useful. As it stands, students of business ethics often seem oblivious to these issues. This chapter might help change that. If it encourages defence of the corporate model as it exists, that too would be a welcome addition to the literature.

## Notes

1. This chapter has a long and winding history, so I am unable to recall all of those who helped in some form, whether reading and commenting on previous versions, or talking about the ideas herein. The following are just some of whom clearly deserve – and have – my appreciation: Andy Altman, Spencer Banzhaf, Jason Brennan, David Ciepley, Michael Douma, Seena Eftekhari, David Farici, John Hasnas, Garth Heutel, Michael Kates, Dale Miller, JP Messina, Govind Persad, Abe Singer, James Taggart, Matt Zwolinski and audiences at the 2019 PPE Workshop of the College of Charleston Center for Public Choice and Market Process. Audiences at the 2017 PPE Society Conference and the Georgetown Institute for the Study of Markets and Ethics (2015) and the University of New Orleans gave useful feedback to older versions of this chapter.
2. This section is adapted from my 2017, pp. 826–828. Importantly, I do not claim that Mill himself reads the harm principle as strictly as is discussed

## The Harm Principle and Corporations 213

here. I spell out my view in my *Toleration and Freedom from Harm* (Routledge, 2018).
3. I defend this view in view in my 2018 and my 2014.
4. The four-volume *The Moral Limits to the Criminal Law* (see, e.g., Feinberg, 1984, p. 36). On Feinberg's view, the harm principle is only part of the core of liberal thinking.) Recent thinkers argue against Feinberg's understanding of harm being in Mill's work (see Jacobson, Miller, and Turner). I put this aside as I am not interpreting Mill. Ben Bradley argues that the existing definitions of harm are a "mess" so "it should be replaced by other more well-behaved concepts" (Bradley, p. 391). His treatment of Feinberg's definition is, though, unsatisfying (see, in particular, footnote 10, p. 395). I defend a modified Feinbergian understanding of harm in my 2018 but cannot include that defence here.
5. Some would suggest we understand harms in terms of rights violations. I eschew rights talk, as I have no theory of rights. What I say throughout should be compatible with all philosophical accounts of rights on offer. I suspect, though, that we do best to talk about rights violations when someone has a justified complaint because an interest of theirs has been set back. For "harming as right violating" (see Feinberg, 1984, pp. 109–114). For this reason, I am sympathetic to theories of rights that take rights to be a species of normative constraints. For two different accounts I am sympathetic to, see Mack (2000) and Rainbolt (2006).
6. See my 2014 and 2018.
7. Government imposed "generosity" requires coercion to collect the needed resources and what is transferred with coercion is not transferred *generously*. Generosity requires willing and knowing agreement on behalf of the provider; forcing assistance will, at best, result in acquiescence, not generosity. Moreover, if a government were successful in its policies of "generosity" – e.g., aiding the poor – it would reduce the opportunities for individuals to develop the virtue. Put simply, we do not act generously when we are forced to give. Of course, some argue that taxation for redistribution is a matter of justice, but again, it would beg the question to assume that government is meant to interfere to help where there is no harm.
8. For our purposes, we can understand "interference" to be any act that has the effect of impeding or preventing (even partially) an agent from doing as they wish, intend, or will. That is, it is hindrance or obstruction. Importantly, some instances of interference will be wrongful and thus harms; while interference may be permitted as a response to harm, wrongful interference is not. On the view discussed here, only interference to prevent or rectify harm is ever warranted. Hence, on this view, interference to gather the resources to provide aid where no harm is present is wrongful.
9. Even if these are paid for with voluntary donations, if the laws are effective, they coerce. (See footnote 35.) Some will argue that there can be government actions – for example, the institution of what H. L. A. Hart calls "secondary rules" (essentially, the rules that apply to the rules that apply to citizens) – that are not interferences of any sort and so compatible with the view that harm alone justifies interference. Insofar as these are a necessary part of a system of preventing and rectifying harm, though, they do not provide a counter-example.
10. There will be disputes about when harm exists in these sorts of cases. I assume here that in cases of genuinely consensual prostitution, e.g., there is no harm, but I am not here taking any further stand on the issue. In particular, I realize that what counts as consensual in these cases can be rather difficult to clarify.

11. I ignore the possibility that voluntary payments (whether directly for state services or as charitable donations) could suffice. I also ignore the possibility of anarchism. I do not deny the theoretical possibility of anarchic states, but such would not permit corporations as I will understand them later (in accord with the general legal understanding) – because anarchic states have no state law and hence no state corporate law. The possibility remains of a self-funding law – i.e., one wherein the institution, promotion and guarantee of the law is paid for by those who benefit from it. I admit to having less of a problem with this myself, but it still not justified by the harm principle.
12. I mean to narrow the definition of criminals to include only those who commit serious harms since on this view, interference is only permitted to prevent or rectify harms. The intension of the term here is the same as in any other society: those who break the law. The extension is much narrower since there are fewer laws, making fewer acts – only those that cause serious harms – illegal.
13. Douglas Husak's discussion of inchoate offenses and the use of criminal law to reduce risks of harm may be of interest to readers (see Husak 2008, pp. 159–177). Husak offers "four distinct principles to limit the authority of the state to punish persons who engage in conduct that creates the risk of harm" (p. 161).
14. The "corporate veil" can be pierced. Bill's assets might be attached to the settlement if, for example, he were found responsible for ABC Corporation's acts. If, though, Bill has had no active role in ABC for years, his private assets are not likely to be touched even if he owns 51 percent of all shares in ABC.
15. See Hansmann, Kraakman, and Squire (2006). Also important is what David Ciepley (2013) calls "asset lock-in" which prohibits an investor from taking assets of the corporation. Armour, Hansmann and Kraakman call this a rule of liquidation protection and see it as part of a strong form of entity shielding, which they consider to be part of the legal personality of a corporation (see Armour et al 2009). Note that to parallel the term "entity shielding," Armour et al also indicate that limited liability is a form of "owner shielding" (ibid, p. 9). While the one shields the firm from the debts of owners, the other shields the owner from the debts of the firm. Together entity and owner shielding amount to asset partitioning (ibid, p. 10). Armour et al see legal personality and limited liability as two of five basic elements of corporations; the other three are the transferability of shares, delegated management with a board structure, and investor ownership (ibid, pp. 5–16).
16. As with Bill (footnote 14), there are ways the Corporations assets could be attached to a settlement. The default, however, is that they are not. Of course, Jay's shares in DEF could be used to satisfy his debt; his ownership of DEF would transfer. Although that might mean the person Jay was indebted to is made whole, that person might prefer not to have to sell the shares. In any case, that the shares would be transferred makes the Jay case less problematic, I think, than the Bill case. This may be why limited liability seems more problematic than entity shielding.
17. According to the "grant" theory of the corporation, "A corporation is an artificial being . . . existing only in contemplation of law. Being the mere creature of law, it possesses only those properties which the charter of its creation confers upon it" (John Marshall's decision in *Dartmouth College v. Woodward*, 17 U.S. 518; 4 L. Ed. 629; 1819 U.S. LEXIS 330; 4 Wheat. 518). This is not currently the most accepted theory of the corporation, but for a convincing defence of the view that it is the best such theory, see Ciepley op. cit. According to Ciepley, this view means corporations are neither private individuals nor reducible to a "web of contracts" among individuals.

The Harm Principle and Corporations   215

18. It reduces transaction costs through limited liability and entity shielding as well as default contract provisions (see Armour et al., op. cit., pp. 20–21) making unnecessary a large web of bi- and multi-lateral contracts.
19. It is also unclear how to limit the liability of investors to those who are not customers, suppliers or employees. (See note 21.) Still, the default contract provisions corporate law creates clearly help.
20. Armour et al claim that entity shielding, along with authority rules (indicating who runs the firm), and procedure rules (who can determine when the firm's contracts are not abided by and can sue on behalf of the firm, etc.) – that together make up the legal personality of a corporate firm – *cannot* "feasibly be replicated" by contract. They suggest other elements of corporate status can (op. cit., 8; the "feasibility" qualifier is removed at 19). See footnote 15. Interestingly, "[l]imited liability did not become a standard feature of the English law of joint stock companies until the mid-19th century, and in . . . California shareholders bore unlimited personal liability for corporation obligations until 1931" (op. cit., 9, n. 25).
21. Armour et al: "The compelling reasons for limited liability *in contract* generally do not extend to limited liability *in tort* – that is, to persons who are unable to adjust the terms on which they extend credit to the corporation, such as third parties who have been injured as a consequence of the corporation's negligent behavior. Limited liability to such persons is arguably not a necessary feature of the corporate form, and perhaps not even a socially valuable one" (op. cit., 11). In the text, I call these involuntary creditors. For more, see Kraakman et al., chapter 5. But see next footnote.
22. See Hansmann and Kraakman (1991).
23. That said, I am inclined to think we should accept it and am inclined to think libertarians in particular ought to accept it for reasons that will be clear in the last section. David Brink rejects the idea that a proper Millian understanding of the harm principle is libertarian (2013, p. 186).
24. See Armour et al., op. cit., p. 9.
25. If, per footnote 20, Armour et al are correct that legal personality *cannot* be replicated by contract, then entity shielding would *not* be possible without corporate law. In any case, even if limited liability can be, the costs of a firm doing business would be higher. Transaction costs would be higher.
26. Putting this point differently, we do not need legislation to have contracts; individuals can make up a contract on their own. If one party failed to lift up to the agreement without consent of the other party, this would seem to be a wrongful setting back of the other party's interests – a harm – and thus permit interference according to the harm principle. This is why state interference to uphold contracts is permissible, though state interference to create a system of corporate law is not. To be clear, this holds for multiple party contracts as well, so if possible, firms would be permitted to mimic the benefits of corporate law using only contracts and then state interference to uphold those contracts would be permissible.
27. Just as this chapter is about the incompatibility of the harm principle and corporations that exist due to the corpus of corporate law, not firms that happen to be large and engage in many contracts.
28. I say "sort of a reductio" rather than a reductio as no logical contradiction is involved; the thought rather is that the consequences of the assumption are so bad as to warrant rejecting it (or its action-guiding force).
29. The problem may be worse as the view expressed in premise 1 does not allow for the provision of even public goods that are not necessary for harm prevention or rectification. Roads that make the transportation of goods possible, for example, would not be built by government agencies if they could not be justified by their relation to harm. (Armour et al seem to consider

corporate law itself a public good [op. cit., p. 20].) Of course, (a) it is disputable whether roads and such *are* public goods and (b) it may be that roads and other goods usually provided by governmental bodies in contemporary society help with harm prevention and rectification. Jethro Lieberman provides some arguments in favour of something like (b) (see his 2012, especially pp. 117–118). Perhaps some would argue that corporations help with harm prevention and rectification (I am sceptical.) The more likely response here, I think, is that although not having corporate law (and thus corporations) would not mean creating harms, it would mean leaving people in far less good situations than they are or would be in with corporations and that such is immoral. Those making such an argument might interestingly invoke legal moralism (of some form). This, of course, is to deny premise 1.

30. This might be a state similar to Rawls's ideal of a property-owning democracy or Jefferson's ideal agrarian regime. I would suggest, though I won't here defend the claim, that the provision of corporate law fosters what Rawls calls systems of welfare-state capitalism rather than in what he calls property-owning democracies (see 2001, p. 139).
31. It began in 1792, when 24 New York City stockbrokers signed the "Buttonwood Agreement" (www.theice.com/publicdocs/ICE_at_a_glance.pdf, accessed 22 December 2014); for more, see Werner and Smith, 1991, esp. Chapter 2.
32. I do not deny that we have greater material wealth due to reduced transaction costs and the lower marginal costs of production that corporate law allows. There simply are smaller percentages of people living in poverty than ever before. (Of course, there are also higher rates of suicide and depression.)
33. See my 2014, 63 ff. The principle first appears in Feinberg's, 1984, p. 27. As noted in note 29, appeal might instead be made to a form of legal moralism. See my 2014, 75ff.
34. Of course, if in providing benefit to some, the government set back the interests of others, it risks harming those others and thus risks running afoul of the harm principle itself. Interference in such a government's actions, then, would be justified according to the harm principle. This is why the benefit to others principle here is thought of as Pareto efficient and not Kaldor-Hicks efficient. (This may also raise questions of state legitimacy.)
35. See Hart, 1961, esp. pp. 20–26. Still, if a particular law or set of laws is not coercive, one might wonder why it must be law at all – i.e., if people want to abide by the rules in question, one would not think they must be instituted or supported by government. This may be an example of what is called a stag hunt problem in game theory (see Skyrms, 2004).
36. For some work on the possible efficiency of such a program, see Bryan (2005), Pressman (2005), Widerquist and Lewis (2006), Ackerman, Alstott, and Van Parijs (2006), as well as the journal *Basic Income Studies*.
37. Murphy and Nagel, 2002, p. 15.
38. See footnote 29.
39. This is a question of *predistribution*, as is the proper shape of property rights.

# References

Ackerman, B., Alstott, A. and Van Parijs, P. (2006). *Redesigning Distribution: Basic Income and Stakeholder Grants as Cornerstones for an Egalitarian Capitalism*. New York: Verso Books.

Armour, J., Hansmann, H. and Kraakman, R. (2009). Chapter 1. In: R. Kraakman, J. Armour, P. Davies, L. Enriques, H. Hansmann, G. Hertig, K. Hopt, H.

Kanda and E. Rock, eds., *The Anatomy of Corporate Law*, 2nd ed. Oxford: Oxford University Press, pp. 6–9.

Bradley, B. (2012). Doing Away with Harm. *Philosophy and Phenomenological Research*, 85(2), pp. 390–412.

Brink, D. (2013). *Mill's Progressive Principles*. Oxford: Oxford University Press.

Bryan, J. (2005). Targeted Programs vs. the Basic Income Guarantee: An Examination of the Efficiency Costs of Different Forms of Redistribution. *The Journal of Socio-Economics*, 34, pp. 39–47.

Ciepley, D. (2013). Beyond Public and Private: Toward a Political Theory of the Corporation. *American Political Science Review*, 107(1), pp. 139–158.

Cohen, A. J. (2014). *Toleration*. Oxford: Polity Press.

Cohen, A. J. (2017). The Harm Principle and Parental Licensing. *Social Theory and Practice*, 43, pp. 825–849.

Cohen, A. J. (2018). *Toleration and Freedom from Harm: Liberalism Reconceived*. New York: Routledge.

Feinberg, J. (1984). *Harm to Others*. New York: Oxford University Press.

Hansmann, H. and Kraakman, R. (1991). The Uneasy Case for Limiting Shareholder Liability in Tort. *Yale Law Journal*, 100, pp. 1879–1934.

Hansmann, H., Kraakman, R. and Squire, R. (2006). Law and the Rise of the Firm. *Harvard Law Review*, 119(5), pp. 1333–1403.

Hart, H. L. A. (1961). *The Concept of Law*. Oxford: Clarendon Press.

Husak, D. (2008). *Overcriminalization*. Oxford: Oxford University Press.

Jacobson, D. (2000). Mill on Liberty, Speech, and the Free Society. *Philosophy and Public*, 29(3), pp. 276–309.

Lieberman, J. (2012). *Liberalism Undressed*. Oxford: Oxford University Press.

Mack, E. (2000). In Defense of the Jurisdiction Theory of Rights. *The Journal of Ethics*, 4, pp. 71–98.

Mill, J. S. (1859/1978). *On Liberty*. Indianapolis, IN: Hackett Publishing.

Miller, D. (2010). *J. S. Mill*. Cambridge: Polity Press.

Murphy, L. and Nagel, T. (2002). *The Myth of Ownership*. Oxford: Oxford University Press.

Pressman, S. (2005). Income Guarantees and the Equity-Efficiency Tradeoff. *The Journal of Socio-Economics*, 34, pp. 83–100.

Rainbolt, G. (2006). *The Concept of Rights*. Dordrecht: Springer Publishing.

Rawls, J. (2001). *Justice as Fairness*. Cambridge, MA: The Belknap Press of Harvard University Press.

Skyrms, B. (2004). *The Stag Hunt and the Evolution of Social Structure*. Cambridge: Cambridge University Press.

Turner, P. N. (2014). 'Harm' and Mill's Harm Principle. *Ethics*, 124(2), pp. 299–326.

Werner, W. and Smith, S. (1991). *Wall Street*. New York: Columbia University Press.

Widerquist, K. and Lewis, M. (2006). An Efficiency Argument for the Basic Income Guarantee. *International Journal of Environment Workplace and Employment*, 2, pp. 21–43.

# 12 Gypsy Traveller Nomadism and State Tolerance

## A Liberal-Egalitarian View

*Marcus Carlsen Häggrot*

### Introduction

In the United Kingdom there live an estimated 300,000 persons who identify as Gypsy Travellers, and of these an estimated 100,000 pursue a nomadic life, typically living in caravans, travelling mostly on circuits within the country, and refusing to settle in a geographically fixed abode (Niner, 2003). In France, the population of Gypsy Travellers is estimated to 400,000 persons and according to estimates about half of them maintain a nomadic lifestyle, also mostly on circuits that run within the national territory (Cossée, 2007; Robert, 2007, p. 188).

How should states such as the British and French treat these mobile populations and respond in terms of public policy to the fact of Gypsy Traveller nomadism? In this chapter, I want to go some way towards answering this question, concentrating on the idea of tolerance. That is to say, I shall examine whether tolerance might constitute an appropriate state response to Gypsy Traveller nomadism, and I shall argue that from a broadly liberal-egalitarian viewpoint, it does not. Insofar as one commits to broadly liberal-egalitarian principles, one cannot accept that the state tolerates Gypsy Traveller nomadism.

When denying that Gypsy Traveller nomadism is an appropriate object of state tolerance, I do not, to be clear, suggest that the state may be intolerant of this practice and may legitimately proscribe it. Instead, the argument pulls in the opposite direction: The thought is that for tolerance to occur, one (tolerating) agent must find objectionable the beliefs, attitudes, or actions of another agent, but voluntarily refrain from interfering with those beliefs, attitudes, or actions (cf. King, 1976, chap. 1; Forst, 2003, pp. 71–73; Cohen, 2004, pp. 78–79), whereas liberal-egalitarian principles have the implication that a state cannot permissibly hold and express objections to nomadism, thus making it impossible for the state to be tolerant in the proper sense of the term.

Further, it is worth noting that the present critique of tolerance is limited in several important ways. It relates only to the idea that the *state* might be tolerant of Gypsy Traveller nomadism, and it only speaks to the nomadic lifestyle of the Gypsy Travellers of Western Europe. As such, the present critique is no comprehensive critique of tolerance in general;[1] it does not articulate any particular view on tolerance exercised by private individuals or groups; and the argument also leaves to the side all Gypsy Traveller practices beyond the nomadic lifestyle itself.

Its limitations notwithstanding, the argument of the chapter is important. Liberal political theory has in recent decades taken an intense interest in the practices of cultural and religious minorities and the accommodations and the public recognition these might be owed.[2] However, the scholarship on minority groups and their potential moral rights has paid preciously little attention to the case of the Gypsy Travellers of Western Europe and the practice of nomadism more generally.[3] So insofar as the present chapter offers a normative discussion of nomadism and the appropriate state response to it, it fills a gap in the normative minority rights literature.

In addition, the chapter constructively contributes to philosophical scholarship on the idea of tolerance. As it is framed in the terms of tolerance and specifically examines in how far the state should *tolerate* Gypsy Traveller nomadism, the present discussion aligns with the work of theorists who seek to identify the cases and conditions in which tolerance is an impermissible, a permitted or, indeed, a required state response to particular practices (e.g. Kymlicka, 1995, chap. 8; Forst, 2004, 2013, chap. 12; Song, 2007; Nussbaum, 2012; Waldron, 2012; Galeotti, 2014). And since to date, this literature has overlooked the practice of nomadism – whether practised by Gypsy Travellers or other populations – the present discussion is set to enrich our understanding of when tolerance is, or is not called for, especially on the part of the state.

To develop the liberal egalitarian critique of state tolerance in relation to Gypsy Traveller nomadism, I shall in the next section distinguish between two practically distinct regimes of tolerance: reporting tolerance and multi-domain-non-accommodation tolerance. I will also relate these regimes to 20th-century policies in France and the UK respectively. In the third section, I focus on multi-domain-non-accommodation tolerance, and show how it is rendered impermissible by important liberal-egalitarian commitments, notably the commitments to general health care provision and the right to vote. After this, I turn in the fourth section to reporting tolerance, arguing that it might not only be objectionable on freedom-of-movement grounds, but also and mostly importantly violates a foundational negative ideal of non-humiliation. In the fifth section I examine an important consideration that seems to tell in favour of reporting tolerance after all, and I explain why this is not in fact the case. The sixth section concludes.

Before this is developed any further, though, it is worth elaborating on two preliminaries. First, the present analysis of tolerance and Gypsy Traveller nomadism takes for granted a normative outlook that is broadly liberal-egalitarian. As such, it follows a prominent strand in contemporary political theory and takes for granted a commitment to individual liberty and the basic moral rights that are standardly espoused by liberals, e.g. rights to free speech, free movement, freedom of assembly and freedom of association, freedom of conscience, and so forth. And as an egalitarian perspective, it is also committed to the views that all members of society deserve to be treated as equals in the sense that their interests and well-being are owed equal consideration and that the distribution of rights, resources, opportunities and the rules of social cooperation more generally, should reflect this fundamental equality.[4] However, the argument presented does not presuppose a particular formulation of liberal-egalitarianism, such as the theory of justice developed by Rawls (1973, 2001), the liberal luck-egalitarianism espoused by Arneson (1989) and others (e.g. Cohen, 1989; Barry, 2001), or Anderson's (1999) democratic equality view. Instead, the chapter aims at ecumenism and proposes to cite considerations and to develop conclusions that are presumably acceptable from within any particular articulation of liberal egalitarianism.

And secondly, some clarifications on the people I have so far denominated as Gypsy Travellers. Western European societies contain a number of minority groups that are often referred to in common parlance as 'Gypsies', but who themselves identify in other ways. In the British Isles, for example, there have for centuries lived groups that respectively identify as (1) English Romanichals (also Romani Gypsies), (2) Welsh Romanichals (also Welsh Kale), (3) Irish Travellers (also Pavee) and (4) Scottish Travellers. Similarly, France has long been the home of groups that respectively identify as (5) Manouches, (6) Yenisches, (7) Kalé (also Gitans) and (8) Sinté.

Historically, these population groups have been peripatetic service nomads (Fraser, 1992, pp. 216–223; cf. Taylor, 2013) – i.e. nomads who make a living by selling goods and services (e.g. seasonal agricultural labour) that are in demand from the settled community but cannot be provided economically by stationary suppliers (cf. Berland and Salo, 1986). A large part of these populations is now settled, but they reportedly remain committed to what has been called an 'ideology of travelling' (Adams et al., 1975, p. 145). As such, they maintain that mobility is a constituent element of the good life and a central venue for expressing a Gypsy Traveller identity. (Adams et al., 1975, pp. 44–45; Okely, 1983, pp. 128–129; Liégeois, 1994, p. 83; Robert, 2007; Matras, 2015). Those who are settled accordingly remain open to the possibility of resuming mobility, and in Britain, France and (to some extent) Ireland, small but not insignificant parts of these groups continue to maintain a nomadic lifestyle, typically living in towed caravans and travelling on relatively stable circuits within the respective countries (cf. Okely, 1983, pp. 125–126; Robert, 2007).

In order to characterize fully the groups listed, more should be said about their respective histories, linguistic practices, and various other customs.[5] It should be noted, too, that they have long been victims of severe stigmatization, grave oppression and outright persecution, both in the UK and France, and Europe more generally (cf. Fraser, 1992; Lucassen, 2008; Taylor, 2013, 2014). But as these matters play (almost) no role in the subsequent argument, I shall say no more about them here.

In Western European countries, there also live recent immigrants from Eastern Europe who generally identify as Roma. In the eyes of the general public, these are often assimilated to the groups listed previously, and it is relatively common that all these groups are confused and indiscriminately referred to as Gypsies or, alternatively, Roma. However, (migrant) Roma from Eastern Europe are conceptually distinct from the groups 1 to 8, not least because their movements involve the crossing of national borders and because, unlike the groups 1 to 8, they are typically *not* citizens of the Western European states in which they live. So when I here utilize the term Gypsy Travellers, I use it as an umbrella denomination for groups such as 1 to 8 only, and the chapter focuses specifically on persons within this category who maintain a nomadic way of life. This means also that the chapter exclusively deals with a form of nomadism that is practised *by citizens, within the territory,* of the relevant state. Non-citizen nomadism and cross-border nomadism (as it occurs in other parts of the world) are beyond the scope of the chapter.

Armed with background and clarifications, we now can turn to distinguish between two forms of state toleration; forms that have actually been practised by European states.

## 1. Two Forms of Tolerance

Between 1969 and 2017, French law featured a particular piece of legislation that has no counterpart in any other liberal democracy (Garo, 2007), namely the *Loi no. 69–3 du 3 janvier 1969 relative à l'exercice des activités ambulantes et au régime applicable aux personnes circulant en France sans domicile ni résidence fixe* (henceforth: Act of 1969). Being specifically tailored to persons older than 16 who had no fixed residence *and* lived in a vehicle, caravan or another form of mobile shelter, the law principally applied to the Gypsy Travellers in France who maintained a nomadic, travelling way of life (Aubin, 2001; Garo, 2007) – although it was well-known among sociologists, ministry-of-interior officials and others working close to this population, that the Act applied also to persons who did not identify as Gypsy Travellers but nevertheless had a lifestyle such that they met all the material conditions specified in the Act.

In any event, the Act's main target population became known formally as *gens du voyage*, and within that category were distinguished two subgroups which were assigned differentiated legal duties. *Gens du voyage* with a regular source of income were required to obtain a special identification document known as *livret de circulation*, which, in order to remain valid, had to be countersigned by police authorities[6] once every year. *Gens du voyage* without a regular source of income were obliged to obtain an identification document known as *carnet de circulation*, which had to be countersigned, also by police authorities, on a three-monthly basis. And in the event that persons of either category failed to hold a properly countersigned document (of the right sort), they were liable to fines up to 1,500 € or imprisonment for up to one year (Garo, 2007).

As I shall note later, the 1969 Act made a number of further provisions, too, about the conditions under which *gens du voyage* could exercise civil, political, and social rights such as the right to be married, the right to vote and various social service rights. But for present purposes it is the duty for nomadic Gypsy Travellers to report regularly to the police that is central, for it constitutes an instance of toleration on the part of the state. I elaborate on this point subsequently, but first it is in order to note that the Act of 1969 is no longer in effect.

In 2012, the Act of 1969 was reviewed for constitutionality by the Constitutional Council and parts of the Act were, indeed, struck down, notably the distinction between *gens du voyage* with and without a regular source of income. Judging the distinction to be an unlawful discrimination that was not based on material and rational criteria, the Council abolished the *carnets de circulation* along with the associated reporting duties, and in 2017 the parliament finally repealed what remained of the Act, including the duty for *gens du voyages* with a regular income to report on an annual basis to the police (Möschel, 2017).

But during the roughly 40 years in which the Act of 1969 was in full operation, it was an important structuring element in the relationship between the French state and its nomadic Gypsy Traveller population. And insofar as the Act specifically created a duty for nomads to report regularly to police authorities, it constituted a form of state tolerance vis-à-vis their nomadism. This is so for a combination of several reasons.

First, insofar as the reporting duty operated against the background of a fundamental permission or legalization of nomadism, there was an important sense in which the French state refrained from interfering with practice of itinerancy and purposely allowed people to engage in this practice if they so wanted. Yet, the state was everything but enthusiastic about this practice. Subjecting nomadic Gyps Travellers to a duty to report regularly to *police authorities*, the state treated nomads in a way that is unusual and reminiscent, indeed, of how states treat criminal suspects on bail and/or convicted criminals on probation. As such, the reporting duty arguably revealed a certain apprehension, a malaise, on the part of the state vis-à-vis the practice of nomadism, and we may thus interpret the reporting duty for nomadic Gypsy Travellers as an instance of toleration as it is standardly conceptualized – i.e. a condition where one (tolerating) agent finds objectionable the beliefs, attitudes, or actions of another, but still refrains, voluntarily so, from interfering with those beliefs, attitudes or actions.

I have described now an important way in which the state can be – and has indeed been – tolerant towards nomadic Gypsy Travellers and their mobile life. But state tolerance towards nomadism can take another form also. The state might permit the practice of itinerance, but instead of expressing its apprehension through a reporting duty that assimilates nomads to criminals, the state might express its misgivings about nomadism in a manner that is more diffuse and dispersed over a range of public policy domains. That is to say, the state might permit nomadism, but systematically refuse to provide nomads with accommodations where this is necessary for them to access important institutions, rights, resources or state services.

To better understand this idea, consider the example of voter registration and polling in parliamentary elections.

If, as it is the case in many representative democracies, voter registration and polling in a parliamentary constituency are predicated on permanent residence in the relevant district, nomadic Gypsy Travellers are not able register and vote in *any* district, as they do not reside permanently *anywhere*. For them to be included into the electoral process, it is thus practically necessary[7] that the state introduces some workaround provisions that allow nomadic Gypsy Travellers to register in a constituency without being permanent residents there. For instance, the state may have to add provisions into the electoral law such that nomadic Gypsy Travellers can register as voters in one constituency of their choice. And by refusing to put in place such special accommodations in the electoral law, and in a range of other public policy domains too, the state may now express in a manner that is diffuse, but unmistakable, that although it allows Gypsy Travellers to pursue a nomadic life, it really does not approve of that choice and does not encourage it.

To distinguish this second form of tolerance from the one described initially, I shall refer to it as *multi-domain, non-accommodation tolerance* and I shall label the first form as *reporting tolerance*. Thus stated, the distinction might be taken to suggest the existence of two distinct conceptions of tolerance, but nothing such is intended: the two forms described merely represent different ways of *implementing*, in concrete policy, the conventional concept of tolerance.

Finally, in relation to multi-domain, non-accommodation tolerance it is worth noting that, as reporting tolerance, this form has an empirical basis, too. During the 20th century, the British state never operated anything akin to the French reporting duties and the Act of 1969: Gypsy Travellers were unconditionally free to practice a mobile way of life (Taylor, 2013). Still, in a number of policy areas, the British state was reluctant to insert special mechanisms for the inclusion and benefit

Gypsy Travellers who were mobile. In relation to voter enrolment and polling, for example, it is only in 2000 that the electoral law was reformed with a view to integrate nomadic Gypsy Travellers (and other homeless persons) into the electoral process. Previous to that, permanent residence in a constituency was a *sine qua non* for voter enrolment and nomadic Gypsy Travellers were simply excluded from participation in parliamentary elections (Khadar, 2013; cf. Representation of the People Act, 1983, p. s4).

Similarly, there continues to exist an important connection in the UK between residence in a location and access to primary health care. To consult a general practitioner (GP), one normally needs to be registered with the GP relevant surgery. Registration, in turn, is usually subject to the condition that one is a permanent resident of the geographic area for which the relevant surgery is responsible. For nomads, this means that they may face difficulties in accessing primary care. Yet, there have not, to my knowledge, been any systematic efforts on the part of the central government to exempt nomads from the ordinary requirements for GP registration, or to otherwise secure reliable GP access for nomadic Gypsy Travellers. Indeed, it is well-documented that nomadic Gypsy Travellers in the UK are severely disadvantaged in terms of primary care access, have a generally worse health condition, and an average life expectancy that is almost ten years shorter than the UK average (Feder, 1989; Parry et al., 2004; van Cleemput, 2012; British-Irish Parliamentary Assembly, 2014).

In France, by contrast, the state has to some extent tried to forestall such exclusions. The Act of 1969 featured provisions, indeed, to ensure that the *gens du voyage* would be able to register as voters, and poll, in one parliamentary constituency even though they did not live there permanently. Similarly, the Act contained provisions to ensure that the *gens du voyage* would qualify for a number of social services and would be able to exercise the civil rights that, according to French law, can be exercised only in one's municipality of residence, such as the right to be married (Garo, 2007).

Before its definitive repeal, the inclusionary provisions of the 1969 Act were also transplanted – sometimes with modifications – into a range of other Acts such that they remain in effect till this day.[8] So whilst reporting tolerance is clearly and directly related to the historical practice of the French state, multi-domain-non-accommodation tolerance is related to and illustrated by, British state practice.

To say that British public policy instantiates perfectly the approach I call multi-domain-non-accommodation tolerance would probably be an exaggeration for in some policy domains, the British state has a record of trying to support and sustain the nomadic lifestyle. In particular, there has since 1968 existed a policy such that public funds are used to provide Gypsy Travellers with caravan sites.[9] But as seen, there has simultaneously been a tendency in British politics to *not* accommodate Gypsy Traveller nomadism in a range of policy areas – for example in the areas of electoral policy and health care policy. And to that extent it is legitimate to regard 20th-century British policy towards nomadic Gypsy Travellers as an example, though an imperfect one, of multi-domain-non-accommodation tolerance.

## 2. Against Multi-domain-Non-accommodation Tolerance

Moving on to the normative assessment now of the idea that Gypsy Traveller nomadism might be the object of state tolerance, we may note first of all that from a broadly liberal-egalitarian viewpoint, multi-domain-non-accommodation tolerance is presumably impermissible.

To be clear, I do not think that the problem with this form of tolerance is that it is generally inconsistent with the normative commitments of egalitarian liberalism. Without specific information about the particular domains and the ways the state might refuse to accommodate Gypsy Traveller nomadism, it is virtually impossible to gauge in how far multi-domain-non-accommodation tolerance complies with liberal-egalitarian principles or, indeed, any other normative principles. As the saying goes, the devil is in the details.

But as soon as one begins to consider the particulars, indications accumulate that liberal-egalitarian principles counsel against multi-domain-non-accommodation tolerance. To better appreciate this, consider the case where residence in a particular location is a condition for GP registration and primary care access. If, as in Britain, the state here fails to put in place an accommodation mechanism for nomadic Gypsy Travellers, they will have poor or no access at all to GP services. More generally, nomadic Gypsy Travellers will be disadvantaged in relation to the good of primary care, which in the view of a liberal-egalitarian is morally suspect. In particular, it stands directly in tension with the view defended by Rawls (2001, pp. 174–175), Anderson (1999, p. 317) and others (e.g. Daniels, 2008; Barry, 1995, p. 97, 2001, p. 109) that certain primary resources, and health care especially, should generally be provided to all members of society.

In defence of a non-accommodation, it might be retorted here that some liberal-egalitarians do not, in fact, demand that people be insulated completely from disadvantage. Luck-egalitarians, in particular, think that it is 'morally fitting to hold individuals responsible for the foreseeable consequences of their voluntary choices' (Arneson, 1989, p. 88; Cohen, 1989, p. 920; Barry, 2001, p. 114) and consequently they accept relative disadvantage that results from an informed, voluntary choice – e.g. a choice to take a risky gamble.[10]

In addition, some luck-egalitarians insist that if actions and choices bottom in religious or cultural beliefs or commitments, they still count as voluntary. Barry in particular is infamous for being adamant that such commitments are not "some sort of alien affliction" or "an encumbrance . . . in . . . the way in which a physical disability is an encumbrance" (Barry, 2001, p. 36). And pulling together these two thoughts, some might now think that from the perspective of a Barry-type luck-egalitarian, it is no moral problem that nomadic Gypsy Travellers, on account of their mobile lifestyle, have poor primary care access. From this specific perspective, their primary care disadvantage appears like a voluntary and therefore unproblematic forfeiture.

However, this retort or qualification, fails to persuade. One important reason for this is that in the case of children, Gypsy Traveller nomadism cannot plausibly be seen as a voluntary choice. And even with adults, there is reason to be cautious in judgment. As noted in the introduction, nomadic Gypsy Travellers generally see the mobile way of life as a constitutive element of their group identity. But often, this cultural dimension of nomadism has stacked on top of it an economic dimension as well. As the introduction also noted, Gypsy Travellers frequently pursue economic activities that are compatible and, indeed, profitable only in conjunction with mobility, e.g. itinerant trading or seasonal agricultural work. Accordingly, nomadic Gypsy Travellers cultivate and collect professional skills and resources that are specific and especially well attuned to the conditions of mobility. Itinerant traders, for example, may cultivate a geographically dispersed client base. But this specialization also means that they may *not* develop skills and resources that are helpful for making a living in conditions of permanent settlement, e.g. a geographically concentrated client base. As such, nomadic Gypsy Travellers may not be able to afford economically the transition into settlement, and the status of Gypsy Traveller nomadism is therefore mixed, at best. The mobility of (adult) Gypsy Travellers may in part rest on cultural and identity-related considerations, but in many cases it is underwritten by economic (and perhaps other)[11] constraints, too, and thus one cannot plausibly see it as perfectly voluntary lifestyle, not even if one generally accepts the view of Barry that culturally motivated choices count as voluntary.

In turn, these considerations suggest that insofar as nomadic Gypsy Travellers are not accommodated in relation to GP registration and come to lack primary care access, the luck-egalitarian conditions of legitimate disadvantage are probably not properly satisfied. Prominent exponents of luck egalitarianism in fact stress that persons should *not* be asked to suffer a disadvantage if, among other things, they made the relevant underlying choices in a context of restricted or costly options, as in the case at hand (cf. Arneson, 1997, pp. 332, 343; Barry, 2006, pp. 97–98; Stemplowska, 2009, pp. 243–244). And thus, the liberal-egalitarian position is categorical: The non-accommodation of Gypsy Traveller nomadism in relation to GP registration runs counter to the liberal-egalitarian presumption in favour of general health care provision, it does not satisfy the conditions that luck-egalitarianism recognizes as conditions for legitimate disadvantage, and thus liberal-egalitarians of all stripes must concur that such a non-accommodation is impermissible.

A similar conclusion applies to voter registration and polling for parliamentary elections. As I have argued at greater length elsewhere (Carlsen Häggrot, 2018), nomadic Gypsy Travellers are directly disenfranchised and excluded from the electoral process if permanent residence in a constituency remains a *sine qua non* for voter registration and nomadic Gypsy Travellers are not afforded any special workarounds. In turn, this disenfranchisement undercuts nomadic Gypsy Travellers' status as members of the political community who are politically, socially, and morally equal to others. And since moral equality is treated by egalitarians as a fundamental moral value and the normative basis of the (moral) right to vote (cf. Christiano, 2008; Waldron, 1999; Kolodny, 2014), egalitarian liberals are thus compelled to regard it as an unacceptable violation of the (moral) right to vote if nomadic Gypsy Travellers are not afforded any accommodations in the domain of voter registration and polling for parliamentary elections.[12]

In response to the arguments developed over the last few paragraphs, an advocate of multi-domain-non-accommodation tolerance might charge that these arguments are fine as such, but do not show what they purport to show. If successful, so the charge goes, these arguments show that liberal-egalitarian commitments rule out the non-accommodation of Gypsy Traveller nomadism in two particular policy domains. But, so the critic continues, they do not establish that liberal-egalitarian rights and principles rule out the non-accommodation of nomadism in other domains and multi-domain-non-accommodation tolerance more generally.

To some extent, this is a fair point. However, notice that the arguments of the preceding paragraphs are not designed to show that every state failure to accommodate Gypsy Traveller nomadism is impermissible. Rather, the suggestion is that liberal-egalitarian principles specifically prevent the state from taking a tough, non-accommodationist line in the policy domains in question, and that egalitarian liberalism thus has built into it a restriction on the domains where the state can permissibly refuse accommodations to nomads. Within these restrictions, the state may well refuse to accommodate Gypsy Traveller nomadism, but then it is no longer certain that we are looking at a form of tolerance proper. When the non-accommodation of Gypsy Traveller nomadism is no longer generalized and invariant, when nomadic Gypsy Travellers are in fact provided with accommodations in the realm of voter registration, in relation to GP registration procedures and maybe in other domains, too, the absence of accommodations in other policy domains no longer serves a clear indication that the state disapproves of the itinerant lifestyle. The varied character of the state response to nomadism effectively empties the response of a clear "objection component" (King, 1976, p. 44) and thus it qualifies no more as a form of tolerance.

To restate the point more generally perhaps, this section does not argue not that liberal-egalitarian principles oppose multi-domain-non-accommodation tolerance because they object to non-accommodation in every possible form. Rather, the thought is that such principles prevent the state from clearly indicating that it objects to Gypsy Traveller nomadism. Liberal-egalitarian principles make it impermissible for the state to invariantly refuse accommodations to nomadic Gypsy Travellers. In turn, this means that the state is prevented as well, from expressing clearly, through a wide-ranging, invariant refusal to accommodate Gypsy Traveller nomadism, that it fundamentally disapproves of such a mobile lifestyle. And insofar as there is no discernible disapproval of nomadism, there can be no question of tolerance either (cf. King, 1976, p. 56; Katznelson, 2014, pp. 40–41).

## 3. Reporting Tolerance and Liberal Non-humiliation

Moving on now to the evaluation of reporting tolerance, a first question to ask is whether such a policy response to itinerance can be consistent with the right to free movement, which is part and parcel of any liberal political philosophy (cf. Carens, 1992; Waldron, 1993; Rawls, 2001, p. 44). A duty for nomadic Gypsy Travellers to regularly report to police authorities does not, for sure, proscribe frequent movement. But it subjects such movement to coercively enforced conditions. As such, the policy departs from freedom of movement, and liberals might be sympathetic, therefore, to the position of Mr. Jean-Claude P., who in 2012 brought the Act of 1969 before the Constitutional Council, complaining *inter alia* that the duty to report violated constitutionally entrenched freedom-of-movement rights (Conseil Constitutionel, 2012, §16). Indeed, liberals might charge that reporting tolerance is undesirable because incompatible with the liberal *right* to free movement.

So phrased, however, the critique is unsatisfactory. The geographic mobility of persons in liberal states is hedged and limited in a myriad of ways. Traffic regulations are one case in point; property rights of others are another. But limitations and conditions such as these are not usually – and rightly so – taken to be contrary to the liberal right to free movement (cf. Miller, 2005; Hosein, 2013). So, just because a policy limits, or conditions, people's geographic mobility, it is not necessarily at odds with the liberal right to free movement. The conditions for there to be such a violation are more demanding.

Presumably, the conditions must at minimum be that the relevant policy (P) burdens the exercise of free movement but does so for no compelling reason, or that P limits free movement for compelling reasons, but that the sought objective could be achieved with means less restrictive than P.[13] And thus, a freedom-of-movement critique of reporting tolerance has to show either (a) that the reporting duty serves no compelling ends, or (b) that it is an excessively restrictive means to achieve ends that are compelling by themselves.

Claim (a), however, is difficult to make in relation to the reporting duty. As I develop in the subsequent section, the reporting duty can be seen as way to bring about regular contacts between the state and its nomadic citizens – which is fair enough from a liberal-egalitarian point of view. A rights-based, freedom-of-movement critique must thus revolve around (b) and show that the compelling outcomes of the reporting duty can be had, too, with means that are less restrictive. This might also be done successfully – in the fifth section, I will, indeed, indicate at least one policy that is less restrictive than the reporting duties of the 1969 Act. But for the time being, I want to bracket the issue of freedom of movement[14] and focus on a problem with reporting tolerance that is much more conspicuous than its potential incompatibility with the liberal right to free movement.

In her seminal essay *The Liberalism of Fear*, Judith Shklar noted that liberal principles such as basic individual rights, proprietorship, and the rule of law can help to avert great evils and on that basis, she famously offered a re-interpretation of liberalism as a normative doctrine that has baked into it a foundational commitment to avert a *summum malum* consisting of "cruelty and the fear it inspires, and the very fear of fear itself" (Shklar, 1989, p. 29).

In a subsequent development, Jacob Levy has extended and deepened this approach in two important ways. For one thing, he has shown persuasively that the concern to avoid the *summum malum* has an especially important role to play in normative analyses of public policy in ethnically and religiously diverse societies (Levy, 2000, pp. 28–31, chap. 2). But no less important, he has argued as well that the *summum malum* described by Shklar actually involves two phenomena that are related, but conceptually distinct: cruelty and humiliation (Levy, 2000, pp. 23–25).

What is humiliation? Levy adopts a definition by Margalit, which describes humiliation as a "behavior or condition that constitutes a sound reason for a person to consider his or her self-respect injured" (Margalit cited in Levy, 2000, p. 24). And in light of this definition, we can see now what is conspicuously problematic with reporting tolerance: A duty for nomadic Gypsy Travellers to report regularly to police authorities is humiliating and falls short of the foundational liberal commitments to non-cruelty and non-humiliation. This is so for at least two reasons.

First, in a broadly speaking liberal society, people are not normally required to regularly report to law enforcement agencies. Requirements of this kind exist, but they are typically reserved for persons who are in (potentially) bad standing with the law, e.g. suspects on bail or convicted criminals on probation. So, when nomads are required to report to the police, they are inevitably placed in the symbolic vicinity of, and publicly associated with, (suspected) criminals, which surely is a reason for any (law-abiding) person to not only feel offended, but to be properly injured in their self-respect.

Further, settled communities are often deeply prejudiced against mobile populations (cf. Scott, 2009) and in Western Europe it has been a persistent trope in folk views that Gypsy Travellers are *voleurs de poules* (chicken thieves), inveterate delinquents prone to every possible form of deceit and petty crime: shoplifting, pursue cutting, horse stealing, poaching, and so on (Clark, 2001, pp. 72–73, 76–88). So, to the extent that nomadic Gypsy Travellers are obliged to report regularly to police authorities – much in the same way as criminal suspects or convicts – they can plausibly interpret that obligation as a legal, public affirmation of the prejudice they suffer at the hands of the settled majority. And this again seems a sound reason to lose self-respect.

## 4. Mobility, Burden Sharing and Non-humiliating Alternatives

If the argument developed so far is correct, liberals – egalitarian or otherwise – should not condone reporting tolerance. And yet – is there not something to be said for a policy instrument that enables the state to regularly access and communicate with those of its citizens who are mobile and cannot, therefore, be counted upon to receive mail and/or visits by officials at a permanent address?

The French Constitutional Council thought as much. It upheld as constitutional the duty for *gens du voyage* to report at six-month intervals, and the explicitly stated reason for this was that such a duty served a valuable purpose in that it "for purposes civil, social, administrative and judicial, enables the identification and search of persons who cannot be expected to be found at a permanent residence and also creates a means of communicating with these persons" (Conseil Constitutionel, 2012, §18; my translation)

From a broadly liberal-egalitarian perspective, this is a compelling view, too. For reasons that will shortly become clear, liberals need not think that a reporting duty as implemented in France is consistent with the liberal right to free movement. But the deeper view that it is valuable for the state to have regular contacts with its nomadic citizens is congenial to a liberal-egalitarian perspective.

Egalitarian liberalism is characterized in part by an insistence that at bottom all members of society are owed equal concern and treatment. A familiar implication of this view is, of course, that all members of society should be granted the same basic rights (cf. Barry, 1995, pp. 82–85; Rawls, 2001, pp. 42, 45; Anderson, 1999, pp. 317–318). We have also seen that, on several prominent accounts, equal treatment is taken to imply that certain primary resources and health care in particular ought to be generally provided.

But the ideal of equal treatment cannot be coherently restricted so as to apply only to the output-side of social co-operation. If one is to genuinely treat people as equals, one must surely look to the burdens of social cooperation and demand that the burdens, too, be shared in ways that are fair and reflect equality. As Rawls put the point, "when a number of persons engage in a mutually advantageous cooperating venture according to certain rules and thus voluntarily restrict their liberty, those who have submitted to these restrictions have a right to a similar acquiescence on the part of those who have benefitted from their submission. We are not to gain from the cooperative efforts of others without doing our fair share." (Rawls, 1973, p. 343)

Now, what it means exactly to distribute fairly the costs of social cooperation can be debated. Some might think that only an equal sharing of the costs is fair; others might argue that a distribution is fair insofar as it is proportional to individuals' varying capacities to contribute to the maintenance of the co-operative scheme. Either way, though, the shared, basic understanding is that each and every one ought to contribute to the maintenance of social life.

Getting nomadic Gypsy Travellers to contribute their fair share can be challenging, however. Because of their mobility, nomadic persons are not easily 'legible' for the state (Scott, 2009), and they cannot be counted upon to reliably receive by mail their tax slips, parking tickets, judicial summons, conscription notices, etc. In turn, this means that nomads may remain unaware of, or forget about, fiscal and other contributions they owe to the wider political community, and from an egalitarian perspective it is desirable, therefore, that there be an arrangement that can substitute for the role that postal communication plays in the relation between the state and sedentary citizens. That is to say, egalitarian liberals will find it desirable that there be a reliable vector between the state and its nomadic Gypsy Travellers for general information, tax slips, and other relevant documents – and direct, legally mandated contacts seem to be just such a vector.

This is not to say, though, that liberal-egalitarians must align with the Constitutional Council and come around to seeing reporting tolerance as desirable after all, or at least as permissible. Rather, it is to say that the liberal commitment to fair burden-sharing implies support for the *general* view that *in some form*, there ought to be regular contacts between nomads and the state. Reporting tolerance is one way, of course, to implement such contacts, but since it fails to satisfy a basic non-humiliation principle, egalitarian liberals cannot pivot back to support this policy after all.

Instead, liberals ought to look into the alternatives, which exist indeed. For example, regular contacts between the state and nomadic Gypsy

Travellers might be created by a legal duty for the nomads to report regularly to a specified branch of the fiscal authority, or some other agency that does not primarily and ostensibly manage crime. Digitized communication – for example through a state-provided digital inbox (digi-box) – and an obligation for nomadic Gypsy Travellers to utilize that digi-box might be another alternative. These are the implementations that liberal egalitarians ought to support, for they enable a fair sharing of the burdens of life in a political community without being humiliating for those Gypsy Travellers who maintain an itinerant lifestyle.

Finally, is it not a form of reporting tolerance, too, if nomadic Gypsy Travellers are subjected to a digi-box or modified reporting duty? I think not, for the following reason. As we have had occasion to remark at an earlier point, tolerance conceptually requires the presence of an objection component. But insofar as nomadic Gypsy Travellers are required to utilize a digital inbox service or to report to a civil authority, there is no such objection. Nomadic Gypsy Travellers are, for sure, subjected to a particular legal duty, and in the modified reporting scheme, they must regularly present themselves before state authorities. However, the state does not here apply to nomadic Gypsy Travellers the treatment and the duties that are otherwise reserved for persons who are in bad standing with the law: Nomadic Gypsy Travellers are not asked to report to the branch of government that is primarily and ostentatiously in charge of combatting crime, and so there is no clear expression on the part of the state that it harbours an objection to the practice of Gypsy Traveller nomadism.

## Conclusion

This chapter has developed critiques against the two ways in which a state might tolerate Gypsy Traveller nomadism. It has argued that insofar as the state permits Gypsy Traveller nomadism, but refuses to accommodate this mobile lifestyle across a broad range of policy domains, it fails to realize important normative goals, such as general health care provision and the right to vote. And insofar as the state permits Gypsy Travellers to practise nomadism, but requires them to regularly report to police authorities, it subjects them to humiliating treatment. Both these considerations should appeal to theorists of a broadly liberal-egalitarian inclination and the overall liberal-egalitarian view is, accordingly, that Gypsy Traveller nomadism is no proper object of state tolerance.

This conclusion does not mean, though, that the state may be intolerant of Gypsy Traveller nomadism in the sense that it rejects and, therefore, proscribes the practice. The suggestion is rather that from a liberal-egalitarian viewpoint, it is wrong for a state to object to Gypsy Traveller nomadism and to operate policies that express the objection.

*Gypsy Travellers and State Tolerance* 233

The critique does also not mean that the state must abandon attempts to maintain regular contacts with nomads and that the state cannot permissibly try to ensure that nomadic Gypsy Travellers bear their part of the burdens of social life. The upshot is rather that fair burden sharing should be secured by digitized communication, a modified reporting duty, or other means that do not humiliate nomadic Gypsy Travellers and do not constitute a form of state tolerance in the proper sense of the term.

Finally, it is worth noting that as a negative argument, this chapter has not comprehensively outlined the particular policies that it would be appropriate for a state to implement in response to Gypsy Traveller nomadism. But insofar as the chapter has succeeded in removing from the table the option of the state being tolerant towards Gypsy Traveller nomadism, it has advanced our understanding of the cases and conditions where tolerance is, or is not, an appropriate state response to particular practices, and it has filled an important lacuna in liberal theorizing about the normative claims of minority groups and nomadic populations in particular.

## Notes

1. For such a comprehensive critique of tolerance see, e.g. Brown 2006.
2. The contributions to normative minority rights theory are too numerous to be cited comprehensively here. For particularly prominent contributions that give relatively broad accounts of minority groups' entitlements, *see* Kymlicka 1995, Carens 2000, Levy 2000, Parekh 2006, Song 2007 and Patten 2014. See also Barry 2001 for an important critique of contemporary minority rights theory.
3. Exceptional in this regard are a set of articles by Testino (2010), Guérard de Latour (2011) and Guérard de Latour and Bessone (2014), but note that these primarily examine how the cases of the European Gypsy Travellers and Roma relate to the distinction between national and ethnic groups theorized by Kymlicka (1995). They do not give any determinate account of the rights or entitlements that Gypsy Travellers can legitimately demand. Attempts to theorize such entitlements in relation to voter registration procedures and the public provision of caravan sites have been made by myself (cf. Carlsen Häggrot, 2018, 2019).
4. For prominent liberal egalitarian accounts in addition to those cited in the next sentence, see Dworkin 2000 and Christiano 2008.
5. For elaborations on the historical, linguistic and broader cultural matters, see Liégeois 1994, Okely 1983, Fraser 1992, Robert 2007, Taylor 2013, 2014 and Matras 2015.
6. NB: The obligation for *gens du voyage* to regularly report to police authorities was not enshrined in the Act of 1969 itself, but specified in auxiliary, administrative regulations, cf. *Décret no. 85–684 du 8 juillet 1985 modifiant le decret 70708 du 31–07–1970 portant application du titre i et de certaines dispositions du titre ii de la loi 693 du 03–01–1969 relative a l'exercice des activites ambulantes et au regime applicable aux personnes circulant en france sans domicile ni residence fixe.*

7. Notice that at this point, I express no view about the *moral* necessity of such accommodations. The point is merely that unless some special arrangement is put in place for them, nomadic Gypsy Travellers are as a matter fact unable to register and poll.
8. The provisions enabling nomads to register as voters have, for instance, been incorporated into the electoral law; cf. *Loi no. 2017-86 du 27 janvier 2017 relative à l'égalité et à la citoyenneté; chapter IV, section 6, art. 193 and 194.*
9. In relation to the British caravan sites policy, it should be noted that the policy has changed considerably since its instauration in 1968, and that it is widely criticized for failing to provide a sufficient number of sites. For a recent example of this critique, see Friends, Families and Travellers (2017).
10. Similarly, Rawlsians accept disadvantage and inequalities under the conditions that basic liberties are secured, that the inequalities are 'attached to offices and positions open to all under conditions of fair equality of opportunity', and that the inequalities 'are to the greatest benefit of the least-advantaged members of society' (Rawls, 2001, p. 42). However, it is difficult to see how the disadvantage at hand might help to improve the lot of those most disadvantaged: If it is nomadic Gypsy Travellers who are identified as the most disadvantaged, it is absurd to claim that their lack of access to primary care is for the good of the least well off. And if it is another population category that is identified as overall least well off, it is still hard to see how nomads being relatively deprived of primary care would help to improve the lot of those most disadvantaged.
11. In the British context it is sometimes thought that some nomadic Gypsy Travellers are mobile because although they would like to settle in a permanently parked caravan, they are unable to access a space to permanently place their caravan.
12. Notice, that once it is recognized that nomads cannot justly be excluded from the electoral system, serious questions remain about how exactly they ought to be integrated into the electoral system. In Carlsen Häggrot (2018), I describe and evaluate several means for inclusion.
13. These minimal conditions are in different ways recognized by a range of constitutional courts, including the European Court for Human Rights and the US Supreme Court (cf. Möller, 2012).
14. Similarly, I leave to the side another potential problem which is that the reporting duty might be discriminatory, as was also charged by Mr. Jean-Claude P.

## References

Adams, B., Okely, J., Morgan, D. and Smith, D. (1975). *Gypsies and Government Policy in England: A Study of the Travellers' Way of Life in Relation to the Policies and Practices of Central and Local Government*. London: Heinemann Educational.

Anderson, E. S. (1999). What Is the Point of Equality? *Ethics*, 109(2), pp. 287–337.

Arneson, R. J. (1989). Equality and Equal Opportunity for Welfare. *Philosophical Studies*, 56(1), pp. 77–93.

Arneson, R. J. (1997). Egalitarianism and the Undeserving Poor. *Journal of Political Philosophy*, 5(4), pp. 327–350.

Aubin, E. (2001). L'evolution du droit francais au droit applicable aux Tsiganes. Les quatres logiques du législateur républicain. *Etudes Tsiganes*, 15, pp. 26–56.

Barry, B. (1995). *Justice as Impartiality*. Oxford: Clarendon Press.

Barry, B. (2001). *Culture and Equality: An Egalitarian Critique of Multiculturalism*. Cambridge: Polity Press.
Barry, N. (2006). Defending Luck Egalitarianism. *Journal of Applied Philosophy*, 23(1), pp. 89–107.
Berland, J. C. and Salo, M. T. (1986). Peripatetic Communities: An Introduction. *Nomadic Peoples*, 21-22, pp. 1–6.
British-Irish Parliamentary Assembly. (2014). *Travellers, Gypsies and Roma: Access to Public Services and Community Relations*. London: British-Irish Parliamentary Assembly.
Brown, W. (2006). *Regulating Aversion: Tolerance in the Age of Identity and Empire*. Princeton, NJ: Princeton University Press.
Carens, J. H. (1992). Migration and Morality: A Liberal Egalitarian Perspective. In: B. Barry and R. Goodin, eds., *Free Movement: Ethics in the Transnational Migration of People and of Money*, 1st ed. London: Harvester Wheatsheaf, pp. 25–47.
Carens, J. H. (2000). *Culture, Citizenship, and Community: A Contextual Exploration of Justice as Evenhandedness*. Oxford: Oxford University Press.
Carlsen Häggrot, M. (2018). The Right to Vote and Nomadic Voter Enrolment. *Citizenship Studies*, 22(7), pp. 725–744.
Carlsen Häggrot, M. (2019). Public Caravan Sites for British Gypsy Travellers: Kymlicka and an Argument from Expropriatory Compensation. *Ethnopolitics*, pp. 1–18. [online] Available at: www.tandfonline.com/doi/full/10.1080/17449057.2019.1628515?scroll=top&needAccess=true [Accessed 27 Apr. 2020].
Christiano, T. (2008). *The Constitution of Equality: Democratic Authority and Its Limits*. Oxford: Oxford University Press.
Clark, C. (2001). *Invisible Lives: The Gypsies and Travellers of Britain*. Doctor of Philosophy. Edinburgh: University of Edinburgh.
Cohen, A. J. (2004). What Toleration Is? *Ethics*, 115(1), pp. 68–95.
Cohen, G. A. (1989). On the Currency of Egalitarian Justice. *Ethics*, 99(4), pp. 906–944.
Cossée, C. (2007). Tsiganes, 'gens du voyage' et statistiques. In: J.-P. Liégeois, ed., *L'accès aux droits sociaux des populations tsiganes en France*, 1st ed. Rennes: Editions ENSP, pp. 223–226.
Daniels, N. (2008). *Just Health: Meeting Health Needs Fairly*. Cambridge: Cambridge University Press.
Dworkin, R. (2000). *Sovereign Virtue: The Theory and Practice of Equality*. Cambridge, MA: The Belknap Press of Harvard University Press.
Feder, G. (1989). Traveller Gypsies and Primary Care. *Journal of the Royal College of General Practitioners*, 39, pp. 425–429.
Forst, R. (2003). Toleration, Justice and Reason. In: C. McKinnon and D. Castiglione, eds., *The Culture of Toleration in Diverse Societies: Reasonable Toleration*. Manchester: Manchester University Press.
Forst, R. (2004). The Limits of Toleration. *Constellations*, 11(3), pp. 312–325.
Forst, R. (2013). *Toleration in Conflict: Past and Present*. Trans. Ciaran Cronin. Cambridge: Cambridge University Press.
Fraser, A. M. (1992). *The Gypsies*. Oxford: Blackwell.
Friends, Families and Travellers (2017). Joint report to the United Nations Universal Periodic Review of the United Kingdom 2017 (3rd Cycle). *Friends Families and Travellers*. [online] Available at: www.gypsy-traveller.org/resource/

joint-report-united-nations-universal-periodic-review-united-kingdom-2017/ [Accessed 8 Mar. 2020].
Galeotti, A. E. (2014). The Range of Toleration: From Toleration as Recognition Back to Disrespectful Tolerance. *Philosophy & Social Criticism*, 41(2), pp. 93–110.
Garo, M. (2007). L'accès aux droits du citoyen. In: J.-P. Liégeois, ed., *L'accès aux droits sociaux des populations tsiganes en France*, 1st ed. Rennes: Editions ENSP.
Guérard da Latour, S. (2011). Y a-t-il une minorité rom? Un enjeu de typologie normative dans le cadre du multiculturalisme libéral. *Revue Philosophique de Louvain*, 109(4), pp. 723–746.
Guérard da Latour, S. and Bessone, M. (2014). Political, Not Ethno-Cultural: A Normative Assessment of Roma Identity in Europe. In: G. Calder, M. Bessone and F. Zuolo, eds., *How Groups Matter: Challenges of Toleration in Pluralistic Societies*, 1st ed. London: Routledge, pp. 162–181.
Hosein, A. (2013). Immigration and Freedom of Movement. *Ethics & Global Politics*, 6(1), pp. 25–37.
Katznelson, I. (2014). Toleration as a Layered Institution. In: C. Stepan Alfred and C. Taylor, eds., *Boundaries of Toleration: Religion, Culture, and Public Life*, 1st ed. New York: Columbia University Press, pp. 37–58.
King, P. (1976). *Toleration*. London: George Allen & Unwin Ltd.
Khadar, L. (2013). *Access to Electoral Rights: United Kingdom*, San Domenico di Fiesole: EDUO Citizenship Observatory. Available at: http://eudo-citizenship.eu/admin/?p=file&appl=countryProfiles&f=1310-UK-FRACIT.pdf [Accessed 26 Oct. 2016].
Kolodny, N. (2014). Rule Over None II: Equality and the Justification of Democracy. *Philosohpy and Public Affairs*, 42(4), pp. 287–336.
Kymlicka, W. (1995). *Multicultural Citizenship: A Liberal Theory of Minority Rights*. Oxford: Oxford University Press.
Levy, J. T. (2000). *The Multiculturalism of Fear*. Oxford: Oxford University Press.
Liégeois, J.-P. (1994). *Roma, Gypsies, Travellers*. Strasbourg: Council of Europe Press.
Lucassen, L. (2008). Between Hobbes and Locke: Gypsies and the Limits of the Modernization Paradigm. *Social History*, 33(4), pp. 423–441.
Matras, Y. (2015). *The Romani Gypsies*. Cambridge, MA: The Belknap Press of Harvard University Press.
Miller, D. (2005). Immigration: The Case for Limits. In: A. Cohen and C. Wellman, eds., *Contemporary Debates in Applied Ethics*, 1st ed. Oxford: Blackwell Publishing, pp. 363–375.
Möller, K. (2012). *The Global Model of Constitutional Rights*. Oxford: Oxford University Press.
Möschel, M. (2017). Race in French 'Republican' Law: The Case of Gens du Voyage and Roma. *International Journal of Constitutional Law*, 15(4), pp. 1206–1225.
Niner, P. (2003). *Local Authority Gypsy/Traveller Sites in England*. London: ODPM.
Nussbaum, M. C. (2012). *The New Religious Intolerance: Overcoming the Politics of Fear in an Anxious Age*. Cambridge, MA: The Belknap Press of Harvard University Press.

Okely, J. (1983). *The Traveller-Gypsies*. Cambridge: Cambridge University Press.
Parekh, B. (2006). *Rethinking Multiculturalism: Cultural Diversity and Political Theory*. Cambridge, MA: The Belknap Press of Harvard University Press.
Parry, G., van Cleemput, P., Peters, J., Moore, J., Walters, S., Thomas, K. and Cooper, C. (2004). *The Health Status of Gypsies and Travellers in England: Report of Department of Health Inequalities in Health Research Initiative*. Sheffield: School of Health and Related Research, University of Sheffield.
Patten, A. (2014). *Equal Recognition: The Moral Foundations of Minority Rights*. Princeton, NJ: Princeton University Press.
Rawls, J. (1973). *A Theory of Justice*. Oxford: Oxford University Press.
Rawls, J. (2001). *Justice as Fairness: A Restatement*. Boston, MA: The Belknap Press of Harvard University Press.
Robert, C. (2007). *Éternels étrangers de l'intérieur? Les groupes tsiganes en France*. Paris: Desclée de Brouwer.
Scott, J. C. (2009). *The Art of Not Being Governed: An Anarchist History of Upland Southeast Asia*. New Haven, CT: Yale University Press.
Shklar, J. N. (1989). The Liberalism of Fear. In: N. L. Rosenblum, ed., *Liberalism and the Moral Life*, 1st ed. Cambridge, MA: The Belknap Press of Harvard University Press, pp. 21–38.
Song, S. (2007). *Justice, Gender, and the Politics of Multiculturalism*. Cambridge: Cambridge University Press.
Stemplowska, Z. (2009). Making Justice Sensitive to Responsibility. *Political Studies*, 57(2), pp. 237–259.
Taylor, B. (2013). *A Minority and the State: Travellers in Britain in the Twentieth Century*. Manchester: Manchester University Press.
Taylor, B. (2014). *Another Darkness, Another Dawn: A History of Gypsies, Roma and Travellers*. London: Reaktion Books.
Testino, C. (2010). 'Nomadism' and Housing Policies: Roma in Italy, a Hard Case for the Theory of Minority Rights. *Notizie di Politeia*, 26(99), pp. 97–112.
van Cleemput, P. (2012). Gypsy and Traveller Health. In: J. Richardson and A. K. Tsang, eds., *Gypsies and Travellers: Empowerment and Inclusion in British Society*, 1st ed. Bristol: Policy Press.
Waldron, J. (1993). *Liberal Rights: Collected Papers 1981–1991*. Cambridge: Cambridge University Press.
Waldron, J. (1999). *Law and Disagreement*. Oxford: Clarendon Press.
Waldron, J. (2012). *The Harm in Hate Speech*. Cambridge, MA: The Belknap Press of Harvard University Press.

## French Statutes

Loi no. 69–3 du 3 janvier 1969 relative à l'exercice des activités ambulantes et au régime applicable aux personnes circulant en France sans domicile ni résidence fixe. Available at: www.legifrance.gouv.fr/affichTexte.do?cid Texte=LEGITEXT000006068336&dateTexte=20090101 [Accessed 8 Apr. 2017].
Loi no. 2017–86 du 27 janvier 2017 relative à l'égalité et à la citoyenneté. Available at: www.legifrance.gouv.fr/affichTexte.do?cidTexte=JORFTEXT000033934948&categorieLien=id [Accessed 11 Mar. 2020].
Décret no. 85–684 du 8 juillet 1985 modifiant le decret 70708 du 31–07–1970 portant application du titre i et de certaines dispositions du titre ii de la loi 693

du 03–01–1969 relative a l'exercice des activites ambulantes et au regime applicable aux personnes circulant en france sans domicile ni residence fixe. Available at: www.legifrance.gouv.fr/affichTexte.do?cidTexte=JORFTEXT000 000309688&categorieLien=id [Accessed 11 Mar. 2020].

### British Statutes

Representation of the People Act of 1983. Available at: www.legislation.gov.uk/ukpga/1983/2/contents [Accessed 8 Apr. 2017].

### Judicial Decisions

Conseil Constitutionel. (2012). Décision No. 2012–279 QPC du 5 octobre 2012. Available at: www.conseil-constitutionnel.fr/decision/2012/2012279QPC.htm [Accessed 14 Mar. 2020].

# 13 Toleration as a Deep Practice, Legitimate Expectations and Refugees

*Gottfried Schweiger and Clemens Sedmak*

## Introduction

In political philosophy there has been far more research on the question of whether refugees should be admitted than on how refugees should be treated fairly after they have been admitted. It is obvious that integration (if it is at all clear what that should mean) is not an easy task – and that both refugees and the population of the host society sometimes endorse different particular norms and practices that conflict with each other. In this chapter, we want to outline the theoretical field in which this question can be meaningfully addressed as a question of the legitimate expectations of both sides and examine to what extent toleration as a deep practice is concerned here.

In the first section we will explicate toleration as deep practice. Such a deep practice includes a moment of adversity (experience of resistance), a moment of intensity (experience of effort and engagement) and a moment of commitment (an experience that requires endurance). Analogously, we could say that it is a form of deep practice of toleration when we can be tolerant under adverse circumstances. In the second section, we will look at toleration from the perspective of value pluralism and its intrinsic and instrumental value for societies. After all, toleration as a deep practice is not an empty formal action, but rather is committed to certain moral goods, which are expressed and protected by this practice on the one hand, and which, on the other hand, are excluded from arbitrary changeability. In the third section, we want to examine the question of the extent to which toleration as a deep practice is a legitimate expectation that both refugees and the population of the host society can place against each other. So we are dealing here with the criteria of legitimacy under non-ideal circumstances, in a particular asymmetric relationship. This asymmetry exists with regard to relevant factors: power, participation, neediness, status, and also concerns the possibility of forming and exercising toleration as a deep practice. In the fourth section we will consider empirical research data from the stake holders of the second Humanitarian Corridor in Italy that brought 500 refugees on a legal pathway to Italy between November 2017 and February 2019; the management of the expectations of social workers, refugees, volunteers and local politicians has been identified as a key factor in the integration efforts with distinct challenges to attitudes and practices of toleration. We will reflect on this empirical material using the theoretical framework developed in previous sections. In particular we want to examine toleration conflicts and the limits of toleration as a deep practice.

## 1. Toleration as a Deep Practice

Values are "conceptions of the desirable". They motivate as well as orient our actions. The concept of "tolerance" or "toleration" is a second-order value; that is to say that the concept needs to make statements about values (commitments) and statements about statements about values (assessment of commitments). Tolerance means saying "yes" to something that would normally be rejected by the speaker. An example: a visitor asks his hosts over dinner in their home whether he is allowed to light his pipe. Saying "yes" to this request by the hosts (who are non-smokers) is an act of tolerance. In a non-smoking household not smoking is not only preferred, but desired, so much so that this desire will be managed with explicit requests (and maybe sanctions) to avoid the frustration and violation of this desirable state. The goods at stake here are the life and lifestyle choices of people who control their private sphere. In the case of a visitor there may be a higher good – the good of hospitality (or other goods such as social harmony or even long-term advantages). Saying "yes" to something that one actually rejects is a case of tolerance.

Toleration is a dynamic triggered by competing moral goods and solved by a hierarchy of moral goods. A particular value X is violated in a particular context because of a higher value Y that is at stake. Respecting Y can mean disrespecting X in a particular situation. In this sense, toleration requires "moral literacy", a sense of how to read the relationship between values and situations and how to read the relationship between different values. The "moral literacy"-requirement is made more demanding by the fact that toleration has limits and requires judgment. You would not want to tolerate sexual harassment or exploitation or corruption even though there may also be the possibility of dynamics of competing higher goods in these cases. And then there are borderline cases – Maud Deckmar, for instance, describes a situation where she decided not to tolerate her mother's behavior. Maud had asked her mother to look after her four-year-old son Fred, who had been diagnosed with autism. Maud entrusted her mother with Fred's care for a night.

When Maud returned the following morning to pick up her son she got very angry because her mother

> had tied one end of a long rope around his tummy and the other end round the trunk of a big tree. She had a lot to do, hanging laundry and couldn't stop doing all the chores around the place. . . . My baby. A captive.
>
> (Deckmar, 2005, p. 33)

She could not tolerate the situation, untied her son and became very angry at her mother who did not think much of it. Should Maud have "tolerated" the fact that her son had been tied to a tree (given the moral goods of her relationship to her mother and the respect for her mother's care taking style)? He was safe and close to his grandmother – but deprived of his liberty.

Toleration is a demanding value, but it could be so much more than that – it could be a defining feature of a person's life. Swiss philosopher Peter Bieri has developed the idea that our understanding of human dignity facilitates and constitutes a particular form of life, a particular way of experiencing the world (Bieri, 2017). The "work" the concept of human dignity is able to do affects our judgments and our perceptions. "Doing dignity" lays the foundation of a form of life. Similar considerations can be developed with regard to tolerance and toleration.

The concept of toleration needs to be nurtured by appropriate practices of doing toleration, of practising toleration. In reflecting on memory, Milan Kundera observed that memories have to be watered just like plants to be kept alive and thrive; and we water our memories by sharing and talking about them (Kundera, 1999); in other words: values need to be part of communicative memory and current practices in order to be kept semantically alive. Values need to be "culturally anchored". If they are not anchored and nurtured by human practices, values will ultimately lose their vitality and colour, or die. The litmus test of the plausibility and comprehensibility of a value is practice, especially practice in the everyday. Nancy Rosenblum has reflected on the connection between the everyday life of neighbours and democracy (Rosenblum, 2016). Everyday practices of respect, proper consideration of the other and an attitude of solidarity and cooperation serve as the basis of democracy in the ordinary. The same can be said about toleration that needs to be practised in the everyday. Without an appropriate environment (a "form of life") values lose semantic plausibility. Values are vulnerable. There has to be access to a proper variety of practices and there has to be stability ("semantic security") which translates into "paradigm security", that is, the stability of certain examples remaining good examples in connection with toleration.

Toleration is a value that is challenged and required precisely in times of a value conflict, namely, in morally demanding situations. Toleration is a value that is not meant for the morally flat situation – it is, in this regard, more similar to "courage" than to "attentiveness". It is a value that does its work in morally sophisticated situations. We could call values like "courage" and "tolerance" that come into play in morally challenging situations beyond the moral conduct of the everyday (that also requires a set of values) adversity-based values. Adversity-based values are necessary to maintain a moral culture even under challenges.

Let us introduce the concept of deep practice here; Dan Coyle coined the term in his observations on high achievements (Coyle, 2009); he wondered about the remarkable soccer talent in Brazil and considered that training under adverse circumstances (rough ball in an uneven favela lot) would constitute a "deep" way of appropriating a practice; if you have mastered the art of playing soccer with a rough ball on a landfill site, how much easier would it be for you to excel in soccer on a real soccer field using a real soccer ball? "Adverse conditions" and "deep commitments" are characteristic for deep practices.

Deep practices require strong commitments and endurance; there is a sense of "moral resilience" in deep practices, the idea of creating flourishing moral practices even under pressure and in adverse circumstances. It is comparatively easy to be tolerant if the stakes are low and the costs are insignificant. Tolerating a loud neighbour in a restaurant or harmless religious jokes in the media or the cheap perfume of a colleague in the work place is not a case for a deep practice of tolerance. There is no need to use the value "toleration" if we are not talking about a matter of robust concern and sincere care. There has to be a real commitment to value X and a real commitment to value Y in the dynamics of toleration that requires the abrogation of X because of Y in a particular situation. It is also worth mentioning that it is not only a moral issue whether a person is tolerant or not, it is also a moral issue whether a person feels the need to be tolerant. Toleration is, as said, an adversity-based value. If one construes "adversity" too quickly, this becomes a moral issue in itself. If a person is "tolerant" when having a conversation with a transgender person, this will not be the kind of "adversity-based" use of toleration that the value is understood to enable.

What we are looking for is a form of life, committed to higher order values even under adverse circumstances, when stakes are high and when commitments are costly. Toleration as an adversity-based value points us to a deep practice of toleration. We could list three consequences of deep practice of toleration: (i) there is no standard account of toleration; (ii) any understanding of toleration is constantly being challenged and faced with disruption; (iii) deep practice can change other practices. Enacting toleration in deep practices will change our social perspective – our outlook – on the world.

Deep practices of toleration can be identified by looking at "especially vulnerable people" and "morally disruptive practices". There is a link between the deep practice of human dignity and the deep practice of toleration. Showing respect for a person under adverse circumstances is an expression of a deep practice of human dignity; not reducing a person to a means to an end, even if it is difficult, constitutes a deep practice of human dignity. Showing respect for a person under adverse circumstances (the established moral fabric has been disrupted, established moral routines have been broken, moral comfort zones have been challenged) is an expression of a deep practice of toleration; the latter has to be based on a fundamental value that abrogates other values. We suggest that this value be respect for the dignity of the person. This respect both justifies and motivates toleration. This respect structures a deep practice of toleration. Reductionism of all kinds (reducing people to numbers, to expenses, to achievements, to problems, to illnesses, etc.) undermine the possibility for deep practices of human dignity – and toleration. Real encounters with real people make it more difficult to engage in reductionist approaches, but also at the same time pose real challenges to the deep practice of toleration. That is why we will further explore the challenges through refugees as a case study.

## 2. Toleration and Values

Toleration does not take place in a vacuum and it has several aspects. Firstly, toleration is functionally important for coexistence in a pluralistic and ideologically differentiated society. This concerns the relationship of citizens and communities to one another, people who should behave tolerantly towards such ideologies, convictions and social norms and practices that they do not share. But this also applies to the relationship of the state and its institutions to the population and the various groups that exist within it. The state's requirement of toleration is also very important because it has a monopoly on the use of force and resources that can be a threat to minorities and vulnerable groups in particular. Toleration is therefore also an eminently political virtue, which is part of a democratic-liberal ethos without which a liberal society and state cannot be maintained (Ferrara, 2014).

Secondly, however, as we have already shown, toleration is also intrinsically valuable. It not only refers to the fact that it makes it possible for coexistence and for the state to function, but we also see it as part of a moral attitude to be tolerant. Even if the functioning of society and state cannot be ensured by tolerant practices, it is morally right to behave in this way and adopt toleration as a value. This is also connected with our thesis that toleration is part of a good life, i.e. the experience of being tolerated and even tolerating others is valuable for one's own biography. The experience of being tolerated is an experience of respect and recognition, which is not necessarily a positive affirmation, but conveys the belief that one is seen and respected as an autonomous and sovereign subject (Galeotti, 2015). Toleration is an experience of difference, whereby difference is necessary according to the theory of recognition in order to experience oneself as a unique individual. The stance of toleration towards others is also only possible as an experience if one perceives oneself as independent and consolidated. This is also what a plural, liberal and just society wants to make possible for its citizens, namely to facilitate such experiences so that they can perceive themselves as autonomous and respected citizens. One can also speak here of the idea that toleration goes hand in hand with the experience of relational justice and the awareness of not being dominated (Pettit, 2012).

Third, toleration is interwoven with other values. Other values limit toleration on the one hand and support it on the other. They limit them, for example, by determining which social norms and practices are appropriate to toleration and for which it is not the adequate reaction, but rather which demonstrate intolerance. Examples of such disputes are well known, especially in the context of migration and refugees. Should social norms and practices that devalue women be tolerated? What about the legitimacy of violence against children or the rejection of democratic decision-making processes? What can be done if toleration itself is rejected as a value and instead intolerance and hatred are advocated? The concept of toleration cannot determine its limits on its own. This requires recourse to other values. The debate as to whether these values should be thin or thick, that is, whether it is sufficient to be politically liberal or whether recourse to perfectionist values is necessary, remains undecided (Nussbaum, 2011). Nor can we detail or trace them here. Rather, we want to confine ourselves to mentioning a few central values that are necessary for the political and everyday functioning of toleration as a deep practice.

Toleration is closely linked to the value of pluralism. It is about recognizing that there are legitimate differences in worldviews and beliefs that cannot be resolved without violating liberal standards. If there were no legitimate pluralism, the value of toleration would also be greatly diminished. Toleration continues to be closely linked to the value of human dignity. To tolerate someone means to recognize that their values and their norms and practices are not one's own, but are legitimate expressions of an autonomous person. Human dignity itself is a complex concept with different connotations (Killmister, 2017). Human dignity refers to a person's autonomy to shape his or her own life and to be respected for it. Toleration is required when the other person has at least, to a meaningful extent, autonomously chosen to adopt and embrace the values and norms that are to be tolerated. But human dignity also has a strongly defensive character, and is thus connected with the claim not to be humiliated (Kaufmann et al., 2011). Toleration also plays an important role here: toleration as a deep practice is also always such behavior, which does not humiliate the counterpart, even if one does not agree with the values and practices and does not share them. Toleration therefore also has its limits, which should be guaranteed by the state, and the state also provides the means to promote toleration: through education, opportunities for public debate, and through the exemplary effect of its representatives.

Fourth, toleration is a deep practice confronted with change – a change that also affects the values that support and limit toleration (Inglehart, 2006). The limits of toleration can shift and often norms and practices that have been widely accepted have slowly but surely become those that are no longer accepted. There are many examples of this: the respect for homosexuality, religious differences, equal rights for men and women or the prohibition of corporal punishment for children. Here, in most liberal societies, a fundamental change in values has taken place, one which now demands toleration towards many social norms and practices, where there used to be rejection or even state persecution, while on the other hand certain social norms and practices now have less toleration shown towards them. There are various normative models for dealing with these changes. They can be understood as an indication of relativism that toleration and the values on which it is based do not ultimately have an ahistorical and universal core, but are always contextual. It is therefore more or less arbitrary and bound to the respective society and culture what is tolerated and what is not. Against this relativism we want to propose a different model, which has the idea of moral progress, which is not linear and knows regressions, but has taken place in recent decades. The moves behind this moral and social progress are struggles for recognition (Honneth, 1996) and the extension of the sphere of human dignity and justice to more and more population groups. Which social norms and practices should be regarded as valuable and worthy of protection, i.e. also as tolerable, is an open social process, but the expansion of autonomy and respect for the human dignity of the individual provide standards here.

Fifthly, we ultimately also want to address toleration as a global and international political value (Tan, 2011; Jones, 2009). Firstly, the globalization of toleration is questionable, i.e. to what extent toleration can be demanded and disseminated outside liberal societies. Toleration can also be misunderstood as a colonial, Western idea that is imposed on other societies and cultures against their will. The other side of the coin here is wrongly understood as toleration towards such social norms and practices that are oppressive and violate human dignity and the respect of other people. Thus, in our opinion, there is no toleration required for practices such as the circumcision of girls or the stoning of adulterers; indeed, it would not be toleration at all, since it is not located within the normative boundaries that we have just discussed. Rather, this would be appeasement policy or even complicity. Secondly, it is precisely large migration and refugee movements that bring these global lines of conflict into liberal societies and turn them into inner-societal conflicts (Kaul, 2019).

## 3. Legitimate Expectations and Refugees

Migration and flight represent a particular challenge for toleration. On the one hand, migrants and refugees bring new cultures and worldviews to the host country. The host country and its population are therefore confronted with new fellow citizens, of whom they should be tolerant. On the other hand, the culture and values of the host country are new to many migrants and refugees and they must learn to deal with them. It may also be a new experience for them that toleration is a lived practice and a value to be cultivated and practised in a country. It can therefore be assumed that major migration movements from countries with different social, cultural, political or legal norms and practices will lead to conflicts that test the toleration of all groups of people involved and of the state and its institutions.

So far, from a philosophical perspective, there has not been much reflection on the legitimate demands that should be made of migrants and refugees. We would like to make six points in this regard. First of all, we think it makes sense to differentiate between migrants and refugees. Migrants come voluntarily to the host country. Refugees, on the other hand, have left their homes involuntarily and have a moral and legal right to be admitted and protected. That is why the relationship between refugee and host country cannot, like that of other migrants who enter voluntarily, be understood in the sense of a contract to which both sides are committed. In the case of the refugee, the receiving state has no other morally or legally acceptable option than to admit the refugee (Gibney, 2018). It is questionable which behavior of a refugee can legitimize the refusal or revocation of this asylum. In any case, this seems to be subject to narrow limits, since the consequences of expulsion for a refugee are in any case more life threatening and more serious than for other migrants who can return to their home country. For refugees, the question is what can legitimately be expected of them, when they legitimately expect to find almost unconditional protection and reception (if they meet the conditions for asylum).

Second, what is actually meant by the state's demand that refugees develop and implement toleration as a deep practice? We think that it makes sense first to limit the demand that refugees learn to act in a tolerant way. They should learn to identify situations where toleration is the appropriate reaction. These are already two demanding aspects. Only in a second step, however, can refugees be empowered to accept toleration as conviction and value through a long and open learning process. This persuasion and education for toleration is fragile and it is uncertain whether it will lead to success (Heyd, 2018). In particular, people who have been socialized and enculturated differently for a long time, i.e. who have to learn toleration later in their lives and have incorporated intolerant values, will sometimes not be convinced that toleration is an intrinsic value which they should accept as their own. However, it is important that those who have intolerant attitudes and values learn when to be tolerant and how to behave as such. To use an analogy, it would certainly be better to be able to convince a misogynist that men and women are of equal worth, but you can nonetheless demand that they do not devalue women through their actions and that they behave towards women as if they were worth the same as men. For the long-term functioning of living together in a plural society and the functioning of a liberal state, however, it will not be sufficient if large sections of the population merely fake toleration and merely act as if they were tolerant. This will lead to undermining processes and intolerance will then emerge in other forms and eventually become apparent. In addition, the state is practically, legally and morally limited in its control functions. That someone educates his children to become tolerant fellow citizens and lives toleration in his personal environment and everyday life is all the more probable if it has been adopted as a value and is honestly affirmed. It is then more resistant to social change and political demagogy and will be lived even when society and the state have no means to control and sanction.

Thirdly, the question of legitimacy, that is, why the state or society can demand that refugees develop toleration, must be clarified. Here there is a close connection to the political values which are made possible and protected by toleration and which are necessary for the functioning of a plural society. We see three reasons for making toleration a legitimate expectation. Firstly, the liberal state and its people have a legitimate interest in continuance. After all, it is not some form of institution and coexistence, but it is supposed to be essential to establish social justice. These goals of justice are not only worth it, they even require it to be protected, and if that means making demands of tolerant behavior, then these are just as legitimate. We will say something later on about the legitimacy of the means; here we limit ourselves to the legitimacy of the objective of demanding tolerant behavior from refugees. Secondly, toleration can be expected from refugees to the extent that other people are humiliated by intolerant behavior. What is at stake here, then, is the expectation that refugees will not violate the human dignity of others by attacking and insulting their reasonably justifiable lifestyles. This argument aims at the value of the good life and well-being of those who are tolerated here and one can expect refugees to respect this. This respect expresses itself as toleration. Thirdly, toleration is a legitimate expectation of refugees insofar as they themselves benefit from it; hence it is about reciprocity of the relationship. Although refugees are always in a socially and politically weaker position, it is precisely in this position that they benefit from a tolerant host society. To this end, it seems legitimate to demand from them the same toleration that is shown to them.

Fourthly, it is a question of clarifying who may and should demand toleration here. So far we have spoken quite indiscriminately about society or the state or the population. This, however, needs to be differentiated, especially with regard to legitimate means. All members of society can expect toleration insofar as they meet in private and public life. It is therefore a matter of social coexistence. Here, however, there are unclear boundaries between what should fall within the realm of morality and what should also fall within the realm of law. And also, in the area of morality, a distinction must be made between those cases in which toleration is obligatory and those in which it seems morally correct but not necessary. Finally, toleration can also overtax. Here, too, human dignity, i.e. respect for life plans and the autonomy of others, is the appropriate yardstick, as is refusing to humiliate others. Stricter criteria must be applied to the state than to social coexistence, since the state has a monopoly on the use of force and is equally obliged to all citizens. It therefore not only has a superior principle of toleration, but it is also not a partner in dialogue like other fellow citizens. The state must therefore demand toleration and enforce it for others, while it is not itself an object of toleration, in the sense that it would develop worldview norms and practices for which it could demand toleration. The state does not possess human dignity either, but is the guarantor of it. The state therefore does not demand toleration for itself, but for the common good and the entire population, whereby it must in particular protect vulnerable groups and minorities who are least able to defend themselves.

Fifthly, we now want to clarify the question of the legitimate means of demanding toleration from refugees. We are confining ourselves to state resources. The state modifies the behavior of its citizens and certain groups in different ways. It can enact laws that determine what is allowed and what is forbidden and impose different sanctions. But that alone is not enough. In order to become socially effective, laws must be monitored and violations prosecuted and sanctioned. But that, too, is not enough. It is efficient and best in the long term if the laws are accepted by the population and regarded as meaningful and if they are therefore largely complied with without supervision or punishment. Politics and law are involved in the creation and maintenance of the social climate, just as they are co-determined by it and politics and law always follow social trends and conventions. One example of how laws and social discourse work together to bring about changes in behavior and values in the general population is the ban on corporal punishment of children, which has been enforced in many European countries in recent decades (Zolotor and Puzia, 2010). It is clear that widespread and legitimate behavior – the physical punishment of children – can change through the interaction of law and campaigning and education. By now, in all states that have enforced the ban on corporal punishment of children, the majority of the population there shares this value and, even without strict monitoring or prosecution, corporal punishment is largely rejected and no longer applied. Legitimate means of enforcing toleration will therefore always have to be measured against several criteria: how good and efficient are they in achieving the goals, whether they violate or endanger other values and freedoms, whether they are used in such a way that they do not unfairly discriminate against certain groups, and what short- or long-term consequences are associated with enforcement. With regard to the refugee group, these questions must be asked in a particularly sensitive way, since the state has special access to this group and has a great deal of power over it.

We believe that it is justified and sensible for the state to inform refugees as early as possible of the expectations it has of them. However, these expectations are not a one-way street and refugees have a right to be helped and supported in fulfilling these expectations. These rights can be justified by the fact that refugees have a right to find sufficient opportunities and possibilities for a successful life in the host country and that their basic needs are provided for as long as they cannot do this for themselves. Refugees find themselves in a particularly precarious and vulnerable situation and are confronted with a variety of health, psychological and social problems (Hynie, 2018). This has an impact on what can be expected of them, as legitimate expectations should always be those that can be met and not be overburdensome. The legitimate means for the state to demand toleration from refugees are therefore certainly not only coercive means of surveillance and punishment in cases of transgression, but above all educational offers and opportunities to deal with those refugees within a secure and benevolent framework (Fives, 2013). This requires both long-term commitment on the part of the state and offers that are not only compulsory but also bring positive experiences and advantages for the refugees. In a social atmosphere that is hostile and intolerant towards refugees this will be all the more difficult.

Sixthly, there is also the question to what extent toleration towards illegitimate social norms and practices can be expected under non-ideal conditions. A number of different perspectives have to be distinguished. Firstly, there are different degrees of immorality and injustice. It makes a significant difference whether someone thinks it would be okay to slap his child every now and then or whether someone thinks it is legitimate to circumcise his daughter. While a liberal society and the state can still show a certain toleration towards the first practice, even if it is rejected and sanctioned, toleration towards the second practice would be inexcusable. Second, there is the component of enlightenment and self-empowerment. If it is true that toleration is both instrumental and intrinsically valuable, then all people have a right to acquire and cultivate that value. The expectation that people will act tolerantly is only one side of the coin, the other is the right to education for toleration as part of the right to moral education. It could also be said that toleration is part of a good life. So when refugees come from countries where they have been denied the possibility of education for toleration and the exercise of the deep practice of toleration, they have been unfairly deprived of what they are entitled to. The host country then has to give them the opportunity to make up for this and to compensate for an injustice they have suffered, similar to when it gives illiterate people the opportunity to learn to read and write. Thirdly, there is the question of compromises (Rostbøll and Scavenius, 2017). There is a need sometimes to compromise between different values, for example the value of protecting refugees from persecution, even if they find it difficult to fulfil expectations of toleration or other values and virtues, and if it must be assumed that the admission of larger groups of refugees will lead to toleration conflicts. Such compromises are also difficult because it is often impossible to foresee how social conflicts will develop. In any case, they should be open to public discussion and reasonable consideration; even if under non-ideal conditions (e.g. fake news and echo chambers) they seem almost impossible today. Nor should rotten compromises be made that ultimately undermine both the stability of liberal society and the trust of both the population and refugee groups. Fourthly, there is the issue of transitions and the time needed for integration and the adoption of toleration as a deep practice. The state has an interest in long-term stability, which is unfortunately often sacrificed by politicians to the short-term success of elections. The migration issue is a particularly good example here. Toleration as a deep practice requires education and practice, especially if it is to be re-learned and internalized by an adult with different values and habits. The integration of the next generation also plays an important role here. In many European societies, such as Germany or Austria, no value has been placed on this, which has led to problems for the children of migrants, because it has not been recognized that they are legitimate fellow citizens whose culture should not be ignored.

## 4. The Human Corridor Project: Limits of Toleration, Societal Conflicts and the Integration of Refugees

Bringing different cultures together, managing expectations from various stake holders, negotiating social norms – these are all obvious building blocks of a context that requires a deep practice of toleration. Such a context has been created by a "Humanitarian Corridor" initiative in Italy: prominent religious organizations in Italy (Caritas Italy, the Catholic Bishops' Conference and Sant'Egidio) have partnered with the Italian government (Ministero dell'Interno) to establish legal and safe pathways towards citizenship ("humanitarian corridors") for a selected group of refugees. One particular humanitarian corridor opened in fall 2017 to provide a total of 500 visas within the course of a year for vulnerable Eritrean, South Sudanese and Somali refugees living in Ethiopian camps. The United Nations High Commissioner for Refugees (UNHCR) is consulted in the identification process, ensuring a non-discriminatory selection process based on internationally recognized criteria of vulnerabilities. This initiative is a manifestation of a new system of community-based and private sponsorship; the method adopted by Caritas Italy is a personalized method of accompaniment working with a host community that will receive a family or small group of refugees for a minimum term of one year (irrespective of their religious affiliation). The first concern of this initiative is *safety*: for the past years thousands of migrants have been risking their lives crossing the Mediterranean Sea to reach Europe, a tragic situation identified by many as a "humanitarian crisis". The legal basis of the program is Article 25 of the EUR-VISA Code which allows European Member States to grant visas with Limited Territorial Validity for humanitarian reasons.

The faith-based organizations involved offer pre-departure cultural orientation to both refugees in Ethiopia and the hosting communities in Italy as part of this "accompaniment" model. Communities are directly involved on a volunteering basis, which offers ordinary citizens a privileged and direct opportunity to act and engage responsibly with refugees. This also leads to frictions and challenges for toleration. The Humanitarian Corridor shows the reality of the challenge of a deep practice of toleration. There are a number of adverse circumstances in this context of accompaniment efforts.

One major adverse factor is the *mental health* of the refugees. Traumatizing or challenging experiences could have happened in the country of origin, during the flight to Ethiopia, in the refugee camp, but also in the unfamiliar Italian context (with an experience of isolation). Mental health challenges have been recognized as an important aspect of working with refugees. Fleeing from conflict areas increases the likelihood of having been exposed to a number of traumatic events, thus arriving in a new country with severe mental health challenges (Acarturk, 2015; Bärnhielm et al., 2017). Moving to an unknown context with significant family responsibilities is a challenge for anybody – but this challenge is aggravated if there is a cultural and linguistic barrier, and a discrepancy between one's role in the family (provider and decider, responsible adult, role model) and one's role in society (asylum seeker, dependent recipient of support). Acculturation-related stressors, insecurity, economic uncertainty and the experience of discrimination add to post-arrival mental health challenges (George et al., 2015). A significant number of refugees in the Humanitarian Corridor suffer from mental health issues that have to be properly diagnosed and treated. Undiagnosed, underdiagnosed or misdiagnosed mental health challenges increase the risk of further struggles. Since the refugees are dispersed all over Italy (the key idea of the accompaniment model: small units are accompanied by small units), a number of refugees find themselves in small towns or rural areas without trauma-sensitive organizations and with no proper professional care. Trauma leads to unpredictable or socially non-desirable behavior and dysfunctional interactions. There is no doubt that mental health challenges increase the accompaniment needs and the resources required and also reduce the person's constructive contribution to the new context. Even without a history of trauma the process of integration is challenging. Lintner and Elsens describe the social aspects of the subjective well-being of asylum seekers and the lack of valued and meaningful occupation during the asylum application process. They show that "social isolation, supported by the spatial isolation [. . .] significantly increased a state of loneliness, disclosure and mental fragility, with consequences for the physical well-being of asylum seekers" (Lintner and Elsens, 2018, p. 84). Catarci, reflecting on the Italian intercultural approach to immigration, highlights the importance of employment and psychological support for immigrants. He also stresses that "interventions (including educational or cultural efforts) cannot be directed solely towards asylum seekers and refugees but should be also addressed to the other side of the relationship: the natives" (Catarci, 2016, p. 33).

A second adverse factor is *expectation management*. Many volunteers in the Humanitarian Corridor expect gratitude for the support they provide. They fail to recognize the opportunity costs – every single refugee left people, places, possessions behind. One interviewee in our research tells us: "We have my father, with 5 children, who is living in America, and my old sister is living in America" (IJECB18–1). Another refugee has one wife in the United States (with two of his children) and one wife in Israel. Many had to leave family members behind in the camps. This means that their arrival is "ambiguous," their cultural gain is "ambiguous gain". This is to say that they have only partially arrived. American psychologist Pauline Boss has coined the term "ambiguous loss" to talk about families with a displaced family member – the missing family member is physically absent, but mentally very much present (Boss, 1999, 2006; Boss and Yeats, 2014). In a similar sense, many refugees in the Humanitarian Corridor are physically present, but mentally absent, since they think of their loved ones and the people and things left behind. There is only "partial arrival" and "ambiguous cultural gain". This leads to frustration on the part of the volunteers and social workers who work hard, and give time and resources, to support the arriving refugees to "fully arrive and integrate". This leads to a dynamic whereby the stakeholders in the Humanitarian Corridor Project bring different expectations to the process. There is the challenge of distorted expectations because of lack of knowledge and ignorance (social workers: lack of knowledge about the culture; migrants: lack of knowledge about the social care system including the tax system). Expectations have been frustrated with regard to school and education (there are issues with the recognition of diplomas and qualifications and capabilities). There is also the challenge of an "entitlement-attitude" that clashes with an "expectation of gratitude". Many refugees expect to be supported while, at the same time, claiming autonomy. This ambivalent situation of adult refugees who find themselves in child-like roles of dependency while at the same time claiming autonomy has proven to be a source of frustration. Frustrated expectations lead to socially challenging patterns of behavior, thus making the accompaniment ambition of the stakeholders difficult.

A third adverse factor is the overall *political climate* – a number of our interview partners commented on the generally xenophobic political climate in Italy. Many people, so the interviewees found, see migrants as a danger to society. The experience refugees have is one of not being really welcome and of encountering a macro-climate of suspicion and rejection; refugees are pushed into roles where they have to justify and explain their presence. The discourse on migration in Italy under Salvini has been redefined from an understanding of humanitarian emergencies and human tragedies into a language of security. This has created a climate of fear and a politics of fear that has led to new forms of intolerance (Nussbaum, 2012). Many refugees act defensively to these challenges and even though they may appreciate efforts on the micro-level they feel the pressure to move on and leave Italy as soon as possible. This again leads to further frustrations in the relationship between refugees and the accompanying communities and families since the moral motivation to invest in people is usually based on long-term perspectives and the expectation of finding grateful refugees who seek to be integrated in Italian society.

There are more factors that could be listed; but it should be sufficient to say that refugees within the context of the Humanitarian Corridor disrupt the lives of the people who work with them (and for them). Some refugees have left over night without any notice; some refugees have complained about the way they are being treated. Some refugees have not managed the transition into the labour market well – in one particular instance, a volunteer organized an employment possibility for a refugee through his social connections (thus "burning social capital"), but the refugee did not honour the contract and was not able (or willing) to fulfil the employer's expectations. Needless to say, this has frustrated the person who secured this job.

Toleration is challenged in all these instances. The highest moral goods at stake are an understanding of the human person as human and the respect for the dignity of the person as inviolable. For the sake of these high moral goods disruptive behavior has to be accepted – "accepted" in the sense of "second and third and fourth chances." Refugees are people who have not won in the birth lottery. If one takes seriously the argument that people who are privileged can be asked to do more for the global community, one can argue that those who are disadvantaged have a different level of what can reasonably be expected. This is not to say that the category of contributive justice is not a key aspect; refugees are agents; they should be invited and expected to contribute to the common good. But their contribution can be a healthy disruption of established patterns. Tolerating these disruptions is clearly a case of a deep practice of toleration. And this deep practice can lead to a rethinking of morally questionable standards.

## References

Acarturk, C., et al. (2015). EMDR for Syrian Refugees with Posttraumatic Stress Disorder Symptoms: Results of a Pilot Randomized Controlled Trial. *European Journal of Psychotraumatology*, 6(10), pp. 1–9.

Bärnhielm, S., et al. (2017). Mental Health for Refugees, Asylum Seekers and Displaced Persons: A Call for a Humanitarian Agenda. *Transcultural Psychiatry*, 54(5–6), pp. 565–574.

Bieri, P. (2017). *Human Dignity: A Way of Living*. Oxford: Wiley.

Boss, P. (1999). *Ambiguous Loss: Learning to Live with Unresolved Grief*. Boston, MA: The Belknap Press of Harvard University Press.

Boss, P. (2006). *Loss, Trauma, and Resilience: Therapeutic Work with Ambiguous Loss*. New York: Norton.

Boss, P. and Yeats, J. R. (2014). Ambiguous Loss: A Complicated Type of Grief When Loved Ones Disappear. *Bereavement Care*, 33(2), pp. 63–69.

Catarci, M. (2016). Challenging Interculturalism: The Inclusion of Asylum Seekers and Refugees in Italy. *Australian & New Zealand Journal of European Studies*, 8(2), pp. 21–33.

Coyle, D. (2009). *The Talent Code*. New York: Bantam Books.

Deckmar, M. (2005). *My Son Fred: Living with Autism*. London: Jessica Kingsley.

Ferrara, A. (2014). *The Democratic Horizon: Hyperpluralism and the Renewal of Political Liberalism*, 1st ed. Cambridge and New York: Cambridge University Press.

Fives, A. (2013). Non-Coercive Promotion of Values in Civic Education for Democracy. *Philosophy & Social Criticism*, 39(6), pp. 577–590. [online] Available at: https://doi.org/10.1177/0191453713485723.

Galeotti, A. E. (2015). The Range of Toleration: From Toleration as Recognition Back to Disrespectful Toleration. *Philosophy & Social Criticism*, 41(2), pp. 93–110. Available at: https://doi.org/10.1177/0191453714559424.

George, U., et al. (2015). Immigrant Mental Health, a Public Health Issue. *International Journal of Environmental Research and Public Health*, 12, pp. 13624–13648.

Gibney, M. J. (2018). The Ethics of Refugee. *Philosophy Compass*, August, e12521. Available at: https://doi.org/10.1111/phc3.12521.

Heyd, D. (2018). Education to Toleration. In: C. McKinnon and D. Castiglione, eds., *The Culture of Toleration in Diverse Societies*. Manchester: Manchester University Press, pp. 196–207. Available at: https://doi.org/10.7765/9781526 137708.00018.

Honneth, A. (1996). *The Struggle for Recognition : The Moral Grammar of Social Conflicts*, 1st ed. Cambridge, MA: MIT Press.

Hynie, M. (2018). The Social Determinants of Refugee Mental Health in the Post-Migration Context: A Critical Review. *The Canadian Journal of Psychiatry*, 63(5), pp. 297–303. Available at: https://doi.org/10.1177/0706743717746666.

Inglehart, R. (2006). Mapping Global Values. *Comparative Sociology*, 5(2–3), pp. 115–136. Available at: https://doi.org/10.1163/156913306778667401.

Jones, P. (2009). International Toleration and the 'War on Terror'. *Globalizations*, 6(1), pp. 7–22. Available at: https://doi.org/10.1080/14747730802692450.

Kaufmann, P., Kuch, H., Neuhäuser, C. and Webster, E. (2011). *Humiliation, Degradation, Dehumanization : Human Dignity Violated*, 1st ed. Dordrecht and New York: Springer.

Kaul, V. (2019). Sources of Toleration: Individuals, Cultures, Institutions. *Philosophy & Social Criticism*, 45(4), pp. 360–369. Available at: https://doi.org/10.1177/0191453719843767.

Killmister, S. (2017). Dignity: Personal, Social, Human. *Philosophical Studies*, 174(8), pp. 2063–2082. Available at: https://doi.org/10.1007/s11098-016-0788-y.

Kundera, M. (1999). *Identity*. Trans. L. Asher. New York: Harper Collins.

Lintner, C. and Elsens, S. (2018). Getting out of the Seclusion Trap? Work as Meaningful Occupation for the Subjective Well-Being of Asylum Seekers in South Tyrol, Italy. *Journal of Occupational Science*, 25(1), pp. 76–86.

Nussbaum, M. (2011). Perfectionist Liberalism and Political Liberalism. *Philosophy & Public Affairs*, 39(1), pp. 3–45. Available at: https://doi.org/10.1111/j.1088-4963.2011.01200.x.

Nussbaum, M. (2012). *The New Religious Intolerance: Overcoming the Politics of Fear in an Anxious Age*. Cambridge, MA: The Belknap Press of Harvard University Press.

Pettit, P. (2012). *On the People's Terms: A Republican Theory and Model of Democracy*, 1st ed. Cambridge and New York: Cambridge University Press.

Rosenblum, N. (2016). *Good Neighbors: The Democracy of Everyday Life in America*. Princeton, NJ: Princeton University Press.

Rostbøll, C. F. and Scavenius, T. (2017). *Compromise and Disagreement in Contemporary Political Theory*, 1st ed. New York: Routledge. Available at: https://doi.org/10.4324/9781315317823.

Tan, K. (2011). Two Conceptions of Liberal Global Toleration. *Monist*, 94(4), pp. 489–505. Available at: https://doi.org/10.5840/monist201194425.

Zolotor, A. J. and Puzia, M. E. (2010). Bans against Corporal Punishment: A Systematic Review of the Laws, Changes in Attitudes and Behaviours. *Child Abuse Review*, 19(4), pp. 229–247. Available at: https://doi.org/10.1002/car.1131.

# Contributors

**Andrea Baumeister** is Senior Lecturer in the Division of History and Politics at the University of Stirling. Her main research interests lie within the area of liberal political philosophy, with a focus on questions of legitimacy, democratic participation and citizenship in contemporary pluralist liberal democracies. In this context her work addresses questions of toleration and recognition, group differentiated rights, the relationship between gender equality and cultural justice, and the role of religion in the liberal public realm. Recent publications include: The Use of "Public Reason" by Religious and Secular Citizens: Limitations of Habermas's Conception of the Role of Religion in the Public Real, *Constellations* 18 (2); Empowering minority women: Autonomy versus participation, *Contemporary Political Theory* 11 (3); and Religion and the Claims of Citizenship: The Dangers of Institutional Accommodation, in *Religion and Political Theory*, J. Seglow and A. Shorten (eds.), ECPR Press/Rowman & Littlefield (forthcoming).

**Andrew Jason Cohen** is Professor of Philosophy and Founding Coordinator of the Bachelors of Interdisciplinary Studies Program in Philosophy, Politics and Economics at Georgia State University. He is the author of *Toleration and Freedom from Harm: Liberalism Reconceived* (Routledge, 2018) and *Toleration* (Polity, 2014) as well as articles in journals like *Ethics*, *The Canadian Journal of Philosophy*, and in new reference works like *The International Encyclopedia of Ethics* and *The Cambridge Companion to Liberalism*. Increasingly, he is looking at toleration (or the lack thereof) in our system of criminal law and in business ethics. He also blogs at www.bleedingheartlibertarians.com/. (CV and papers available at https://andrewjasoncohen.academia.edu.)

**Johannes Drerup** is Professor of Philosophy of Education at the TU Dortmund as well as a guest professor at the Free University of Amsterdam. His research interests include philosophy of education and childhood, moral and political philosophy and applied ethics. He is a cofounder of the open access journal *On Education* and coedited a handbook on the philosophy of childhood (together with Gottfried Schweiger; 2019, J. B. Metzler). Other recent publications include *Education, Epistemic Virtues, and the Power of Toleration*. In: Critical Review of International Social and Political Philosophy (CRISPP), 2019: https://doi.org/10.1080/13698230.2019.1616883; *Education for Democratic Tolerance, Respect and the Limits of Political Liberalism*. In: Journal of Philosophy of Education, 52, 3, 2018, 515–532.

**Marcus Carlsen Häggrot** is a postdoctoral researcher at Goethe University Frankfurt. He holds a DPhil from University of Oxford (2017) and has held teaching positions at the Institut d'Études Politiques de Paris. His recent publications include 'The Right to Vote and Nomadic Voter Enrolment', *Citizenship Studies* 22(7) (2018), 725–744; and 'Public Caravan Sites for British Gypsy Travellers: Kymlicka and an Argument from Expropriatory Compensation', *Ethnopolitics* (forthcoming). His current research project explores how parliamentary constituencies should be configured, especially in relation to émigré voters and in the context of EU parliamentarism.

**David Heyd** is Chaim Perelman Professor of Philosophy (emeritus) at The Hebrew University of Jerusalem. His main fields of research are ethics, political philosophy, bioethics. He is author of *Supererogation* (Cambridge, 1982), *Genethics* (California, 1992) as well as editor of *Toleration* (Princeton 1996). His articles on toleration have been published in *Canadian Journal of Philosophy* (2001), *Nomos* Series (2008), and in a collection edited by C. McKinnon and D. Castiglione (Manchester 2003). For full CV and list of publications, see http://pluto.huji.ac.il/~msheyd/site/.

**Mark A. Hutchinson** is Research Fellow in the Department of Politics at the University of York, as part of the Leverhulme funded project "Rethinking Civil Society: History, Theory, Critique". Prior to taking up his current position, Mark was a Lecturer in early modern history at Durham University (2016–17) and Lancaster University (2015–16). He has also held both a Mid-Career Fellowship (2017–18) and a Junior Fellowship (2014–15) at the Lichtenberg-Kolleg, the Göttingen Institute for Advanced Study, Germany, and a Government of Ireland Fellowship at University College Cork (2011–13). Mark is particularly interested in the implications of Reformation views of humanity for early modern political thought and culture in Ireland, England and the Palatinate in the Holy Roman Empire. His publications include *Calvinism, Reform and the Absolutist State in Elizabethan Ireland* (2015; paperback 2017).

**Anniina Leiviskä** works as a postdoctoral researcher at the University of Helsinki, Faculty of Educational Sciences in Finland. Her major areas of research are theories of democracy and citizenship education. She is particularly interested in the topics of political legitimacy, educational justice, and inclusion and participation in the context of political education and democratic politics. Her current research project *Democracy, Education and the Challenge of Inclusion: Reconstructing a Theory of Citizenship Education for Contemporary Democracies* (2017–2020) is funded by the Academy of Finland.

**Jon Mahoney** is Professor of Philosophy at Kansas State University. His primary research interests are in political philosophy and philosophy of law. Recent publications include, "Wedding Cakes and Muslims: Religious Freedom and Politics in Contemporary American Legal Practice," "Religion, Identity, and Violence," and "The Politics of Religious Freedom." Jon is also interested in international education and has had three Fulbright Grants to the Kyrgyz Republic, including for 2018–19.

**Cillian McBride** is Senior Lecturer in Political Theory at the School of History, Anthropology, Philosophy and Politics, Queen's University Belfast. He is the author of Recognition ((Polity, 2013) and editor (with Keith Breen) of Exploring Republican Freedom (Routledge, 2018). He is currently working on a book on republicanism and the idea of social freedom.

**Andrew R. Murphy** is Professor of Political Science at Virginia Commonwealth University. He received his B.A. from the University of North Carolina at Chapel Hill, and his M.A. and Ph.D. from the University of Wisconsin-Madison. Murphy's scholarship focuses on the interconnections between politics and religion, in both historical and contemporary contexts. He has explored the emergence of liberty of conscience in England and America, and the interconnections between political theory and practice, from his first book, *Conscience and Community: Revisiting Toleration and Religious Dissent in Early Modern England and America* (2001), to his more recent focus on the life and career of William Penn: *William Penn: A Life* (2019); a co-edited collection *The Worlds of William Penn* (2019); *Liberty, Conscience, and Toleration: The Political Thought of William Penn* (2016); and an edition of Penn's political writings in the Cambridge Texts in the History of Political Thought series (2020). Murphy's research has also explored the interconnections between religion and contemporary American politics, most particularly in *Prodigal Nation: Moral Decline and Divine Punishment from New England to 9/11* (2008) and (as co-author) *Political Religion and Religious Politics: Navigating Identities in the United States* (2015).

**Roberta Sala** is full Professor of Political Philosophy and Public Ethics at the Faculty of Philosophy, University Vita-Salute San Raffaele, Milan, Italy. Director CeSEP, Center of Studies on Ethics and Politics,

University Vita-Salute San Raffaele, Milan, Italy, 2016 on. Scientific Chief Unity University Vita-Salute San Raffaele, research project "Enhancing Social Innovation in Elderly Care: values, practices and policies" – INNOVAcaRE (1-caRE), Fondazione Cariplo "Aging and social research: people, places and relations 2017 Project", principal investigator prof. A. M. Chiesi, University of Milan. Member Scientific Committee Interfaculty Center Gender Studies GENDER, University Vita-Salute San Raffaele, 2016 on. Member Scientific Committee SWIP Italia, Society for Women in Philosophy, 2018–2021.

Publications (selection). Books: *Bioetica e pluralismo dei valori*, Liguori, Napoli, 2003. (ed.) *Scritti sulla tolleranza*, La Nuova Italia, Milano, 2004. *La verità sospesa. Ragionevolezza e irragionevolezza nella filosofia politica di John Rawls*, Liguori, Napoli, 2012. *Il silenzio di Dio*, Edizioni San Paolo, Cinisello B., 2014. Articles: (2019) "Modus Vivendi and the Motivations for Compliance". In (a cura di) J. Horton, M. Westphal, U. Willems, *The Political Theory of Modus Vivendi*, pp. 67–82, Heidelberg: Springer International Publishing. (2018) "A Religious Reading of Rawls's Works Paul Weithman's Rawls, Political Liberalism and Reasonable Faith". *Filosofia e questioni pubbliche*, vol. 8, pp. 53–66, ISSN: 2240–7987. (2018) "Call it Public Metaphysic: A New Way for Liberalism in Sebastiano Maffettone's Works". In (a cura di) G. Pellegrino, Legitimacy, *Democracy and Disagreement. Essays in Honour of Sebastiano Maffettone*, pp. 39–50, Roma, Luiss University Press. (2015) "May Joint Commitment Stabilize Modus Vivendi". *Phenomenology and Mind*, vol. 3, pp. 172–180, ISSN: 2280–7853. (2013) "The Place of 'Unreasonable' People Beyond Rawls". *European Journal of Political Theory*, vol. 12, pp. 253–270, ISSN: 1474–8851.

**Gottfried Schweiger** is Senior Scientist (permanent position) at the Centre for Ethics and Poverty Research of the University of Salzburg since 2011. Schweiger was Visiting Researcher at the philosophy departments of the University of St. Gall, Switzerland, for the winter semester 2014 and of the University of Bochum, Germany, for the summer semester 2016. Schweiger published extensively on (global) justice, poverty, childhood, the capability approach and migration. Among other work in externally funded projects, he was the PI of a major research project on "Social Justice and Child Poverty", which developed a capability-based theory of social justice for children and was funded by the Austrian Science Fund (FWF) from 2014 to 2017. With Gunter Graf he co-authored two monographs on the philosophy of childhood: *Ethics and the Endangerment of Children's Bodies* (Palgrave Macmillan 2017) and *A Philosophical Examination of Social Justice and Child Poverty* (Palgrave Macmillan 2015). Other recent publications include the co-edited volumes *Absolute Poverty in*

*Europe* (Policy Press 2019, with Helmut P Gaisbauer, Clemens Sedmak) and the papers "Ethics, Poverty and Children's Vulnerability" (*Ethics and Social Welfare*, online first) and "The Duty to Bring Children in Conflict Zones to a Safe Haven" (*Journal of Global Ethics* 12 (3) (2016), 380–397). Schweiger is founding co-editor of the open access journal *Zeitschrift für Praktische Philosophie [Journal for Practical Philosophy]* (since 2013), founding co-editor of the Book Series "Philosophy and Poverty", published by Springer (since 2018) and Associate Editor of the open access journal *Palgrave Communications* (since 2017). In recent years, he acted as reviewer, among others, for *Philosophy Compass, Ethical Theory and Moral Practice, Review of Social Economy, Social Theory and Practice, Journal of Poverty, Journal of Global Ethics, International Theory, Ethical Perspectives* and *Review of International Studies*.

**Clemens Sedmak** is Professor of Social Ethics and holds a joint appointment in the Keough School of Global Affairs and the Center for Social Concerns at the University of Notre Dame, IN. He is also the FM Schmölz OP Professor for Social Ethics and head of the Centre for Ethics and Poverty Research, University of Salzburg.

**Timothy Stanton** is Professor in Politics at the University of York. He has written about Locke, liberalism, and other figures and themes in the history of political thought and is editing Locke's unpublished manuscript reflections on the nature of churches (1681–82) for the Clarendon edition of his works. He is currently leading a five-year research project "Rethinking Civil Society: History, Theory, Critique", funded by the Leverhulme Trust.

**John Tate** teaches politics and international relations at the University of Newcastle, Australia. His primary research interest is political theory, political philosophy and history of political thought. He has published in these areas in journals such as *American Journal of Political Science, Political Theory, Political Studies, European Journal of Political Theory, Philosophy and Social Criticism, Journal of European Studies* and *Telos*. He has also published a monograph, *Liberty, Toleration and Equality. John Locke, Jonas Proast, and the Letters Concerning Toleration* (New York: Routledge, 2016).

# Index

Note: page numbers followed by 'n' refer to notes.

Abrams, Philip 32n1
Abts, K. 170, 173
acceptance component of toleration 105, 152, 196n3
adoption services 142
adversity-based values 242
agonistic pluralism 6, 163, 168–170, 173–174, 177, 178n6
American Muslims 121
Anderson, E. S. 102–103, 225
Andrew, Edward 61
Angle, Stephen 124
Anglicans 41, 57, 60
anti-Catholicism 41–42
*Antigone Dilemmas* 119
Armour, J. 214n15, 215n20, 215n25
Arneson, R. J. 220
Ashcraft, Richard 26, 50n3
asset lock-in 214n15
authority: government, Locke on 17, 18, 25–26, 33n10; and medieval Christianity 61; political 17, 119, 122, 124; religious 124; and republican toleration 110; and respect recognition 109; and social recognition 107–108
autonomy 1, 60, 99; personal 83, 86, 135–136, 186, 187, 188, 190, 191; political 97, 130, 133, 135, 136, 138, 144n9; and recognition/non-domination 111; of refugees 253; religious 58; respect for 101, 156

Balint, Peter 88, 95n8, 116, 144n15
Barry, B. 226
Baumeister, Andrea 5, 129
Baxter, Richard 56, 57

Bennett, James 59
Betz, H.-G. 171
Bieri, Peter 241
Bilson, Thomas 15
Bogue, David 59
Boss, Pauline 252
Bradley, Ben 213n4
Brink, David 215n23
Brinsley, John 65–66, 72
burdens of citizenship 5, 129, 136; burden shifting 141; intelligible reason requirement 136–138; legal exemptions 138–139, 141; and public reason 130–136; unequal distribution of 136, 138
burdens of judgement 84
Burnet, Gilbert 57–58

Calvin, John 64, 66
Calvinism 63–64, 65–66, 68
Caritas Italy 251
*carnet de circulation* 222
Case, Thomas 15
Catarci, M. 252
Catholic Adoption Agencies 142
Catholicism: Catholics, Locke on 24; Catholics, Penn on 41–42; political implications of 42; writings on human dignity 132, 144n8
change, and toleration 245
charity 89–90, 92
Charles I 19, 47
Charles II 26
Chillingworth, William 57
Christianity 116, 121; Christian arguments of toleration 38; concept of dignity 134, 197n10; and liberty

of conscience 40, 41, 43, 50, 124; medieval, characteristics of 61; true religion 14, 31
church and state, separation of 185
Church of England 16, 39, 48, 49, 54, 56
Cicero 99
Ciepley, David 214n15, 214n17
civic religion 97, 99
civil peace: fragility of 18; and right of resistance 26; and toleration 13, 14, 18, 20, 23, 24, 29, 32
Civil Rights Movement 122
civil society 24; associations, legal exemptions for 141, 142; and public justification 167
Clarendon Code 56, 57
coexistence: and modus vivendi 150, 151, 156, 157; and toleration 115, 116, 151, 243, 248
Coffey, John 15, 57
Cohen, Andrew Jason 1, 7, 202
Collins, Jeffrey 53
commitments, and deep practice of toleration 242
common good, and legal exemptions 139
*Compassionate Samaritane, The* (Walwyn) 66, 68
comprehensive doctrines 84, 85, 88, 132–133, 159n3, 165
conditionality of esteem recognition 108
Confucianism 124
conscience, individual: Anglican view of 60; and Christian arguments 38; and Locke 22–24, 25; and Penn 40–41, 48; puritan view of 60; *see also* liberty of conscience
conscientious disorders 22
consensus-oriented politics 169
constitutional essentials (Rawls) 71, 72, 84, 167
contemporary regime of toleration 5, 102–105
contract law 208
Conventicle Act 39, 40, 46
Cooper, Anthony Ashley 30
Corbet, John 56, 57
corporal punishment of children, ban on 248–249
corporate law 7, 202, 207, 208, 210–211
corporations 7, 202, 214n17; blurring of public and private life of employees 103–104; business ethics 212; contract law 208; justification for government action 204, 207, 210–211, 212; legal incorporation 205–206; and lobby groups 104–105; and power 102–104; reduced welfare without 208–211; social media 105; weak benefit-to-others principle 210, 211
Coyle, Dan 242
Cross, Ben 178n6

Deckmar, Maud 240–241
deep practice, toleration as 7–8, 239, 240–243, 244–245; Humanitarian Corridor in Italy 250–254; legitimate expectation and refugees 246–250; values 244–245
deliberative theory of democracy 6, 165–166
democratic pluralism 165, 169
*Discourse of Ecclesiastical Polity, A* (Parker) 39
discourse principle 166
Dissenters 29, 38, 45, 46–48, 49, 54, 57
domination: and corporations 103, 104; and permission conception of toleration 100; and republican toleration 101, 110; and respect recognition 110; and social recognition 107
Drerup, Johannes 1, 6, 79, 183
Dunn, Mary Maples 37

ecclesiastical arguments of toleration 39
Edwards, Thomas 56
egalitarian liberalism 98, 102, 225, 230; *see also* Gypsy Traveller nomadism
Elsens, S. 252
*England's Present Interest Discovered* (Penn) 37
English Civil War 18, 19
enthusiasm 55
entity shielding 205, 206, 207, 214n15
entreployees 104
epistemological toleration 38, 39, 84
equality: and justificatory neutrality 133; and liberal toleration 120–123; and liberty of conscience 67, 69

equal recognition approach 120, 122, 123
equal respect, principle of 130, 137, 152–153, 185; and headscarves 187, 190, 192, 194–195; and republican toleration 101, 108, 109; and secularism 184; *see also* respect conception of toleration
*Essay concerning Human Understanding, An* (Locke) 55
*Essay Concerning Toleration, An* (Locke) 17, 22, 23, 24, 26, 27, 28
ethical pluralism 5, 123–125
extremism, *vs.* populism 171

fair equality of opportunity 122, 123
false religions 14, 15, 30
family courts 92
Fanon, Franz 107
Fateh-Moghadam, B. 197n10
Feinberg, J. 213n4
Ferrara, Alessandro 176–177
Finnis, John 132
forbearance, toleration as 5–6, 149, 153
forced assimilation 116
forgiveness 89–90
Forst, Rainer 58–59, 99, 115, 168, 172; on limits of toleration 174; on minimal moralism 126; respect conception of toleration 117, 162–163, 164; on symbols 192; on toleration 111n1, 195–196n2
Forster, Thomas 54
*Fourth Letter for Toleration* (Locke) 16, 17
*Frame of Government* (Penn) 44, 45
France, Gypsy Travellers in 7, 218, 220; Act of 1969 221–222, 224, 228; reporting tolerance 222–223, 228, 230; social services 224
France, headscarf ban in 189, 193
free assembly, right of 39–40
freedom of conscience *see* liberty of conscience
freedom of movement 7, 228–229, 230
freedom of thought 61, 84, 110, 118, 119
French Revolution 98
fundamentalism 166
Furly, Benjamin 36

Galeotti, A.-E. 106, 120, 121
Galston, William A. 60, 173

*Gangraena* (Edwards) 56
*gens du voyage* 221–222, 224
Germany, crucifix controversy in 193
global philosophy 123, 126
Glorious Revolution (1688) 46, 55, 57
Goethe, Johann Wolfgang von 140
Gokalp, Ziya 124
Goodwin, John 63
government: action, corporations 204, 207, 210–211, 212; authority, Locke on 17, 18, 25–26, 33n10; generosity imposed by 213n7; Penn on 44–46, 49; and religion, distinguishing 44
*Grand Remonstrance* (1641) 69
Gray, John 150, 153–154, 158
*Great Case of Liberty of Conscience, The* (Penn) 4, 37, 39–40, 41, 42, 43, 44, 47
Gypsy Traveller nomadism 7, 218–219, 220–221; access to primary health care 224, 225, 226–227, 234n10; burden sharing 231–232; digitized communication and modified reporting duty 231–232; economic dimension of 226; liberal-egalitarian principles 219–220, 225, 226–227, 228, 230–231; multi-domain-non-accommodation tolerance 223–228; non-humiliation 229–230, 231; reporting tolerance 222–223, 228–230, 232; voter registration and polling 223, 224, 227

Habermas, Jürgen: on burdens of citizenship 136; deliberative theory of democracy 6, 162, 163, 164–167, 168, 170, 172–173, 175, 176, 177; on public reason 132
Häggrot, Marcus Carlsen 7, 218
Hansmann, H. 214n15
harm principle 7, 152, 202–204, 211; and contract law 208; Feinberg's understanding of harm 213n4; justification for government action 207, 209–210, 212
Hart, H. L. A. 213n8
Hartley, C. 137
Hashemi, Nader 124
headscarves, ban in kindergartens/public schools 6, 183, 186–187; and bullying 197n14; double

fetishization 193–194; double standards in ethics of autonomy 191–192; equal respect 187, 190, 192, 194–195; meaning of headscarf 187–188; pedagogical relevance 190–191; personal autonomy 187, 188, 190, 191; political context 186–187, 191; political costs 189; state neutrality and political value of pluralism 193–195; symbolic politics 187, 192; traditional interpretations of Islam 188
*Healing of Israels Breaches, The* (Brinsley) 65–66
Heins, V. 187
Heyd, David 2, 4, 79
Hindus 124
historical arguments of toleration 38, 39
*History of the Dissenters* (Bogue & Bennett) 59
*History of the Puritans* (Neal) 56
Hizb ut Tahrir 141
Hofstadter, Richard 122
Hooker, R. 64
horizontal toleration 91, 99, 101
Horton, John 90, 94n1, 150–151, 153, 154, 158, 159n10
human dignity 134, 197n10, 248; Catholic writings on 132, 144n8; and conscience 22, 23; deep practice of 243; and form of life 241; and social recognition 108; and toleration 244
human rights 83, 90, 134
Hume, David 55–56
humiliation, and reporting tolerance 229
Husak, Douglas 214n13
Hutchinson, Mark A. 4, 53

*Idea of Public Reason Revisited, The* (Rawls) 167
illiberal toleration 115–116, 125
inchoate offenses 214n13
incorporation 205–206
indifference, and toleration 86–87
individual liberty, and Locke 16, 17, 20–22, 26, 27, 29
internal colonialism 116
intolerance 90, 122, 155, 244; and equality 120–121; ethical 164; Habermas on 172; and mandatory pledge 118; non-tolerant people 146–147, 153–158; and respect conception of toleration 164; sectarian 97; towards minorities 116; *see also* right-wing populism
Islam 124, 187, 188
Israel, Jonathan 60–61
Italy, Humanitarian Corridor in 8, 240, 250–251; expectation management 252–253; mental health of refugees 251–252; political climate 253; safety 251
itinerant traders 226

James II 36, 38, 46
Jamin, J. 171
Jehovah's Witness 116, 117
Jesus Christ 38, 41, 69, 71
Jones, Peter 87–91, 95n8, 95n10, 138
justice as fairness 61, 165
justificatory neutrality 5, 129, 130, 133, 139; burdens of citizenship 130–136; and principles of justice 140

Kant, Immanuel 80
Kemalism 124
King, P. 54, 59, 72, 95n8
Kippis, Andrew 54, 55, 59
Kok-Chor Tan 94n6
Kraakman, R. 214n15
Kühler, Michael 79
Kukathas, Chandran 126
Kundera, Milan 241

Laclau, Ernesto 175
Laegard, S. 94n4, 94n5
Larmore, C. 158n1
latitudinarians 57
Lecky, W. E. H. 57
left populism 175
legal exemptions 138–142
legitimate adversaries, right-wing populists as 163, 169, 173
Leiter, B. 139
Leiviskä, Anniina 6, 162
*Letter Concerning Toleration, A* (Locke) 3, 17, 21, 22, 24–25, 30, 36, 43–44, 59
*Letters from a Gentleman in the Country* (Penn) 38
Levy, Jacob 229
liberal colonialism 2

liberalism 1–3, 53, 79, 102; egalitarian 98; and grand narrative of toleration 53–54; multicultural 120; muscular form of 2; and respect for rights 82; right-based 80; toleration-based 87–91
liberal moralism 149–150
liberal multiculturalism 101, 102, 105, 106, 107, 108
liberal-pluralist regime of secularism 185, 193
liberal state(s) 4, 83–88, 91–92, 93–94, 95n7; cultural community within 156; geographic mobility of persons in 228; Habermas on 172; persecution of minorities in 116; political toleration 129, 140; public education in 184; secularism 185
liberal toleration 5, 97, 98–101, 114–115, 116–120, 125; and equality 120–123; and ethical pluralism 123–125; selection bias 126
liberty of conscience 3, 4, 15, 59–60, 99, 100, 185; and Calivinism 63–64, 65–66, 68; definition of 40; and equality 67, 69; and headscarf ban 189, 194; and legal exemptions 138; and liberty in political sphere 62, 65, 67–69, 70; Locke on 16, 17, 20–21, 22; and Penn 37, 38, 39–49; Pennsylvania 44; and pledge of allegiance 117; and Protestants 63; and reason 64–65, 66–67; and religious conformity 20–21; right to 58; and toleration 69–70; and will 63, 65, 66
liberty of judgment 21
liberty of the will 21
liberty of thought 66, 118, 119
Lieberman, Jethro 216n29
Lightfoot, J. B. 62
Lilburne, John 69, 72
limited liability 205–206, 207, 214n15, 215n21
Lintner, C. 252
*livret de circulation* 222
Locke, John 3, 13, 57, 59–61, 62, 72, 123; boundaries of imposition and obedience 16, 23–25, 26; denial of toleration 24; empirical re-evaluations 27–30; on enthusiasm 55; on government 33n3; and individual conscience 22–24, 60; and individual liberty 16, 17, 20–22, 26, 27, 29; and liberalism 4, 50, 54; and moral challenge of toleration 30–31; and Penn 36–37; on persecution 99; persistent interest in toleration 16–17; political philosophy, continuities in 17–18; pragmatic and normative arguments for toleration 31–32; and Proast 31, 33n12; on religious divisions 15–16, 27–28; and religious truth 24–25; right of resistance 25–26; secular grounds for limits of toleration 17, 18, 20, 23, 24–25; shift from anti-tolerationist to pro-tolerationist position 27–30; on state authorities 33n10; on true religion 30–31, 33n11; *Two Tracts on Government* 16, 17, 18, 19–20, 21, 23, 27, 32n1; *Two Treatises of Government* 25–26, 27; on understanding 43–44; volatility of religion 18–20
London bombings (2005) 141
luck-egalitarianism 225–226, 227

Maclure, J. 184, 185, 188–189, 194
Mahoney, Jon 5, 114
Maloyed, Christie L. 49
March, Andrew 124
McBride, Cillian 4–5, 97
mental health of refugees 251–252
Meyer, T. 196n4
Mill, John Stuart 7, 92, 104, 116, 123, 202–203
Milton, John 55, 56
minority groups/cultures 80, 122, 124; illiberal toleration 115–116; positive acceptance of 105, 106–107; and status inequalities 120; and toleration-based liberalism 88; *see also* Gypsy Traveller nomadism
modernity 49, 60, 61, 102
modus vivendi 5, 115, 146–147, 158n1; as a form of inclusion 154–158; Hobbesian 148–149; Rawlsian 147–149, 153, 155; Rawlsian, criticisms 149–151; and social order 157; stable 156,

157; and toleration 153–154; transitional 148, 149
Molyneux, William 55
Montesquieu 98
moral challenge of toleration 13–15, 30–31
moral literacy 240
moral minimalism 126
moral pluralism 2, 83
Mormons 116
Mouffe, Chantal 6, 162, 163, 168–170, 173–175, 177, 178n5
Mudde, C. 173
multi-domain-non-accommodation tolerance 7, 219, 223–228
Murphy, Andrew R. 3, 4, 36
Murphy, Liam 211

Nagel, Thomas 211
nationalism 169, 171
Native Americans 116
Neal, Daniel 56
negative toleration 5, 146, 149, 151, 152
neo-Roman republicanism 97
Nettesheim, M. 197n8
neutral state 83–86, 92, 129
Newey, Glenn 89
New York Stock Exchange 209
non-domination 97, 101, 111, 139, 140
non-tolerant people, inclusion of 146–147, 153–158
Nozick, Robert 82, 92
Nussbaum, M. 119

objection component of toleration 105–106, 109, 152, 196n3
*One Project for the Good of England* (Penn) 38
*On the Political* (Mouffe) 169
Ottoman millet system 100, 115–116
overlapping consensus 131, 146, 147, 148, 155, 165, 184
Overton, Richard 67–68
Owen, John 43

Paine, Thomas 80, 110, 140
paradox of toleration 152
Parker, Samuel 39, 41
Patten, Alan 120, 122, 123
Peace of Westphalia 100

Penn, William 3–4, 36, 50; career of 37–38; on Catholics 41–42; on church and state 45; early political writing 39–44; on government 44–46, 49; on human nature 42; on imposition 40–41; and James II 46; liberty of conscience 37, 38, 39–49; and Locke 36–37; on persecution 41, 47, 48; power of interest in politics 47–48; reliance on Scripture 41; religious arguments of toleration 48–49; on religious dissent 47–48; on religious divisions and political stability 47; on religious judgments and understanding 42–43; on repealing penal laws 46–47; Restoration political argument 38–39; on suppression of moral vice 45
Pennsylvania 44, 45–46, 49
*Peoples ancient and just liberties asserted, The* (Penn) 37
perfectionist state 86–87, 92
permission conception of toleration 4, 99–100, 115–116, 196n3; and corporations 103–105; and recognition 107–108
persecution 55, 99; in liberal states 116; Penn on 40, 41, 47, 48; and permission conception of toleration 100–101; and Restoration era 57
*Persecution and Toleration in Protestant England* (Coffey) 57
personal autonomy: and headscarves 186, 187, 188, 190, 191; and neutral state 83, 86; and public reason justifications 135–136
*Perswasive to Moderation, A* (Penn) 4, 38, 46–49
Pettit, P. 98, 103, 111
philosophical toleration 84, 85, 94n6
pledge of allegiance 117–118
pluralism 2, 3, 5, 70, 87, 158; across traditions 125; democratic 165, 169; ethical 5, 123–125; and liberal toleration 123–125; moral 2, 83; political value, and headscarves 193–195; and religious toleration 61; within a tradition 125; value pluralism 123, 126, 150, 244
political, the (Schmitt) 168, 169, 170, 173

political arguments of toleration 38
political autonomy 97, 130, 133, 135, 136, 138, 144n9
political conception of justice 131, 132, 135, 140, 153, 165, 167
political liberalism 4, 89, 93, 158n3; political conception of justice 131, 132, 135, 140; public reason justifications 137; Rawls 6, 72, 84, 85, 135, 159n5, 165, 172
*Political Liberalism* (Rawls) 71–72, 165, 167, 172
political liberty 5, 114, 116–117, 119–120, 122
political morality 5, 118, 123, 125, 126
political toleration 5, 82, 84, 129, 130, 139; burdens of citizenship 136–139; and legal exemptions 140–142; normative commitments 140, 143; and prudential non-intervention 140–141; public reason 130–136
polling, Gypsy Travellers 223, 224, 227
Popple, William 36, 59
populist moment 175
positive toleration 152–153, 157
power: and corporations 102–105; political 84–85, 129, 130, 131, 138, 144n9, 165, 174; and recognition 107; and vertical/horizontal toleration 91
pragmatic arguments of toleration 38
Presbyterians 56–57, 67, 68, 69
primary health care, access of Gypsy Travellers to 224, 225, 226–227, 234n10
Proast, Jonas 16, 17, 31, 33n12
Protestants 41, 42, 65, 116, 121, 124; arguments of toleration 38; conception of religious doctrine 124; conscience 61, 62, 63; and grand narrative of toleration 54
prudential arguments of toleration 38
public justification 136–137, 138, 139, 140, 143, 167
public reason 72, 129–130, 131–132, 139, 143, 143n5; constitutional essentials 167; element of restraint 131; exclusionary character of 133, 136, 138, 139, 140, 141, 142; language, translation into 132, 134; legal exemptions 138–139; Rawls on 131, 132, 165, 167, 178n4;

religious reasons 132, 133–135; and right-wing populism 172
puritanism 56, 57, 59, 60

Quakers 40, 42, 45

racial inegalitarianism 171
racism 140, 173
Rawls, John 61–62, 70–72, 116, 121, 168, 220, 225; on constitutional essentials 71, 72, 84, 167; democracy theory, respect conception of toleration in 164–167; on intolerant doctrines 163; on modus vivendi and toleration 147–149, 153, 155, 158; political liberalism 6, 135, 159n5, 165, 172, 175, 176, 177; on political power 144n9; property-owning democracy 216n30; psychological principle 172, 175; on public reason 131, 132, 165, 167, 178n4; and right-wing populism 172, 173; on social cooperation 230; on state 83; on toleration in liberal state 84–86, 94n6; on unreasonable people 146; view of modus vivendi, criticisms 149–151
Raz, Joseph 86
realism 149–150, 151, 153, 158, 159n5
*realpolitik* 26, 29
reasonableness 84, 151, 155, 158–159n3, 165
reasonable pluralism 70, 184
reciprocal justification 163, 165, 172, 174, 176
reciprocity 131, 165, 166, 167, 172, 247–248
recognition 6, 101, 120, 243–244; equal recognition approach 120, 122, 123; and modus vivendi 157; respect 108–111; social 105–108, 157; and status inequalities 121–122, 123
Reemtsma, J. 192
Reformation 13, 15, 61
refugees, and legitimate expectations 7–8, 239, 246–250; compromises 250; degrees of immorality and injustice 249; enlightenment and self-

empowerment 249–250; Humanitarian Corridor in Italy 250–254; integration/adoption of toleration 250; legitimate means of demanding toleration 248–249; members demanding toleration 248; question of legitimacy 247–248; refugees *vs.* migrants 246; toleration, state's demand for 246–247; toleration under non-ideal conditions 249–250
regimes of secularism 185
regimes of toleration 5, 98, 101–105; respect recognition and republican toleration 108–111; social recognition 105–108
religion: bigotry 120–121; conflicts 19–20; and government, distinguishing 44; rituals 124, 125; volatility of 18–20
religious arguments of toleration 39, 48–49
religious assembly 39–40
religious conformity 14, 15, 16, 17; and conscience 66–67; and disorder 28–29; and individual liberty 20–21; Penn on 48
religious dissent 38, 39, 47–48
religious neutrality 117
religious pluralism 65, 66, 183–186, 192
religious toleration 3, 6, 13, 58, 61, 172, 183; boundaries of imposition and obedience 16, 23–25, 26; and civil peace/state security 13, 14, 17, 18, 20, 23, 24, 29; continuities in Locke's political philosophy 17–18; and individual conscience 22–24; individual liberty 16, 17, 20–22, 26, 27, 29; moral challenge of toleration 13–15, 30–31; motives and ambitions of ruling authorities 14–15; Peace of Westphalia 100; and Penn 41–42; right of resistance 25–26; *Two Tracts on Government* (Locke) 18, 19–20, 21, 23, 27; *Two Treatises of Government* (Locke) 25–26, 27; volatility of religion 18–20; *see also* headscarves, ban in kindergartens/public schools; Locke, John
*Remonstrance of Many Thousand Citizens* (Overton) 67

reporting tolerance 7, 219, 222–223, 228–230, 232
republican regime of secularism 185, 189, 193–194
republican toleration 4–5, 97, 101; and respect recognition 108–111; and social recognition 106–107
respect 243–244; for autonomy 101, 156; and deep practice of toleration 243; and legitimate expectation of toleration 247; for rights 82–83, 84, 88, 89, 90, 92, 94n5
respect conception of toleration 4, 99, 101, 121, 162–163, 174, 196n3; and justification 164, 165; and liberty 117–118, 119; in Rawls' and Habermas' theories of democracy 164–167; and republican toleration 108–111; unconditioned moral respect 173, 174, 176
Restoration era 56–57
Restoration tolerationist arguments 38–39
rights: and harm 213n5; human rights 83, 90, 134; respect for 82–83, 84, 88, 89, 90, 92, 94n5; right of free assembly 39–40; right of resistance, Locke on 25–26; system of rights (Habermas) 166, 167, 178n3
right-wing extremism 171
right-wing populism 6, 162; and consensus-oriented politics 169; and Habermas 172–173; as intolerant doctrine 162, 170–172; issue, effective response to 176; and Mouffe 173–175; new populist moment 175; proto-totalitarian logic of 170–171, 172, 173; and Rawls 172
Robinson, Henry 55
Roma 221
Rosenblum, Nancy 241
Rousseau, J. J. 97, 98, 99
rule of faith 22
Rummens, S. 170, 173

Saint Augustine 5, 99
St. Paul 38
Sala, Roberta 5–6, 146
Salvini, Matteo 253
Sandys, Edwin 15
Schmitt, Carl 168, 170
Schweiger, Gottfried 1, 7–8, 239

*Seasonable Caveat against Popery, A* (Penn) 41–42
secondary rules 213n8
secularism 6, 183–186, 192, 193–194
Sedmak, Clemens 7–8, 239
self-determination 122, 123
sexual orientation 120
Shiffrin, Seanna 118, 119
Shklar, Judith 229
Sidney, Algernon 36
*Sittlichkeit* 174
small-scale economies 209–210
social esteem, recognition of 106–108
social media corporations 105
social networking 103–104
social recognition 105–108, 157
sole proprietorship firms 205
Sommerville, Johann 60
Spinner-Halev, J. 124
Stanton, Timothy 4, 53
state(s): agent of 119; anarchic 214n11; authoritarian 115–116; and church, separation of 185; generosity, and coercion 213n7; and harm principle 202–204, 207; Jones on 87; legitimate expectations and refugees 246–250; neutrality 6, 83–86, 88, 183, 184, 185, 186, 193–195, 196n3; oppression 116; and permission conception of toleration 100, 102, 104; Rawls on 83; toleration 88, 89, 90, 91, 95n7, 243, 248; *see also* Gypsy Traveller nomadism; liberal state(s)
state security: and right of resistance 26; and toleration 13, 14, 18, 20, 23, 24, 32
Sunni Islam 124
symbolic politics 187, 192, 196n4
system of rights (Habermas) 166, 167, 178n3

Tate, John William 3, 13
Taylor, Charles 106, 108, 120, 184, 185, 188–189, 194
Taylor, Jeremy 57
Thaler, Mathias 173–174
theological arguments of toleration 39
*Theory of Justice* (Rawls) 70, 165, 172
thinker-based approach 118, 119, 124–125
toleration 1–3, 53, 63, 79–80, 93, 151–153, 240; as attitude 4, 80, 82–83, 87, 88–89, 99, 157, 243; -based liberalism 87–91; concept 80–81; concept, deconstruction of 168–170; deontic status of 89–90; discretionary character of 87, 88–89; and general culture of liberal society 91–92; globalization of 245; grand narrative of 53–54; horizontal 91, 99, 101; impersonal standpoint regarding 87; institutional concept of 87, 94–95n6; interest and 46, 47–48; of intolerable 92; intrinsic value of 243–244; and liberal state 83–88, 91–92, 93–94, 95n7; limits of 1–2, 5, 6, 17–18, 109–110, 140–142, 152, 164, 165, 166–167, 169, 170, 172, 174, 175, 177, 245; and modus vivendi 153–154; mutual toleration between groups and individuals 92–93; philosophical debate over 195–196n2; Rawlsian 147–149; respect for rights 82–83, 84, 88, 89, 90, 92, 94n5; revival of traditional toleration 154, 159n10; supererogatory account of 89, 92; toleration of the intolerant 172; universalist justifications of 2; varieties of 115–120; vertical 91, 101; *vs.* tolerance 88, 95n8; Walwyn on 69–70; without limits 126; *see also* liberal toleration; religious toleration
Toleration Act 37, 57–58, 59
*Tolleration Justified, and Persecution Condemned* (Walwyn) 69–70
Toprak, A. 197n14
transitional modus vivendi 148, 149
true religion 14, 15, 21, 30–31, 33n11
Trump, Donald 103
*Truth Exalted* (Penn) 41
*Two Tracts on Government* (Locke) 16, 17, 18, 19–20, 21, 23, 27, 32n1
*Two Treatises of Government* (Locke) 25–26, 27
Tyrrell, James 36

UK Equality Act (Sexual Orientation) Regulations 2007 142
United Kingdom, Gypsy Travellers in 7, 218, 220, 234n11; access to primary health care 224, 225, 226–227; lack of special

mechanisms 223–224; multi-domain-non-accommodation tolerance 224–225
United Nations High Commissioner for Refugees (UNHCR) 251
unreasonable people (Rawls) 146, 148–149, 151, 153, 154–155

Vallier, Kevin 136, 137, 139
value pluralism 123, 126, 150, 244
value(s) 240, 241; adversity-based 242; change in 245; social norms/practices 244, 245; and toleration 242, 243–246
Vaughan, R. 57
vertical toleration 91, 101

volatility of religion 18–20
voter registration, Gypsy Travellers 224, 227, 232

Waldron, Jeremy 133
Walwyn, William 55, 66–67, 68–70, 72
Walzer, Michael 81
Washington, Booker T. 108
Washington, George 49–50
Weimar Republic 72
*West VA v Barnette* (1943) 117–118
William of Orange 57
Williams, Roger 55

xenophobia 253

Printed in the United States
by Baker & Taylor Publisher Services